No Sequel to Life

From the Heart of a Bush Pilot

Jerry J. Jacques
Alaska Master Guide License #110

&

CS Norwood

PUBLISHERS CATALOGING-IN-PUBLICATION DATA

Jacques, Jerry J. / author; Norwood, CS / coauthor

No sequel to life: from the heart of a bush pilot /

by Jerry J. Jacques and CS Norwood

True and fascinating stories from Alaska master hunting guide #110, whitewater explorer and guide, as well as bush pilot flying the unpredictable Alaska skies. His adventures include special ops pilot in conflict zones around the globe.

Enhanced / Revised Edition

BIOGRAPHY & AUTOBIOGRAPHY / Adventurers & Explorers / Aviation & Nautical / Memoirs

Regional themes - 4.0.1.6.1.0.0 Alaska / -1.6.17.0.0.0.0 Ukraine

Paperback

358 pages / 60 17.78 x 25.4 x 1.5 cm / 120+ illustrations

Includes biographical references and index.

ISBN: 979-8-9884470-8-5

Library of Congress Control Number: 2024911528

Cover design by CS Norwood

Illustrations in this book were enhanced using Topaz Gigapixel AI for clarity.

Printed in the United States of America

adventure writers ink
Bay Minette | Twin Falls

Contents

Dedication

This book is dedicated to all the teachers, coaches, and mentors who go the extra mile to help kids succeed in the fundamentals of education.
Thank you for giving part of your life to help!

"Learning to read was the greatest gift of my life!"

—*Jerry Jacques*

This is the Beaver float-plane I fly the most and one of my favorite photographs!
(Photo Bob Chiu)

All photographs unless otherwise noted were taken by friends and family, and
sometimes, in the wilderness, we just set up a camera and a tripod, and
we took photos of ourselves.

Acknowledgments

Art Wolfe: *friend, photographer, and contributor*

Caleb Jacques: *my son and contributor, dog trainer, and guide*

Christian Elwell: *friend, contributor, guide, and author*

Dave Moore & Sterling Beckland: *helped me get the lodge up and running*

Diana Schieber: *friend and chief proofreader*

Erin O'Connell: *my daughter and curator*

Jack Baker: *friend and essential link*

James Wesley, Rawles: *friend, podcaster, and contributor*

Jason Jacques: *my son and contributor*

Joanna Bailey: *librarian advisor*

John Cassidy: *contributor and author*

Kerry Pride: *beloved wife of Zach Babat and contributor*

23 SRB (a Separate Rifle Battalion in Ukraine)

Rebecca M. Sweet, MD: *friend and proofreader*

Sam Carter: *contributor and podcaster*

Victoria Yeager: *friend and proofreader*

All those who helped along the way, and

Most importantly:

Laura Z. O'Connell: *my lovely wife, attorney, and wonderful mother.*

We made every effort to verify the correct spelling of names of individuals and places included in this book as well as verify dates.
We are sincerely sorry if we got something wrong.
Many of the photos included are old. We have made every effort to make them as sharp and clear as possible.
Some hyperlinks may no longer be extant, and a few names were changed for various reasons.
Finally, please let us know if your story was not included here. We are writing a sequel.

Foreword

*By James Wesley,
Rawles
Novelist, and
Founder of
SurvivalBlog*

In writing biographies—or obituaries—the words "Legendary" and "Larger Than Life" are often over-used. But when describing Jerry Jacques, those words are truly apropos. His countless adventures are the stuff of legends. I can safely say that he has crammed several lifetimes into his nearly seven decades walking this Earth. It is no exaggeration to describe him as a genuinely expert bush pilot, an expert military STOL pilot, and an expert hunting guide. His narrow escapes have been many, and his lessons learned have been hard-won. He relates both in this book.

Jerry Jacques has signed numerous nondisclosure agreements for his work with American government three-letter agencies. So, not all his stories can be revealed until declassification dates that I assume are in the 2050s or beyond. But, nonetheless, what is between the covers of this book will truly amaze and captivate you.

I'll be bold and make an assumption about who is reading what I'm now writing: You are standing in a Barnes & Noble bookstore, and you are presently debating whether or not you should buy this book. Let me make that decision easy for you: Flip forward through about 200 pages to Chapter 22: Escape from Chad. Take a few minutes to read that. Now picture Jerry Jacques in that situation: Flying an aging twin-engine prop plane with no autopilot, single-handed, leveling it off at 12,000 feet, reducing the plane's airspeed to just over the stall limit, carefully setting the plane's trim wheel, and then pushing his torso out the window into a buffeting 100 mile-per-hour slipstream to refuel the plane through a rubber hose. Repeatedly. Feats like that are truly Larger Than Life. And men who survive to tell such tales are surely few and far between.

Born in 1957 in San Jose, California, Jerry Jacques was a rambunctious child fascinated by aviation from an early age. He threw his youthful vigor into kayaking, whitewater rafting, and mountain climbing. In 1974, he first visited the Talkeetna River, and he immediately felt that was where he was destined to live. With "more guts than brains" and insufficient camp stove fuel, he attempted to climb Mount McKinley (Denali) at age 19.

Soon after, Jerry started a whitewater rafting business. He spent his first winter in Alaska, 1978-79. He ran a trap line that winter, living in a remote and poorly stocked, dirt-floor cabin. After many hard

lessons learned, he emerged the next spring more experienced, more level-headed, and weighing a lot less.

The next year, he began training as a pilot. He flew for eight years with only a student pilot license and logged over 1800 hours before the FAA caught him flying passengers without a license. After a six-month suspension, he was awarded his license, but only by the good graces of a couple of very understanding FAA officials. Surely, that would not happen with today's FAA.

From there, Jerry embarked on several decades of adventures around the world that had him rubbing shoulders with famous musicians, world-class big game hunters, an NFL quarterback, and Gen. Chuck Yeager—the first man to break the sound barrier. Jerry's journeys have been as far flung as Belize, Chad, Afghanistan, South Africa, and Australia. He spent so much time hunting big game in South Africa, in fact, that he qualified to become a licensed hunting guide there.

In 1997, one of his guiding clients, Marvin Winter, shot the Safari Club International (SCI) world record bear. That grizzly scored 31 2/16" (skull measurement). As of this writing, it still holds the all-time SCI record for the biggest brown bear ever recorded. (See Chapter 17.)

The piloting, hunting, and fishing stories that Jerry tells are truly amazing. For most of us reading this book, any one of these stories would be the pinnacle experience of a lifetime. But for Jerry, they are just another day in a very busy life.

It has long been said: "There are old pilots and there are bold pilots. But there are no old, bold pilots." Thankfully, Jerry learned many important lessons early in his flying career. He soon became a sage at reading the weather. And he learned early on to have the discretion to firmly say no when judging flying conditions and so-called landing strips. Jerry has also gained the wisdom to calculate forced landings in just a moment's time. This has saved lives, more than once. Jerry puts it bluntly: "Planes can be replaced, people can't."

The dozens of stories that Jerry relates about his backcountry guide and air service are told with humility and candor: enormous and ferocious bears, out-in-the-middle-of-nowhere close calls with death, drunken millionaire clients, finicky engines, watery avgas, unforgettable sunsets, and unforgiving Alaskan winters. He also describes how he came to faith in Christ and how he met the love of his life, Laura.

In more of a shorthand fashion, Jerry describes some of his work as a STOL pilot ferrying troops and supplies in Chad and Afghanistan. Given the secrecy of the missions, he only hints at the extent of his covert work, while in the employ of the famed Blackwater/Academi/Constellis/Xe Services military contracting company.

I first made contact with Jerry in 2009, when he kindly wrote an article on "Grub and Gear" for my preparedness blog, SurvivalBlog. I only later learned more about his first few winters as a solo trapper in a very remote corner of Alaska. Those stories—including some very harrowing details—are included in this book.

In a 2009 letter, Jerry wrote me:

"I often get a chuckle from people that think they can fill a backpack and head into the woods and survive long term with [only] what is in a backpack. Until recently I spent most of my life guiding in Alaska and in Africa. I spent an average of 110 days a year living out of a backpack under a tarp or in a pup tent, and another 180 days each year living in a remote cabin without electricity or running water.

In an uninhabited game-rich environment with a rifle and only a backpack of gear I could survive for a period of time. How long could I survive? I do not know, as there are too many variables."

This is not just a book for private pilots. And it is not just a book for hunters, fishermen, or military-history buffs. It is a book for anyone who enjoys a rousing biography or autobiography.

Journeying into Alaska's backcountry in a small plane with tundra tires or floats can be life-threatening in any month of the year. But admirably, he has prevailed in all seasons and invariably he does so with a big grin on his face. This man is indeed larger than life. Jerry Jacques most certainly embodies the spirit of the Alaskan Bush.

And I'm proud to call him my friend.

—*James Wesley, Rawles*

Foreword

By Art Wolfe

Jerry Jacques is a hardworking and honest man. I really have respect for people who don't just talk about who they are and what they do, but actually live up to their own words. Jerry exemplifies somebody who rolls up his sleeves. There's virtually no obstacle in his way that he does not tackle with confidence. As far as flying with him, I've flown with a lot of pilots into backcountry all over the world, and I can't think of any pilot I feel safer with than Jerry Jacques. I like my pilots sober and gray-haired. And that is who he is today.

Way back in 1979, however, Jerry and I were both a bit younger. He wasn't gray-haired yet, but he certainly was living his dream, even then. That July, a couple of my high school friends and I headed to Alaska looking for some adventure. We wanted to raft the Copper River. The Copper was virtually an unknown river wilderness area even in the late '70s. Having never floated a river before, my two friends and I contacted a young guy by the name of Jerry Jacques. At the time, Jerry

owned a small whitewater guide business based in Talkeetna, Alaska.

It's been so many years since that occasion that I've forgotten how and where I met Jerry, but the memories that are strong include rendezvousing in Chitina, Alaska, near the headwaters of the Copper River and meeting Jerry for the first time. I can remember with such clarity that he was a young, wiry, bushy-haired man who had a tall, lanky assistant named Tom Turner. The two of them led me and my friends on a very memorable and very long trip down the river as it cut through the rugged Chugach Mountains.

That first evening, Jerry, showing off his nineteen-year-old status, took a very large knife, held up a head of lettuce, and, with one stroke of the blade, chopped through the lettuce all the way into his hand. Virtually on our first meeting, Jerry had cleaved his hand open.. He was stitched up and bandaged up; yet, he was so nonchalant about it, that I knew this guy was tough.

The following day we got packed and on the river. For me, it was a great trip, floating the Copper River was a fantastic way to see the wildland, and, for the next twelve days, we saw no other humans.

I also remember multiple glaciers were calving icebergs into the river. It was magnificent to see, but we constantly had to avoid the falling ice and navigate around floating icebergs during our raft journey.

Towards the end of the trip, we had to float virtually under the terminus of a glacier that was constantly calving huge slabs of ice into the river. So, were we feeling lucky at the time? I guess, because we floated right in front of these walls of ice and miraculously got through it without any injury. Of course today, nearly fifty years later, the glaciers have receded and are no longer a threat to any raft travel. But back then, it was quite an occasion and something that we really had to deal with. It was a great trip.

Later that summer, another set of friends and I decided to go to Anchorage and align again with Jerry Jacques. This time, he convinced us to float the Talkeetna River Canyon, which had never been rafted before. And so there I was with Jerry once again. At the start of our next adventure, Jerry and another pilot loaded us all in the back of his Piper Super Cub and flew us up above the canyon to a narrow strip along the river.

The Piper Cub is a very small, light plane that can get people into the backcountry, landing on non-runways. Bush pilots can land these planes on glaciers and snow fields when the aircraft is outfitted with skis, as well as on makeshift airstrips cut out of the Alaskan tundra when it's coming in on big tires. It can even take off and land on lakes and large ponds with its floats attached. It's quite a versatile airplane.

On this particular trip, we landed the aircraft on a rough gravel river bar. My pilot was very young. I don't think he even had hair under pits at that time, he was so young, The first landing on the tiny gravel bar there was not a clear landing path, running over some brush ripped open a hole in the fabric underbelly of the Piper Cub. When I was introduced to my pilot, I learned his real name was Don Lee, but what I vividly remember is his nickname—*Crash*.

Over a process of multiple flights in, we were able to get the two whitewater rafts, Jerry's kayak, and me and my two friends and, again, Tom, Jerry's tall, lanky whitewater guide onto the rafts. But, at this point, the rain started falling quite heavily, and, by the time we hit the Canyon, the river was at flood stage. There is a series of very dramatic drops in the river as it's pouring through this narrow canyon. I seemed to recall a kayaker attempted it the fall before and disappeared on the river. So for inflatable rafts to go down this narrow, twisting, rapid-filled river was an adventure. In the first set of rapids, we virtually had the entire eighteen-foot Avon raft filled with water which meant it was almost impossible to control. We started bouncing off the walls, promptly ripping open one of the four air compartments of the raft. We made our way eventually onto the side of this steep canyon where we bivouacked for the next two days. This allowed us to repair the rafts. Jerry was ahead of us in a kayak and not able to climb around the vertical cliffs to try helping us, but he had confidence in Tom and knew that we were okay and delayed because we simply had damage done to our raft.

So, those were my first two trips with Jerry Jacques. I wrote an article about the trips for *The Seattle Times*; that article helped Jerry get many new clients.

As most are aware, people drift apart over time. Three decades passed before I would hear from Jerry again. By that time, I had a TV show called *Travels to the Edge*. We sold this program to seventy countries around the world, and Al Jazeera broadcast the show throughout the Middle East.

Now thirty years after our first encounters, Jerry was flying in Afghanistan. From what he told me, he was in a facility taking a few days R&R. The TV was on although he had his back turned to it. *Travels to the Edge* was on, and even though he wasn't watching, he still recognized my voice some thirty years later; my voice was still imprinted in his brain. He turned around, and seeing me on TV after all those years, decided on the spot that when he returned to Alaska he would reach out and communicate with me, which he did. By now, he had a lodge on Lake Iliamna and owned multiple floatplanes. He convinced me to come up, and we had a great time, which led to decades of hanging out with Jerry while leading my workshops photographing the bears of Katmai and Lake Clark.

Jerry virtually changed his life by phasing out the fly-fishing business at his lodge and converting the lodge into a destination for wildlife photographers. I love this kind of story, reconnecting with friends and people from the past.

Life is short; the more we can hang onto our friends and our acquaintances the richer our years become. I cherish the fact that Jerry reached out to me, and it changed my life as well. We've had great times together leading brown-bear photo safaris from Jerry's beautiful lodge next to Katmai National Park. And now it's time for my dear friend, Jerry Jacques, to tell you the rest of the story. It's just about all here in *No Sequel to Life: From the Heart of a Bush Pilot.*

—*Art Wolfe*

Art Wolfe
WWW.ARTWOLFE.COM
Seattle | v +1 206 332 0993 | f +1 866.212.6793

Preface

There's a four-inch corrugated metal plate screwed firmly into the vertebrae in my neck. People have been telling me for years that I have a few loose screws, hopefully this fixes that. I got hurt at FOB Sharana, Afghanistan, in 2010. I walked away from the incident, but I'd been in some pretty rough pain ever since. As a last resort, I consented to neck surgery in 2012. So with a little recovery time on my hands, I began my book. I gathered old notes together and wrote some, but I was soon feeling a little better. I don't sit still very well, and writing's not nearly as much fun as flying clients around the Alaskan bush. But this story needs to be told, if for no other reason than perhaps it may light a spark—a yearning for adventure—in some young heart.

As for me and my story, I guess I've led three different lives. I'm a whitewater guide and wild river explorer, a hunting and wildlife photography guide in Alaska and Africa, and a bush pilot on four continents. I've also flown special ops in my career, but we'll get into that later. What I most want to tell you about is my story of a wildly adventurous life.

Friends and clients had been telling me for years that I should write a book.

My brothers John and Jim; my kayaking partner, Rob Lesser; high school wrestling coach, Mike Cohen; photographer Art Wolfe; my doctor, Darryl Wilkins (my biggest rival in high school wrestling); and Gen. Chuck Yeager, himself, have all been telling me that I need to write a book about my adventures. Well, I am not sure anyone will believe most of the things I've done—all the things that I have been lucky enough to experience and a few adventures that I was lucky to have just barely survived. However, I do have pictures, movies, witnesses, magazine articles, and scars to prove it all.

A few years ago, while going through some old boxes of gear, I found my food supply lists and notes from my first winters in the Alaskan bush. I guess these are the start of my book.

My problem is, I would rather be involved in new adventures than sitting down writing about past ones. The other problem is I cannot spell to save my life and have no writing skills. In fact, the best grade I ever earned in high school English was a D. So, finally, in 2022, I found someone who wanted to help—the sister of my old friend, Ron

Sutphin.

CS Norwood emailed me:

"If you ever want your stories recorded, let me know, and we'll get to work. I believe we're all a little richer when these stories are actually written down and preserved for the record," she emailed. If she was fishing for my story, I took the bait. With her brother's book *(Covert Skies: Ron Sutphin's Road to Civil Air Transport (CAT) and Covert Operations in Laos)* finally published, she's helping me complete mine.

My own brother, John told me there will be "no sequel" to my book. So that gave me the name for the book, *No Sequel to Life*. A friend recently suggested the name: *From the Heart of a Bush Pilot*. I think a combination of the two will work. Now with title, old notes scattered about, and a co-author and editor...I think I'm practically finished!

The longest journey starts with the first step I'm told, and I know this to be true from my years of wilderness survival. Now, at exactly the right time in my life, I stepped out in faith into this different kind of venture—compiling my stories into a book in hopes of inspiring someone else. Unlike my coauthor and editor, who sees the possibilities before the last page is completed, I do not think anyone besides my family and friends will read it, but if I have my way, this book will inspire my kids and my grandkids to stop watching TV, incessantly playing video games, and talking about TV shows and those games like they are true adventures. They are not. I want to inspire my kids and grandkids to live their own adventures—or to at least venture out, away from that video screen for even a little while.

I will have succeeded if my kids and grandkids, and perhaps yours, as well, decide to explore their own possibilities, writing their own stories, one day inspiring their own offspring. Nothing needs to be left behind. I've had it all: family, friends, and the life of adventure I had always dreamed of living. Little successes can happen often, but real success is what you create over a lifetime.

My friend, Jay Baldwin, always called me Triple J because of my initials, JJJ. He was the only one in my life who called me that. Jay stayed at my lodge many times. He wrote the book *Survival Flying: Bush Flying Tales & Techniques as Flown and Taught in Alaska*.[1]

Jay was going to help me with my book; he wrote the following notes in 2015 just before he died:

---

[1] [*Survival Flying: Bush Flying Tales & Techniques as Flown and Taught in Alaska*, Baldwin, C. Jay, Ortland, Stephen, Newsham, Rick, Baldwin, Sandy, Baldwin, C.Jay, eBook - Amazon.com]

Since 1974, Triple J has been exploring the world's wildest places by bush plane and whitewater raft, logging first descents down extreme whitewater rivers, and pioneering radical off-airport landing spots.

Triple J spent his early winters alone as a trapper in remote Alaska. Later, after gaining a reputation as a bush pilot, he spent many winters flying in war zones across the globe, but Triple J is best known as one of Alaska's best wilderness guides and bush pilots.

Triple J managed to survive 48 years in harm's way in the world's most dangerous places. Like a moth drawn to a flame, if there was adventure to be had, he was all in.

Five decades of extreme risk all over the planet came with a cost: many of his closest friends didn't survive, a failed marriage, and thirteen wrecked aircraft are all part of his past.

Triple J's book will take you through plane crashes, being shot at, mauled by a bear, stranded, and twice left alone in a war-torn country where he could not speak the language.

Somehow, Triple J lived through those desperate survival situations and life-threatening injuries.

During his career, he performed several rescues and had his own life saved by pilots who risked their lives helping him.

I am not sure it was worth it, but you decide for yourself, read No Sequel to Life.

—Jay

Introduction

When I first met Jerry, he was changing a tire in the rain and mud. We were in front of Nagley's store in Talkeetna, Alaska.

Back then, Talkeetna was a dirt road that dead ended at the confluence of the Susitna and Talkeetna rivers. Moms drove to town on four-wheelers with babies on their laps and with their shotguns at the ready on the handlebars. People wore sidearms to avoid being eaten by bears while doing their milk run. Families took planes to go on picnics.

I was twenty years old, and I thought Alaska was about as cool as it could get. I guess I'd read too many Russell Annabel stories as a kid and just couldn't find what I was looking for in the lower forty-eight. I'd been fishing for a week with a buddy and had made it back to town for more supplies. I was planning on heading back out when I spotted this burly looking guy cursing at a tire, or a tire iron, or maybe a malevolent jack. He bore a striking resemblance to the photo of a wild man holding up a ten inch bear paw pictured on the front of a

"Helio 295 Juliet Alpha, Approaching Christiansen Lake for Landing"
By
Christian Elwell
© 2023 Christian Elwell

brochure that I'd been staring at for half a year. "Jerry?"

Jerry had gotten my number from an elk-hunting client of mine in Montana and called me the winter before. It had not been a long conversation.

"Would you like to come up and pack for me this season—get some Alaska experience—then guide for me once you get your license?"

"Yes," was my only answer. I knew Jerry's reputation as an honest, hardcore, bad-ass from both the whitewater and hunting communities. Of course I was going.

"Can you be here mid-August?"

"You bet."

A lot of life has happened for the both of us since that call thirty years ago. When I hung up the phone, I had a hunch, but didn't yet know just how pivotal working with Jerry was going to be in terms of guiding the direction of my life and how our time together would give me some of my finest memories and friends in Alaska.

I was not inexperienced when I rolled into Jerry's lodge at twenty years old. I had grown up in the woods and had two years of experience guiding hunters in Montana and Idaho. Great experience, but in Alaska, every adventure is ratcheted up by several notches. There is no basecamp to return to in that wilderness—no one to call for help or ask for advice. If you don't get back to your camp by supper, there will be no one waiting for you, looking for you, and no one caring for that matter, at least until your scheduled pickup date. Once you hear the last fading sound of your drop-off plane's engine as it flies away into that big Alaskan sky, you're left with only a big silence, usually magnified by the loud buzzing from big Alaskan mosquitoes. And that's it.

You are on your own until unpredictable weather and schedules allow the pilot to land again, sometime near the end of your hunt. Taking courses and getting certified in things with the word "wilderness" in them may provide some nifty tricks, but that's about it. The kind of grit, patience, and sound decision-making abilities a guide really needs can only be learned by doing. I got lucky. By signing on with Jerry, I had someone who was both willing to teach me what he could plus give me lots of opportunities to learn—usually the hard way—on my own. There were a lot of trials-by-fire to be sure.

Being an Alaskan Outfitter means different things to different people. To Jerry it meant being highly skilled as a hunter, pilot, climber, white water boater and survivalist. If there was a river Jerry wanted to run, he'd fly to it and run it. If there was a log jam in that river that needed moving, he would rappel off a cliff, bust it open and climb out. The words "can't" and "too difficult" just weren't in Jerry's vocabulary.

A person would be lucky to master just one of those disciplines in a lifetime and Jerry was an expert in all.

He was so calm in stressful situations that we'd joke about them being his happy place. On top of that, he was a natural leader and teacher. Jerry truly wanted to help people, and he never judged them without giving them a chance. He was always willing to share what he knew with anyone willing to work for it——really work for it. Which meant that those of us who trained with him had at least one essential thing in common, which was handy when we found ourselves relying on each other in some difficult situations.

When I made my way to the lodge that first night, I found a giant log home on the edge of a lake with a floatplane tied to a dock. There was a guy sitting on a picnic table fleshing a Dall sheep cape. Here I was looking at a real set of Dall Sheep horns! Zach Babet sat hunched over, working bits of meat and fat off the hide, cursing the mosquitoes biting at his eyeballs and not particularly interested in the overly-social new guy. After a fresh application of bug spray and an offer to help him with the hide, Zach and I soon found common ground in our guiding experience in Montana. We shared a sense of humor, and passion for wild places unburdened by a lot of the rules and regulations the lower forty-eight seemed choked with, at least to us. We soon began a friendship that would become one of the more meaningful relationships in my life which lasted until Zach's untimely and tragic death twenty-some years later. He died while we were working together in Western Alaska.

Jerry called his business Jacques Adventure Company; it was an apt name. Our time at Jerry's place was a cross between boot camp, a twenty-four-hour-a-day job, and a paid vacation. He was our commander-in-chief, employer, father figure, and chief nemesis. We adventured big in big country. Jerry provided us with plenty of uncomfortably high-stake situations during which we honed specific skill sets as we developed a resilience-under-stress that can only be garnered by pushing yourself through high-pressure situations—often. In those days we were navigating without a GPS during long roaming trips across huge country. We were happy to eat one MRE a day but joked about their origin and how Jerry had gotten his hands on so many.

On long nights in camp, we wrote letters. We gave them to our clients to mail for us when they flew out and were left to wonder if the letters to our sweethearts ever showed up or if they would want to read them after not hearing from us for weeks on end. Lucky for us, enough of our letters found their way to our sweethearts that we each married the love of our lives some years later.

Jerry's Lesson number one: It's all about the airplane.

"I don't care if you're in the middle of taking a crap, if you hear a plane about to land, you come running." We didn't have satellite communication in those days, and Jerry's favorite pastime seemed to be landing at my camps at unexpected and inopportune times. Glad we covered this right off the bat. I have never had a plane wait on me since that first year. If I am near an aircraft, my sole purpose, for that time of my life, is to facilitate all activities involving getting that plane back in the air or tied up. The difference of a few minutes can not only have bad consequences for that particular flight, with weather or daylight, but can cause chaos with all the other flying that needs to happen. A missed flight today means one more tomorrow, and the weather might be bad tomorrow. Client A needs to get flown out to catch his flight home, client B's moose meat needs to get to a cooler, and Client C has been sitting in town for two days waiting to start his adventure. It's all about the airplane.

Now I'm the one who will come unhinged if someone I'm working with is too inexperienced to pick up on the program. Satellite communication has forever changed logistics in Alaska. There are generations of new guides who have been spared the trauma of jumping every time a mosquito flies by their ear thinking it's a plane that may-or-may-not be landing for them. But if satellites fail, I'm ready.

Everything we learned from Jerry had a system and a purpose. We all became familiar with checking the sumps on the wings and belly of the planes before every take off, same with pumping water out of all the float lockers, every time, and unless you want to feel like one of the dumbest humans on the planet and the likely reason the plane was going to crash, you'd better wipe the windshield in a smooth one directional manner.

"Yes, boss."

Jerry would take the time to explain why and how he wanted something done and the consequences of doing it differently, attention to detail was important. Because of him, I am now confident questioning any pilot about any details of their safety protocols or deciding not to fly with them. I am forever grateful for all these lessons and try to make a point of sharing what I can to people who want to learn, in a similar fashion. Many of them were fundamental skills, the base skills that other skills are built upon.

Will that rope uncoil perfectly from your throw bag when you need to rescue someone?

I'd pay good money now to watch someone on a float trip with Jerry use a throw bag to tie a raft up or not clip their life jackets to something at the end of the day.

Did you lose most of your gear at the start of a ten-day wilderness float, or was it locked in with the bags rolled tight?

Can a pilot look at all your gear laid out and immediately know how they want to load a plane.

When we were in town we were generally at the hanger. For a young guy like myself wanting to be a professional hunter, it was an impressive sight. There were sheep horns, moose horns, wheel skis, climbing gear, rafting gear, guns, planes—and lots of blue tubs which would plague Zach and me for years. We were constantly loading and unloading, packing and repacking gear, organizing and reorganizing food. It was often boring work. The boring work that helps you become a proficient professional down the road. Especially if you were doing it for Jerry. Our time in the hanger or basecamps provided much of the material for Zach's and my off-kilter humor.

Mr. Funnel is the trade name of a wide mouth funnel that we always used to run our fuel through anytime we transported fuel for the planes. One day, I was wearing hip boots, standing on my tiptoes to keep water out with Zach on my shoulders. It was blowing forty-five miles per hour, and we were trying to get wing covers on the Cub outside of Cold Bay when Jerry, dressed in Nomex, with the ever-present cocked and locked 1911 on his side, yelled, "Who moved Mr. Funnel?! Mr. Funnel lives here! In this tub!" Jerry's reprimands often strengthened the bond between me and Zach. Mr. Funnel became one of the longstanding jokes we shared. By the end of that trip Mr. Funnel had a whole backstory and family all its own.

Jerry created a family for us, too. In the evenings, when everyone was at the lodge, we ate family-style around a large table. Jerry would say grace and we would be one large goofy close-knit group sharing food and life. This was the case whether there were guests or not. Jerry was not one of the outfitters who felt it was necessary to put himself on a pedestal by having the "help" eat in the kitchen. After dinner, we sat up late sharing stories and learning about weapons and gear.

You know you're family when you get in trouble for breaking the rules, too. If we were just back from an extended trip, Zach and I, as well as any other guides who were around, might try to get to town for a few beers away from the boss. Jerry was fine with this, but he had a secret weapon to make sure we didn't get back past the unspoken curfew without risk.

Jager was a ninety pound *Schutzhund*-trained Rottweiler. He was loving, kind and loyal, and would rip your leg off at Jerry's command. This was part of the training that dog and his master reveled in. Jerry wanted to know, did I want to help with Jager's training? You bet. Did I

Dugout campsite

want to wear body armor—um…why? Was that necessary? I "helped" a couple times, then did what any sensible person would do, which was try not to snicker whenever Jerry found the next unsuspecting victim. It was fun enough, except for his signature move of whacking you in the balls while leaping for your protected arm. Jerry swore he didn't teach Jager this trick, but I'm not sure I believed him.

Jager slept in the arctic entry to the lodge. As he got older, he slept more soundly. Dare to show up after the lights were out at the lodge and you had two options: The first was to sleep outside amidst the mosquitoes all night, or second, risk startling a trained killer who might not recognize you as you step over him. Jolting Jager out of his sound sleep didn't seem like the best option. We got used to the bug bites.

When the wind's blowing fifty, at least there are no bugs.

Jerry always said the second most important thing to remember when hunting for brown bears in the Alaska Peninsula is your shovel. Jerry had been out when it was worse-than-bad plenty of times. He taught us how to survive those times. We learned to take hunting the tip of the Alaskan peninsula for brown bear seriously. It's the land that never got finished and where weather starts. It doesn't take a meteorologist to guess you might get a bit of wind while camped in a narrow strip of mountains between thousands of miles of frigid open ocean.

Jerry taught us to dig deep pits in the ground and pile the sand around us so that the tents were completely underground. We used four-foot pieces of rebar as tent stakes. My first year there, we had wind at the airport strong enough to peel half inch steal back like the top of a sardine can. It was blowing so hard that a vacuum was created over top our hole powerful enough to lift a tent full of three large guys off the ground vertically. I got lucky seeing that right off the bat. You cannot take weather seriously enough on the Alaskan Peninsula. Jerry taught us that no matter how long it takes or how difficult it is, dig in, and batten down the hatches.

Every so often we got a really big blow on the peninsula during bear season. I don't know of another outfit that buries their tents. Even today, if you happen to be flying the Peninsula after a big blow, you will see tents torn and scattered all over the place, some of them miles from where they were intended to stay. None were ever ours, though. We always had our shovels—second only to our rifles.

One trip that really brought all my training with Jerry together was in the Talkeetna mountains. Some of the finest hunting I had done for Jerry happened in that area. I took some tremendous animals over plenty of long nights. I was mostly cold and wet and always hungry. Sometimes I had unsuccessful hunts, difficult clients, or got lost. But it was fair-chase, remote-wilderness hunting, and always worth it. Our trips were often ten-day cross-country backpack hunts. From one glassing spot in the Talkeetna's at a single assessment, I spotted black bear, grizzly bear, Dall sheep, moose, caribou, wolf, and wolverine. I often spent a few days where my clients and I had been dropped off before we struck off in whatever direction that made sense. When Jerry flew over, I'd coordinate with him via a handheld VHF regarding where to pack meat and hides or the location of our pickup point. That site could be a wheel strip or a lake, or, on multiple trips for me, it was a gravel bar and a raft.

One particular hunt was with Klaus, a client from Germany. We started out hunting the big benches above the Talkeetna River for moose and bear. We shared a two person tent, carrying all our gear on our backs, living lean. We'd left most of our food and nonessentials at our drop-off strip. We cooked only what was necessary for the evening meal over a small fire. Breakfast was cold instant oatmeal and lunch was a granola bar. Somewhere in the middle of our trip Klaus killed a grizzly, fat on blueberries. Hunger may make the best sauce, but I still think of that evening meal as some of the finest meat I have ever eaten.

Jerry picked up Klaus' bear before we took a detour into the mountains to look for rams. Several days of scrambling over rotten scree found us perched on a ledge unable to climb higher and with a sketchy descent that required zigzagging for hours between cliffs. With a snowstorm rolling in and the rams having left the country, we decided to fly out and have one more go at finding a good moose.

We thought this was our best option with only a few days left of our fourteen-day hunt.

I took off in the Cub with Jerry during a snowstorm headed out of the mountains to the Talkeetna River late in the afternoon. Klaus would wait for Jerry to make the round trip. Jerry described a valley he'd taken some nice bulls out of in the past as, "one side covered in spruce, about a quarter mile down from where Crazy Woman dumps in on the right." He hoped to get us two hunting days, but "if I can't get Klaus to you tonight, you'll have to float tomorrow and that will give you just the one day of hunting. If you get a moose, float your-selves back to town."

This was the end of the season, the only real food I'd had in a bit was that grizzly; the only sleep, when I could grab it, had come in handfuls—and wait—did Jerry just tell me to float back to town, as in through the gorge? As in one of the longest continuous rapids in the world at high water? Hopefully, with a moose? Hang on! Where were the giant moose that are supposed to just show up at camp to the sound of pans banging together, love struck, and not too happy about a rival bull doing dishes in his valley? For a flash, I fantasized about being one of those mythical outfitters who do all their hunts out of cabins on lakes. As I unloaded the gear, Jerry said, "you'll be fine.

Photo of me with a big bull moose. (Christian El-well, Talkeetna Mountains 1997)

Should be pretty straight forward at these water levels. Read and run and watch out for sweepers." Right.

Klaus got dropped the next day. We loaded our gear in the old sixteen-foot bucket boat and headed downstream on a cold, clear, fall day. The next morning, we worked our way uphill in the dark. We only had the one day to hunt, we were tired, hungry and wet, but midday found us lying in the sun, warm for the first time in a while. We lounged on our backs as we debated if the ridge beneath us looked "mostly covered in spruce" and how many creeks came in on the right. I had spent part of the morning doing my best to sound like a lonesome cow, but there was no hope of something moving in the midday heat. My stomach making noise woke me up from snoozing with my binoculars stuck to my face. Only it wasn't my stomach—it was a huge slab-sided bull-of-a-moose trotting out of the spruce right at us. With cover, high ground, and the wind, my biggest concern was waking Klaus up in time. (Years later I wonder if the old bull wasn't coming in to the sound of Klaus' snoring.) After finding a suitable stick to poke him with, it didn't take Klaus long to assess the situation and do his part of the business. We thanked the giant old bull for his life and took a moment to really look around and realize just how far we had climbed that morning. There was a god-awful amount of country between us and that river we had to get back to.

Sometime before dark, as I was loading the moose cape in my pack, we saw Jerry fly over. He was truly excited for our success, which he deserves equal credit for. Three hours later, using a flashlight to see my compass, standing in a beaver pond, a torn-up, worn-out German police officer with low blood sugar behind me——I was admittedly not thinking about team spirit. I was grateful for the moose and the hunt but had already switched focus to the problems of moving seven-hundred pounds of meat and the canyon we had to float it through. *Have faith, oh ye of little hope.*

It was late and cold and dark when we made it back to the raft. We were surprised to find that Jerry had dropped Klaus' hunting buddy off upstream with his guide, my buddy Greg Smith. They had taken a catboat down and were snoring in their tents when we threw our packs down.

Season was over, our tags were punched, the sun was out. We were four friends in the mountains with a moose to pack out and a four-day float through a gnarly gorge for our highway back to town. Pack, build fire, eat tenderloin, sleep, repeat. They were glorious days. Greg and I had more fun than you should at work going through the canyon. With house-size holes and huge wave-trains the clients in the front had a cold, wet time of it. I believe I heard muttering in a German accent "not in contract" several times. Nothing a giant driftwood fire, stories, and moose meat didn't cure though. The leaves were yellow on the cottonwood and willow as we floated out of the mountains on fast, blue glacial water. It was a nice way to go back to town after a time in the woods. We walked up the dusty dead-end street late in the afternoon. It was real quiet when we went in the bar to use the pay phone to let folks know we were back.

That night, while swapping stories with a few other guides who were still around, they laughed, shook their heads and said "Jerry…" As in, of course you started in the high-country chasing rams, ran a canyon in one day that other expeditions take a few to do, and then floated all the way to town. Pretty sure they all hunted out of cabins with the aforementioned love-struck bulls lining up for pancakes.

In the early years, a guide's career success is often measured in trophy size, the number of animals taken, and how quickly this all happened. The major promoters of the industry all supported this ideology and largely still do, which is unfortunate. Every young guide wants to "tag out" and get to town for a hot shower and beers, while recanting stories of the hunt. I don't think this ever happened to me while working for Jerry, and, years later, I am forever grateful. We were almost always successful, mainly because we had ten-day hunts and hunted hard. Back then, it was easy to be jealous hearing stories of guides who never had to hunt more than a few days before they were back in their lodge with a pocket full of tip money. Now when I share some of my stories with other guides, I'm speaking of how we hunted with Jerry, they listen in wrapped amazement. Guess I got what I was looking for.

*My dog Josey &
me showing off our
trophy bear paw*

From pulling into Jerry's driveway the first time, thousands of miles away from everyone I knew, until I started my own outfitting business in Alaska, I felt like I was part of a team with Jerry as our leader. There was much to learn to become a professional hunter in Alaska. There were (and still are) all the requirements the state has; a written exam, unit exams, first aid, CPR, and hunting and fishing laws and regulations are all things that can be studied by a warm fire somewhere. Then there are the skills that are going to allow you to thrive in the wilderness and survive while earning a living doing a wilderness business.

Zach and I were so fortunate to have Jerry as both a mentor and friend. He always considered us part of the team, took the time to teach us what he could, and provided us with lots of big adventures. We had our share of predicaments, but, over time, problems became challenges, and the sky still got light in the east, and we were doing some of the coolest trips in Alaska. Jerry led from the front and we trusted him and liked him. Good or bad, wet or dry, we were in things together, and we wanted Jerry to succeed because he wanted us to succeed.

Zach Babat & I grew up in the wilderness together with Jerry

Zach & me with a big bear skin

Jerry
Jacques

I.
Whitewater & Coming of Age in Alaska

From his first flight in a classic Stinson aircraft, to two harsh winters alone in the Alaskan wilderness, to a daring escape from captivity in the jungles of Guatemala, Part I tells the story of Jerry as a kid bound for adventure like few will experience in an entire lifetime—but these are still early days.

—CS Norwood

1.
How Dreams Begin

Devils Canyon lives up to its name in every raging, boiling rapid of that wild Alaskan stretch of the Big Susitna River. And I was going to be the first person to successfully raft it. It was considered the Mt. Everest of whitewater, and at twenty-one, I thought myself man enough and resourceful enough to run it solo. Somehow, I managed to successfully navigate the biggest set of rapids at the confluence of Devils Creek and the river canyon. I was master of my own destiny, right up to the middle of the canyon at a place called Screaming Left Hand Turn where I lost control and the raft flipped. My raft was upside down now, but I wasn't about to let go; it was more than a life raft to me. While I hung on helplessly, the cascade propelled me over big rapids and little rapids; I was swept downriver for miles. Eventually, and only by the grace of God, the raft finally hung up in an eddy long enough for me to tie off to a rock.

Being alone and trapped in the canyon scared me less than losing that raft. I hadn't finished paying Vladimir for it yet. It took me two nights to get the raft turned right-side up and repaired. Youth has its own special dispensation for dealing with near-death experiences; being a kid who was still in one piece, finally back at base in Talkeetna, my first Devils Canyon run got chalked up to just one more terrific adventure in my life—but this was early days.

Flash forward about five years to 1981. I was leading my clients on a six-day Talkeetna River whitewater raft trip. We had stopped at my prospector friends' tent at Disappointment Creek. I was tired and feeling sick but needed to help Marvin who was alone and being plagued by a black bear. I ran her off once, got back in my bunk and was asleep the minute I laid down under the two old heavy canvas sleeping bags. The next thing I knew—like something from a really bad dream—a bear was standing over me for the second time that night. She was so close, I could feel and smell her hot, stinky breath on my face. Very slowly I moved my left hand toward my pistol, but before I could get to it, she grabbed my arm and started shaking me while trying to pull me out of the tent. I fought back hard, trying not to let her drag me out before getting my free hand on that pistol. Once, twice, I fought my way almost to it, only to be dragged away again. It was on my third desperate try that I finally got hold of my Colt 1911 / .45 ACP. I hadn't aimed yet when she started shaking me even harder. I felt like a sticky old piston in an old motor, thrust up and down by this savagely determined bear. At the top of the next up-stroke, I put the gun to her head and almost pulled the trigger. I stopped short when I realized I was about to put a bullet into my own arm as well as the bear's head. I hesitated only a fraction of a second, put the gun to the base of her neck, and pulled the trigger. She instantly let me go and fell backward out of the tent. I fired off two more rounds at center mass through the opaque plastic that was now hanging between us. I got up and went out just as Marvin and Ed Wick came running up. I put a third round in her to make sure she was dead and then collapsed; my two friends caught me. I didn't escape this one without some real damage.

While episodes such as this are the stuff of terror-filled nightmares for almost everyone on the planet, for me, my life is a dream come true. But every dream starts somewhere, somehow, in circumstances defined by place and time...

Back to the Beginning

I was born in 1957 in San Jose, California. I have no idea what sort of infant I was—I hope, for my parents' sake, that I was a good little kid, easy to care for—a happy baby. But that might be doubtful. My first recollections in life are of constantly being in trouble. I was the kid who most neighborhood parents did not want their kids to play with.

Our neighbors told other parents, as well as my own parents, that they were cursed to be living next door to that little "Jacques Boy." They all said they would trade me for Dennis the Menace[1] any time and that Mr. Wilson was lucky to have Dennis the Menace as his neighbor rather than that Jacques kid.

As a six-year-old kid, I watched the last salmon run to ever return to the San Tomas Aquino Creek behind our house in Santa Clara. Perhaps I didn't understand the full environmental impact of what was taking place at the time, but I know now. People did not realize that the weir dams built upstream along with digging the creek to twice its normal depth for flood control, would kill the salmon runs. Sadly, this natural wild salmon run was gone forever.

It seems so long ago that I attended a Catholic school for first and second grade. Even at that young age, I was always getting into trouble for fighting and generally being a lousy student. Mother Superior and her paddle knew me well. Halfway through second grade, I was expelled from Saint Clair's Catholic School for being incorrigible. It probably did not help that I had locked one of the nuns in a storage closet.

---

[1] (contributors, Dennis the Menace (1959 TV series) n.d.)

My parents had divorced, and Dad was suddenly gone. Without the healthy fear of my dad, I was out of control and always getting into trouble. The frequent paddling I got from the nuns or the switch my mom used was nothing I feared. The only thing I feared was my dad's iron hand.

I was so out of control that my grandparents on my dad's side took me to Canada for two months. My mom had told them that she could no longer handle me. But being banished to Canada was no punishment for me. Now I was living my dream! My Uncle Walter Will (my grandmother's brother-in-law) would take me fishing for trout and gave me my first exposure to guns.

When we returned to California, I stayed with my grandparents for most of third grade.

I was soon back in Canada with my dad, though. He had just remarried. My new stepmom's name was Lois Chancellor, a PE teacher from Nevada. She was an excellent stepmom, and I felt lucky. Happily, we spent most of the summer living in a camper while traveling western Canada, stopping by to visit relatives.

Still, it wasn't quite enough. Even at my young age, I knew something was wrong, and I soon realized that Santa Clara just wasn't the right environment for me. This was perhaps because as far back as I can remember, I had heard stories from my great grandfather, grandfather, and my dad as well as my uncle about their lives in Alaska and the Yukon and about our family's history in the north.

North!

"They were the good old days up there!" They reminisced fondly of the grizzly and moose hunting, the fierce winters, the ramshackle towns, and open tundra of those wild far-away lands. Despite all the hardships, there was always a note of longing in their voices for their days in Alaska and the Yukon, the land that had shaped and hardened these men I loved so dearly. They had been forged in that land, and that's where I wanted to become a man, as well.

After listening intently to them tell and retell their adventures in the northern wilderness, I soon had it all figured out. I knew for certain that I was in the wrong house, wrong school, wrong town, wrong state—I was supposed to be in Alaska!

First Flight

Rudy Buchser was my dad's best friend from high school and college. When I was six years old, he flew us to Monterey, along the California coast. It was a very memorable trip. I was told most of the details and compared notes with Rudy when he worked as a pilot with me in 1997-98.

Rudy and Dad planned our takeoff from San Jose Reid Hillview Airport in a classic Stenson 108 Voyager airplane.[2] This was my first time being near an airplane as well as my first flight. I vividly remember the battery was dead and Rudy had to hand prop the plane to start it while my dad had his feet on the brakes. After takeoff, we flew over top my parents' house. Seeing our home with the creek, farms, and orchards on one side and the city on the other side made a huge impression on me. I suddenly became oriented in my small world from this bird's-eye view. And at that moment, I knew I would always fly, but never in a million years did I think I could ever become a pilot. The cost of lessons and plane rental was not possible for me, and my family had no interest in aviation.

Although this marked the beginning of my lifelong love affair with aviation, paradoxically, it also marked my first-time experiencing the death of a man.

We had landed on a beach south of Monterey where Rudy and my dad promptly offloaded their clamming tools and buckets and headed out into the surf. A Japanese lady was contentedly watching me and Rudy's daughter play while her husband was also clamming. He was wearing waders and had a large steel rake tied to his waist. We idly watched as he waded deeper into the surf, raking the sand ahead of him for his clams. Another wave hit him as he had ventured waist-deep into the water, but this wave filled his waders. The instantaneous and powerful force of receding surf suddenly took him under. He virtually disappeared before our eyes and was gone, carried out to sea. His wife screamed in panic. My dad and Rudy were at least a quarter of a mile away but heard her cries, dropped their tools, and came running.

It was too late; he was nowhere to be found. The sea had claimed him. Rudy and my dad were in wet suits and started diving into the surf looking for him. After half an hour, Rudy came back and, without a word, lifted his daughter and me onto the plane. We all started looking for the man from the air, but we never saw him. His body was found a week later with that big steel rake still tied to his waist.

About the time we returned to California from our Canadian camper trip, to my deep dismay, Dad and Lois both made it clear that they were anti-gun parents, so anything having to do with guns was off limits. I had saved enough money I earned by pulling weeds for the lady next door to buy a cheap .22 rifle at a garage sale. The guy holding the sale made me bring my dad to pick it up, though.

"No way!" Dad said. I was heartbroken, but Dad and Lois did let me buy a re-curve bow instead.

We lived on the edge of the city. So out the front door was city

---

[2] For photos and Aircraft History, see: (Pacific Coast Air Museum 1996)

life and out the back door was San Tomas Aquinas Creek as well as farmland. Sadly though, the farmland and orchards were quickly disappearing into what became known as the Silicon Valley.

Fighting was the only thing I was good at in the city. I was a failure at football and baseball. I took on Glen Street, the school bully and got my butt whooped. So, I took him on again a few weeks later when I still would not back down, and to everyone's surprise—including mine—I beat him this time. I fought him every week for the rest of the school year. Sometimes, I came out on top; sometimes I took a beating. Eventually, we called it even and became friends.

By the time I was in fourth grade, my favorite uncle, Satch Carlson, moved to Alaska. Before he left, though, he gave me a bolt action .22 rifle. I was thrilled of course, but my parents were a little worse than upset with Uncle Satch. At first, and to my utter dismay, I was not allowed to shoot it. They were obstinate, but so was I, and I kept at it until they finally gave in. My hunting career had begun.

I shot my first rabbit in a huge open field with the grass only a couple of inches high. I shot the rabbit with my .22 rifle from one hundred yards while prone on top a levee. It took many rounds to get the range down before I hit it. It was my first kill, and I cried when I picked it up and realized what I had done. My parents did not know how to clean or skin it, so I had to figure it out myself. They made me do everything, including cook it.

I was alone in my new world. I had no one to teach me anything about hunting. I had listened to my grandfather's talk, but, as a kid, I never got to hunt with anyone but myself.

During spring of my fifth-grade year, I ran away for the first time. I wanted to go to Alaska but there were no offers from anyone to take me there. I was on my own. I did remember my grandfather saying that our creek opened to the San Francisco Bay and that ships in the bay often went to Alaska. So the bay was my first destination. I did make it to the bay, but there were only mud flats and no ships near where the creek emptied into the bay in Santa Clara. I don't remember how I got caught. I just remember my dad picking me up and being mad. He must have been more scared than mad, though, because I didn't get spanked that time.

My wild lifestyle at that very young age eventually caught up with me, however. School teachers soon discovered that, even in the fifth grade, I could not read. Mr. Vern Alexander, the school principal, took me and three other kids out of class the hour before lunch and during lunch hour. He gave up two hours of his day for the whole school year to give four kids extra help to learn to read.

I had started that year with a first-grade reading level. After one school year with Mr. Alexander, my reading was at twelfth-grade level. Years later I found out that I am very dyslexic. There is no doubt in my mind that without the help of that dedicated teacher, my life would not have turned out very well.

Thank you to all the teachers, coaches, and mentors who give part of your lives to help kids like me! This book is dedicated to you—the teachers, coaches, and mentors who go the extra mile to help struggling kids succeed.

Several years ago, I started looking for Mr. Alexander to thank him. It took me ten years, but I finally found him. He was living in Texas.

We talked on the phone and wrote several letters back and forth. I told him that without his help and what he had done for me, my success in business and learning to fly would never have been possible. At the time I called him, I owned four planes and a successful hunting, fishing, and rafting business. He was pleased that a former student remembered him and was modest regarding what he had done for me. He was a talented teacher who gave me one-on-one time and figured out a way to calm me down. He never made me feel bad for being slow in learning to read. I still get tears when I think of what he did for me and how it changed my life; it was the greatest gift of my life. To this day, he remains one of my heroes.

After learning to read, I would spend lunch in the school library reading any magazine article about hunting, fishing, shooting, or survival I could find. I started reading books on explorers and pilots. I listened to my grandfather's stories of Alaska and the Yukon every chance I had and always asked him many questions.

While I was still in fifth grade, my dad and mom (Lois) bought a cabin in the Sacramento delta. We spent most weekends and all summer there. I spent most of my time building docks and pounding pilings by hand. The reward was getting to escape and go hunting early mornings and after the day of manual labor. Dad worked me and my two brothers hard but then gave us time to play in return.

Sixth grade came and went, and we were back in the cabin for the summer of '69. I spent all my free time exploring our part of the delta in an eleven-foot skiff with a three-horsepower motor that I had saved up to buy. (I still have the old three-horse, and it still runs.) I tried again to run away at the end of that summer. I knew the delta fed into the bay and that I could get to the ships in the bay using the skiff. I figured I would stow away on a ship bound for Alaska.

With the three-horse outboard I made it forty miles toward my Alaskan dream before my dad caught up to me in his ski boat.

By the time I started seventh grade in 1969 I was running away from home more often. I wanted to become a mountain man in Alaska or the Canadian Yukon. But at the age of twelve, I never made it far; I kept getting caught and my captors always sent me back home.

Also, by the ripe old age of twelve, I had been in and out of trouble more times than I can remember. The final straw for my parents and teachers was when I acted as the lookout for a gang of older guys while they robbed a liquor store. In a last-ditch effort, my parents packed us all up and moved to the hills above Redwood City to keep me away from the gangs of San Jose and, hopefully, keep my younger brother from following my footsteps straight into delinquency.

As an eighth grader, now with no gang to hang out with, I joined the Boy Scouts. My best friend, Robert Reid, took me along with him to a meeting at the start of the school year. The Scout troop was sponsored by the Mormon Church.

Bruce Lister, the Boy Scout leader, asked all the boys if they wanted to build fiberglass whitewater kayaks. Robert and I were the only ones interested enough to start earning the fifty dollars it took to buy the supplies, though. The church got donations and had a mold built as well as getting most of the supplies donated. The twenty-five dollars we each earned was only a fraction of the actual cost. Someone else in the church let us use their garage for the winter, and Robert and I helped Bruce finish building the mold. Bruce helped us build wood and fiberglass paddles as well as our kayaks. Working three nights a week, building those two kayaks took most of the winter. Now I was finally doing something that really interested me. In the spring, our brand-new kayaks loaded and ready for their first river run, our scout troop headed for the Russian River. Our feeling of accomplishment was almost overwhelming when we put our own craftwork in the river. Robert and I were the only ones who didn't have to rent canoes; we ran the Russian River in our own kayaks.

More than that, on that first run, I was instantly hooked on whitewater. That raging river supplied the wildly daring adventure I craved. It soothed all that pent up frustration I carried with me everywhere. I was genuinely happy and totally focused while running the Russian River that day; whitewater settled me like nothing else could, and though I never did become a member of the LDS church, I will be forever grateful to the Mormons for the exposure they gave me to whitewater and the outdoors. They were good role models. That church and scouting taught me to be prepared. The LDS teachings to have a year's supply of food stored at home made sense to me. Building my own kayak taught me that remarkable things can be accomplished through hard work and pursuing your goals and your dreams. I owe my brothers and sisters in the Mormon Church much for the positive influence they had on my life.

At my young age, I was explosive when confined in school and town. Looking back, I think I was one of those rare kids who needed to be set free to face a challenge, to wander and explore.

At the start of my freshman year in high school, Dad and Lois divorced. I had not seen my birth mother for a few years; she had moved away. I was devastated most by the loss of Lois, though. She had been good to me. Dad had been having an affair with another woman and, shortly after Lois moved out, the other woman moved in.

Like a logjam in whitewater, events often have a way of blocking our plans and altering our course in midstream.

Two months into my freshman year in high school, I had already been suspended twice for fighting and was back in the principal's office, again on the verge of expulsion. The vice principal had had enough of my behavior by that time, so he dragged me to the wrestling room in the gym. He said, "If you think you're so tough, show me with these guys."

The coach was all in with the challenge and put me with a small guy named Steve Madena. I sized him up and figured it would only take me a few seconds to whoop him. Steve took me down so hard it knocked the wind out of me. I wasn't done, though. I wanted a second chance at him. He took me to the ground hard again, and again—two more times. Mike Cohan, the wrestling coach, let me pick myself up and said, "So, tough guy, want to learn how to defend yourself from that move?"

"Yes," I had sense enough to say, even though what I really wanted was to learn how to do those moves to the next guy I wanted to fight. The vice principle took me aside and told me to join the wrestling team. He said, "Get rid of all your aggression in the mat room or be expelled." It was my choice now. I joined the wrestling team. With morning and after school practice, I had no energy left to get into fights.

After the wrestling season ended, I reverted to my old ways, getting into trouble, and now I was at odds with my dad again.

It was near the end of my freshman year, while I was still just a fifteen-year-old with home life in turmoil, that I determined to get to Alaska. I also decided that I wanted to join the Marine Corps, even though I was too young. I walked into the Marine Corps recruiting station in Redwood City thinking they would have a base in Alaska. The Corps did not have a base in Alaska, but I decided I wanted to join anyway. I lied about my age and now I had to come up with documents to prove I was eighteen. I hitchhiked back to San Jose where one of my friends had an uncle who made fake IDs, including birth certificates good enough to fool the government. Next, I got a Social Security card using the fake birth certificate.

Recruiters were trying hard to get guys to volunteer and sign up. My phony birth certificate and Social Security card said that I was eighteen, but I still needed a high school diploma or a GED. The draft was still in place for the Vietnam War, and California was one of the hubs for anti-war demonstrations, so I think they were happy to have a kid come in who actually wanted to join. The recruiter loaned me books and gave me advice to help me pass my GED. I passed, and I thought I was set; he signed me up. I had my physical test and induction in Oakland, California.

Two weeks later, he drove me back to Oakland. A group of us were sworn in, then loaded on a bus on our way to boot camp. The bus had just started to move when it jerked to an abrupt stop; the recruiter got on the bus with a scowl on his face meant just for me. My dad had discovered from my little brother that I had joined the military and was on my way to boot camp. Dad had managed to quickly track me down and inform the Marines that I was only fifteen. It was not a pleasant ride back to Redwood City, but just before we got back, the recruiter started laughing so hard, he had to pull over. When he stopped laughing, he told me that he now had the distinction of having recruited and signed up the Marine with the shortest career on record. "Come back and join as soon as you turn eighteen," he said after he quit laughing.

My parents were at their wits end with me. As probably the last of their last hopes, they explored sending me on a twenty-three-day Outward Bound wilderness survival course run by Tim Hansel and Dick Savage.

Tim Hansel was the director for California Outward Bound and a teacher at my high school. After learning what Outward Bound was and that I was headed for the High Sierra Nevada Mountains, I thought it was the next best thing to joining the Corps. I wanted to go. My dad decided it was silly and would not help in any way. Trying to figure out how to pay for the course, I offered to work in exchange for the course. Tim offered me a fifty-percent scholarship if I would eat fifty percent of a banana slug to prove to him that I had the intense desire to go. I went out and found a banana slug and, in front of him, ate the half-slug without hesitation. Five minutes later, when no one was looking, I was in the bathroom throwing up.

Lois paid for the rest of the Outward Bound course. She also drove me the five hours to the starting point. She saw how compelled I was to spend my time in the wilderness and was supportive, even though she and my dad had split up. That wonderful lady who supported my dreams and was a fantastic role model will forever have my love and gratitude.

I learned so much during those twenty-three days. Mostly, I loved rock climbing, rappelling down vertical cliffs, and traveling cross country in the rugged mountains. Near the end of the course, each student was left alone to survive for three days and three nights at a six-thousand-foot elevation in the High Sierras—no sleeping bag or tent. Students were allowed to take six matches and a pocketknife. On the third morning, I killed a marmot with a sharpened stick and a big rock. I ate all the meat. When the instructors picked me up at the end and offered me food, I told them that I wasn't hungry. They were surprised until they found out what I had done, then they were not happy with me. Looking back, I realized it was, after all, in California and in a national park. Killing the marmot was probably not the best idea.

Overall, it was a life-changing experience for me. I saw that not all Christian men were soft or led boring lives. These amazing role models helped lead me to Christ, becoming a Christian and ultimately becoming a professional guide and business owner. That logjam I had been up against was beginning to break up.

After the Outward Bound course, I moved in with my former step-mom and her two roommates and started my sophomore year of high school.

Hitchhiking with a backpack with climbing and camping gear was not a problem but getting my kayak to the rivers was a challenge, so I concentrated on climbing.

It was easy to hitchhike with my climbing gear to Yosemite National Park for weekend climbs. I'd skip school on Friday and be in Yosemite Valley at Camp Four by nightfall, climb all day Saturday and Sunday, skip school on Monday while I climbed half the day, then hitchhike back to the bay area. Four weeks before my sixteenth birthday, I had met a climber who was an old man—I was sixteen years old, and he was thirty-five—so, yeah, he seemed like an old man to me. He was some sort of high-tech computer person living in San Jose, right next to the place that had become known as Silicon Valley.

We had already climbed together on two occasions and found that we were compatible. He was a better climber and had more experience than I did, but since he didn't have a climbing partner, he agreed to climb with me again one particular weekend. My dream climb was to

Lost Arrow
Climb, 1973

climb Lost Arrow on my sixteenth birthday and, after completing the climb, exit the tip via the Tyrolean traverse.

There was a very famous climbing poster at the time that showed a group of climbers accomplishing the Tyrolean traverse. This was a spectacular visual of a rope tied to bolts on the top of the Lost Arrow Spire with the other end of the rope secured to a tree on the other side. The climber has his climbing harness clipped onto the rope with a pulley and carabiners as a backup. Then, if you're the climber, you just pull yourself all the way to the other side.

I had first seen this poster in The North Face store in Palo Alto and thought it would be the ultimate climbing experience.

My plans were made to head to the valley. A friend from high school, Rick Gottwald, wanted to come with us and do the hike from the valley floor up the Yosemite Falls trail and cross Yosemite Creek to the point where we were across from Lost Arrow. The hike up from the valley floor was strenuous. We had multiple climbing ropes and all our climbing hardware, along with our camping gear for the trail. It was a warm day, and we were all hot and sweaty. Our climbing racks clanked like windchimes in the still air. Any conversation ceased as the trail narrowed to follow-the-leader, and I was the leader. Soon the awareness of my surroundings also narrowed to my steady rhythmic pace upwards on the path and the sounds we made as they drifted away into the vastness around us. I was in that sort of mission-focused state, when I came upon a man lying in the middle of the trail with his feet propped upward toward the rockface and his head resting downwards towards the abyss. By his side sat an open gallon jug of wine, a notepad lay on his chest, and a backpack propped up his head. With binoculars he was staring upwards at the rockface, above and basically between his feet. There was no way to walk around him, either. I would not have disturbed him in whatever was his business, except the trail was so narrow at that point that the only way we could advance was for him to move or for us to step over him. He had obviously heard us coming from the clanking of our gear, but there he lay, unmoving, studying that rockface. We waited. Finally, he looked over at me.

Warren Harding! I immediately recognized him from pictures I'd seen in books and climbing magazines. He was one of my climbing heroes! Warren Harding and I had never met, until now.

After looking at me for a second or two, he blurted out, "Do you know who I am?"

This hero just plummeted from the towering rockface I had put him on. I had not heard of him being an arrogant person, just a kind of rebel.

"No," I answered blandly disinterested now. "Who are you?"

He picked up the gallon jug of wine and said simply, "I'm Donald Duck. Do you want a drink?"

Hero status restored. I was now laughing so hard I almost fell off the trail.

Turns out he was using his binoculars to study and map out a possible route. All these years later, I don't recall the name of the route; it was either the Black Wall or the Forbidden Wall. I don't know if he ever accomplished that climb, but it was my first meeting with the legend.

He moved out of the way then and asked us what we were going to go climb.

"Lost Arrow!" I blurted out.

He thought it was pretty cool that a young kid was heading to do Lost Arrow. He told my climbing partner and me to have fun as we parted ways.

We continued our hike; topping out on the valley rim, we crossed Yosemite Creek and went to the edge to look down on Yosemite Falls. From more than a couple of thousand feet above the valley floor, the vertical view was amazing as the water plunged one-thousand four-hundred and thirty feet down the rockface of the upper fall. Overall, its two-thousand-foot, directly-downward course takes it to the valley floor where the creek soon joins the Merced River. Looking out at the panorama before us, we could see almost the entire Yosemite Valley, across the snaking Merced to Glacier Point, Sentinel Dome, and beyond to the Yosemite Wilderness area. It was a majestic sight on a beautiful day! For my once-in-a-lifetime sixteenth birthday, I could not have wished for any better gift for myself, and I was more than ready for this climb!

From the falls, we hiked the rim until we were across from Lost Arrow where we found a place to camp for the night. The next morning, we had some decisions to make. In order to climb the Lost Arrow Spire Tip, we first had to rappel down a significant distance from the rim to get into what's called The Notch. From there we would cross over to the tip of the spire and start the climb. It is completed in three pitches.

Trying to figure out how we were going to get the rope so we could do the Tyrolean traverse after we had completed our ascent of Lost Arrow was an issue, however. We didn't have any directions on how previous climbers had done it. I'd only seen the pictures and read the climbing guide on the actual difficulty of the climb.

We had brought along some light cord with a weight attached to one end, and, after trying for about fifteen minutes, I finally landed the weight on top of the Arrow where it stayed. It had actually hit the top and bounced over the far side and was just suspended there. We tied the other end of the rope off and used a length of Goldline, an older style climbing rope, to rappel down. We left it fixed in case we had to jumar back up if we failed to summit the Arrow.

The rappel wasn't as exposed as I had thought because you're looking down into this notch. It wasn't horrible yet it was still intimidating to go backwards off that cliff and down into The Notch. All-in-all, going backwards off that cliff and down into The Notch is not a big deal for a rock climber. We rappelled onto The Notch. I stayed roped up and crossed the notch calling this pitch one or P1. Years before there had been a climber who had fallen off the notch and died.

I took the lead on that easy first pitch. Next, my partner took the lead making it to a ledge called Salathé Ledge. To continue, he traversed to the far edge of the Salathé Ledge.

This is where a commitment move must be made. You must reach out, grab, and swing away from the ledge. At that moment, you're looking straight down about two thousand feet or more to the valley floor. I remember seeing these really tiny little valley shuttle buses scurry passengers around for a look at the falls—pretty intimidating. Well, my partner got to the edge of the ledge; looked at that move, and asked flatly, "Do you want to lead this pitch?"

It looked like a pretty cool pitch to me.

"This is your sixteenth birthday," he said. "If you want, why don't you lead. It would be quite an accomplishment for a sixteen-year-old!"

I was jazzed! I went ahead and reorganized the climbing rack to my sling. Then I looked around the corner, froze, then retreated.

Fifty years later, I still remember that first commitment move; the climber has to step off the ledge and reach around the corner with a straight-down vertical exposure of a couple of thousand feet; it was and, I'm sure till is, a very intimidating commitment move. It took me a while, but I pulled it together, made the move, and continued. From that point, I discovered that there were quite a few fixed pitons and so the aid climbing was actually quite easy. All I had to do was clip into one fixed piton then on to the next. It wasn't that difficult. Previous climbers had already done the hard work.

At the time, I had a brand new, or relatively new, one-hundred and sixty-foot climbing rope. In the day when the Lost Arrow climb was first done, I believe they had only had one-hundred and twenty-foot climbing ropes. I got to the top of what should have been the pitch and it looked to me like it wasn't that long of a pitch, so I figured I could make it to the top in one pitch. I continued my ascent, but the rope drag kept increasing. Now just forty feet from the summit, there was so much rope tension that I couldn't go any farther. I hadn't used long enough runners and I'd been making some mistakes in how I placed my protection. I literally couldn't pull the rope anymore. Now I was stuck. I was yelling at my climbing partner to give me slack, he was yelling back that the rope was slack on his end, but I wasn't pulling the rope.

I had just made a simple mistake and was now in trouble. My solution was to tie the rope off to a fixed piton. From my position, it was not far to the top and wasn't very steep; but still, if I slipped and fell from that point, it was a certain death sentence. I took my climbing *etriers*, which are little webbing ladders, and put them together. Using all my runners, I put them together and tied that to the piton and my rope. That gave me enough extra length that I could be pretty safe climbing the rest of the way to a fixed bolt near the summit, I was then able to clip myself onto the bolt. Even though I pulled with all my might, I still couldn't make the rope come up. I yelled down to my climbing partner that both the rope and I were clipped in and secure, but I couldn't really belay him because of the rope tension. He was able to climb up the rope using jumars, pulling my webbing runners and carabiners as he ascended.

When he got to me, he bawled me out for not using enough runners. "You should have done it in two pitches, not one! You created too many zigzags in the rope. That's why the tension was on the rope, and you couldn't pull it up!" he scolded.

Then he saw what I'd done with the etriers and the runners and realized that I really hadn't done anything that unsafe. He understood that I had just made novice mistakes and rectified them as safely as I could.

We had just completed a successful ascent of the tip of the Lost Arrow Spire, rated 5.7 A2 in difficulty, and now we were sitting on the summit about two hundred feet above The Notch and 2,380 feet above the valley floor, just admiring the spectacular view once more. I remember there was a little metal box there containing a notepad and pencil. The notebook had names and short notes from climbers who had been there before us. I wrote something, I don't remember what, but I did include my name and the date. My climbing partner did the same. If that notepad is stored somewhere by the Yosemite Park Service, I would happily pay to have a copy.

Then we started yelling to Rick Gottwald, who had remained on the rim. He had become bored waiting for us and was taking a nap.

When he finally showed up, the plan was to have him pull our ropes to his side using the parachute cord that was still on the summit. We attached one end of our two climbing ropes. Rick pulled them over and secured them on his side. About this time, two other climbers showed up on the rim alongside Rick. I remember one of them was called "Mouse." I don't remember the other climber's name.

After we had the ropes set up, my climbing partner went first, clipped onto the rope on the Tyrolean traverse; the old Goldline rope which we had drug up with us was now used to pull. Now the three of them, Rick and the other two climbers, pulled from the other side and pulled my climbing partner across the chasm between the Lost Arrow Spire and the wall. It was spectacular to watch!

After he got to the other side, he let Rick put on his climbing harness, and Rick was able to accomplish his own Tyrolean traverse over to me! We both sat on the peak and admired the view. We knew that what we were experiencing made us the two most privileged and luckiest San Carlos High School students ever. Rick crossed back over, and I traversed last; kind of like the last to leave my birthday party.

We took a few pictures, but I don't have a clue where the photos went, so I wasn't going to even include this story in the book.

A few days ago, however, on Facebook, Brian McCullough, a well-known mountaineering and climbing guide based in Talkeetna, posted photos of Lost Arrow and the Tyrolean traverse. I've known Brian by name for thirty-five years but never had a conversation with him. On occasion, we may have said hello to one another in the Talkeetna Roadhouse or at the airport. Possibly less than ten words were ever spoken between us in all that time. I'm not even sure how we became friends on Facebook.

So today, as I was driving to the shooting range to do some practice, I decided to give him a call and ask permission to use one of his photos of Lost Arrow. I didn't know if he would say yes or no, but I figured it was worth a try, and the conversation would take a total of maybe five minutes. We ended up talking for an hour on the phone.

It turns out he is also from California. He's a few years younger than I am and had also climbed Lost Arrow for the first time when he was in high school. We had many mutual friends from Talkeetna, and both admired some of the same famous climbers of the day when we were kids. Cheerfully, he gave me permission to use his photos. After hanging up, I felt a small wave of regret. All the years that I've bounced between Iliamna and Talkeetna, I've known Brian McCullough by name only. He's a climber, adventurer, outdoorsman, and a master carpenter, but for some reason we just never connected. We never had a conversation that would allow us to realize how much we had in common, but I think if we had had that conversation, we'd have become friends, probably even sharing an adventure or two. Maybe it's still not too late, though, when I think about it. This is just my first book.

Brian McCullough on
Tyrolean traverse from
Lost Arrow Spire
to the rim
(Photo courtesy of
Brian McCullough)

Brian exiting
Lost Arrow
(Photo courtesy of
Brian McCullough)

VK   Robert Reid, being a few years older than me, taught me how to ride motorcycles and how to maintain them. His dad was a World War II vet and an escaped POW, although he never talked to us about it until I was in my thirties. I always respected Mr. Reid immensely and knew he had his own incredible survival story to tell.

On holidays and weekends, Robert's dad would fly or drive us to Bradford Island in the Sacramento delta. As an exercise in becoming men, his dad always made us forage for our own food. We had to catch or shoot something or go hungry. He helped us become skilled hunters. Catching catfish, crawdads, and shooting ducks and pheasants. He made us poach under the nose of game wardens and the private duck and pheasant club managers on the islands that we could reach by canoe. Occasionally, he let me fly his plane after we were in the air. When Robert and I were not at Bradford Island, we were with my parents in their cabin thirty miles away or in the delta. It was a Tom Sawyer and Huck Finn life, and we loved it.

VK,
Vladimir Kovalik

I had my climbing rope coiled and climbing rack on the outside of my pack while hitchhiking to a climb one day, when this guy in a black Porsche stopped for me. I hopped in, glad for the fancy ride. The guy introduced himself as Vladimir Kovalik.[3] "My friends call me VK," he said. The climbing rope was a giveaway. He said that he had also been a climber, but now he owned a whitewater rafting company called Wilderness World. He told me about his wild river trips, and I told him I was a kayaker as well as a climber but had no one to kayak with. I had an instant connection with this tough, assertive guy. Before he dropped

---

[3] Photo courtesy of Boatman's Quarterly Review and VK's son, Kyle Kovalik (Kovalik, Kyle, & Steiger, Lew 2005-2006). See also: (Collier 2022)

me off at my climb, he said he had a trip starting next Friday on the Stanislaus River. He told me I could follow his guides and clients in my kayak.

That next Friday, Robert Reid drove me and my kayak to the Stanislaus River. I had planned a three-day run down the Stanislaus with its Class III rapids. Robert would pick me up at the end of the trip. We got there after VK's raft company had already gone down river.

I foolishly launched alone. I did not know how to do an Eskimo roll, so every time I tipped over, I had to swim my Kayak to shore, bail out the water, then start over. Thank goodness for flotation bags in the bow and stern.

Two miles after I launched, I had already tipped over about four times, but I was still undeterred; I loved it. At Rose Creek, I met the guides working for Wilderness World. They were providing lunch for their clients and invited me to join them. I ate a fancy lunch while a few of the guides played in my kayak at the rapid just above the lunch spot. After lunch, I followed them downriver. They invited me to camp and to eat dinner with them that night. I only had a pack of Top Raman, so their dinner was a lot more appealing.

That night was the wildest party I had ever seen, and the first time I saw people smoking pot and women with their tops off. The next morning, one of the raft guides was so hung over, he just walked out to the road and left. This left a raft with no one to row it. The head raft guide figured that if I could kayak the upper river, which was Class III, then I could row an empty raft down the lower river which was Class II. As the clients were eating breakfast, he gave me lessons in the eddy next to camp. He put the clients on the other rafts and had me row an empty raft and follow them. My kayak was tied onto the back of the raft.

The next day, they had a one-day trip down the upper river. They invited me to row an empty raft again. This was a way for me to start learning to become a river guide, so I jumped at the chance. It was the start of my rafting career.

Wilderness World, VK's company, was an international whitewater rafting company with operations all over the world, including Alaska. I figured I was living my dream when he gave me a part-time summer job working as a whitewater raft guide in California. No pay, but I learned a lot that summer about the rafting business.

I worked long hours, but it was still a dream come true for a young kid. I was only sixteen and got to run the Stanislaus River three more times that summer. I became proficient at rafting Class IIIs.[4]

My Dad told me that if I stayed in school and passed my classes, I

---

[4] To learn more about the different classes of river rapids, see: (OBrien 2021).

could live as I wanted. And so I did; I now lived a nomadic life. Some nights I stayed at Lois's house and some nights at Mike Cohan's (my wrestling coach) house. Some nights I camped in the woods where I shot a duck or rabbit for my meal. I cut firewood for money on Coach Cohan's property. Coach was a part-time tree surgeon. He taught me how to use tree climbing spurs and ropes to remove problem trees near houses and would pay me to help him on jobs, this also made me some good money on occasion, but I had another side job, as well.

Type I Mae West life jackets were used by most raft companies. These had bladders inside for flotation. The problem was the bladders were fragile under continued commercial use. VK gave me over three hundred of these life jackets with one bladder ruptured. I bought a used Singer Model 20U commercial sewing machine and started fixing the life jackets and selling them. With the sewing machine, I also made tie-down straps for rowing frames and large cargo bags for the back of rafts.[5]

I enjoyed my jobs and the nomadic life I was leading, but I hated school and barely passed my classes. I never went on a date or to a dance, a party, or a movie, and I never ate in a restaurant. None of that held much interest for me. I was looking for something else, I suppose. I wanted the wilderness; I wanted the whitewater rivers; I wanted Alaska—I wanted adventure; yet, somehow, I stayed in school that year.

During spring break in 1974, I started working for Wilderness World in California. I was learning more about professional raft guiding, making twenty-five dollars a day on the river and loving it.

Vladimir Kovalik, Vic McLean, and Bob Volpert all became mentors. Vic told me he believed Alaska was the best place for a young person to start a raft company, and I was already hooked on Alaska from my grandfather's stories. As soon as school was out, I went back to working raft trips on the Stanislaus River, but now I knew where I was headed.

In August, VK offered to let me join him in Alaska. He was going to explore the Copper, Alagnak, and Nenana rivers. I was to be the trip photographer and a raft guide on the river expeditions—without pay! I was working for the privilege of being on the trip. In retrospect, I got the better end of the deal.

After exploring several rivers, VK left his two rafts and gear stored in Talkeetna at Don Sheldon's hanger and headed back home to California.

Personally, I had no plans of ever leaving Alaska, but mid-September, my dad had different plans and contacted the Alaska State Troopers to send me back to California.

---

[5] I still own and use the Singer 20U sewing machine.

The trooper who found me confiscated my phony IDs but took real pity on me. At least, he talked to me like he understood my predicament.

"Son, you're welcomed back as soon as you turn eighteen, and I will help you any way I can," he said. "Until then, you have to go home."

Back in school in California again for my senior year, all I could think of was whitewater trips, rock climbing, and Alaska. My plan was that as soon as wrestling season was over, I was going to drop out and head back to Alaska; I figured by the time the troopers caught up with me again, I would be eighteen.

It was a good plan from my perspective, but Coach Cohan convinced me that, as the newly elected wrestling team captain, I owed it to the team to finish high school.

I hated school and wanted nothing more than to head back to Alaska, but Coach was persuasive. Finally, I promised him I would stay in school and try to graduate.

I'm not sure I could have stuck it out till graduation, though, if it weren't for my senior project. Ilios was an alternative program within our school utilizing an open study program that let individual students choose what they studied and complete their studies at the pace they learned best. What I studied the most and learned the quickest was anything that had to do with wilderness adventures. As my senior project, I was allowed to start and teach a wilderness class, providing a teacher would sponsor me and attend every class. Rod Linear, Coach Cohen, and teachers from the Ilios program agreed to help.

First, I had to produce an outline of what I proposed the class was about, then post it to see if at least twelve kids would sign up.

I promised the kids that they would get to do field trips and get hands-on experience with backpacking, rappelling, rock climbing, kayaking, and whitewater rafting.

Over forty kids signed up, so the class was a go.

I was required to write lesson plans for every day of class. I had to write the plans detailed enough so that the sponsoring teachers could teach the class if I were not there.

I arranged to have guest speakers once or twice a week for the whole school year. Getting experts to come talk to high school kids wasn't hard. My bosses in the kayaking, rafting, and climbing business were more than willing to come and speak. Contacting places like North Face, REI, and the local sport shops and ski slopes, I was able to get several of their experts to come as guest speakers, as well. It was great! I learned something new from every speaker who presented to my class.

The first multi-day field trip that I organized for the class was a cross country ski trip. The school administrators had to approve it, and they put my plans through a lot of scrutiny.

As a seventeen-year-old kid, I had to rent ski equipment, rent a large enough place to sleep twenty-eight kids and four adult chaperones, hire instructors, and plan a food menu for three days. I had everything planned out and written down. The cost to the kids was a third of what the ski resort was charging for a similar trip. The school approved the trip, and it was a success!

The kayaking, climbing, and whitewater rafting field trips also took a lot of work to put on and were also big hits with the kids. The class was a huge success, and it kept me in school for my senior year.

I did not plan it, but somehow each trip I had organized for the high school made me a small profit. I worked for VK weekends and organized trips with high school students to raft the Stanislaus River.

VK agreed to pay me a fifteen-percent commission for each person on the trip.

To my parents' surprise and relief, I graduated San Carlos High School with the class of 1975.

By the time the summer of '75 was over, I had worked rivers in both California and Alaska. I was incredibly lucky to have learned the ins and outs of the whitewater rafting business from Vladimir Kovalik, Bob Volpert, and Vic McLean who were free with advice on how to start and run a rafting business.

I had made nineteen hundred dollars in wages and commissions. I wanted to stay in Alaska, but my parents and Coach Cohan talked me into going to college.

During my first semester, I wrestled for the College of San Mateo and won eighty-five percent of my matches. But my heart was not into wrestling, and I still hated school. Before the second semester started, I had a different plan, my plan!

VK had two whitewater rafts with all the gear stored in Talkeetna. He was downsizing his business and agreed to sell me his Alaska rafting operation for four thousand dollars. We agreed on nineteen hundred down and twenty-one hundred dollars over the next three years.

My goal was to run the whitewater rafting company ferrying my clientele (mostly wildlife photographers) to remote places inaccessible to ordinary tourists. I was on my way north to Alaska.

2.
Coming of Age & North to Alaska

Following My Dream North

I had agreed to also buy one of VK's prototype whitewater rafts called a Havasu. Because it was an early prototype, it didn't have the cosmetic stripe on the side, so he sold it to me with the promise that I would pay him another eight hundred dollars by year four. I loaded everything that I owned in an old pickup and headed to Alaska.

Already in Talkeetna was the gear I was buying from VK: two fifteen-and-a-half-foot long rafts, two rowing frames, a dozen dry boxes, a few coolers, life jackets, and a few dry bags.

After traveling around Alaska all summer, running rivers, looking for the perfect river, I saw that Talkeetna, listed not as a town or village, but as a census-designated place (CDP), was a very cool little collection of shops and Nagley's Store at the end of the road system. Already inhabited by the Dena'ia people, it was established in 1916 as a district headquarters for the Alaska Engineering Commission. Some bush pilots made flights available for hire and Talkeetna Air Service had been in business since 1947. People looking for wilderness adventure gravitated to Talkeetna. With its proximity to Mt. McKinley, it was the hub of the Alaskan climbing scene, and at the confluence of the Susitna, Chulitna, and Talkeetna rivers, it was a perfect spot to base my new raft company. I was now living out of my truck as a gypsy and running river trips anywhere I could get clients. Life was good

Ray Genet the King of the Talkeetna Climbers

I arrived back in Talkeetna in June of '76. Since it was the center of the Alaskan climbing scene, I thought I had to prove myself, so I devised a two-fold plan. First, I wanted to climb Mt. McKinley. Second, to prove myself as the premier river guide, I would raft through the un-runnable Devils Canyon on the Big Susitna River.

To iron-out that first fold—the McKinley climb—I called my two rock-climbing partners in California, Gary Gissendainer and Roger Mead.

They were happy to try the climb. Gary had to lie to his parents and tell them he was just going to be climbing in Yosemite for a month.

McKinley was a good goal, but the truth was, I was a typically clueless teenager. I knew everything—right!!! While trying to plan the McKinley climb with my friends, Gary and Roger, we met Ray Genet, already a legendary mountaineer in Alaska. He figured out that we were experienced rock climbers but didn't have enough mountaineering experience to climb McKinley. When he gave advice that I dismissed as silly, Ray and I ended up in a screaming argument.

I don't remember now whether it was Gary or Roger who made the plans with Ray Genet, who was, at the time, the only climbing guide on Mt. McKinley. We didn't want a guided trip as none of us could have afforded it, anyway. But Ray had offered, for a fee, to provide planning and supply the food and gas.

Ray's idea of logistics, however, varied greatly from mine. His idea was to give us a hand-drawn map of a route to the summit with some basic notes on it, where to camp, and at what elevations—that was his logistical support, along with arranging with Jim Sharp to fly us and our gear onto the glacier. Ray showed us two refrigerator boxes, cut in half, so four big boxes full of all kinds of dried food: Mountain House, Richmoor, along with packages of Japanese food that was obviously left over from other climbing expeditions.

"Just take the amount of food that you think you guys need," he said. Then pointed to some cans of Coleman white-gas fuel which were rusted on top, and said, "You probably need this many gallons of fuel." And for that, the leftover food, and rusty cans of fuel, if I remember correctly, he was charging us three hundred bucks a person—for that. We still would have had to pay for the flight.

I thought it was ridiculous and said so to Gary and Roger.

"Hey, we can just go back to Anchorage and get all this stuff new and not use leftover and must pay all this money—three hundred dollars each! This is ridiculous!"

Ray heard me. I was about to cost him nine hundred dollars, and that's what caused the argument.

There was no previous agreement. Either Gary or Roger had just contacted him over the phone, and that was what their plan was.

When I heard logistical support, I expected something like a day-by-day, step-by-step itinerary. How much food and fuel we would need at each camp, for example. I had expected that Ray would have the food organized into what we needed, and he would school us on our expected consumption. I wanted Ray to tell us to use this much food up to this point, cache this much at this point. I expected a detailed itinerary of what we should do, and this wasn't happening. It was just "here's the food, there's the white gas." You should take this amount of white gas, and take whatever food you need, and this hand-drawn map, which you could get the same thing from Alaska Mountaineering and Hiking store in Anchorage!

I think you can still get the map there in fact. They had a calendar with the same map if I recall. Although that's the most common route to climb Mt. McKinley, Ray, I'm sure, did it from memory, and he may have even consulted with them on the map that was on their calendar.

But I was too broke to pay Ray three hundred dollars for what he was offering.

So, when he took offense, I stood my ground. Ray had an extraordinarily strong personality and a temper to match; he was a hot head. It was, after all, nine hundred dollars.

Jim Sharp, the bush pilot, had to break us apart. The next day, we went to Jim to get him to fly us to McKinley, but he refused because of what had happened with Genet.

"Good first week in Talkeetna!" Gary said. "You made an enemy of the climbing king and now the bush pilot won't fly us."

I suppose Sharp took pity on us, though. After a few minutes, he said, "Go talk to Cliff Hudson. He might fly you up there."

Hudson agreed to fly us to the Kahiltna Glacier where we could basecamp on the southeast slope of Mt. McKinley, now more commonly known as Denali. We started our climb from there. The Kahiltna Glacier is at an elevation of 7,200 feet. There's still more than 13,000 feet to climb to reach the summit; Mt. McKinley peaks at 20,320 feet. During the next twenty-one days, I learned the hard way that Ray was right, I really did lack the experience to climb McKinley. Even though my climbing partners had more experience than me, it was still not enough.

We had clear weather but did not make it anywhere close to the summit.

Several years later, I told Ray's wife, Kathy, the story about our argument; she just chuckled and said, "That's so much like Ray. I was in the background and heard it, ignored it, because it was so in-character for him." Kathy and Ray's two sons, Taurus and Adrian (Ado) are still friends of mine today.

Even more in character, according to Kathy, was that, after I went up and tried to climb (even though we weren't successful), Ray's temper was short-lived; he didn't hold grudges.

The climb was actually a nightmare for me because I had only worn crampons on my feet once before. On top of that, I was pretty shocked that, when we flew in, the first thing we had to do was hike downhill to get down to the glacier fork, which was where we began our assent. From the drop-off point, we hiked down the mountain then turned right and began our ascent. I suppose I expected Hudson would drop us off on the glacier right on the immediate climb route. It's only about 7,200 feet at the Southeast Fork of the Kahiltna Glacier where our pilot dropped us off. My next disappointment came at our 14,000-foot basecamp in the form of altitude sickness. That kind of surprised me. That first night, I had a headache and felt nauseous, even though it was not that high in altitude. We were going to be on the mountain for at least two weeks and, thankfully, my altitude sickness was gone by the next day.

There were already other climbers on the mountain when we arrived. I don't know their experience level, but we just didn't know what we were doing. Both Gary and Roger had far more mountaineering experience than I did, although we all had about the same technical rock-climbing experience. But Ray was right, none of us had the experience or expertise required to do what we were doing. Roping up—none of us had ever encountered crevasses before. We were in good physical shape for rock climbing, but this was Mt. McKinley—Denali—the highest mountain in North America, and we weren't mountaineers![1]

Mt. McKinley, also known as Denali (ArcticHokie 2003)

Regardless of our lack of experience, we were resolute, remaining undeterred, at least in the beginning. We backpacked our equipment and gear in three trips from our basecamp up to high camp, until we had our high camp established with enough food and fuel that we could wait there for the right weather to make our summit push.

Fuel was—and still is—critical for melting snow for drinking water. Dehydration is a big deal, and we all got dehydrated because we just didn't have enough water intake and that, again, was because of our inexperience.

---

[1] South view [from Boeing 737 flight] of Mt. McKinley from 27,000 feet. By ArcticHokie.

At high camp, we had our sleeping tent set up with another tent cached with all our supplies. If we were able to summit and return to high camp, if the weather closed in on us at that point, we needed to have at least three- to six-days-worth of food and more than that of fuel so we could wait for the weather to clear enough to get back down to basecamp and our flight out.

The three of us decided by consensus that we had had enough adventure this trip and were going to try later. This was inexperience: the day that we should have made our summit push, we really thought that the weather was coming in. Even though two other groups were going to go up, and they did summit, we just thought "No, this weather's coming in." We had heard the stories about getting trapped up there and the visibility being so bad you couldn't see and people dying because of that and the extreme weather and not being able to even walk because they couldn't see anything. The three of us kept looking and thinking, "No, I think this weather's comin' in. It's gonna change." We were right that the weather was changing, but there was more than enough time for a summit push. The weather we were looking at was more than a day or so out.

We did manage to climb past our high camp, which was around 14,000 feet (known as 14K camp on the maps). The highest elevation we made was some point just over 16,000 feet.

My friend, Rob Lesser will tell you that as a kid, sometimes I had more guts than brains. There were many rivers I kayaked down that I really had no business attempting. A few of those rapids were really above my ability, but I did it anyway. Usually, I could pull it off. I had climbed numerous rock faces before but had never attempted anything like a mountain. As novices, Gary, Roger, and I had attempted to climb Mt. McKinley—we failed.

Shortly after getting back to Talkeetna with my tail between my legs, I crossed paths with Ray Genet again. To my amazement, he was friendly and said that we did a respectable job for our first time on the mountain. He bought me an orange juice drink at the general store.

I told him that I was planning on rafting Devils Canyon. He told me he guided hunters near there in the fall and knew the canyon well. He asked questions about my rafting experience and wanted to see the rafts that I had. To my surprise, after showing him my best rafting gear, he told me that he thought I should give Devils Canyon a try. He also told me that if I made it, I would be the first to make it in a raft. He also told me to look at the Talkeetna River Canyon above Iron Creek. He said it had never been run by anyone in kayak or raft, and it would be a first descent. He told me that it might be more of what I was looking for in a river to take clients down. The three weeks and the failure to make it to the summit of Mt. McKinley gave me years' worth of maturity, so this time, I listened to every word Ray Genet said.

First Descent of the Talk-eetna River

In July, pilot Mike Fisher and I were flying over the Susitna River through Devils Canyon. At low level in the float plane that view of the river was intimidating. The size of the waves and holes were huge; that I had expected, but the technical difficulty of the routes and the length of the rapids far exceeded what I expected to see. Gary and Roger did not have much river experience but were worried by the huge waves and holes. They let me decide to go or not go. I knew we were not ready for Devils Canyon and so I said, "No go." It was the first time in my life that I had ever backed down from a challenge.

We had already paid for the flight, so from the air we looked at the Talkeetna River Canyon and decided to run it instead. Mike landed the plane at the headwaters on Stephan Lake then went back for the rest of our gear.

After inflating the seventeen and a half-foot raft, we attached a rowing frame, loaded all our gear, and launched. In a short amount of time, we were at the end of the lake and starting down a tiny sliver of water so shallow we had to drag the raft for the first half mile.

John Ireland and his friend Jody Lee (Photo by Cliff Hudson)

Both Gary and Roger thought I was silly for bringing two guns along for bear protection and never missed the opportunity to tease me as if I was just being paranoid.

The creek flowed into a small lake called Murder Lake. As we rowed past a small cabin on the lake a Sourdough named John Ireland came out and said hello. He invited us to have a cup of tea. He was impressed with the size of the raft and how we had it rigged but said there was a nasty canyon with a waterfall downriver. He told us no one had ever even tried to run the river in all the years he had lived here.

"If you plan to make it all the way back ta Talkeetna, you boys'll have to carry that raft and yer gear."

To make it back to Talkeetna, he said we would have to portage around the canyon for ten miles. Whitewater was a very new sport in the 1970s and his advice was common. He wished us a safe trip and said he would be praying for us.

The outflow of Murder Lake is Prairie Creek, heavily populated with king salmon in the spawning season. Half a mile downriver, we came to a large log jam that had to be portaged. A quarter mile later, there was another log jam that we also had to carry the raft over.

By the time we had carried around the third log jam we had seen four grizzly bears.

We set up camp early, but we were nervous with so many grizzlies close by. All three of us slept in our one small tent that night. The tent belonged to Roger, and he would not let me bring the shotgun into the tent, but my .44-mag revolver was okay with him, as long as it was in an ammo box.

Early the next morning I got up, put my .44-mag revolver into my shoulder holster, and started fishing. I wanted one of those salmon. I did hook several kings who put up a fight good enough that I could not get them to shore. After two hours of trying to land a king salmon I had lost all my lures. When I walked back into camp, Roger was holding my single-shot H&R 12-gauge shotgun, and Gary was looking extremely nervous. A grizzly had walked nonchalantly through the middle of camp shortly after I left. They panicked and went through my dry bag to find the shotgun slugs and quickly figured out how to load the single-shot 12-gauge. Roger had pulled the hammer back but did not know how to safely release the hammer without firing it, so he just held it until I got back. Seeing him there, holding that hammer back, told me that the lesson for the day would be on how to handle the 12-gauge. Gary and Roger both shot the 12-gauge and my .44-mag. They never again said a negative word about me bringing guns on the trip, and Roger even slept with the loaded shotgun next to him for the rest of the trip.

It took us three days to raft down Prairie Creek to the Talkeetna River. Although I never landed a king salmon on that trip, Roger did bring in several, Gary landed two, and we all three had a great time fishing down the river.

In total, there were fourteen log jams on Prairie Creek that we had to portage around, so our progress was slow.

At last at the confluence of Prairie Creek and the Talkeetna, we were surprised to see how silty the river was and how fast its current flowed. Our relatively placid little creek suddenly joined one big river, but we were curious, not worried. After a few hours of rafting, we came to the corner with the big rapid we had seen from the air four days before. We pulled over and scouted it. It was an easy Class III, and we ran it with no problem, but we took some time to relax after it was behind us. We thought that what we had just run was the biggest rapid on the river, at least it looked that way to us during the flyover.

Gary fell asleep and Roger started reading a book. I was rowing and enjoying the scenery and looking for wildlife, especially grizzlies. I wasn't paying enough attention to the river hydraulics as we floated around a bend. We were picking up speed. Unwittingly I had, to our misfortune, entered the biggest rapid on the river without scouting it! With the roar of what lay ahead, Gary was instantly awake; Roger was yelling to get to shore, but it was too late. Now we were in for it—we were committed to running this monster blind!

The first drop on that stretch of the Talkeetna is a river-wide ledge with a big hole. I turned the raft to go over the drop straight and hit the center of the hole. The force of the impact knocked me completely out of the raft; I tumbled so wildly that I couldn't tell which way was up or down. Still in the raft, Gary and Roger were stuck in the hole. As the raft spun violently around in the deadly current, they jumped from high-side to high-side trying to keep from flipping. At one point in all the commotion, Roger saw my foot alongside the raft and grabbed it. Together they pulled me back into the raft, threw me into the rowing seat, and yelled in unison *"Row!"*

I needed to get reoriented fast, or we were screwed.

The current spun us a few more times with me at the oars. Roger and Gary scrambling from high-side to high-side was the only thing keeping us from flipping.

God must have pitied our plight as the whole river suddenly surged. I realized the advantage, dug the oars in, pulled with all I had, and rode the surge out of the powerful vortex. Now the raft was full of silty water and totally swamped as the river picked up speed, narrowing to only thirty feet. The lofty, wooded canyon walls morphed into sheer rock cliffs on both sides as the river funneled—pushing us uncontrollably along for the ride. The bright daylight dissipated into deep shadows and the sound of raging river engulfed us as a solid wall of rock loomed dead ahead. Here, the mighty Talkeetna slammed into the cliff face that it had failed to carve a path through despite ages of onslaught, and the rock wall forced the river into a sharp ninety-degree turn to the right.

In the full grip of a raging river, it was up to me to get us through. From where I sat with my friends, the view was intimidating. We were in for it. I read the river course as quickly as I could and pulled the oars with all the strength I could muster. I managed a perfect ferry angle[2] with the current, but it made no difference. The raft bent in half as we slammed into the wall. The impact catapulted Gary, body-slamming him onto the vertical rocks. For an instant he clung spread-eagle on the wall before falling into the boiling water beneath him. I was in the rowing seat when the bow hit me in the chest so hard it knocked me backwards out of the raft—one more time. With me swimming once again, the raft bounced off the wall. I remember thinking the front tubes had to have been ruptured by the impact. My proprietary thoughts were roughly interrupted, however, when Roger grabbed me and threw me back into the rowing seat for the second time in only minutes, next he salvaged Gary with one quick pull. In a second or two, the river spit us out of the narrow funnel between the vertical walls.

Miraculously, the raft had sprung back to its original shape with the tubes still holding air! Even though I was still pretty busy at the moment, I was ecstatic that my raft had survived intact. I also noted that it was now only fifty percent swamped; the impact with the wall had dumped out half the water.

The force of the river was evermore relentless, though, and there was no time to celebrate. Just a few yards downriver were more big rapids with big rocks that had to be rowed around as well as two holes to miss. I did manage to avoid the rocks and first hole but bulls-eyed the last biggest hole. For the third time in under three minutes, we struck rocks, and I was thrown out of the raft and into that hole. The river sucked me to the bottom of the vortex, held me there, then spit me back to the surface. I swam hard. Gary threw me a rope, then hauled me back onboard, and, for the third time, I was plunked back into the rowing seat and commanded to row. I pulled on the oars again for all I was worth, and we cleared what I hoped was our last monster hole. At this point, we were at the bottom of the rapids, and the raft was again one-hundred percent full of water. I rowed another half mile though, before I could get us into an eddy so we could bail it out. Gary managed to jump ashore with the rope and tied us off to a tree.

---

[2] Ferry angle is the position of the raft in the current, so that when you row you move from side to side in the river to position the raft where it needs to be.

We were all stunned and wet.

"What the hell just happened!? Where did that rapid come from?" Gary queried aloud for all three of us like the true adventurer he was. We finally realized that the rapid we had scouted before was not what we had seen from the air. We had scouted the wrong spot then drifted blindly into the biggest rapid on our entire Talkeetna course!

Being the first to run a river (and survive to tell) gives you the privilege of naming the rapid. We decided to call that rapid The Entrance Exam. We decided that we had failed that test—The Entrance Exam—by not scouting the correct rapid.

The wall we called Gary's Gate.

They said that I had been in the first hole for at least sixty seconds before Roger saw my foot and grabbed me. I told the guys that I felt like I had been flushed down a toilet and was circling the bottom.

Roger said that, after my three trips out of the boat, I looked like a giant turd that kept going down the toilet bowl but somehow kept popping back up to the surface. We never intended on that name for the rapid, but when word got out with the story of our trip, the name The Toilet stuck. Forty-five years later that is what everyone still calls that big hole in The Entrance Exam rapid.

Unfortunately, we discovered that both of our bail buckets had washed away when we hit the last hole. That presented only an inconvenience compared to what we had just experienced, however. Without those bail buckets, we improvised, using my ammo can and a dry bag to bail the raft. It took longer to bail but gave us a little break off the river.

I suppose we should have been prepared for the unexpected by now, but the amount of continuous Class III whitewater[3] we encountered over the next twelve miles was a real shock. We had not realized from the plane how big the rapids were going to be. Still, we had a wakeup call at The Entrance Exam, and now we were on top of our game. Even so, we did a lot of bailing.

Ray Genet met us at the end of the village airstrip in Talkeetna. He congratulated us on the first run of the Talkeetna River. He wanted to know everything we had seen and what we thought of the river.

"The Talkeetna's the river I'm looking for," I told him. "It's a perfect commercial whitewater run. We just need to go back with chainsaws and cut out all those log jams on Prairie Creek,"

Hunting guide and pilot, Larry Rivers, along with Don Lee, and a few local Talkeetna people were my next victims to run the river. It was a good trip with no incidents—nothing I couldn't handle in my first official guided raft trip down Prairie Creek and the Talkeetna River.

---

[3] (OBrien 2021)

Ray sent me three Germans for my next six-day Talkeetna raft trip. He also offered me a job as a moose packer in September. Sadly, not long afterwards, Ray Genet died while descending the summit of Mt. Everest.[4] I still miss him.

---

[4] (contributors, Ray Genet n.d.)

Back to Alaska

Mid-Summer

VK and Vic McLean sent me a few rafting clients each summer in Alaska. With my little raft company, I bounced my business between Talkeetna and Lake Iliamna. My uncle, Satch Carlson, helped me keep my old truck running and let me use his shop. He also let me stay in his home when I was in Anchorage. Larry Rivers did the flying for my Talkeetna raft trips and became a mentor, teaching me how to fly a PA-18 Cub and how to run a small business. Carl Jensen had me work as his assistant on hunts after the rafting season was over and before trapping season started. I was getting by.

Hardcore Alaska Bush Pilot

Still new to Alaska and a total cheechako or greenhorn, despite my blunders, through sheer grit and determination, I was building a whitewater rafting business in Alaska. Between raft trips, I traded my labor to a pilot who flew my raft supplies and clients into the headwaters of the rivers that I was taking the clients down. I kept his planes fueled, washed, helped load and unload, cut firewood for him, and did whatever else was needed.

One morning, Sunny, the pilot, told me that I was going to work on an airstrip for a day or two. I was handed a list of things to gather and told how much gas to put into his Piper PA-18 Super Cub.

Sunny's list included a shovel, pick and ax, a prybar and chainsaw, a tool bag and one five-gallon plastic bucket. Those were my work supplies. He also included a large roll of nylon cord, a tarp and sleeping bag, and food for two-to-three days.

From the back of the fuel shed, he told me to bring him an old propeller that was full of nicks and dents, it was a horrible looking piece of junk. Strangely, he took off the good prop from the Cub and installed the funky prop. Sunny certainly did not live up to his name in the disposition department; he was a grumpy old man. I knew not to ask questions and just followed his directions. He had me help him tie the good prop, shovel, pick and pry-bar outside the plane on the wing struts. On the other side, he tied a pair of landing-gear legs.

The rest of the gear loaded along with me into the Cub with the chain saw on my lap. The Super Cub looked a whole like the packed-up car in the Beverly Hillbillies[1] as it left their mountain home. Like their

---

[1] Title of a 1962-71 TV sitcom ("The Beverly Hillbillies").

old wreck, we were loaded-up and all strapped-down; the only difference was, this old jalopy was airborne.

Cigar in his mouth, resolute Sunny got us off the ground into the air, and off we flew into the mountainous Alaskan wilderness. After an hour in the air, he descended into a small valley and started circling above a small stream. He made four or five lower passes, then told me to tighten my seat belt.

What seat belt?! He had removed my seat belt to use as one of the tiedowns to lash his good prop onto the strut. I could see there was no place to land, and I was not at all clear about what the hell was going on. The next thing I knew, we were five feet above the creek heading straight at a patch of willows. His wheels touched down on a short sixty-foot piece of gravel bar. We skidded for a second with rocks flying off the tires before we crashed into the willows. The prop cut through the willows like a giant weed whacker, with me feeling like I was getting myself chopped up right along with the bush. Mercifully, we came to an abrupt stop, but the propeller was still turning. Knowing the plane would burst into flames any moment, I jumped out and was fifty feet away in an instant.

Turning back, I was shocked to see that old pilot still sitting in the plane, calmly smoking his cigar. I cautiously walked back to the plane to see what the hell was going on! Only then did he explain to me that he needed a new air strip here because the creek had washed away the old one.

There was no place long enough to land in this valley, so, using the willows to stop the plane was his plan from the start. That's why he had put his bushwhacker prop on before we left.

We unloaded the gear and spent the next few hours making a crude airstrip with the chain saw and tools. When he was satisfied with what we had done, he put the good prop back on and took off. I was left behind with the tools to continue improving the airstrip. In a day and a half, I had completed a five-hundred and fifty-foot strip safe for landings and take off. Two days later, Sunny landed on the new strip. After he completed his inspection, we loaded up, and flew to my next project. In the middle of nowhere, I was to cut down trees and build a wall-tent frame, dig an outhouse hole, build the outhouse, and put in a set of tie-downs for the plane. When he finally returned to pick me up, it was time for me to start another whitewater trip.

As agreed, Sunny flew me and my raft, all my gear, and all my clients to the Koktuli River. I reckoned we were more than square on the deal.

I was desperately trying to build a clientèle in 1978 when I met wildlife and nature photographer Art Wolfe. Our friendship quickly developed, and we started doing Alaskan wildlife and wilderness photo expeditions together. I could take us into places that no one else could access, while Art took amazing photos to show the world. He published an article with some of his photos from our trips giving me ample credit for getting him access for his incredible work. Those photos and that article marked the turning point for my struggling company.

Art Wolfe

There were other photos and articles, as well, and the publicity from Art's work brought rafting and fishing clients from around the world. This made exploring the wildest places in Alaska by kayak and raft possible for me.

Still, these were early days. Kayaking and rafting took us only so far expending a lot of time and effort to arrive at our destinations. I needed to fly.

I started exploring new territory for my clients now, and one of the trips I did was an attempt to become the first person to successfully raft Devils Canyon. It was considered the Mt. Everest of whitewater.

Devils Canyon Run

Looking for partners in the quest I wanted Gary Gissendainer and Roger Mead. Roger wanted no part of Devils Canyon, and sadly, I learned that my friend, Gary, had died in a climbing accident on Quarter Dome in Yosemite. (His fall happened May 28, 1978, and he died on June 3, 1978.) No one else I trusted was willing to attempt rafting Devils Canyon with me. With no other options, I was foolish enough to try to run it solo. Somehow, I managed to get through the biggest set of rapids called Devils Creek. In the middle of the canyon at a place called Screaming Left Hand Turn, I flipped the raft. Hanging onto the now upside-down raft, I was dragged over big rapids and swept down river for miles. Eventually the raft hung up in an eddy long enough for me to tie it to a rock.

Being alone and trapped in the canyon scared me less than losing the raft. I will admit my biggest fear at that time was having to face my old boss, Vladimir, and tell him that I lost a raft—the one I had not finished paying him for. It took me two nights to get the raft turned upright and repaired. By the grace of God, I did make it back to Talkeetna but never considered the run a successful run. When you're clinging to an upside-down raft at the mercy of the river for half of the biggest rapids, it is not a successful run.

My First Alaskan Winter, 1978

I had much to learn and learned most things the hard way. I was incredibly lucky to survive the first few years in the Alaskan bush. With all the stupid mistakes that I made, the only explanation I have for my survival is that the hand of God was on me.

The first couple of Alaskan summers owning my raft company were spent trying to find clients and guiding the few raft trips I could book. In the fall, I worked at hunting camps; every penny I made went to pay down my twenty-one-hundred-dollar loan for the rafting gear I had bought from Vladimir.

I was always in the field and had no home to live in. I had an old pickup truck that had been put together from parts bought cheap at a wrecking yard. I also had a twelve-foot trailer that held all my earthly belongings including my rafting gear; I could not even afford to rent a cheap apartment because I put all my money back into my business. I lived the life of a nomad.

During that first winter, I needed a place to live, I decided to go trapping because I could live for free in one of the cabins that my grandfather had helped build decades before.

I met my grandfather's old Alaskan trapping partner in October. He told me that the cabin was fully stocked with everything including food. Enough food and supplies for at least one winter. When I started asking him questions on how to trap, he said, "Sonny, I have not got the time to teach you, and since you don't have to build the cabin, you will have time to figure it out." Then I heard him add half under his breath, "…providing you don't do something stupid like shoot yourself or get lost and freeze to death."

He also said something to the effect that if he had not owed my grandfather a favor, he would never give his half of the cabin to a long-haired hippie kid from California. I had to promise the old sourdough that I would have all his traps flown back to town at the end of the trapping season or buy the traps from him.

I had never spent a winter in a cold environment before and that first attempt proved to be a life-or-death disaster!

To get to the trapping cabin necessitated a flight in a bush plane. The cheapest way to fly to the cabin was in a Piper PA-18 Super Cub on tundra tires. The pilot told me he could carry one passenger and two-hundred pounds of supplies or a total of four-hundred pounds of supplies and no passenger. Cost ninety bucks, cash only.

The cabin was by a small lake; the pilot circled, pointing it out to me. I got out of the plane with a full backpack of gear, a duffel bag of supplies, and a .30-06 rifle. Before leaving, he gave me a compass heading and pointed to a few landmarks to help me find my way, then said goodbye and took off. Alone in the wilderness now, I had to walk miles to the cabin. I left the duffel bag in a tree to retrieve later. With a full backpack and my rifle, I walked as fast as I could to the cabin. I was excited to see "My Cabin" at last. What a shock I had when I saw the cabin. The old trapper had lived many winters in the cabin and told me it was built strong. What I found was a tiny log shack with a dirt floor and sod roof. The cabin's only furnishings were a woodstove, a hand-built bedframe, a table, and an old two-inch-thick bed mattress suspended by wire from the rafters. There were traps, snowshoes, an ax, a bow saw, a one-man crosscut saw, some files, a lantern, and the other basics that are needed to survive the Alaskan winter as a trapper. The old trapper had not been to the cabin for at least four years. At least sixty percent of the food supply that I was counting on had been eaten by rodents or had spoiled.

First lesson learned! Don't count on food to be there when you need it, you'd better make sure you have the proper kind of food that's stored in a very secure way, or you will go hungry and perhaps starve to death.

Most people think it must have been boring spending those four and a half months alone in my cabin. The reality was that I was too busy just trying to cut enough wood to stay warm, skin the martin, fox, or wolf that I trapped or shot, to be bored. I was always cold, usually hungry, and exhausted most of the time. I never had the time to get bored. Being a greenhorn at trapping, I only averaged one animal a week, and it was usually shot instead of trapped.

As soon as I walked into the cabin, I knew I was in trouble. I did not have the four-to-five-month supply of food I needed. I had a topo map of the trapping area only, but I did not have the maps I might need to get me back to any kind of civilization.

Second lesson! Make your egress plan before you head off into the wilds and have at least two good contingency plans.

Thankfully, there were two sixteen-gallon drums with snap-ring lids in the cabin that were full of dry goods, as well as some cans of dried goods on the shelves—also still good. The list of what was still edible is sparse, though. In all there was:

    20 lb Bisquick
    50 lb dried beans
    25 lb white rice
    10 lb dried lentils
    10 lb oatmeal
    10 lb coffee
    25 lb salt
    2 lb black pepper
    10-lb can Crisco
    4 lb honey

Those supplies, my provisions for my first winter as a trapper in 1978-79, along with a young moose I shot, did keep me alive, but it was no fun. Fortunately, I had youth and enthusiasm on my side and knew the situation was only temporary. I decided to just make it a challenge and kind of live some of my grandfather's stories firsthand for myself. I had put a roll of toilet paper in my pack for the trail, but there was none at the cabin.

Third Lesson! Birch bark, snow, or small pinecones do work to wipe your posterior but make a very poor long-term substitute for real toilet paper. I also learned later that winter that at negative twenty-degrees Fahrenheit, your butt will freeze to a wooden toilet seat in the outhouse. Note: Making your toilet seat for the outhouse out of hard blue Styrofoam will make using the outhouse much less of a pain in the butt over an Alaskan winter.

As fall quickly turned to winter, the lake next to the cabin froze and the temperature continued to drop. The high-quality mountaineering boots I had used in the California High Sierras were not anywhere near warm enough and did not have removable liners. Those boots were hard to dry.

Fourth lesson! Pack boots with two sets of liners or bunny boots are must-have items working outdoors in cold and snowy environments.

Many times during that winter, I could have shot grouse or ptarmigan if I had had a .22 pistol. That would have added much-wanted variety to my menu. I also learned that if I got a wolf or wolverine in one of my traps, my .30-06 blew too big a hole in the hide and destroyed most of the value of the fur.

Fifth Lesson! A .22 rifle or pistol is a must-have firearm in the wilderness.

After two months my clothes were in bad shape. Most light-weight high-tech clothing used for backpacking or mountaineering is not designed for day-to-day hard use and mine certainly did not hold up to the rigors of outdoor work for the long haul. Over time, I learned that high-quality wool clothing does a lot better over a rugged winter and is not susceptible to melting next to a fire like nylon is. Yes, wool is heavy and takes longer to dry but, in my opinion, for working in the woods, wool is the way to go.

Sixth lesson! Clothing made for loggers, surveyors, and commercial fisherman may be heavy, but it passes the test of durability over a long haul a lot better than sporting gear. Filson is the best.

My boring diet was starting to get the best of me, and I was always hungry. After two months of my four-and-a-half-month stay, I started getting sick and my teeth seemed to be getting loose. It finally dawned on me that I had no intake of vitamin C, and I thought I had scurvy. Remembering something I learned from my grandfather, I started eating rose hips that were dried and still hanging on a few bushes near the cabin. Thankfully, there was no deep snow that year, so I could find a few rose hips. I was lucky!

Seventh Lesson! Make sure you have a source of vitamin C.

Every time I took my rifle inside the warm cabin, condensation would form on the steel barrel and working parts. My rifle was getting really wet.

Eighth Lesson! If you bring a rifle into a warm cabin from a below-freezing environment, condensation will form on it which promotes corrosion if the entire rifle isn't dried and oiled properly and at once. If the moisture stays, the bolt may be frozen the next time you are outside in the cold. So, if you do bring a weapon in from the cold, strip it down, dry it and clean it. I quickly learned to leave my rifle outside next to the door for most of the winter and only brought it in to clean.

One morning there was a small earthquake. For some reason that got me to thinking of my family and the outside world. I started feeling very alone. I started thinking, "What if the Russians had dropped the bomb? I wouldn't know it!"

Ninth Lesson! Being able to at least hear what is going on in the outside world helps your mental attitude a lot. A radio to listen to the news was something I longed for.

Snowshoes are easy to use and almost anyone will figure them out quickly. When you are working on snowshoes, however, you will fall now and then.

Tenth Lesson! Tape the muzzle of your rifle to keep snow out of the barrel when you take the inevitable header into the snow. I use electrical tape or put a condom over the muzzle of all my rifles in the field to keep everything out of the barrel. It will not affect accuracy unless you are shooting over three-hundred yards.

Although my first winter as a trapper in Alaska was full of hardship and big education, there are many good memories about that season of my life. Given another chance, however, I would not want to repeat that adventure. The fact that I survived my first trapping season in Alaska was an accomplishment, but I would not have succeeded even that without the sudden appearance and intervention of sixteen-year-old Kevin Jensen, proud member of the *Dena'ina Athabascan* people.

April and May are the "starving months" in Alaska, even for Alaskan wildlife. Everything edible from the previous year has already been devoured. The salmon are not running, and any small game becomes fair game for alpha predators such as bears and wolves. Unless you are eminently prepared and well provisioned until the very end of spring and on into early summer, your luck's run out.

By the advent of early spring 1979, I was still cold, lonely, and very hungry. In my youthful zeal to live the life of my grandfathers, I was close to starving to death. I had failed to assure a flight out, and no one was checking on my well-being. To seal my fate, the last of my moose meat showed a glossy green veneer, a deadly sign that my food stores had run out. I shaved off the rancid layer, hoping the meat beneath was not yet tainted.

I suppose it's true that the Lord watches after the foolhardy, especially, those who trust Him, because just about that time, Kevin showed up at my cabin. He was exploring far from home along the Iliamna River when he saw smoke up the valley from his camp and hiked in to see what was up. He located the cabin and found me.

We instantly became friends. The next day we took the long walk back to his boat and camp. The following day he took me home. Walking into the house, his parents were understandably shocked to see me—a filthy, skinny white boy whose clothes were in shambles.

Kevin said to his parents "A stray *Guzik* (white guy) followed me home. Can we keep him?"

Carl and Marge Jensen welcomed me into their home and made me feel like part of the family. They became like parents to me. Over the years, they taught me how they blended their traditional native way of life with the best of the white man's ways. Carl Jensen was of the *Dena'ina Gghayi* clan. An expert in many trades, he was a commercial fisherman and carried the mail with his dog sled. He was a big-game guide, as well as a power-plant operator.

I learned the traditional native ways and much of what I know from the Jensen's.

After returning to Anchorage in June, I sold my furs. The fur buyer could tell I was a cheechako by the way I had prepared the pelts. I got twenty cents on the dollar for my pelts, and I think that was generous on the part of the fur buyer. After four and a half months of hard work, and, after paying the bush pilot along with the money I still owed the trapper, I would have less than one hundred dollars.

The old trapping partner of my grandfather met me at the fur buyer, he was now very friendly and asked me many questions. He encouraged me to go back for at least one more winter. He told me to go get a bath and haircut and meet him at the White Spot Cafe down the street in downtown Anchorage, and he would buy me a good meal. While we were eating, he handed me a list.

80 lb Bisquick
50 lb beans
50 lb rice
25 lb salt
25 lb lentils
25 lb oatmeal
10 lb sugar
10 lb lard
10 lb powdered milk
10 lb split peas
10 lb Tang
10 lb coffee
1 case tomato paste
5 lb strawberry jam
4 lb honey
2 lb pepper
5 gallons white gas
4 large boxes of wooden matches
24 large plumber's candles
8 roles toilet paper
6 lantern mantels
7 lb trapping wire
gun oil
trapping lures and scents

The list of supplies that the trapper had the pilot bring to the cabin each spring when the plane came to pick him up was enough to fill what would have otherwise been an empty plane. In early April, the lake next to the cabin was still frozen, so the plane would land on skis and taxi next to the cabin. The pilot and trapper would put the supplies into the cabin, then the pilot would fly the trapper back to town.

The trapper then informed me that he had purchased the supplies for me and was having them flown to the cabin along with two more steel drums to safely store the supplies in. He encouraged me to return to trap the next winter.

With my first Alaskan winter under my belt, I drove my old truck back to California to pick up work as a raft guide on spring trips with Vic McLean and VK..

Epilogue—

Kevin Jensen saved my life when he found me starving on the Iliamna River that spring day so long ago. He led me to his home and his parents who welcomed me from that day on as a member of their family. Kevin became a brother to me as we both learned from his dad, Carl Jensen, how to survive in the Alaskan wilderness. We learned how to fish in the teeming river. He taught us how to hunt the caribou, Dall sheep, black bear and moose that roamed close by the Iliamna in Kevin's boat. Later we elevated our hunts to espying our quarry from my 1957 Piper Cub. These were the things we loved and shared.

Kevin was a very talented musician and singer as well as a whiz on computers. When Kevin was in the wilderness things were always good for him. He was in his element—the place where he thrived. He was honest and one of the warmest, friendliest people I've ever known. But in town, in what we called "civilization," Kevin struggled. City temptations were just too strong for him, and he was soon torn between two different worlds and could not reconcile himself to their separateness. He succumbed to the temptation and escape from reality that drugs offered him. They—the illicit drugs—eventually took over his life and, sadly, after a lifelong battle, that is what killed my dear brother Kevin. I have lost many friends in aircraft crashes and in war zones, but losing someone you love to drug addiction is even harder for me to handle. I still struggle to justify this loss—because I can't. I still miss my brother, Kevin Jensen.

Alaskan Winter of 1980-81

My crazy uncle, Satch Carlson had an even crazier dentist friend who raced cars, ice-raced motorcycles, and flew bush planes... Uncle Satch introduced me to Charley Connell. Of course, we talked airplanes and motorcycles for hours. I needed dental work but did not have the money for a dentist. Charley agreed to see me and let me trade a raft trip for the dental work. A few days later, as I sat in his dental chair, Charley told me he was a partner in a remote gold mine near the headwaters of the East Fork of the Chulitna River. He told me that all the supplies and fuel had to be flown in; there was no road leading to the mine.

Charley asked me if I wanted to fly fuel and supplies to the mine. I was trying to build flight time anyway I could, so this sounded good.

I told Charley I did not even have my private license yet. He said, "That's not a problem. The plane's not a hundred percent legal anyway."

Charley owned a single-engine Pilatus Porter PC-6/350 aircraft, registration number N4913.[1] He told me that one of his business partners was a former fighter pilot and Air America® pilot whose name was Ron Sutphin. He said Ron would check me out in the Porter and, if I was skilled enough, I could fly it back and forth to the mine.

Early that summer, Charley told me the mine desperately needed supplies and fuel. He had me meet him at Birchwood Airport, a small municipal airport just east of Anchorage.

Ron gave me instructions on how to operate the Porter and then let me do several takeoffs and landings. I was so excited to get to fly a Porter with these two experienced pilots, and I just did everything I was told.

We made dozens of landings at different dirt strips that day with Ron's instructions. I was having a terrific time learning to fly the Pilatus from Ron and Charley, but at the end of the day, the two men had an argument. All I could gather was that Ron was not happy with the legality of the Porter's paperwork and was washing his hands over the whole matter. He said he would not fly the Porter again unless things were corrected.

Charley told me later that Ron was being overly cautious because of his airline job. Not to be deterred, Charley said, "You can fly light loads on good-weather days in the Porter and you can slowly increase

[1] N4913 Pilatus PC-6/350: Flightaware.com

weight of the loads over time."

That whole summer, whenever I was not guiding trips, I flew. With only a student-pilot license, I flew a hundred and seventy hours in the Porter that summer, making supply trips back and forth to the mine. I also flew an old Super Cub, N8889D,[2] an added two hundred hours that year.

In total, I flew for eight years with only a student pilot license and logged over 1800 hours before the FAA caught me flying passengers without a license.

There are plenty of horror stories about the FAA being unreasonable and unfair to pilots, but my personal experience with the FAA in Alaska was that they treated me very fairly; they have always been fair to me.

When I was caught red-handed flying passengers, the FAA could have crucified me. Instead, they gave me two choices. The first choice was that they would revoke my student pilot privileges for two years and impound my aircraft if I was caught flying it; and the second option they gave me was that, within thirty days, I had to pass the private pilot written test and oral exam, as well as pass the practical flight test with an examiner. After that, I would voluntarily surrender my new license for six months.

When I asked Bart Tiernan, my attorney, if he could help me get out of this pickle, he looked at me like I had lost my mind and said, "Are you nuts? Take the deal before they change their mind!"

I studied for the written exam for three weeks and passed. I also passed the oral exam, but the weather turned bad, and my flight test got canceled several times. My thirty-day window ran out.

When I went back to the guy at the FAA and told him what had happened, he saw that I was doing my best to comply, made allowance for the negative weather, and extended the time deadline. It took another month before the weather cleared, and the examiner was able to let me take my flight test. I did pass and brought the paperwork to the guy at the FAA. He said he would see me in six months.

A long five months later and a week before the start of the spring bear-hunting season, I desperately needed to be back in business flying my plane! Lesson learned! I had been grounded long enough! I went back to the guy at the FAA and asked if there was any way—any way at all—I could get my license back early. I needed to fly to get to my guiding area. He studied me thoughtfully for a minute.

"Bush flying in Alaska is a very risky business," he said finally. "There's a very high death rate among guides flying Super Cubs, and in most Cub wrecks, head injuries are the cause of death for the pilot."

---

[2] N8889D Piper PA-18A 150: Flightaware.com

He paused to let that sink in, then he offered me another deal.

"If you promise me that you'll wear a flight helmet any time and every time you fly," he continued, "I'll give you back your license now." He knew my situation pretty well and told me where I could buy a surplus flight helmet cheap.

Of course I took the deal! I gave him my word, bought the flight helmet, and with license restored, I was on my way to Cold Bay for the spring bear hunt three days later.

To this day, I always wear a flight helmet. The FAA guy was right. I can bear testimony to the fact that flight helmets saved the lives of two of my close friends.

5.
Guatemala

1981 After Thanksgiving, my trapping season in Alaska started. I got a message one night over KCAM 790 radio station through Caribou Clatters.

The message said only:

"To Jerry on the Iliamna River" From Vladimir VK"
"I would like you to work a raft trip in Central America during Feb-
ruary and March"
"Call VK as soon as possible"

But that was enough. I cross-country skied two long days to Mom-and-Pop Jensen's home at Pedro Bay (the closest phone to my trapping cabin) and called VK.

"Hello VK! This is Jerry Jacques; I got your message."

"Good Jerry! How are you my friend," VK said. "Are you still in Alaska?"

"Yes! I'm at Lake Iliamna." I replied.

"Good! I wish I was there with you. Jerry, I need one more guide for an expedition in Guatemala and Mexico. Are you available in February and March?"

"What're the details of the trip?"

"Jomo and Jimmy Hendrick are coming. I have a group of archae-ologists as clients, and we're going to float from the Guatemala high-lands through a couple of rivers down into the Rio Usumacinta. We're going to stop along the way to explore Mayan ruins. It's pretty easy whitewater but a long trip in the jungle." VK's clients were archaeol-ogists from the Peabody Museum of Archaeology and Ethnology at Harvard University in Cambridge, Massachusetts. Our purpose was to stop along the way to explore Mayan ruins considered inaccessible by other means.

"I'll pay you seventy-five dollars a day for every day we have cli-ents," he continued. "I'll also pay you fifty dollars a day before the trip if you want to work in my warehouse repairing and making some new equipment." He paused a second to let that sink in. "Jerry, I need a commitment soon."

A winter river trip in a warm climate that promised to make me more money than a winter trapping season in Alaska sounded perfect.

It took me less than five seconds to make up my mind.

"Sounds good! I'm in. When do we start?"

"Any time after the first of January. Come to my warehouse in Monterey."

"Okay, VK; you have my commitment. I'll see you right after the first of the year."

"Good Jerry, but part of the deal is you have to bring me some smoked salmon from Alaska."

"Okay VK; I'll see what I can do about that!" I laughed, and our conversation ended.

If I would have had a way to see into the future, at that moment, that conversation might have ended with something like, "No. Sorry, VK; I can't make this one."

Acting on all the info I had about this trip, I pulled my traps and got myself and my pelts to the fur buyer in Anchorage. From Anchorage, I drove the six days down the ALCAN Highway to California, first to see my girlfriend and then to meet up with VK in Monterey. I worked in his warehouse for a month, using his sewing machine to repair equipment until the trip got underway.

Early in February, I drove with VK and his two other guides, *1982* Ken Ward (aka Jomo) and El Swisso (originally from Switzerland), to Flagstaff, Arizona. VK had another warehouse in Flagstaff for his Grand Canyon operation, and we met another guide there, Jim "Jimmy" Hendrick (aka Lean Elk). We picked up all the raft gear and loaded it into a custom built 4x4 high-clearance van and a tricked-out 4x4 Bronco, then drove south. Driving almost non-stop, we were soon in Central Mexico and having to cross military checkpoints every fifty-to-seventy miles. The guards at the checkpoints expected to be paid bribery money. With a fancy van towing a 4x4 Bronco and a ton of whitewater equipment, the cost of these bribes at each checkpoint could have been high. VK, however, was a brilliant expert at devising unconventional ways of dealing with these sorts of things.

He had come up with a unique strategy for getting us through the checkpoints; it was quick and cheap—and it worked. VK, always in the lead van, had brought along two cases of old Playboy magazines. He always had one of the magazines conspicuously placed on the dash and opened to the centerfold. It was interesting to watch, and the same scenario played out almost identically at each checkpoint.

We'd pull to a stop and hand over our passports. After checking us all out, the guard would start looking through the windows of the van and would at once zero-in on the magazine with the conspicuously placed nude photo.

VK would wait for the precise moment of the guard's piqued

interest, smile, feign nonchalance while conversing with him in perfect Spanish, pick up the magazine and hand it to him. Soon a second soldier would be looking, and VK would grab another Playboy magazine, handing one out to each checkpoint guard. Apparently, magazines with nude-women photos were something these young soldiers did not have much access to. As soon as they were fully engrossed in the pictures, VK would tell them the mags were a gift and call out his farewells, something like: "Adios, amigos! Disfrutar!" while easing away, then driving off and paying nothing. All-in-all, it was a good strategy and worked well at the time.

We arrived in Palenque three days later and met up with the archaeologists who were to be our clients.

Collage of Palenque Mayan ruins (Ricraider 2012)

We spent a day with them walking around the Palenque ruins. With the Peabody archaeologists giving the tour, it was incredible. I had never been around any man-made construction so old in my life. Those archaeologists talked the whole time about the history of the ruins. It was an experience I will never forget. Because they were archaeologists from Harvard, they were given free rein to explore anything and everything inside and outside the ruins. We even got to go deep into the burial chambers.

We left the Palenque ruins the next day and drove a day and a half on rough dirt and muddy roads. We were able to drive the vans and Bronco through many of the smaller streams without bridges. Now I understood why Vladimir had those special four-wheel-drive vans built.

Our destination in the Guatemalan Highlands was a small, clear stream perhaps sixty feet wide that VK called the *Tres Naciones*. We camped there for the night and launched the next morning. The stream was shallow with barely enough depth for the rafts to float comfortably as we rowed downstream.

VK, Jomo, and Jim Hendrick had run this river the year before; El Swisso and I were the new kids. With most river companies, the new guides get most of the work to do at camp. With VK's company, however, everyone including VK shared all the chores equally. We rowed for about seven hours that day, eating lunch while floating down the river. We camped that night on the banks of the river next to a small native village; the residents came out to greet us.

The people of this remote river corridor in the jungle were of the *Lacandón* Maya tribe, direct descendants of the Mayans. It was interesting that the elders dressed in white robes and, even though this was an incredibly remote area with no road access, the village and all the villagers were extremely clean and tidy. They did have trade and contact to the outside world, yet they lived a primitive life. Their subsistence had an obvious agricultural base. There were chickens, a few goats, and gardens with melons and corn growing along with other things I couldn't name. For the size of the village, it was obvious to me that not all their food came from the tiny tract of land they were working. I soon learned they were also hunters and gatherers in their surrounding jungle.

The people of the village were all very friendly to us. The person who seemed to be in charge had obviously met Vladimir before and gifts were exchanged.

It was on our third day on the river that we stopped at midday and walked to a hill above the river where there were several Lacandón huts. We spent the next two days exploring in the jungle with the natives as our guides.

The archaeologists were excited as they found several hills that were obvious Mayan ruins with one being an undiscovered pyramid. They also marked the location of a group of huge stones with visible carvings. I really enjoyed these honest Lacandón people and their simple lifestyle. I had every intention of returning to learn more from them later that winter.

Every second day, we would reload the rafts and head downriver which was now increasing in water volume from the different side streams flowing out of the jungle; the channel was getting deeper and wider. Even the trees in the jungle got taller. We were now under a triple canopy rainforest. Scarlet Macaws lived in the top-most trees, which are among the tallest trees in the world. Below this top layer is the canopy. We could hear howler monkeys above us now. The thick canopy acts like an umbrella and does not allow significant light for the forest understory layer with all its mosses, ferns, and lichens. Orchids also grow in this layer. Iguanas were with us everywhere on the jungle floor. Spiders and snakes thrive on the rainforest floor as well, and once or twice, we even saw jaguar tracks in the sand along the river.

Most nights the Lacandón's would find us at our camp. They were looking for Vladimir. He would trade or buy artifacts from the Lacandón's who had been gathering them for the year since VK's last trip.

The Tres Naciones, the little river we had started on, eventually flowed into the Usumacinta River. The first problem we ran into was after the river turned into the Mexico-Guatemala border. We were camping on the Mexican side that night when we got checked out by a small cadre of Mexican Federales. Although the overall check went fine, they looked me over closer than anybody else on our trip. I had long curly hair and a long beard at the time, and I reckon I looked suspicious.

There was an incident later that night that really woke me up to hard, cold reality. Apparently, military troops from the Guatemalan side had made a deal to trade Guatemalan wine for Mexican beer. The Guatemalans sent the wine across, but the Mexicans didn't send the beer. During the night, they were shooting across the river at each other in retaliation. We found out later that one of the Guatemalan soldiers was killed in the exchange of gunfire. This was the first time I realized how cheap life could be in a third-world country. Someone dying over a few cases of beer seems largely incomprehensible in our society but, to them, I suppose it was a source of pride.

We got back on the river as early as possible the next morning and rowed downriver as fast as we could.

There were two or three sections of whitewater to navigate before camp that night. The rest of the trip we spent stopping at countless uncharted ruin sites as well as more well-known Mayan sites like Piedras Negras and Yaxchilan. The upper sections of the river were very safe, but after we rafted below the whitewater sections, the river was accessible by dugout canoes or cayucas. Most of these dugout canoes were used by the natives, but we had to be careful because the bandidos and the drug runners were also accessing this lower part of the river in cayucas with motors on them. We did have one run-in with the bandits near the end of the first trip. Jimmy was watching the boats when two bandidos showed up, cut the rope on one of the rafts and headed downstream. Jimmy yelled, and with machete in hand, he went running downstream at full speed through the jungle. Ten minutes later, Jimmy found our raft onshore surrounded by four bandits; they were all armed with rifles. Time to retreat! They hadn't spotted Jimmy, so he quickly turned around and went back to camp and told Vladimir that one of the rafts had been stolen. Thankfully, this took place at the end of the trip. Somehow, Vladimir was able to buy back the raft as well as all the rafting equipment. VK was glad none of us got shot.

I was so sick that I couldn't go on the second trip VK had scheduled. I holed up in a cheap hotel in Villahermosa, while VK and the guides went on. I was told that the trip also went well, but VK needed to go back to pick up some stuff he had left behind. His rafts were too full to float out everything he had accumulated on this trip.

VK made a deal with me to return with a young Spanish and *Lacandón*-language interpreter whose name I could not pronounce. He just told me to call him Steve; Steve and I were to raft out the rest of the stuff VK had stashed.

This was a more complicated trip than the earlier one. It started out fine, but things soon started turning bad. Not far from the Lacandón villages, we started seeing dead people floating in the river. There had been rumors of the Guatemalan military committing genocide on the Lacandón people, but I was horrified to see this firsthand. I knew I was witness to an atrocity. Sadly, Steve had seen this before and was not surprised. We rafted downriver to the same village where I had admired the people so much on my last trip. What we found was devastation. We were told that a military helicopter armed with machine guns had swept in and the gunners killed over a third of the people; many others were wounded. One of the surviving elders came to us urging us to leave.

"It is not safe for you to be here," he said.

I figured that the helicopter had already left so it was probably safe now. I was an EMT, and I wanted to stay and try to help the wounded, but the elder insisted Steve and I leave. Two of the survivors started walking us back to the river, but it was too late. Soldiers/mercenaries were at our raft. What happened next was pandemonium.

More of the villagers were being shot, and they captured Steve and me as well as some more of the villagers. They beat the crap out of me, gave me rotten food to eat, and did other unspeakable things to me. Steve said that, since I was from the US, they were planning to hold me for ransom thinking that I must be a rich American who had people who would pay to get me back. Eventually, they kind of lost interest, and I was able to escape. The escape was nothing spectacular; they just weren't bothering to watch me closely. When no one was looking, I just ran into the jungle, jumped into the river, and started swimming downstream. With the help of VK's Lacandón friends, I made it to a safe place where he and my dad arranged to pay to get me home.

Steve never made it out.

Witnessing the military mercenaries in service of the Guatemalan government commit genocide on the Lacandón's so they could take their land and being captive in the hands of belligerents had a profound impact on me. In hindsight, the whole sordid episode negatively affected my soon-to-come marriage. I still struggle with this trauma today.

I learned years later that all the historical artifacts VK had smuggled out of the jungles of Guatemala and Mexico were returned to the Mayan people. That helped ease my guilt somewhat for the part I had played. If it helps at all, at the time, militia were destroying the artifacts they found. Conversely, it could be noted that Vladimir's actions helped preserve the artifacts for the Mayan people.

Although he was no saint, Vladimir Kovalik was both a mentor and a good friend to me. Like all of us, he was human and had his faults; still, my admiration and respect for VK continues to this day.

Reserva Ecológica "Cañon del Usumacinta", municipio de Tenosique, Tabasco (Photo Alfonsobouchot 2009)

Second Winter in the Alaskan Bush

July is when the sockeye salmon return and it's the most important event of the year. Salmon is subsistence food in Alaska. We put out a small net every day for the month. Each day the net is hauled in, and the fish collected. The fish are carefully prepared and processed. We have over thirty different ways we preserve our fish, but the three most common methods are smoking, canning, and freezing.

When the Sockeye Salmon Return

To smoke salmon the traditional Native Alaskan way, we remove the ribcage but leave the two halves attached to the tail (so the fish can hang on the poles). Next, we put the fillets into a brine solution for two-to-six hours. After brining, each fillet is carefully hand dried as any amount of moisture left on the fillet will cause mold and can ruin the fish. Finally, we hang them on the poles in the smoke house for three days. With constant smoking for seventy-two hours, the fish is now cured and can be eaten and will last until spring.

Canning fish is also very time-consuming and has too many recipes to list.

Freezing is the fastest way to preserve the salmon, but most people only have limited freezer space and fish can quickly freezer-burn, so only a small percentage of fish are frozen.

August is berry-picking month. We gather blueberries, crowberries, high-bush cranberries, low-bush cranberries, salmon berries, and wild strawberries. A few bears are out but most are still on the river devouring their own salmon catch before the long winter.

September is moose hunting season.

October, November, December, January, and February are the trapping season months.

I spent many Thanksgiving and Christmas holidays with the Jensen's and wound up working with Carl when he took me on as an apprentice hunting guide and moose packer. He taught me how to field dress and butcher moose. From him, I learned how to hunt moose and grizzly. I worked with him every spring and fall as a hunting guide. In the summers, my rafting business continued to grow, and I was flying all over Alaska exploring new rivers while guiding fishermen to trout and salmon streams and clients into wild, rushing rivers for whitewater adventures. Now I was living my dreams.

Pedro Bay Alaska   Thanksgiving dinner in 1981 was great! It was a feast combining the best of Anglo and Native cultural foods. After the meal, Carl and Marge Jensen (like parents to me, I called them Pop and Mom), sat me down for a serious talk. Mom told me I was of age, and she would help me find a good Dena'ina Indian girl to marry. My response was that I was still sweet on my high-school sweetheart, and she was just finishing chiropractic school in California. Mom questioned me about her and asked if she was Indian, I told them she was a Guzik (white) girl. Mom smiled and half-jokingly said that was okay, but I was forbidden from marrying an Eskimo. Pop laughed, but there was an undertone of seriousness to what they said. Back then there was still tension between many of the older Indian and Eskimo people. This conversation led to several life-changing events and me, more-or-less, becoming domesticated.

*Carl & Marge
(Pop & Mom)
Jensen*

Two years after that conversation, in the spring of '83, I returned to California and married my high-school sweetheart. I brought her back to Alaska, intending to finally have the family I'd dreamed of in the place I loved. Problem was, I was barely *housebroke*! I lived in a tiny cabin with no electricity and no running water. To top it off, I was off guiding a hundred and eighty days of the year! I probably hadn't considered how conducive my lifestyle would be to a young wife, fresh from civilization, suddenly dropped into the wilderness.

Before long in our new life as man and wife, we moved into a house in Anchorage. Unfortunately, the marriage was a disaster. I had been plucked straight out of the wilderness, and I didn't fit into her social circles in Anchorage. I did not like night clubs, and (when I could escape the city for my wilderness *office*) I was gone from home far too much. It was quickly apparent between the two of us that she was not at all keen on my chosen lifestyle, and I was a poor fit into her world. To no one's surprise, our marriage soon ended in divorce. I was emotionally devastated by the breakup but overwhelmed with joy by the arrival of our son—one of the best days of my life was the day our son, Jason, was born.

Jason was the most important person in my life, and happily for me, at the conclusion of a long battle, the court decided it was best for him to live with me full-time. Together, my son and I launched a life of adventure on our own. Because Alaska's school system allowed students to do a combination of in-class study and home school, the two of us were free to spend our time wandering across Alaska, staying in hunting camps and venturing down rivers. We traveled outside Alaska to Canada, Central and South America, Mexico, and even spent a few months in Africa where Jason had his own pet warthog that followed him around like a puppy.

By the time Jason was ten, he was already becoming an accomplished outdoorsman. He could navigate with a compass or by the stars, build a campfire without matches or lighter, and was river-wise enough to follow me down Class IIs in his own kayak.

Jason was growing and thriving, but I was lonely. Over the years, I had made some missteps and suffered some tremendous losses. Years passed until, eventually, my life became complete. What I desired most, happened. I desperately wanted a large family, and I believed my desire was not incongruent with my wild wilderness lifestyle. I wanted a loving wife and a large family! And then there was Laura. With all combined, there are seven kids: Matt, Corine, Jason, Kevin, Erika, Erin, and Caleb. Each one is a wonderfully unique person, and I've had so much fun watching them all grow up. I'm proud to call all seven of them my kids, but Laura gets the credit. She's a fantastic mom and has been a better wife than I deserve. Following that long-ago path to its present state shows me that even a convoluted trail, punctuated with some turmoil of my own making, led me to true happiness. But back to my Alaskan winters...

My second winter was a lot better than the first. The first thing I did when I arrived at the trapper cabin was to see that the supplies were all there and in fine shape. I also had my topo maps with the Jensen's home in Pedro Bay located. It was at least a three-day walk, but now I knew how to get there.

As my second winter quickly set in around the cabin, it did not take long to get into my routine. Every day started the same. At approximately 6:00 a.m., the alarm clock went off. I didn't have an alarm clock; my alarm was the stove! When it had only a few coals left, the cabin temp almost immediately dropped below freezing. Every morning, like 6:00-a.m. alarm-clockwork, I had to get up and stoke the fire in my trusty old stove. As soon as I got it going, I'd hop outside into the extreme cold and cut a log into rounds. The stars were still bright, and I was still in the dark at 6:00 a.m. in the Alaskan winter wilderness. Then I'd make my way down to the lake while still in the dark (batteries for the flashlight were too precious to waste and so was gas for the lantern), carefully chip the ice around each of my five fishing lines with a hatchet, pull up the hook, hoping for a burbot (freshwater ling cod), reset the bait, dip my pail, and haul water as well as my frozen butt back to my warm cabin.

If I had failed to catch a fish for breakfast, I'd use the saw to cut off a frozen chunk of caribou or moose meat (depending on what I had killed that winter) from the meat pole next to the cabin. Still in the dark and cold, I would step back into the cabin, warm my frozen hands, dry my gloves, and cook breakfast on the wood stove. Next, I would put the Dutch oven filled with beans or lentils and rice covered in river water on the wood stove to rehydrate while I was gone for the day. Next, I packed my lunch which usually consisted of two pancakes with a slab of cooked caribou or moose meat in the middle; lunch also included one tablespoon of Tang in my insulated water bottle. I filled that with hot water from the pot on the stove. Warm Tang makes a nice midmorning warm-up on the trail, and it's a pretty good source of vitamin C.

By the time I finished my morning rituals, it was just starting to get light, and it was time to get to work. I'd strap on my snowshoes and head out pulling the sled. If it had not snowed overnight, I could walk on top of my packed-snow trail without the snowshoes, but I kept them on the sled. Fresh snow necessitated wearing snowshoes to make any progress.

My routine day was spent dragging my supply sled and checking and resetting traps. I used wire snares and leg-hold traps of all different sizes. I would follow the tracks in the snow to find the path the animals were using and make sets there. I used brush to funnel the animal into the trap. While steadily at work on the traps, I was still alert, constantly looking for a wolf, fox, or wolverine to shoot. Pelts were my livelihood, and these would just add to my cache.

Each day, without fail, I also had to find a dry-standing dead spruce tree to cut down and limb with the ax. I used the sled to haul my firewood and pelts back to the cabin. I knew I must have everything tied down on my sled and back on my main trail before it was completely dark. Days are short in Alaska's midwinter. The sun is up only four-and-a-half hours, yet my flashlight was only for emergencies. Trekking back home after work was not an emergency.

Following a packed trail is easy in the dark, the brilliant snow reflects any light available. Wilderness safety meant remembering a few rules, like always getting behind the sled on any downhill. A packed sled will hit you in the back of your legs and could break a snowshoe—or a leg.

A broken leg in that wilderness, so far from any contact could be a death sentence. You didn't break too many rules out there and survive.

Lesson 11! Cross country skis are no substitute for snowshoes.

The snowshoes at the cabin were old and on their last legs of useful life. Instead of bringing a new set of snowshoes, I had purchased a new set of back-country cross-country skis to use while at the cabin. I thought I would use the snowshoes as a backup. I quickly learned that skis wouldn't do the job in thick brush for doing chores or trapping. They were no substitute for the snowshoes. Skis have their place and can certainly save time crossing country, but they are not a replacement for snowshoes. In snow country, snowshoes are essential while skis are a very nice luxury.

When I finally arrived back home at the cabin each night, I was cold, tired, and hungry. Of necessity, the first thing I did was start my fire and fix dinner as soon as the stove was hot. After dinner, and if I was lucky that day, I would light the lantern and skin whatever I had trapped or shot after it thawed. Finally, all work finished, I was ready for 9:15 p.m.—the highlight of my day! I got to listen to the AM radio for forty-five minutes.

Because I had remembered Lesson Eight so well, I brought along a battery-powered radio this time, always hoping *Caribou Clatters* had a message for me from my family. I had books and magazines with me this trip and allowed myself forty-five minutes to read by lantern or candlelight. At 10:30 p.m., just like cold clockwork, the stove would begin to cool. So, just before candle or lantern light out, I'd re-stoke the fire, then collapse into my cold bed. But that radio, my dinner, and the promise of sound sleep were my reward for the day's hard work.

Around 2:30 a.m., the fire was burned to just a few coals and I'd get cold, get up, put more wood on, and go back to sleep. The next thing I knew, it was 6:00 a.m. again, and the fire had burned to just a few coals, and it is freezing in the cabin. My day started all over again.

Lesson 12! In a frigid winter climate, use no oil in the bolt or trigger assembly of your rifle—it could freeze. On one freezing day while running my lines, I sighted in a perfect shot on a big timber wolf sporting a buff-and-black-colored hide worth four hundred and fifty dollars, but when I pulled the trigger on my rifle, it only went click. The firing pin would not strike the cartridge with enough force to set off the primer. After the second try and another click, the wolf ran off and out of range. That was another very expensive lesson.

On my daily trips to check the fishing lines and get water, I knew the ice on the lake near my cabin was twenty-eight-inches thick and still getting thicker by the week. On one December day when the temperature hovered around minus twenty-seven degrees Fahrenheit, I was crossing the outlet end of a small lake to check out some tracks. Not worrying, I walked across the surface at my usual pace; I thought the ice was twenty-eight-inches thick everywhere—it wasn't. I fell through the ice and found myself waist deep in freezing water. I was two miles from my cabin. Hypothermia is real and deadly, and plunging your body waist deep into subzero water, then having to hike two miles for any relief is deadly serious. I was young and healthy, but it took every ounce of resolve I could muster to make it back to the safety of my cabin.

Lesson 13! Any outlet or inlet of a frozen lake may have thin ice. A warm spring or any number of other anomalies can cause thin ice. To top it off, the fire had gone out in my stove and no coals were left. I was so cold; my hands were shaking, my teeth were chattering, and my lower extremities were numb. I couldn't keep my body steady enough to loft my kindling in the stove to even get a fire organized, much less started. As a last resort, I threw in some larger chunks of wood and doused them generously with some white gas. Although I almost incinerated my cabin, I was warming up again pretty fast.

Lesson 14! Always have the kindling and all the fixings of a fire ready, especially any time you leave your cabin. You never know when someone may be at the end of their strength and need to get a life-saving fire going.

One evening in early January, I returned to the cabin to find a note and care package on the table from the bush pilot. The pilot had brought me a bag of oranges, a fruitcake, and a newspaper. He also left three letters from my family! I felt like I had won the lottery.

As the snow got deeper during the winter, I discovered that many animals liked to use my packed trail. I had already learned never to underestimate the danger of a moose. But now I learned that a moose in the winter has the right-of-way on a packed trail. There is every possibility they will charge you instead of going into deep snow. I had a cow moose chase me up a tree then stomp on my sled, breaking one of my snowshoes just to bring home her lesson.

Lesson 15! Moose are dangerous, especially in late winter. Give them the right-of-way.

In early February, I came across some large grizzly tracks in the snow. I was shocked, as I thought bears would be in the den all winter. I followed the tracks and found the bear had made a moose kill.

Lesson 16! Grizzly bears do not truly hibernate and may be out of the den during any month of the year. Over the years, I learned that if a bear is away from its den in the winter, it will be hungry and grumpy—and nothing to underestimate.

As a kid, I loved watching western movies. I loved to watch the cowboys who wore their handguns in those low-slung, fast-draw holsters; I thought that was cool. But the western style fast draw holsters I tried in the bush were useless. Today, I see that some law enforcement and military teams are using thigh mounted holsters. I am not disputing the tactical points of that method, but if you are working in the northern woods, you will occasionally fall into snow or mud.

Lesson 17! Quick draw holster v. northern woods obstacles of snow and mud. In the Alaska bush, you want your handgun in a full flap holster or in a normal holster worn under the last layer of clothing. Getting your handgun into your hand fast is of no use if it will not fire when you need it.

Lesson 18! Select holsters that will allow you to always carry your handgun with you comfortably and will protect the weapon from the elements. I have tried over forty different holsters and methods of carrying my handgun. I strongly suggest that if you're planning to live in the bush, experiment with different ways to carry your handgun. Find something that works for you. I use different holsters.

I use a full-flap holster when I am working in the bush, and a chest holster when I am flying float planes.

My second winter in the trapper cabin came to an end in March as the bush pilot landed on the frozen lake with four-hundred pounds of supplies. He helped me put the food into the steel drums for the next trapping season then flew me back to town.

I sold my furs to the fur buyer in Anchorage. After paying the bush pilot for the supplies and flights to the cabin and back, I had made

$2700. I had spent one hundred and twenty days alone in the bush trapping.

I learned much that second winter and, over the years, I've refined the old trapper's list to keep me full and a lot happier.

That second winter, I had also visited the Jensen family, Kevin, Carl, and Marge every ten-to-twelve days. This Native American family, living on the shore of Lake Iliamna, welcomed me any time I needed a place to stay.

Carl had been the last person to deliver mail by dog team and sailboat for the US Postal Service. He was an elder of their Village, a trapper, and a hunting guide. Carl and Marge welcomed me into their family and treated me like a son. I learned an incredible amount about the old ways and the traditional Lake Iliamna Village lifestyle from them.

Here in Alaska, we live by the season and the season dictates how we live.

Spring is the time of rebirth in Alaska.

Wood and food supplies are low after the long winter and, as the snow dissipates, life begins again.

In April and May, we start our garden plants in the house, tomatoes, squash, strawberries, and cabbage are some of the things we start growing in the house to transplant them into the garden in late May.

May and June are also the months we cut firewood. This activity takes working five long days a week to get enough wood cut and hauled into the woodshed. Heating the house is by woodstove and, with the long cold winters, it takes a lot of wood to last the year.

II
It Happened Like This...

Jerry Jacques lived every minute of his young life for his next big adventure. Some of his escapades were tremendously successful, while some seemed to take on a life of their own. My sister said after I recounted one of these adventures, "He might be a different way of making a person, according to God."—Lynne Malvoso.

Jerry's friend, Rob Lesser, told me after reading another one of Jerry's whitewater stories that Jerry seemed to have an 'impulsive streak' in his river-exploration forays into the unknown.

From my perspective, the world would be much less rich without adventurers like Jerry—those rare people who live their lives to the limits, even if that adventure doesn't always go as planned.

I never was so adventurous and chose to live my life traveling, much like the poet Keats, in "realms of gold." I can always appreciate those who do risk it all, though, purely for the love of adventure. I'm right there with 'em, snug and warm in my comfy chair, enjoying every death-defying, jaw-dropping, thrilling word!

Enjoy the adventure as you read these fun and sometimes harrowing stories Jerry's included in "It Happened Like This..."
—CS Norwood

Batman on the Tuolumne

John Cassidy is a Stanford graduate and published author. Scan the QR Code below to find his book: Juggling for the Complete Klutz by John Cassidy and B.C. Rimbeaux.

I was on the Lumsden road, driving with two friends to the Tuolumne River for a kayak trip. The plan was to paddle our kayaks on the familiar 18 miles, and then, properly emboldened, take on Cherry Creek tomorrow morning.

"I heard a raft guide got bitten on the lip by a bat a few weeks ago," I said, over my shoulder. "During the day. He was napping at lunch."

Barry and Rimbeaux were in the back. The three of us had known each other for years and been on countless trips on various rivers together, either as professional river guides or on our own in kayaks, as we were today.

"Where?" Asked somebody from the back of the van.

"On the lip. On his mouth."

"No. I mean what river?"

"This one. The Tuolumne."

"I don't believe it. A bat lands on his mouth in the middle of the day and bites him? No. Wrong."

"That's what I heard, At the Clavey."

"Who?"

"I don't know. Some raft guide."

"Ridiculous."

"No, really. It happened."

"No, it didn't."

We passed another mile or two of sparkling repartee like this. Neither of them had the slightest faith in my amazing and fascinating fact. On the river, we were joined by a single boater. He paddled up to Barry who was drifting a bit behind. The two of them fell into conversation.

Hey!" We heard Barry holler after us, "This is the guy that got bit by the bat!"

"Really?" I said, after a pause but happy to take the low road. "But I thought that was impossible. Remember? Back in the van? You guys knew."

Jerry Jacques, it turned out, was very much the guy who'd been bitten by the bat. On the mouth. But as we gathered around him between rapids, listening to him talk, we learned that the bat bite was no more than the opener. What follows was his story.

"Three days after getting bitten, I went to the hospital. There was a mix-up. They gave me the wrong medication. Now the doctors treating me at UCLA Med Center are not sure that the correct treatment was started in time; it is likely that I may die from rabies. So I came up here because I figured, if I was going to die of rabies, I'd rather do it on the river than in a city." It was a good start as a river story and obviously had serious potential.

Jerry's delivery, deadpan and almost weary sounding, removed any doubt about its veracity.

"Early spring I was working a trip here. I was snoozing on my rowing seat when this bat landed on my face and bit me in the lip…drew blood even. A guy on the trip was a doctor, and he said I'd better get to a hospital. What kind of bat bites people in the middle of the day?" The three of us looked at each other and had no answer to that one.

The story went on. "So I drove down to the hospital in San Francisco, where they started the 21-day treatment. After 2 days the shots were to be spaced a few days apart. I convinced the doctors to give me the medication and directions for the future treatments so my doctor in Modesto could continue treating me. I never told them that what I really wanted was to go kayaking. In Modesto, a kayaker friend was a doctor. I brought the meds to him, and we went kayaking on the Stanislaus where he gave me my next shot. Then I drove to LA to visit my girlfriend and wandered into UCLA Med Center to get the remainder of my treatment. The doctor looked at the meds and the directions, got upset, and left the room. When he returned, he told me that the hospital in SF had mistakenly given me the wrong medication and had been trying to find me for the past two weeks. They had to start the whole treatment over from scratch, but if the incubation period had run its course this was bad. No one ever survives rabies; the shots are supposed to prevent rabies. Not cure it. If you are showing any signs of rabies, it turns out, you're a goner. If you get really sensitive to the light, or really irritable and crazy, or some other things like that, you've got it and it's too late. Plus, in the last stages, you get super-contagious, and they quarantine you. Lock you up. Anyway, at UCLA Med Center they started the 21-day treatment with the correct medication. When I finished up all the treatment, they told me there was a strong possibility that the treatment started too late, so they needed to quarantine me at the hospital."

That's when I figured the shots hadn't worked. I figured they were about to drop a net over me and lock me up. There was no way I was letting them do that, so I ran out."

We were bouncing through rapids at this stage but paying far more attention to the story than anything on the river.

"I just got all my stuff together and drove up here." At this point he stopped and there ensued one of those pregnant pauses.

"When?" somebody finally asked. "When did you come up?"

"Last night," he said. "I drove most of the night. I just got here a couple of hours ago."

We let that sink in.

"So you don't know if you have rabies or not? Still?" I asked.

He shook his head. At that point, the river intervened, and we were forced to pay some attention to where we were actually going. We caught a necessary eddy and began the process of reading and running the rapids, Jerry's last line resonating in our heads: "If I'm going to die, though, I'd rather do it here."

The rest of the trip was uneventful. The day was nice, the water was familiar. Jerry, we discovered, was just learning how to kayak. We pulled over for a simple lunch on a beach to ourselves and finished the day without any real mishap. As we were taking out though, we received a surprise.

"Mind if I join you guys tomorrow?" Jerry asked.

We paused for an awkward moment. Jerry was a bare beginner; the three of us had years of experience and were just now ready to take on Cherry Creek. ("Maybe," I thought.)

Today, we'd been able to rescue Jerry and his boat from his swim with little trouble. Tomorrow would be a whole different story. Cherry Creek was six miles of straight-up serious water with a number of Class V rapids. It was a do-not-swim stretch.

"Like I said," he added, looking at us carefully, "this is where I need to be."

Eventually, we shrugged and nodded. "Sure." What else was there to say? Over the course of my kayaking career, I ran Cherry Creek maybe half a dozen times, but I never was able to sleep well at the put-in. But that night, the first night, was probably the worst. I got a couple of hours of restless tossing.

The un-runnable Lumsden Falls[1] was the only rapid you could see from the takeout and the road. Over the years, especially if there was

---

[1] According to Whitewater Guidebook, The Upper Tuolumne River, also referred to as Cherry Creek...is the yardstick that all Class V runs are measured against...Cherry Creek is for experts only...Mile 7: Lumsden Falls (Portage) is a 30 foot drop over boulders that is run by some kayakers and rafters, but it's typically portage on river left. (Cherry Creek 2023)

time on the evening before a commercial trip, we boatmen would sit on the bridge, drink a beer, and check it out, trying to find a runnable line. Eventually, we'd all just shake our heads and head back down the road. It was a monster rapid, starting with a series of steep boulder drops before funneling into an undercut wall. The boulder drops looked at the edge of possible, but nobody wanted to find out what was in the undercut. There were only a few kayakers in the state who'd run Cherry Creek at the time, but none of them had ever run the falls. It was the knock-out punch at the bottom of Cherry Creek. A no-question walk-around. But all that was far from our minds when we put in that morning. Between us and there, we had a ton of Class V, and our focus was very much in the here and now.

We went through the put-in rituals without the usual banter. There were a couple hundred yards of easy warm-up water before the river turned a corner and it all started. We paddled away, agreeing to meet in an eddy just above the corner—the starting line. We had game faces on and none of us was thinking about anything but what was coming. Until we got to the eddy.

"Where's Jerry?" somebody said. We looked upstream. We could see all the way to the put-in. No Jerry. "He's got to be here. I know he put in." Then we saw him. Swimming, hanging onto his boat. Somehow, in the bouncy little Class II stretch we'd just come through, he'd broached his boat between two rocks, bent it in half, and was swimming. A bad sign. We managed to catch him before the real stuff started. His boat was bent in half, "a taco." We could still see the truck at the put-in and we all heaved the same sigh of relief: Jerry would have to take out. There'd be no beginners on Cherry Creek today.

Wrong. Up on the bank, Jerry proceeded to stand inside his boat and jump up and down enough to bend it back to semi straight. A rough-and-ready fix. A few minutes later, he was back in his boat and pulling on his spray skirt. "Are you sure you're up for this?" somebody asked—reasonably, I thought. "Let's go," he said. Confidence? I thought. Arrogance? Indifference? We set up our order and joined the current, one by one. Since it was all new, we ran it eddy to eddy, rapid by rapid, boat scouting over our shoulders where we could and where we couldn't, we pulled over and scouted from the bank. It was slow going. At least it was for us. Jerry had a less laborious approach. He didn't bother scouting, preferring to wait in the eddy while we did the legwork. I don't think he was cocky so much as fatalistic. And logical. Why over-plan a route when your steering wheel is a little sketchy? But the river gods were in a good mood that day. At this distance in time, the rapids blur together, but we must have made the cuts where we had to and squeaked through the must-do chutes.

(Jerry's interjection to the story: "I never told them, but I was in constant pain, all my joints hurt so much I could barely stand it, and the nausea was very intense. I could concentrate on the big rapids and make the life and death moves but lost focus on the little stuff.")

We had a Spartan lunch on a beach mid-way and geared up for the final leg. It must have been getting late when we finally came to Flat Rock. We scouted from the right bank and examined the drop. Steep and skinnier, but the pool below looked clean. If there were rocks in it, they were out of sight. We decided to try it with as much speed as possible. Hit the pool flat. Don't probe the bottom. Rimbeaux went over first, and when he appeared below, intact and upright, we all followed in relieved succession, nothing but water at the bottom. Almost immediately we found the take-out eddy on the right. There was the bridge, startlingly close. The river dropped out of view, and we could hear the ominous roar of Lumsden Falls. We were done. The sense of relief and profound exultation is hard to describe. As we pushed out of our seats and began to shoulder our boats for the climb up the bank, Jerry made an announcement. "I'm going to run it." We looked at him blankly. "Lumsden? You're going to run Lumsden?" It was a shocking moment and for the first time since put-in, I looked at him as I had the day before: a guy who might have a disease, a fatal disease. We mounted a little resistance, putting up the obvious objections, but under the circumstances, we ended up just wishing him luck and offering a last bit of advice: "Stay off the wall," we said, "on the right. About halfway down."

The bridge offered ringside seats, and, as we stood in the middle of it, watching Jerry get ready to pull out of the eddy, I would be lying if I didn't confess to some morbid curiosity.

"Are we watching this? Or rubber-necking?"

Jerry got out into the main current, and, from the beginning, it didn't go well. The only possible line was directly over the boulder drops, hoping for clean exits. Getting pushed to the right meant the wall. We watched him go over the first drop and disappear into the foam. When he reappeared, he was too far right, at the next drop he came out upside down. We saw efforts to roll—unsuccessful—before the current took him hard to the right. He slammed into the wall and vanished. We started to run for our boats when someone shouted: "He's out!" Sure enough. His helmet appeared in one place, his boat another, and his paddle a third, but Jerry made it through. We scrambled down to the river in time. Someone went after his boat while the rest of us helped him out. He was holding half a paddle. Jerry hadn't run Lumsden so much as swum it, but he was here, alive, and we were finally ready to go home.

We separated that evening. Jerry said he wanted to go find another paddle and as he drove off, we bid our adieus, wondering when, if ever, we'd see him again. We met up with Gail, Rimbeaux's friend and our shuttle driver, and, as we drove back home, celebratory beers in hand, related the whole tale. When we finished with our thrilling adventure, she asked what seemed like the most irrelevant question. "What did you have for lunch?"

"Lunch? What'd we have for lunch? Who cares? A sandwich. A couple of apples. Why?"

"Did you share?" Gail was a nurse. Silence.

"Do you know how rabies is spread?" She looked at us. "Saliva. Did you share the apples?"

We felt like kids who'd been caught underage. "Maybe. I don't remember…"

"You shared an apple with a guy who's got rabies." She declared flatly.

The beer suddenly tasted weird. The next day I was working the phones, calling various clinics. "Is it possible to get rabies from somebody by sharing food with them?"

I finally got a doctor to talk to me. "People who have rabies aren't on the street." He responded bluntly.

"Just for argument's sake, let's say somebody was."

It was no use. No one believed me. Rabid people are in horror movies, not kayaking on The Tuolumne River. It got to the point where I started to doubt myself. Maybe the whole story's a crock, I thought, hopefully. Maybe Barry and Rimbeaux were right!

Jerry had mentioned the outfitter he'd worked for. I called him up.

"Does Jerry Jacques row for you guys?" I asked.

"He used to," the man said, "but then he had to go get some shots. A bat bit him." Great. I thought, when I need a guy to be lying through his teeth, he's not.

"Do you know where he is?" the guy asked me. "He ran away before they could finish with him. Some doctor down in LA really wants to talk to him."

I put down the phone a vindicated but unhappy guy. A couple more phone calls and I finally got a nurse friend of mine to look it up. "They have to be showing symptoms," she read to me, "before they're considered dangerously contagious. Sensitivity to light, irritability. And foaming."

Foaming? I didn't remember any of that. And he didn't seem that irritable. A little crazy, sure. But he's a boatman. I was rationalizing, but the days went by, and I failed to do any foaming of my own. Barry and Rimbeaux, for their part, thought I was being completely paranoid.

"You don't have rabies," they said dismissively, "Don't be ridiculous."

It would have been easier to take some consolation from their opinions if they weren't the same geniuses who were so certain nobody'd ever been bitten on the lip by a bat in the first place. But eventually, my paranoia faded away and more trips intervened. As the seasons wore on, the story fell into the pile of all the river stories we'd tell around the campfire. The years passed. I retired my kayak, got married with a family ("the full catastrophe," in Zorba's famous phrasing).

When my kids got to the wide-eyed stage, I used to tell them some of the river lies, including the rabies story, embellishing it without any shame. "Whatever happened to that guy?" they'd ask. "Whatever happened to Batman?" I had to shake my head. I didn't know. No one knew. Until one day the phone rang.

"Hello?" I said.

"Do you remember that time on Cherry Creek when I went down with you guys in kayaks?" the voice said. "Like about twenty years ago?"

"Jerry?"

"I ran/swam Lumsden Falls. Do you remember?"

"Is this Jerry Jacques?" I said.

"Yeah. I need to know if you remember that run."

"Where are you?"

"Alaska."

"You don't have rabies?"

"No. It turned out to be OK. It was only the medication that was making me sick. Nothing ever happened," he said. "But I need a favor…"

Jerry, I learned, had returned to Alaska shortly after the whole incident, running rivers, scuffling a boatman's living, running his own outfit. With hundreds of new adventures, he'd pretty much forgotten that day with the three of us on Cherry Creek. Until just recently.

He and his brother had been in a bar in Anchorage and struck up a conversation with the guy on the stool next to them, a lawyer from California who'd been a big kayaker back in his day. The subject of big bad rapids came up and eventually, as often happens in these circumstances, the name Lumsden Falls surfaced. Jerry must have put his beer down to inform the lawyer that he was talking to the very man who'd run it first.

"After I left you guys, I went and bought a new paddle, went back with my brother waiting at the bottom with a throw rope; I ran Lumsden again. Still not a clean run, but I did make it down upright and still in my boat.

"The jerk didn't believe me or my brother," Jerry explained curtly. I felt a faint wave of sympathy and understanding for the lawyer. And the favor?

"We bet $100. I'm going to give him your number. When he calls you, you know what to say, right? You saw me, right?"

What could I say? I was there.

Jawbone on Cherry Creek (Photo by Zachary Collier 2002)

Follow the link to watch the video
Kayaking Cherry Creek 2021

Mummy on the Stanislaus

For a serious raft trip on the Stanislaus River in California, this one turned into a comedy show with me in the starring role. It was early 1978, and I was on my way to Alaska within a couple of days, but I had one last trip to run. As it turned out, it looked like I didn't have to do the trip. So I dispatched all the guides, and we had extra room, so I told them they could take friends and family down the river just as a reward for them having worked hard all season. Then I got a call from the head office that we had another trip going out that I didn't know was on the schedule. This trip was on a different river. I was told to pull a couple of the guides and boats that I should have had available to go run that one-day trip.

The problem was that I dispatched all the guides and all our boats. We didn't have anything, and my guides were on a two-day overnight trip. So, I got hold of the bus driver, put on a shorty wetsuit, helmet, life jacket, and grabbed my fins and a thing called a surf mat, which is an inflatable mattress about three-and-a-half-feet long and two-and-a-half-foot wide. I was going to have our bus driver drop me off at the head of the river.

It was now dark—very dark. This is on the Stanislaus River in California, long before the New Malones dam was constructed, and about a mile-and-a-half before the put-in I had him stop. I thought I knew where I was. My plan was to hike down with my little flashlight from there to the river. I would be below the major rapids, and I would just paddle the surf mat into camp and then grab one of the guides and two rafts and head downriver where the bus driver was going to pick me up early in the morning. Then we would have time to get over to the other river to conduct that trip.

Well, I missed my mark on where I thought I was. I hit the river with a couple of big rapids still below me. I didn't fully realize it because it was dark. I've done a lot of rafting and a little bit of kayaking in the dark just for fun to challenge myself on rivers, including the Stanislaus River. So, I launched laying on the surf mat; I had my fins on also. I immediately realized that I was in the wrong spot. I went through one rapid that's called Death Rock. I managed to hit Death Rock then bounced off it into the hole. Thankfully, the water level wasn't too high, so the hole didn't have enough power to really keep me trapped.

Eventually, with a couple of rapids downstream, I bounced, grinding my way down, and got to a place called Rose Creek, a tributary of the Stanislaus, which is our normal lunch spot, and I was cold at this point—cold, pretty beat up, and it was dark, and so I decided to pull into Rose Creek. The water at Rose Creek was always ten-to-fifteen degrees warmer than the Stanislaus River. So, I soaked in there for a little bit, and at first it felt warm, but then, after I got to that temperature, I started getting cold again. I figured I was just going to get out and spend a couple hours, warm up, and wait for a little bit of light before I headed back downstream. I didn't have that far to go to where our guides and our crew were camped. I was out of the water, but there was a light breeze blowing, and I got cold again after a bit.

Previously, the BLM had installed cement pads with a wood fence around them where they had porta potties located. BLM no longer had the funding. They had been pulled the year before, but the fence and the pad were both still there. I figured I could get out of the wind by going inside the fence. So, I went ahead and crawled inside. Getting out of the wind helped a little bit with the warmth, but I knew there was a camp there because there were a couple of rafts pulled out. I didn't know where they were camping, up-river or up the creek a little way I guessed.

I was lying there, looking at all those rolls of toilet paper still hanging on the side of the fence but no outhouse there anymore. I figured, you know, that might make insulation, so I took the rolls of toilet paper and slowly wrapped my legs, wrapped my arms, wrapped my whole body with layers and layers of toilet paper which added some warmth, and now I was warm enough I could finally fall asleep.

It was just barely dawn when I heard the creak of the door that led into the fenced-off area. As it creaked open, I sat up and, apparently, I looked like a mummy! There was a loud scream. The door slammed and then I heard somebody yelling in female voice while running away.

"There's a mummy at the outhouse!"

At that point I'm thinking, *"Uh-oh! This doesn't sound good!"*

So, I grabbed my surf-mat, grabbed my fins, ran about thirty feet, jumped in the river before I put on my fins, and started paddling downriver. I could hear the commotion behind me, and I think, "Well, at least I'm out of there!"

Then I look around me and I see in the dawn light, all this toilet paper that were layers and layers all over my whole body is starting to wash off into the river.

"This is pretty disgusting," I thought. *"I'm surrounded by all of this toilet paper floating downstream with me."*

I got my fins on, and it was probably only thirty minutes in the

Rafting on the Stanislaus River North Fork
(Photo ©2005 Dick James http:// www.byways.org)

river from there to where our campsite was—an old campsite on the Stanislaus River. I walked into the campsite, and there's a bit of a smoldering fire burning where we could just do our cooking, and as I'm walking through the trail, a skunk walked right in front of me! I was so tired and so cold and just so at the end my wits that I just put my foot underneath its belly without really kicking and pushed it out of the way. That threw it into the blackberry bushes. For whatever reason, it didn't spray me.

I found a young boatman by the name of Danny Grant. It was his first year as a boatman, but he was an incredibly hard-working, talented kid.

"Hey, we've got a trip on the American River! I need you to grab a boat; I need to grab a boat; we need to get downstream. Our bus driver's waiting for us, and he'll get us over to the American so we can run this trip," I told him.

Danny grabbed his dry bag and his gear, and we launched the two rafts. Off we went downriver. There were plenty of extra rafts for their trip as it was very lightly loaded with people. We rowed the two rafts down the river to this trip's takeout, a place called Parrot's Ferry. The bus driver was already there, and we loaded the gear as quickly as we could. We had already done the shopping for everyone's lunch, and the lunch cooler was already packed so off we went. Danny and I drove like wild men over to the American to our put-in point.

There are two put-in points for the American River, and every time I guided one-day trips, I would launch from the lower put-in. Well, the office sent these clients to the upper put-in point, so we never did get to run the trip—my entire downriver-escapade was for nothing. Danny's and my crazy-rowing and mad-driving ended not at an expectant knot of clientele, but at a totally empty point on the riverbank.

Things have changed significantly in my rafting business since the time of this story. Here in this 2012 photo, my brothers John & Jim join me for a float on the Copper River in Alaska.

I called the company, and they contacted another raft company who was already at the upper site, and that company graciously added our clients to their tour, so everything worked out fine for the clients who probably never knew the lengths we had gone to just to make their whitewater experience so memorable. It was an all-around missed opportunity for our company, but a very hilarious episode for me—the Mummy on the Stanislaus.

Me & the Bears

In June of 1981, I was leading a six-day Talkeetna whitewater raft trip.[1] The trip was a small one with only a few clients. Talkeetna bush pilot and guide, Larry Rivers, flew us to an airstrip that we had built by hand two miles below Yellow Jacket Creek. We saw Dall sheep ewes and lambs while setting up the raft. Ed Wick was the second raft guide. Ed and I worked well together. He was a good breakfast cook, and I did an okay job with dinner. So far, this was an uneventful trip with clean runs down the canyon. The last night's camp on my six-day trip was always at Disappointment Creek. Two prospectors, Bruce and Dennis, lived by the creek. This was the upper limit of jet boats on the Talkeetna River. The Jet boat service run by Steve Mahay, was the only access to this mining claim and it was an expensive charter to get there. Bruce and Dennis were big men, each weighing over two-hundred and seventy pounds. They were Vietnam vets who spent three months prospecting the area each year and ran a suction dredge on the creek. As Disappointment Creek was the last night's camp, I usually had a week's worth of leftover food and produce in the cooler, and it was customary for Bruce and Dennis to join us for dinner. The prospectors were always glad to see me because I had lots of goodies for them and a newspaper that was only a week old, and they always had hot coffee and a hot fire ready for us as we came out of the whitewater canyon, usually wet and often cold. These two were colorful characters and added to the trip for my clients. They had built a nice outhouse at our campsite as well as a cooking shelter for me and my guides to keep us out of the rain. To top it off, Bruce and Dennis would have cut and stacked firewood ready for our arrival.

The prospectors lived in an interesting structure (they called it a cabin, but it was actually a makeshift tent) at Disappointment Creek. Their tent was framed using poles they had cut and sided with clear, heavy-duty Visqueen plastic sheeting cut from rolls. They made a framework from the poles, then stretched the plastic over the entire framework and stapled it to the poles. In other words, they lived in a plastic baggy supported by toothpicks. Every winter, the snow would collapse and tear the plastic. Each spring when they returned, they brought a few new rolls of Visqueen and boxes of staples. The

---

[1] For further information on the route for this trip see: https://www.alaska.org/detail/talkeetna-river.

frame usually was still standing so they only had to re-skin it. They had also made their own beds, tables, and chairs from the poles.

Ten days before Ed and I embarked on this last trip, I had met a friend of Bruce and Dennis named Marvin. He was a bartender at Chilkoot Charlie's in Anchorage. I was not aware this happened, but soon after we met, Marvin was strong armed/kidnapped by Bruce and Dennis who both worked as bouncers at Chilkoot Charlie's during the winter. They spirited him away to their remote claim so he could dry out and get off the booze before he drank himself to death. They did not make him quit cold turkey but cut him down progressively until he sobered up.

So, after our wet ride through the upper Talkeetna canyon (this was before self-bailing rafts), as Ed and I pulled into the eddy at Disappointment Creek, I was surprised at what we found. Marvin was on the beach with three or four campfires blazing around him, a coffee pot, and at least three-hundred cigarette butts on the ground. He was shaking so badly that he could hardly talk. Finally, stuttering, he told us a bear had been breaking into the cabin and chasing him out. Marvin was afraid to shoot the bear because he did not want to get into trouble with Fish and Game or make trouble for Bruce and Dennis, who had left him to finish drying out cold turkey. They were in town buying supplies, selling gold nuggets and, I am sure, having more than a few drinks at Chilkoot Charlie's. Marvin knew I was a hunting guide and had been waiting on the beach for two days for me to show up on my next raft trip. He asked me if I could get rid of the bear and not get anybody into trouble. I told him I would help him after I cooked dinner and as soon as I had taken care of my clients. That night, the clients gave him the nickname Starvin' Marvin. For a skinny little guy, he ate more than we thought possible. As soon as dinner was done, Ed and I walked with Marvin the hundred-and-fifty yards from my camp to the cabin.

I had my rifle and .45 ACP handgun with me. We helped Marvin clean up the mess the bear had made. Marvin told me when Bruce and Dennis left for town that there was some leftover dog food in a bowl. He put it outside, and a black bear ate it that afternoon. He thought that was neat, so he refilled the bowl the next morning. This went on until the dog food ran out.

Then, whenever he was away from the cabin, the bear started breaking in and stealing Marvin's food. At first, Marvin was able to run it off, but the bear soon became more aggressive and eventually it ran him off. After we had things cleaned up, Marvin wrapped a new layer of plastic around the makeshift tent while I made a few snares from cable that they used to tie off their dredge in the creek. Marvin asked me if I would stay until the bear came back. I agreed. There was a bunk on the opposite wall from Marvin's that had four old, heavy canvas sleeping bags on it. Two or three bags were used for cushioning over the poles and the remaining one or two to sleep under for warmth.

I was sound asleep when Marvin's bear poked his head through the plastic right next to me. Fortunately, the tearing plastic woke me. I saw the bear's head for only an instant before it was gone. Because it happened so quickly, I was not convinced there really had been a bear at all. But the hole was there. Marvin woke and confirmed that he had covered all the tent with plastic and no holes were in the sheeting when we went to sleep. With me carrying my .375 H&H rifle, and Marvin packing a .44 Mag, we searched the area around the tent. I noticed that Marvin was still shaking badly. He was going through withdrawals and was still stressed out from being alone in the wilderness, as well as the bear that kept chasing him out of the tent. His hands shook so badly that they looked like a sewing machine needle going up and down. After a fruitless search, we returned to the tent. Marvin stapled a new piece of plastic over the hole, and I went back to bed. I had been feeling sick the entire day and was very tired. I laid down on my back, and sleep overtook me quickly. I'm not certain how long I had been asleep—it felt like only a second, when I was rudely awakened by the sound of ripping plastic and a rank smell of horribly bad breath. I found myself looking up at Marvin's black bear standing over me. She had both front paws on the bed. Out of my peripheral vision, I could see Marvin trying to get his cheaply made Italian .44 magnum revolver out of its holster hanging on his bed frame. I must admit, this was one of the few times in my life that I was terrified. Not of the bear—I was terrified Starvin' Marvin would shoot me with the 240-grain hollow point he had in his six gun. Out of desperation, I swung my fist as hard as I could into the face of the bear, hitting her on the side of the head. She let out a loud *beller*, jumped back, and launched herself out of the same hole she had made in the plastic.

About that time, Marvin cleared leather with the gun.

"Don't shoot!" I screamed. To my surprise, his hands were not shaking. He appeared calm for the moment, but his shaking transferred to me. We both jumped up and ran outside looking for the bear. She had disappeared into the thick alder again.

"Are you okay? Did the bear step on you?" Marvin asked as we made our way back into the tent.

From his perspective, it looked like she had been standing on me. As soon as he realized I was okay, he started shaking again, so now we were both shaking.

"The last thing I expected to see was you actually slug that bear in the face," he said.

"Believe me, with her breath, I was definitely not going to kiss her," I said. What a foul smell a bear has face to face. I realized that the snares I had set for the bear were of no use. Marvin's bear was smarter than my snare-setting ability.

Marvin and I fixed the hole in the plastic by stapling up a sheet over that wall. This time when I laid down, I switched ends and put my feet where the bear had come through the plastic twice before. I figured if she came through again, I'd rather it be at my feet. I had just drifted back to sleep when Marvin suddenly said, "Did you hear that?"

I was instantly awake with my gun in my hand.

"I heard a shot," Marvin said. We both heard the second shot. I was up and running to my camp. Halfway there, I realized I was running through thick alder in the direction of gun shots. I stopped, dropped, and yelled "Ed, I'm coming from the tent. Don't shoot!"

"Come on! It's over," Ed yelled back.

I walked into camp and saw Ed standing over a dead black bear with my clients standing in the pouring rain, looking glum.

I walked up to Ed, got close to his face so no one else could hear and whispered, "It's not good to shoot the wildlife on the hippie trips."

Ed turned to me with a hurt look.

"I had no choice," he whispered back. "I chased that bear off at least five times, but it kept coming back!"

As my tunnel vision opened, I saw the campsite looked like a bomb had gone off. One of the coolers had its lid torn off. The garbage bag had been ripped open, and empty tin cans were strewn all around. A dry box lay upside down, and a dry bag was ripped open with clothes pulled out and scattered.

"I bounced rocks and firewood off that bear's head three times, and it still kept coming back! And it was getting more aggressive each time," he said. Ed told me that the last straw was when a client was chased into the outhouse and the bear would not let her back out.

"Someone was going to get hurt! I had no choice but to shoot the bear," he said finally. The bear was a healthy-looking boar of average size but was skinny as I would expect in the spring.

It was 4:00 a.m., raining, and I was still sick; Ed looked worn out. The two of us would take care of skinning out the bear and cooking breakfast later, in the meantime, we needed to get a few hours of sleep now that we could relax. I went back to the cabin and was asleep the minute I laid down under the two old, heavy canvas sleeping bags.

The next thing I knew—like a really bad dream—a bear was standing over me again. I slowly started to reach for my handgun, but before I could get my left hand on it, she grabbed me by my arm and started shaking me. She was trying to pull me out of the cabin. I fought back hard, trying not to let her drag me out before getting my hand on my pistol. Once, twice, I fought my way almost to it, only to be dragged away again. It was on my third desperate try using my right hand that I finally got hold of my 1911 Colt .45 ACP. She started shaking me up and down. I felt like a piston going up and down in an old motor. At the top of an up-stroke, I put the gun to her head and almost pulled the trigger but stopped when I realized I would shoot my arm as well as the bear. I waited a fraction of a second, put the gun to the base of her neck, and pulled the trigger. She instantly let me go and fell back out of the cabin. I fired off two more rounds at center mass through the opaque plastic that was now hanging between us. One of those shots hit the bear in the top of the head, glanced off the skull, and ricocheted past the heads of Ed and Marvin as they rushed to help me. Marvin said later that it sounded like an angry bumble bee as the bullet split the air right past his left ear. I got up and went out just as the two arrived. I put another round into her to make sure she was dead and then collapsed; Marvin and Ed caught me.

My left arm was dislocated from the shoulder and partly crushed. The heavy sleeping bags over me, along with the fact that two of her canine teeth were broken off at the gum line, had saved my arm from being torn into pieces. Although not as strong as a polar bear or a grizzly bear, the mature black bear has a bite force of well over six-hundred pounds per square inch. That's tremendous biting, tearing, and ripping power. Fortunately, there were only a couple of punctures in my arm, but it still put me out of commission for the next two months as my arm and shoulder healed.

Me with the black bears of Disappointment Creek

I had dropped my guard after Ed killed the first bear, and Marvin's wild stories now made more sense with two bears. The second bear, the one that got me, was an elderly sow and in poor health.

Ed put the two dead bears and me, along with the clients, on his eighteen-foot raft and rowed us all in that overloaded raft, all the way back to Talkeetna.

Polar Bear Encounter   It was 1985 when I had my first polar bear encounter. I left Larry Rivers' summer camp at Red Sheep Creek near the headwaters of the east fork of the Chandalar River. The camp was located in the middle of Arctic National Wildlife Refuge. I had planned to fly my Cessna 180 to Dead Horse, Prudhoe Bay, to buy gas for camp. Because of the weather, I had to divert to Barter Island, a small island, four miles long and two miles wide, just off the Arctic coast of Alaska in the Beaufort Sea. Kaktovik is the village on Barter Island; its other feature is a run- way built on the island in 1953 capable of accommodating heavy-lift aircraft.

On the day I flew in, there was no gas available at the airport. Walt Audi would usually sell gas, but he had run out and was waiting for his shipment to arrive. I had to walk to town, buy some gas cans, buy auto gas at the trading post, and get a ride back to the airport. By the time I did, all this weather closed in, and I was stuck.

I had to spend the night on Barter Island and decided to stay at the Waldo Arms Hotel, an interesting place, but it takes a stretch of the imagination to think of it as a hotel. It is, however, warm and mostly dry and a very fun place to stay. I enjoy the colorful atmosphere and history. Around 3:00 a.m., I noticed the wind had changed direction. My plane was a few miles away, parked at the airport. I got up, dressed, strapped on my .45 ACP, and headed for the airport on foot to check on my plane. The light was poor but not totally dark, and there was a blowing mist. I was walking down the road halfway between town and the airport and noticed movement to my left.

Out of the dark blowing mist lumbered the huge form of a polar bear. She stepped onto the road forty feet in front of me. The bear and I both stopped and looked at each other for what seemed like a very long time. She stood up on her hind legs, testing the cold night mist. My .45 was instantly in my hand—I stayed very still. I think that bear was a sow, but I'm not certain as it was the first polar bear I had ever seen. From my distance, I judged her to be seven-and-a-half to eight-feet tall when standing. We remained fixated on each other until, eventually, she seemed to shrug her shoulders, drop back to all fours, and blithely continue ambling her way toward the airport. I decided then and there that polar bears always have the right of way—my plane could wait to be checked on, so I returned to the hotel with frequent glances over my shoulder to make sure I was not being stalked.

At 8:00 a.m., the weather was still not flyable, but I was able to borrow a truck and go check on my plane. I turned the Cessna to face into the wind, all while feeling a little edgy, but the bear was not in sight.

By late the next afternoon the weather broke, and I was able to fly back to my camp at Red Sheep Creek. As I took off from the Kaktovik airport, I saw my second polar bear from the safety of my plane, but this one was certainly not as impressive as coming face-to-face on the ground at forty short paces.

Don Lee & the Wide-Eyed Trucker

While flying the Pilatus Porter for Charley Connell and Ron Sutphin delivering fuel and supplies to their gold mine, I made many flights up the east fork of the Chulitna River. From the air I saw good whitewater below and wanted to kayak the river. The Chulitna River is a 110-kilometer-long right tributary of the Susitna River in the southern part of Alaska's interior region. Three forks converge to form the river, which itself flows into the Susitna River near Talkeetna. A few years had passed when, in July 1985, Don Lee agreed to fly me and my kayak to the upper east fork of the Chulitna River. It was time I tried to run this river.

First, I drove my truck from Talkeetna to the spot where the Parks Highway crosses the main Chulitna River. At a prearranged time, Don landed his Super Cub on the highway and got off the side of the road with just enough room so the passing cars missed the wings of the plane.

We tied my kayak onto the belly of the plane and took off on the highway. Don pulled onto the road and started his takeoff roll. We were just getting our speed, when a semi-truck appeared on the highway heading straight toward us. Don yanked the flaps, and we staggered into the air flying directly over the truck. We were so close that I could see the shocked expression on the trucker's face.

Thirty minutes later, Don landed on a gravel bar next to the river. "That was crazy with the truck on the road," I said.

Don just shrugged. "It wasn't that close," he said. "You're the one who's crazy for kayaking this river alone."

We untied the kayak from the plane, and Don flew back to Talkeetna. If I did not make it back to Talkeetna in three days, we agreed that Don would start searching for me.

Grizzly fishing on the Chulitna

I carried my thirteen-foot Perception kayak to the river. I put on my dry suit, spray skirt, life jacket, wetsuit booties, and helmet, then launched in some still water off the gravel bar where we had landed. I paddled into midstream to start my solo adventure. My life jacket had a special pouch sewn in that held my four-inch S&W .44 mag. In all the years of kayaking and rafting, I never had to use the revolver, but it sure made me feel better just having it with me.

As far as the whitewater community knew, no one had ever run this section of river before. From the air, it looked like there were several Class III and IV rapids with one narrow spot that could be Class V.

Scouting from the air, though, it's not always possible to judge how difficult the rapids are. First descents are fun. Facing the unknown, discovering the reality of what lies ahead just adds to the excitement for me.

I had picked a relatively calm spot for my ingress, but I was quickly at the point where the canyon narrowed, which meant that now I was committed, and the whitewater began. The narrowing of the canyon walls coupled with the drop in elevation (gradient), create channel hydraulics. The water intensifies, and as the speed of the water increases so does the speed of the kayak. When the rushing water hits a boulder or any other obstacle, it boils back, creating the whitewater effect known as a hole. Holes can be fun, or they can be death traps. Either way, I was committed to running this canyon.

With thirteen years of whitewater experience, this run was just fun and uneventful for me as there were only two Class III rapids and one Class IV drop. I never even needed to get out of my kayak to

Grizzly salmon fishing

Success!

scout. The only challenging part of the whole trip was when I came around a blind bend to find a grizzly intently fishing in the middle of the river right in front of me. I could have easily presented a target, but that magnificent bear had its back to me and was so intent on its fishing expedition that it did not move or show any sign that it was aware of my sudden presence. I knew differently, however. Today, king salmon was on the menu, so I had to back paddle for a full minute before that bear acquired its intended meal and waded out of the river to dine on its catch.

By evening of the same day I launched, I had run the river to its confluence with the main Chulitna River and paddled down to where my truck was parked. By 1:00 p.m. the next day, I was back in Talkeetna having lunch with Don Lee and Larry Rivers. During our conversation over the meal, I told them about my kayak run and the grizzly fishing on the Chulitna.

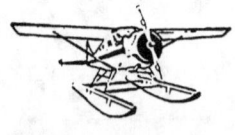

alaska-grizzlies.com

(Photos courtesy of Alaska Grizzly Safaris)

Don & David Lee

I first met David Lee in Talkeetna. As I pulled up to the general store, there was a teenage boy waiting outside.

I could just guess by the body language that he was going to ask me to buy him beer; I'd already made my mind up that I wouldn't do that. I got out of my truck, and, as I walked up, he looked directly at me. *Here it comes*, I thought.

"Are you over eighteen?"

I looked at him a little closer now, confused. Alaska minimum drinking age was twenty-one, not eighteen years of age.

"Yes," I answered cautiously, puzzled about what came next, still thinking it might have something to do with beer.

"Well, I'm only sixteen, and I wanna go moose hunting, but I don't have any ammo. They won't let me buy ammo cause you have to be eighteen to buy ammo…I have a .338 but no ammo to hunt with," he said.

"If I give you the money, would you buy me a box of ammo?"

Nice! I thought. For moose-hunting rounds, I am happy to help!

"Yeah, I can do that," I said with a smile on my face.

I went inside and bought him a box of .338 ammo, came back outside and handed him the box. We got talking and ended up going moose hunting together for the rest of the day. We didn't see anything, but a friendship was started that day outside the general store.

As we had chances to talk on our hunt, I found out David and a friend of his, Steve Johnson, had run away from home in Minnesota and hitchhiked to Talkeetna. They were living with David's older brother Don Lee.

We had covered some ground in our hunt, but it was soon getting too dark to see much, so we called it quits. I gave David a ride home, which meant driving through some pretty muddy 4x4 dirt roads. David's older brother, Don Lee, met us as we pulled up. Don was covered in sawdust from constructing an addition to the one room cabin. He quit his work for the day and invited me in for dinner.

I remember this vividly today; dinner was spaghetti with chunks of meat in it. After a little while, Don went out to go use the outhouse. When he was out of earshot, David and Steve both chimed in with what sounded like a dire warning, "You might not want to eat that spaghetti."

"There's a little sawdust mixed in," I said as I checked out what was left on my plate, "but it tastes fine."

"No! It's dog meat!"

Sounded to me like they were serious.

Their warning was kind of too late, though—I'd already devoured two plates of dog-meat spaghetti.

Now it dawned on me why David was so desperately trying to shoot a moose! About that time, Don returned from his trip to the outhouse, and our conversation stopped.

"Good spaghetti," I said.

It turned out that Don was struggling trying to take care of the two runaway teenagers. He managed to keep them in school. He made sure they were clothed and fed, but Don was only nineteen years old. He was still a teenager, too, yet he was now the guardian of two younger teens. All three of them were living in the one-room log cabin Don had built by hand.

He did not have money for meat, but Don did have this huge dog named Tawny. After the boys moved in with him, he couldn't afford to feed it anymore. He tried to give Tawny away, but nobody was willing to offer such a big dog a home.

He was left with only two choices—he could watch his dog slowly starve to death, or he could shoot it. He shot it.

To my way of thinking, that was a man-sized decision.

But still faced with man-sized decisions, he thought, *this dog's meat is protein; I have hungry teenage boys to feed, and it should not go to waste.* He skinned out the carcass, used the hide for a door on their outhouse, and butchered the meat for their winter supply.

I have known Don for more than forty years now. He loves dogs as much as anyone I know, so it must have been an incredibly painful decision for him to turn his pet into their winter meat supply. I give Don a tremendous amount of credit. You can slowly starve to death in Alaska, or you can grow up pretty fast. With Don looking out for all of them, the two Lee brothers grew up fast as fine men, and Steve remained in Alaska to become a pilot. He worked for the FAA until his retirement.

Over the years Don and David each became very famous Talkeetna bush pilots. David eventually owned Talkeetna Air Taxi, then married Don Sheldon's daughter, Holly, and together they still run Sheldon Air Service. Don Lee started Alaska Floats and Skis, one of the best places to learn about Alaska bush flying.

Don, David, and I have guided and flown together all over Alaska.

We've helped each other out of a few tough spots, and Don and I even worked together in Afghanistan. I'm really proud to say that I have a great friendship with the Lee's that continues to this day

David Lee had one extremely bad year when he owned Talkeetna air taxi. He wrecked three airplanes in one season. The first wreck happened while he was dropping off some Caribou hunters in the Talkeetna Mountains. He landed on a nasty ridge-top strip, hit a hole, and flipped his Super Cub onto its back.

Eric Drinkwalter and Terry Mangione were flown in by Jay Hudson and managed to get the airplane turned right side up and patched back together enough to fly it back to Talkeetna for expensive repairs. A few weeks later, with David's Cub back on line, he flew to Falls Creek Airstrip, which was usually a good strip, but when David flew in this time, the creek had changed course making the strip unsafe for his plane. David had hired a young man to go in and rebuild the airstrip. He landed up above on a tiny gravel bar and dropped the guy off close enough for him to walk down to the little cabin next to the washed-out airstrip. The guy was supposed to rebuild the airstrip and when it was safe to land, he was to hang a blue tarp on the backside of the cabin, that way David would know that the repairs were finished, and it was okay to land.

When David flew over a week later, the blue tarp was there, and the guy was waving for him to land. David lined up and landed. Unbelievably, there were still a couple of big holes right in the middle of the airstrip that had not been repaired. David hit the first hole with the tail wheel, ripping it off the Cub. This was actually not a big deal and an easy repair back at the hanger—but he was in the bush, not at his hanger. David was not happy with the guy he had paid to repair the strip.

The guy had not done what he was hired to do yet he had convinced David that the strip was safe by hanging the blue tarp on the cabin.

Whatever words were exchanged, and David and the young man got the airplane pulled back to the very end of the strip. David was going to take off empty and go back to repair his plane while the guy worked on the strip until the job was completed. It was a good plan, except this guy was totally panicked! He was afraid of being out in the bush alone and refused to let David leave without him.

With little choice, David agreed, against his better judgment, to let the guy get in the back seat of the Super Cub and try to do the takeoff. With the extra weight and without the tail wheel, the tail of the airplane was dragging on the tail spring. This caused considerable drag and extended the distance needed for takeoff. He didn't make it. The plane was really wrecked now, sitting at the end of the strip. It wasn't going to get off the ground in its current condition.

I didn't know David was up there flying. While this was all happening, I was in my Cessna 180, flying loads of rafting gear onto a gravel bar at the confluence of the Talkeetna River and Yellowjacket Creek for the start of an upcoming rafting trip.

After unloading my gear, I took off and was half a mile past the strip when, out of my peripheral vision, I caught a quick glimpse of two people walking through the bush. This was late July and there should not have been anyone up there other than our group. The two people walking up the river looked very out of place, but I had only caught a glimpse.

I went downriver a little further, turned around, came back upriver, and flew over them. This time I could see they were each waving their arms in the attention-seeking pattern. Obviously, something was wrong. I went ahead and landed at Yellowjacket Creek, got turned around, and taxied back. About the time I was getting out of the airplane, David Lee came running out of the bushes. He explained the whole situation to me with the end-of-story being that his wrecked Cub was still sitting up at Falls Creek with no hope of going anywhere from the end of that bush airstrip.

He and the guy that was supposed to have built the strip for him had walked down hoping to maybe catch me between making my loads. Fortunately, they succeeded.

It had taken them four hours of hard walking to get to my drop-off site. David knew we usually only went in with a load and came out empty; the conditions were right.

"I can take you back to Talkeetna so you can get your 185 and come back and get your worker," I told David.

Hearing our plan, the worker suddenly threw an absolute fit!

"I'm going with you! I'm not staying here alone!" He ranted on and on and on.

I'd just heard the story of how David had wrecked his airplane trying to get the guy out of the bush, and I was already mad.

"Didn't you learn your lesson when you crashed in the Cub because the strip was too short to take a load out?" I asked the panicked airstrip worker. But he wouldn't listen. He insisted that he was getting in my airplane and flying back to Talkeetna with me. At this point I got even madder.

"There's no way in hell you're ever going to get in an airplane that I'm flying—not even if conditions were perfect and I had a long airstrip would you ever ride in an airplane with me."

"There's no way in hell you're going to stop me from getting in that airplane when you take off," he shouted back parroting my words. At this point, I just smiled at him, picked up his rifle, took the bolt out of it, and handed it back to him.

"If you try to get in my airplane," I said meeting him eye-to-eye, "it will be putting my life and David's life at risk, and, if I have to, I will put a .45 ACP round from my colt through each of your knees, and if that doesn't work, I'll put the third round between your eyes."

Wisely, he kept silent.

"Now get your shit over to that pile of rafting gear, sit down, and wait for David to come back and pick you up and you better hope that David's airplane starts because there is no way you will ever fly in an airplane with me." At this point, I was done talking to him, and that was okay because it appeared the poor guy realized he was more afraid of me than he was waiting a few hours alone.

I took off with David Lee, using most of the gravel bar before we were airborne. Back in Talkeetna, David packed some of my raft gear into his 185 since he had an empty airplane flying back to pick up this guy anyway.

David immediately arranged to get his Cub out of the bush. However, this time it couldn't be flown out, it had to be helicoptered out, and that was a huge insurance claim.

Fast forward to late September when my hunts and raft trips were finishing up for the season. At the time, I had my two Super Cubs and my Cessna 180 still ferrying gear from campsites when I heard that David had wrecked his 185 at Yellowjacket Creek. The plane had a gear leg failure which is not uncommon with Cessna 185s. Bush airplanes are worked hard, especially if they've been worked on skis. David owned Talkeetna Air Taxi which did a lot of ski work up on Mt. McKinley.

David's an outstanding and extremely safe pilot. Even back then in our younger days, I never hesitated to get into an airplane that David was piloting. Airplanes used in the Alaska bush are not landing on gravel bars or ridge tops just for fun, they're hauling heavy loads of climbers or miners or homesteaders, rafters or whatever else needs hauled in or out, landing and taking off on unimproved or even nonexistent backcountry airstrips. Doing this is extremely hard on airplanes, and airplanes get bent. Unfortunately, it's just part of the business. I personally have bent a baker's dozen of airplanes during my forty-five-year career flying the bush.

Now, with David having bent his third airplane in one season, he was distraught and financially stressed in the extreme. To get the airplane out of the headwaters of the Talkeetna River and back to the hangar in Talkeetna for repair, once again, it was going to take a helicopter to bring it home. I do not remember what the cost was back then, but in today's dollars, that would be at least a thirty-thousand-dollar helicopter trip.

This time, David just couldn't afford the cost of hauling his airplane via helicopter back to the hangar in Talkeetna; he was in a tight spot. He needed his Cessna operational in order to make his living.

Mechanic Eric Drinkwalter went up and assessed the airplane. He told David that it was definitely rebuildable, and that's all we needed to hear. Being the creative geniuses we were, we put our heads together and decided that if we disassembled the airplane where it sat, we could load the pieces onto my whitewater rafts and float the airplane down the seventy miles of whitewater river and back to Talkeetna.

We decided we would put the wings and the control surfaces on one raft and the fuselage on the other raft. After a lot of discussion, we made our decision. Yep, late September we were gonna do this. After all, it was the most economical way for David to rescue his plane and get back to work.

We were friends. David and I had done lots of little business deals back and forth, and I knew he was in financial trouble. I told him all he had to do was pay Jim Hendrick's wage as a raft guide and I would supply the rafts and my labor to help get the airplane taken apart. Hey, we would give this a try! We all knew it was a risky proposition, floating a Cessna 185—wings, fuselage, and everything but the engine—seventy miles downriver in Class III and IV whitewater. But we were young and needed to save some money.

David felt it was worth the risk. I was confident, and Jim Hendrick was confident that we could make it work.

We strapped the wings on Jim Hendrick's raft. We took the rowing frame and moved it to the very back of the raft instead of in the center where it normally would be and attached the wings. It looked like he had a diving board sticking out in front of the raft. The wings stuck out about seven feet in front of the raft and went all the way back to Jimmy's feet. We loaded the fuselage on my raft sideways. I needed to row from the rear, behind where we would normally have the rowing frame. From this position, though, the fuselage completely blocked my view.

I couldn't see anything, so we took off both the pilot and copilot doors so I could kind of see ahead through the cockpit.

On that last day of September, the outside air temperature was below freezing.

Finally, the moment of truth had come, the Cessna was loaded and secured on my two eighteen-foot whitewater rafts. We launched downstream on the Yellowjacket with me rowing the raft with the fuselage and Jim Hendrick rowing the raft with the wings and all the control surfaces. Eric Drinkwalter, Terry Mangione, and Paul Mallory were all onboard for the ride.

From Yellowjacket Creek down to Prairie Creek is just braided, moving water, nothing particularly dangerous, so there was no way we were going to hurt the airplane in that stretch of river. But after Prairie Creek the river flows into the Canyon. From this point on are very significant Class III, pushing Class IV, whitewater rapids. In fact, the Talkeetna River sports some of the longest commercially runnable rapids in the world.

At Prairie Creek we stopped and re-secured everything before launching back downriver. Although our skills were challenged the entire river, we made it all the way through the canyon and all the way to Talkeetna and never put a scratch on the airplane fuselage or the wings—or any of it. I considered it miraculous! By the next summer David's airplane had been rebuilt and was flying again.

In return for the week of my time, effort, and rafting support, David offered to do four flights for me with his 185 anytime I needed it. Sure enough, the next season I had engine problems on my Cessna 180 and David jumped right in. He didn't just do four flights for me, though—he wound up doing six flights for me and never charged me a penny!

That's just the kind of guy David was and still is today. He made an agreement that he would do something, and then he did more than he had agreed to do. That's been the relationship that David Lee and his brother, Don, and I have all had for the past forty years—it's been pretty neat.

Jim Hendrick (l) &
Paul Mallory ready
the raft to float the
Cessna wings.

"We strapped the wings on Jim Hendrick's raft. We took the rowing frame and moved it to the very back of the raft instead of in the center where it normally would be and attached the wings. It looked like he had a diving board sticking out in front of the raft. The wings stuck out about seven feet in front of the raft and went all the way back to Jimmy's feet. We loaded the fuselage on my raft sideways. I needed to row from the rear, behind where we would normally have the rowing frame. From this position, though, the fuselage completely blocked my view.

I couldn't see anything, so we took off both the pilot and copilot doors so I could kind of see ahead through the cockpit." —JJ

The Jim Kelly Story

This is the story of how I made Jim Kelly, the Pro Football Hall of Fame NFL quarterback, scream like a girl.

It's not what you think it would be. I don't have the year right now, but I've got it documented somewhere.

Jim Kelly and his brother, Pat, had booked a hunt in New York through a partner I had at the time by the name of Rex Maurer. They were coming on a brown bear/coastal grizzly hunt in Cold Bay, Alaska. After they arrived in Cold Bay, we went out to sight-in the rifles, making sure they were all still zeroed. As we drove out, we drove past my Super Cub on the lake, the one on floats, and Pat looked over, knowing that Jim did not like flying in airplanes and said, "Ah, that's the airplane you're going to have to fly in Jim."

Thinking it was a joke, they were both shocked when I told them, "Yep, that's the Super Cub. That's what we're going to be flying in, either that one on floats or one on wheels."

They both got really quiet. Later that day, after we sighted the rifles in, Jim did get into my Super Cub, the one on wheels, and we flew out to the hunting area. He barely fit in that airplane. Jim's a big, tall guy, and the Super Cub is a tiny little airplane. Within ten or fifteen minutes of flying around, seeing caribou and sea otters and different sights along the coast, he really started to enjoy the flight and had a good time.

It was about a thirty- to forty-minute flight out to where we had the camp going. My partner, Rex, was the guide at the camp. I dropped Jim off and got his brother and another load dropped off, as well. They had hunted there for a few days when I got a message one evening after I had finished my flying for the day for my other seven camps. Jim Kelly's camp at Hot Springs Bay needed a ride. They had gotten a bear. I was not prepared to fly more that evening, so I ran out just before the fuel service closed, got in line with two other airplanes in front of me, and filled up the right-hand tank of the Super Cub; the left tank was already half full. Then I flew out to the camp. I was in a hurry because I knew the tide was going to be marginal. My runway was a small little beach that I could only take off and land on when the tide was out.

When I arrived overhead, I could see that the tide was already on its way in. There was barely enough beach to land, only 350-400 feet of length from water-to-water, just enough to land and takeoff with a very light load. I got Jim into the airplane, and I told him he could only take his sleeping bag and nothing else, not even his rifle, because it was such a short strip for takeoff. We left everything else with his brother, Pat, and Rex.

I turned the Super Cub around using power, added full power for takeoff and was in the air at about two-eighty or three hundred feet. I had only three hundred and fifty feet of beach to work with at takeoff, but we were airborne. We got about four hundred feet in the air when the engine started coughing and then died.

I did quick emergency procedures, switched fuel tanks, pulled carb heat. The engine was not going to start. I hit the starter—all of this is taking place incredibly fast—but we weren't going to make it.

I yelled at Jim, "Hold on! We're going down!"

I had to make some fast decisions: there were big cut banks, almost cliffs, off to my left and water underneath me. No beach anywhere, and I didn't think I had enough altitude to make it into the tundra on dry ground because we might come in short with that engine having quit. Coming in short was not an option. We'd hit the cut bank, and both be killed. There was no doubt, so I didn't take that risk.

I decided to do an old crop-dusting technique where you ski the wheels across the water. My idea was to try to get as close to shore as I could and get as slow as I could before the wheels caught and the airplane flipped upside down. So I pushed the stick forward. We started skipping off the water, but our speed was steadily decreasing. I got about sixty yards from shore when the momentum finally slowed enough that the wheels stopped skiing and dug in. The Cub nosed down into the sea, the entire airplane went vertical, and then it happily settled back into its upright position. We were still in the water, off-shore probably sixty yards.

"Get to shore! Don't let the current sweep you out to sea," I yelled to Jim.

In an instant, I was going through my emergency shutdown procedures: turning off the fuel, turning off the master switch for the electric, and turning off the mags. Even though there was no chance of fire in the water, I wasn't thinking that. In this high-stress situation, I reverted to my training. As I was completing my emergency shutdown procedures, Jim yelled from behind me, "I can't get it off!"

I had already opened the door, which is like a clamshell effect on the Super Cub, so when I turned around to look at Jim, the water in the plane was already up to his navel; I couldn't see below that, and I thought his seatbelt must have been stuck. I was still in my harness, so I didn't have good maneuverability, but I was able to reach back hard and fast and grab for his seatbelt. Unfortunately, I grabbed the wrong part of his anatomy as I was groping him for the belt, and it obviously hurt.

It was pretty much chaos and pandemonium in that little Super Cub at that moment. Jim screamed at me in a really high-pitched screech. "It's not this! It's the helmet!"

He had every right to add the words "you idiot" in there, but Jim's too much of a gentleman. I let go of his testicles and crotch and everything else, because I was groping for the seatbelt.

At about that time, he got the clip on the flight helmet undone, got the helmet off, and bailed out of the airplane. When he first stepped out, I think he was standing on the tire and then his second step put him above his waist, deep in water. He took one more step and that happened to be where the drop off was, and he went in over his head. At that point, he did exactly what I told him to do. He got to shore. He looked like Mark Spitz swimming just hard and fast, straight towards shore. This was spring of the year in the Bering Sea. That water was iced over just three or four weeks ago, so it was cold, cold water. I think he swam all the way to where his elbows were hitting before he stood up.

I got out second, and I could touch bottom where I was. Aware that there was a drop off there, I was thinking that maybe I could save my airplane from washing out. The seawater came to the middle of my chest. In the back of the airplane, I have an extra storage compartment where I keep things like the tiedown ropes, and I thought maybe I could get that sixty feet of tiedown rope out, hook it to the tailwheel and get closer to shore and maybe save my airplane. Well, as I was doing that, I had to get a Leatherman tool off my belt and open the screws and open that hatch. All this was taking time. Jim, who was onshore, saw that I wasn't following him and thought I was stuck in the airplane. About that time, I heard him yell, "Hold on! I'm coming to help!"

I looked over the tail of the airplane and saw him charging back into that ice-cold Bering seawater to come and help me! He was putting his own life at risk now to rescue me—somebody he barely knew. To me, that says everything you ever need to know about the man. He was willing to risk his own life to come and help somebody else.

About the time he got to the airplane, I finally got the rope out. Then, seeing me for the first time, Jim realized that I wasn't stuck or trapped in the airplane. He helped me tie the rope to the tail of the airplane and then we pulled it around, so the tail was facing shore and the wheels were on the bottom.

Jim's brother Pat and my partner Rex got to us by then, and, between the four of us, we were able to pull and haul the airplane onto shore. With the tide still closing in, there was only about a fifty-foot-long section of beach now; there was no way that I could have landed on that. I had no choice except to land on the water.

We finally got the airplane out and then started assessing ourselves for any injuries. Jim had torn a fingernail off getting out of the airplane in all the confusion, and his hand was bleeding, so we got that bandaged up.

When I was late, a friend of mine flew out to look for me. The beach had been underwater, but the tide had gone back out by then, and he was able to pick Jim up before it got dark and take him back to Cold Bay.

We began to repair the airplane and figured out that the reason for the crash was contaminated fuel from the fuel source. I learned later that all three airplanes that had gotten fuel at the same time wound up with engine failures because of it.

When we hit the water, it bent one prop blade back. We wedged the prop between a couple of rocks and bent the blade straight enough. We pulled the carburetor apart and got it dried out. We dried out all the spark plugs and got rid of the contaminated fuel then added fresh fuel back into the tank. After two days of repairs, we flew my Super Cub back to Cold Bay.

Among his many rules and maxims from the book he and his wife, Victoria published, 101 Chuck YEAGER-isms, Gen. Chuck Yeager included, "Any landing you can walk away from is a good landing. Any landing where you can use the plane the next day is an excellent landing." (Yeager 2022). As crash landings on the open sea went, we were able to swim and wade away from this crash site—that was a good thing. Saving my airplane was a bonus, so I'd call this an excellent landing of sorts.

So that's how I made Jim Kelly scream like a girl—by doing my best to save his life, but, unfortunately, groping him instead. I don't think either of us are really too proud of that moment, but it happened.

12.

Mike Featherstone

The state of Alaska is divided into twenty-six separate Game Management Units or GMUs and sub-units. Hunting regulations are set according to those particular Units and sub-units.

My guide was going to shoot me!

The hunting business had expanded with camps in Units 13 and 14 the Talkeetna Mountains, in Units 16, 17, and 19 the Alaska Range and on the Alaska Peninsula in Unit 9. We had a main camp on Chakachamna Lake which is close to the entrance of Merrill Pass. In June 1991, I was flying supplies and staging gas, food, and equipment for the upcoming moose hunting season that would start on the first day of September. I had approximately twenty plastic five-gallon cans of avgas at the camp. Additionally, I had cases of MREs and Mountain House food cached in bear-proof containers.

After bringing another load of supplies into the camp, I discovered that a black bear had made a mess of the supplies. At least a dozen of the five-gallon cans had bite marks in them. The cans were on their side and the gas had drained out. Not only the cost of flying gasoline into this camp, but the cost of the gas as well as the five-gallon cans being ruined really pissed me off.

When I returned to Anchorage, I remembered that two young men had been calling me asking for a job. Their names were Mike Featherstone and Bill Wernicke. They had been lifelong friends and, shortly after graduating high school, saved enough money to drive to Alaska. They both wanted to become guides and had gotten my phone number. Bill and Mike turned out to be extremely smart, hardworking young men. I told them that I didn't have work for them until September but, if they wanted, I would fly them out to a remote camp on Chakachamna Lake. I would supply their food, pay a small wage, and they could build a better camp, then, by the later part of August we would open the camp.

By the time late August had rolled around, Mike and Bill had built a fantastic camp. During September, we ran approximately twelve hunters through the camp. Altogether, they harvested twelve black bears, eight moose, eight caribou, five grizzlies, and three Dall sheep. It was a fantastic hunting season for both my guides and clients. However, we were being overrun with black bears that were causing lots of problems both at the main camp and in the spike camps. Toward the end of the moose season, the weather took a nasty turn with high winds and torrential rains, yet I was still responsible for moving all the equipment both in and out of camp; I used all three of my planes as needed to get the job done, but I was the only full-time pilot for my business.

My plan was that as soon as moose season ended on 20 September, we would take down the camp, remove everything that wasn't in bear-proof containers, and head to Lake Iliamna where I was leasing a lodge on the Iliamna River from Joe Norris. As plans go, it was a good one, but the best laid plans involving STOL planes are still subject to the weather. We lost so many days due to wind and rain that there was not enough time to fly all the gear out of the camp at Chakachamna Lake. By the time the weather broke, I had to decide if I would move my guides over to the Iliamna River and start the hunts there. The problems mounted exponentially: all the equipment, tents, fuel cans… the black bears would have destroyed everything if I left the camp unguarded. I asked Mike Featherstone if he would agree to stay at the camp to watch it for five-to-ten days.

This would give me time to move the guides, get the hunts started, and everything taken care of at the Iliamna River lodge. Mike agreed that he would stay and babysit the camp. The Iliamna River lodge was built as a hunting and fishing camp by Ron Hayes and Dawn Knighton. Ron Hayes had gone to prison for Fish and Game violations. He was one of Alaska's most infamous poachers.

Joe, who was an acquaintance of Charley Connell and Ron Sutphin, had gotten in touch with me the previous year and asked if I wanted to lease the lodge from him during bear hunting season. So, I flew my Super Cub and landed on a gravel bar in front of the lodge and checked it out that spring. It was a fantastic location with five nice little cabins as well as a separate building for the kitchen with a small dining room. Joe told me that he bought this lodge to run fishing trips during the summer. But Joe was not a registered guide, so he could not run hunts out of it. Joe and I came to a financial agreement, and I leased the lodge from him starting late September and going through the end of October.

The first week after arriving at Iliamna River Lodge, I was able to get four caribou hunting camps out that consisted of four guides and six clients. Mike had been at the Chakachamna Camp alone for one week at this point, and I was getting ready to go pick him up.

One morning while having breakfast with Joe and his maintenance man, Gary, Joe asked me if I would fly my Super Cub to move his caribou camp out of the field. The lake he had used to drop the camp off was too small to haul a load out in the C-185 on floats. It was big enough to drop loads in but did not have enough power to take off with a load unless there was a strong headwind.

In the camp, he had two hunters, a cook, and a guide. This was completely illegal for Joe because he did not have a registered guide license; he only had a Class A assistant license, which meant he could not book hunts, but he did it anyway. It was not an uncommon practice back then. I told Joe that I couldn't help him because I needed to take my wife back to Anchorage, and, on the way, I was going to pick up Mike Featherstone at Chakachamna Lake.

"Well, I need to take my wife to Anchorage, too," Joe said. "How about I take both our wives, and I'll pick up Mike on my way."

That would free me up to use my Super Cup on wheels to get his people and camp out of the field. This trade made sense, and I agreed. I flew my Super Cub and landed on the tundra next to the lake. I picked up one of Joe's clients and flew him to the Iliamna village air- port. I made a second trip, picked up another client, and flew him to Iliamna. I flew the guide and cook along with the camp back to the lodge on the Iliamna River. This took three more trips in my Super Cub.

The guide and the cook were both looking for Joe, and they were angry. They told me they had not been paid all summer long and wanted their paychecks! Joe had not returned from Anchorage yet. This was before satellite phones, so there was no communication with the outside world at the lodge.

After waiting around another day, the guide and the cook asked me if I would fly them to Iliamna. The plan was that Joe had tickets waiting for them there. I had already flown one of Joe's other fishing guides to Iliamna and there was, in fact, a ticket waiting for him so he could fly back to Anchorage where, supposedly, Joe was going to meet him and give him his paycheck for the season. When I flew Joe's hunting guide and cook to Iliamna, there was no ticket for either of them. Nancy, the owner, said she would not extend any more credit to Joe for air taxi tickets. The guide had a personal credit card and was able to put his ticket on the card. The cook did not have a credit card or any money and was now stuck! I gave him enough money to buy the ticket back to Anchorage. Again, Joe had told them that he was going to meet them at the airport in Anchorage where he would give them their paychecks for the season.

For the next month, I ran caribou hunters and bear hunters in the area basing out of Joe's lodge on the Iliamna River. Joe, however, never showed up. I had flown over to Pedro Bay from time to time to pick up my clients as they came and went. While there, I finally reached Joe on the phone from the Jensen's house.

Joe told me he was having issues with his C-185 and would be back as soon as possible. That was the last time I heard from Joe. Gary had agreed to stay at the lodge and work for me as my cook and maintenance person. After the season was over and I'd moved all my clients and guides out of the field and got them onboard the air taxi back to Anchorage, only Gary and I were left at the lodge. We winterized the lodge and on the last load, Gary and I headed to Anchorage. We landed late-evening at Merrill Field in my Cessna 180. I got gas at Spernak's just as they were closing. While Mike Spernak was fueling my airplane, I called my wife and asked her to come pick me up in my truck. She told me she was busy with patients and couldn't leave for another three hours, so I asked her to just have Mike Featherstone use my truck and come pick me up.

"Mike is with you!" she said.

I instantly felt my blood run cold.

"What did you say? Joe told me he picked Mike up when he took you to Anchorage!"

"No! When he flew me back to Anchorage, he was running low on gas. Joe did not pick Mike up," she said. "He said he would pick up Mike on his return to the lodge."

But Joe had never returned to the lodge—an entire month had gone by from the time he had agreed to pick up Mike!

I felt sick, thinking that Mike might still be out there at the camp on the lake. I was processing all this latest info as Mike Spernak finished fueling my Cessna. Instantly, my first priority was to get Mike Featherstone. With Gary's help, I quickly unloaded all the gear, jumped in the airplane, and headed towards Chakachamna Lake. I had a huge knot in my stomach en route over the next forty-five minutes. I didn't know if Mike was still there or even if he was okay. Ten miles out and with the lake in sight, my radio came alive. It was Mike on the camp aviation radio.

"Jerry is that you?" he asked, sounding kind of hopeful and pissed off at the same time. It was just good to hear his voice.

"Yes Mike, it's me," I confessed. "…and I'll make you a deal if you promise not to shoot me or my airplane." I paused for effect, hoping he would take a moment to at least hear my deal before shooting me out of the sky. After all, the only thing he knew was that I had forgotten him, leaving him alone and stranded at the camp for five weeks.

"I'll pick you up, and I'll get you straight back to Anchorage if you just promise not to shoot." For thirty seconds there was silence on the radio.

"Mike, are you there?"

"Yes, but I'm thinking about the deal." There was another long moment of silence.

"I want out bad enough that I'll take the deal. Come on in and land," he said finally, although he didn't sound very enthusiastic.

This was not an encouraging conversation, but I made a straight-in approach (a circling aircraft would have made a dandy target) and landed next to the camp. Mike's bags were packed, and he was ready. We stowed his gear and as much of my camp gear as would fit into the airplane, took off, and headed straight toward Anchorage. During that whole flight, Mike never uttered a single word—not a grunt, not a nod of his head, not anything. He just stared straight ahead the whole flight.

"I swear Mike! Joe told me that he picked you up! I thought you were in Anchorage!" I think I was pleading with him now.

I tried my best to explain the whole thing to Mike—the deal I had made with Joe to pick Mike up in exchange for me moving Joe's caribou camp; Joe telling my wife he was low on gas and saying he would pick Mike up on his return to the lodge. I did not know until that phone call to my wife that Joe never picked Mike up at the end of his agreed-upon week's stay at my camp. I came to his rescue as soon as I knew what happened. Unfortunately, pleading my case wasn't having much effect. Mike seemed resolved to let this grudge fester a little while. Not a single syllable came out of his mouth. The flight back to Merrill Field was downright uncomfortable.

Thankfully, Gary was there when Joe had made the deal to pick Mike up in exchange for me picking up Joe's hunting camp and clients. Gary explained to Mike everything that had happened with Joe. He told Mike that we believed what Joe had told me, that Mike had been picked up at Chakachamna Lake and taken back to Anchorage. We wound up having dinner with two of Joe's fishing guides who also explained that Joe had not paid his staff for the summer and had disappeared after he got to Anchorage.

Thankfully, Mike was able to hear from multiple sources and realized that I had not forgotten him or intentionally left him at Chakachamna Lake for six weeks, which was five weeks longer than he had agreed to be there. There was plenty of food at the camp for Mike to eat and the big wall tent that he stayed in had a heater, so he was comfortable enough and had enough food in his belly to survive, but it was no fun for him.

Mike kept expecting to hear my airplane at any moment and then see me land to pick him up. He never left the camp, afraid that, if he did leave, I'd come in to pick him up, and he would miss his flight home.

Mike worked for me for several more years and, though I don't see him often, we have remained friends. He became a very successful hunting and fishing guide and eventually purchased ten acres of my property near Pedro Bay where he has built his own lodge and is doing very well for himself.

Joe was another story. When Joe returned to Anchorage, the owner of the airplane that he was leasing saw it sitting at Lake Hood and, since the owner had not been paid all summer for the lease, he had his mechanic pull the airplane out of the water and lock it in a hangar.

The owner of the airplane was also one of three investors who actually owned the lodge. They were leasing the lodge to Joe, and, unfortunately, Joe was way behind on the payments. .

Mike Featherstone,
1991 photo

Big Saves on the Big Su

May, 2022—This episode is the 1st of 2 episodes. Some stories stand the test of time. This is one. 1995, Big Susitna River in Alaska, glacial melt, rains in the canyon. Three friends fly deep into the backcountry with plans of a 2 day trip on big water. That day their plans changed & 27 years later they all tell the story. (Sam Carter 2022)

"No Boat No Paddle on the Big Susitna River"
River Radius Podcast
Host:
Sam Carter

Part 1: No Boat No Paddle on the Big Susitna River

Part 2: No Boat No Paddle on the Big Susitna River

July 1995 Rough Draft: Corran Addison, Dean Cummings, Brennan Guth, Jerry Jacques, Chris Spelius.

The success or failure of any expedition is dependent on planning, experience, and the ability of the team members. When Team Timex contacted me with only four-days' notice, wanting me to be their local guide and outfitter for a kayak expedition through Alaska's Devils Canyon, I said no.

I explained to Robbie, the photographer and owner of Polar Bear Productions, that Devils Canyon was considered the Mt. Everest of whitewater. An expedition would take considerable planning, especially since none of his team had ever been to Alaska. Robbie patiently explained to me the team was made up of four of the world's best kayakers who would arrive in Anchorage in three days, and the canyon would not pose a problem for them. Robbie told me they only needed help with logistics, equipment rental, and the flying. This team needed no guide! They did want one more team member, however.

Silver-tongued Robbie soon had me excited and committed to joining the expedition. The next three days passed quickly. I had to arrange transportation to get a six-man team from the Anchorage airport to Talkeetna. I had to fly the camping and cooking equipment to Gold Creek. I needed to help find a helicopter to transport the two photographers into the canyon and provide emergency rescue if needed. All this, yet still maintain my full-time guiding business.

The first two flights I made were from Talkeetna to Gold Creek with all the camping gear, kayaks, extra plane gas, and a generator for recharging camera batteries. All the flying I would do was in a 160-horsepower Piper PA-18 Cub.

The expedition members took the train from Talkeetna to Gold Creek as the road ends in Talkeetna. I met Team Timex at Gold Creek in a small, remote mining camp with no road access located on the banks of the Susitna River. Gold Creek with a population of fourteen is situated at the point the railroad tracks leave the river. Upriver is an extremely remote wilderness along the Susitna River with a particularly death-defying river gorge known as Devils Canyon.

The first team member I was to fly to the put-in above the canyon was Chris Spelius. We flew three hundred feet above the canyon studying the rapids. We made several passes, pre-planning our routes and line on each rapid. I pointed out to Chris my personal nemesis from my last expedition, which was Screaming Left Hand Turn. At the extremely high water we now had, we said it did not look bad, but Devils Creek rapid looked ominous and Hotel Rock was certain death; if anyone went into the hole it was creating, they would not come out alive.

The first major snag in the expedition was that the airstrip I planned on using was washed out due to the high water. I had to find a new spot to land and pioneer a new airstrip. After a lot of looking, I decided a gravel bar six miles above the canyon was the only possibility. There was no good place to safely operate, but there was a spot a hundred and seventy-five feet long that, if I could get stopped on, we could then build a workable strip close by.

The wind was blowing upriver at eight miles per hour. Chris, in the passenger's seat, wisely put on his kayaking helmet. I made seven low passes, and on the eighth, flying downriver and into the wind, I set twenty-degree flaps, approached at forty-five miles per hour, and five hundred feet before the theoretical threshold, full flaps. Speed now forty-one miles per hour, just feet before the threshold, I chopped the power at thirty-eight miles per hour, and we stalled on the threshold. I dump the flaps, no bounce, wheels firmly on the ground. Now we are past the point of no return. I am committed to making this landing work, as there is not enough strip left ahead to get airborne again. Brakes locked, stick full back, we decelerate rapidly. The tail starts to get light—too light. It is in danger of nosing over and flipping on its back! Less brake pressure. End of runway coming fast. The tail is at the critical point of coming over the top. Swerve to miss a hole. Half ounce more brake, and she will flip. I apply just a little more brake?! She starts to come over the top! Less brake! But still the end of land and the river is still coming. Finally! We come to a full stop at last!

I used a hundred and fifty-five feet with twenty feet of gravel bank to spare—no problem. Right! I wipe the sweat from the palms of my hands, get out of the plane and try to figure out what the hell possessed me into thinking that I could land in this spot.

Chris and I spend the next three hours cutting brush, moving driftwood, rolling boulders out of the way, and filling holes. With Chris' help, I taxied the plane to the new strip we had just roughed out. Chris continued to work on the strip. I loaned him my handgun for bear protection, and flew back to Gold Creek leaving Chris alone, sixty miles from base camp and the nearest people.

Right after I flew off, he told me later that he was glad to have the gun as he found fresh grizzly tracks in the sand next to the strip we had just built. He said he thought he heard something in the brush a few times. At Gold Creek, I picked up more team members and flew up the canyon to give them a look at the whitewater and then to the put-in. Corran, Dean, and Chris worked most of the night improving the strip. I flew kayaks and gear the next day along with the last team member. It was midday before I finished flying everything in.

By the time we launched, I was exhausted and glad to be done with the flying. On the last trip, a friend flew me in his Cub to the newly completed strip so I could join the team.

I had never seen the river so high. The high water on this river was going to make things more difficult. At 12,000 to 16,000 CFS the river was going to be the most intimidating that I have ever run. At the current water level of 30,000 CFS, this was going to be the highest this river had ever been attempted. Team Timex was confident and almost cocky. Was I nervous? No. I was scared sick! I had not done much kayaking in the last five months. I was in good physical condition, but would that be enough? Having been in Devils Canyon several times years before, I now rationalized that I would be able to portage the worst rapids if I didn't feel in tune with the river.

As soon as we got on the water, the butterflies in my stomach left; it was good to at last be back home on the river. Ninety minutes after we shoved off, we arrived at Devils Creek. The first and foremost rapid in Devils Canyon starts at the confluence of Devils Creek. This is the crux! Survive through it, and you will most likely exit the canyon alive. We stopped above Devils Creek to scout. Looking down from the cliffs above the river, the group was much more impressed with the size of the rapids than they had been while in my plane. As a group, we decided the safest route was to enter the rapid in the center then move right. This was the route that Dr. Walt Blackadar Jr. and the ABC Expedition had pioneered, and every other successful expedition team had followed.

Our group did discuss the possibility of a run on the left side. The giant waves and holes looked intimidating but possible, as long as you could stay out of the three giant keeper holes at the end. It might be possible to run the biggest stuff and survive. The decision of Team Timex was not to run the left side. This not being my expedition, that I had not been boating for five months, and the fact that I was the least skilled kayaker of the group, I kept quiet.

It was decided that Chris and I would make the first run. What got us elected to go first? Chris being the most skilled Expedition kayaker and me being the only one to actually have run the canyon before. Chris and I pushed off from the safety of the shore. I quickly felt in total control and comfortable. My Perception kayak and I were one with the river. I was at home and in great company. Chris and I paddled together as a team, we moved from one eddy to the next, watching each move. At the start Chris asked a few questions as to which route I had used and what boulder was what. Chris quickly got orientated and took over the lead.

The first third of Devils Creek rapid was easy. On my previous runs, this part had seemed very hard and intimidating. Chris hit a submerged rock and barely caught the most crucial eddy in the middle of the rapid. If he had missed this crux move, he would have been in deep trouble. After having the advantage of seeing Chris struggle, I took a slightly different line and made the eddy with no trouble. After we had negotiated this technical part, we now only had to power to the far right, and we would be out of danger. I thought to myself, *I have been here and done that! Why not go for the left side, throw the big stuff, and not cheat the river? I know it's runnable!*

Call it a brainstorm or, better yet, a brain fart; I was inspired to change the plans.

I yelled over the roar of the rapids to Chris, "I want the left side. It's doable! Let's run it!"

I will never forget the look on Chris' face. His eyes got huge. He shook his head violently—not a single word came out of his mouth, but the discussion was over.

So, Chris finished the run as planned with his typical style of perfect moves. He made the classic run. Robbie filmed him doing it while I waited. After Chris had made it safely into an eddy, Robbie, using hand signals, let me know Chris was okay and in the eddy above the next rapid, the Nozzle.[1] So I pealed out of the eddy on the left and paddled for the first big hole. It was huge and pulsing. Robbie was frantic when he saw me going left, but with his years of being a professional camera-man, he never missed a frame. The first big exploding hole surfed me and let me out still in control. With confidence, I powered through the giant waves and to the next big hole. I hit it with good forward speed expecting to punch it; instead, it body-slammed me violently backward into the hole. Now the river was in complete control, and my fight for survival was just beginning I managed to roll up in the hole and get a breath of air. The turbulence of the hole was intense. I got tumbled and beat up. When the hole released me, I tried to roll. When I did roll, I was in a hole. It's amazing how everything is forgotten when all you want is your next breath of air! Exhausted, out of breath, and disori-entated, I fell sideways into the Death Trap hole which swallowed me.

I knew that I might never come out alive and that I did not possess the skill to escape on my own.

At one point, I was bracing in the hole leaning upstream which is not supposed to work but it did. I got a half-breath of air before the hole surged and slammed me to the bottom of the river. It got dark. The pressure on my ears was almost too much to bear. Apparently, I flushed out of the giant hole from the bottom of the river and rolled upright. Just as I was at last upright, I went sideways into The Nozzle, the next rapid. I slammed the wall so hard it ripped the nose of my kayak off. Now I was ripped from my kayak and forced to swim for my

[1] For a look at Devils Canyon Creek Rapids at 25,000 CFS, watch the video FLOWSTATE S2 Ep1: Devil's Canyon. The Nozzle and Hotel Rock are videoed, starting at 4:15 minutes.

life. I felt like I had exhausted all my strength, but the last eddy before the rapid known as Hotel Rock was my last chance to survive.

I swam into the eddy, just barely making it. Now I had to get to the shore before the hydraulic surges took me out and to the certain death waiting at Hotel Rock. At normal level, Hotel Rock is a huge boulder in the middle of the river. At the high water we had, Hotel Rock was completely underwater. It formed a killer hole—river wide. It was a death sentence for anyone who mistakenly went into the Hotel Rock hole.

With every bit of strength I had left in me, I swam for the shore. I timed the cycle perfectly—almost in reach of the rocks—but missed! The hydraulics and current were too strong. I could not get to shore. I knew now that I was going to die. I had no strength left to fight. I had only seconds to live. I was dying, and I knew it. My thoughts turned to my son Jason without a father—that alone scared me more than death.

Amazingly, and only by the grace of God, I was suddenly given more strength to keep my head above water and to continue to fight. It seemed useless but as long as I could, I would, even if I could not reach the shore. I fought to stay in the eddy for my son, Jason. Finally, a big surge pushed me out to the main current, the death hole of Hotel Rock just forty yards away.

Chopper to the Rescue!, July 1995

With nothing left in my favor, miraculously, arcing around the corner at eighty miles per hour, our helicopter appeared with the door open, Robbie tied in and hanging out. Robbie threw me a rescue line with a gallon jug of water on the end so the helicopter rotor wash would not blow it around. This is a technique I had copied from Walt Blackadar's Devils Canyon Expedition. On the second throw, the rope was within reach. I grabbed the line and clipped it to the harness I was wearing, and the pilot managed to tow me within reach of shore. Five feet from shore, I had to cut loose. I grabbed the first rock and pulled myself halfway out of the water, then I collapsed. I don't know how long I was unconscious, but when a surge started to take me back into the river, I managed to struggle up a little farther so only my feet were in the water. The helicopter had no place to land and had left. I tried but did not have enough strength to pull myself to safety. I did manage to jam my arms into the rocks before I passed out again, but I came to suddenly when a big hydraulic surge in the river began dislodging me. The rocks that I had my arms wedged in were now under water. I was going back into the clutches of the river, and I could not stop. I held on as best as I could, but the surge and current finally dislodged me and I knew again that I did not have the strength to fight the river. I no longer had the strength to even hope I could survive when a strong hand grabbed me by my left shoulder. I looked up into Dean Cummings' resolute eyes. He tried to pull me out by himself, then the famous South African kayaker, Corran Addison joined him, and together they dragged me to safety above the surges of Devils Canyon.

I passed out again—this time in safety. I remained semiconscious for the next hour before I could get enough oxygen back into my body. Slowly, I got enough strength to sit up on my own.

I owe my life to the helicopter pilot, Robbie, Dean Cummings, Corran Addison, and the Grace of God.

Is the left side runnable? Absolutely. It will be run in the future and, in the years to come, kayakers will continue to get better until Devils Canyon is considered just another challenging river trip for the expert kayaker.

Will I run the left side again? No. In fact, I will never get near the canyon again in a kayak, raft, plane, or even walk near enough to the edge that I could fall in, and this is what I told myself at the time.

The team regrouped and portaged Hotel Rock. We saw my kayak stuck in the hole and occasionally visible. Thank God I was not with it. The team finished the canyon in style. Robbie got the film footage he needed, and Team Timex successfully completed Devils Canyon.

Six weeks later: no boat, no paddle, one Helio…

Deep in the Alaska wilderness, the glacier-fed Upper Susitna River plunges into the depths of Devils Canyon. This stretch of the Big Susitna is considered the Mt. Everest of whitewater, and I had joined the Timex Kayaking Expedition for a record breaking 30,000 CFS high-water decent.

Attempting to run a torturous left side Devils Creek Class V route that had never been successfully accomplished, I became yet another victim, sixty seconds from certain death, when a brave helicopter pilot rescued me.

I promised my young son I would never again run Devils Canyon.

Helio Courier & Super Cub to the Rescue!, September 1995

From the village of Talkeetna, I had transported a three-man kayak expedition planning to run Devil's Canyon. It was my third trip in N4319Z, a 160-horsepower Piper Super Cub, landing on a tiny gravel bar in the middle of the Susitna River with Bill "Buckwheat" Overington, Michael "Mikey K" Koehmstedt (or Kehmstedt), and Bill "Bill Q" or "Q" Quitch, all expert whitewater kayakers. Their plan was to kayak downriver through Devils Canyon, after which they planned to camp at a remote gold mine where their friend Connie was waiting with their camping gear. No roads lead to the camp; the only access is by taking the Alaska Railroad to the point where the train tracks cross the Susitna River.

Watching the kayakers disappear downriver, I thought of my recent failed attempt to kayak this river, and of the people who had risked their lives saving me, I was happy knowing I would never again run that river, and I wished them luck. As soon as they were out of sight, I flew back home to Talkeetna.

Bill, Mikey, and Buckwheat had made it only partway through the deep gorge's notorious Class V whitewater when Buckwheat got into real trouble, losing his kayak, and having to swim for his life. Through heroic efforts, his teammates managed to rescue Buckwheat from the raging torrent. Their adventure had now turned into a survival ordeal. They were soaking wet, they were stuck in the canyon with no tents and no sleeping bags, with a cold night to look forward to, and they had very little food.

Early the next morning, they assessed the situation. Buckwheat's kayak was long gone, but Bill and Mikey still had theirs, so it was now up to them to arrange the rescue of their companion—and their first step would be to kayak down the second half of Devils Canyon's extreme whitewater, leaving Buckwheat with nothing but his wetsuit, his life jacket, his helmet, and a few candy bars.

After an adrenaline-filled day of Class V whitewater, Bill and Mikey arrived at the remote gold-mining camp and were reunited with their friend Connie and explained that Buckwheat was stranded upriver. The next day, they managed to flag down the once-a-day southbound train and catch a ride to Talkeetna. It was late evening when the trio showed up there without Buckwheat. Looking glum, they explained the situation to me, and it didn't sound good.

Buckwheat had hoped to make it to an emergency extraction point where he could clear the brush off an old airstrip to make it usable again, but he had been alone in Devils Canyon now for two nights, with temperatures that can hover near or below the freezing mark in September. We immediately put together an airdrop package containing a sleeping bag, food, a large tarp, an ax, and a machete, loading everything into my floatplane, Helio Courier N295JA. It took me about thirty minutes to fly to the overgrown airstrip where we hoped Buckwheat was waiting.

Visibility was diminishing quickly now as evening turned to night. It was getting hard to see, but still, there was definitely no sign of Buckwheat! I made the airdrop anyway, hoping that even though I couldn't see him, Buckwheat would see the equipment drop and find the gear. After the airdrop, I did not have enough daylight left to return to Talkeetna, so I diverted to Fog Lake for the night.

Since it rained all night, the entire upper Susitna valley was fogged in the next morning which made takeoff impossible. My return to

Talkeetna was delayed once again. By the time the fog cleared, it was late morning, and I immediately got into the air: My mission was to go back to see if Buckwheat had made it to the airstrip. As soon as I got airborne, the radio in my plane came alive. "N90X calling N295JA.[2] Are you out there, Jerry?" It was pilot Jay Hudson looking for me—and worried, since I had not returned the night before. Jay told me that he and Bill were in his plane on tundra tires; he was in route to the abandoned airstrip and would check on Buckwheat. With Jay on the way to Buckwheat and my plane low on gas, I returned to Talkeetna.

But Jay and Bill did not find Buckwheat at the airstrip. After searching the canyon for some time, they found him, but he was nowhere near the airstrip or the survival gear; it had proved impossible for him to climb out of the canyon. Still trapped in Devils Canyon with no food or sleeping bag, and unable to climb out, Buckwheat had returned to the same place Bill and Mikey had left him. Jay flew low and airdropped him a radio.

Now, after three cold, rainy nights with no gear, the stranded kayaker was in serious trouble; hypothermia was setting in. A helicopter rescue would be the only way to get Buckwheat out of the canyon alive. Jay radioed his father, Cliff Hudson, the legendary glacier pilot from Talkeetna, and Cliff called the Alaska State Troopers requesting a helicopter for the rescue, then came to me with the update. With a helicopter dispatched to rescue him, I was relieved to know that Buckwheat would soon be home safe. After a quick lunch, I went back to work dropping off rafters at Stephan Lake. While en route to Stephan Lake, however, I learned from Jay's radio that the State Trooper's two helicopters were delayed with two different rescues—no helicopter was available to rescue our stranded kayaker. It would be another day or two before the troopers could go after Buckwheat. But the weather was deteriorating and closing in fast. With the fog rolling back down the valley; before the troopers could arrive, the canyon would again be hidden under a blanket of fog. The odds were stacked against Buckwheat now, and I thought it was unlikely he would survive another night. Alaska nights are long in mid-September, and daylight hours are short with little warmth. The freezing cold, the wet, the exhaustion, the fear of being trapped and alone deep inside the canyon—not to mention the danger of grizzly attack—could lead a man to lose hope, and as hope dies, so does the man. A hopeless man can give up altogether or make reckless decisions which often lead to deadly outcomes.

With my knowledge of the unforgiving wilderness he was trapped in, I knew that Buckwheat would surely die if not rescued soon.

---

[2] Helio Courier N295JA is the aircraft pictured on the front cover of *No Sequel to Life*.

I landed at Stephan Lake, dropped off my load of rafting gear, and discussed the situation with raft guide Jim Hendrick. He agreed that Buckwheat could not survive much longer.

"Can you land anywhere to get to him?" he asked.

"It's remotely possible that a landing could be done in the river, but it would be extremely dangerous," I replied.

Jim offered to fly in with me to help rescue Buckwheat. I knew that if I tried to land, it would be very risky—and I was simply not willing to risk Jim's life along with my own.

"I need to do this alone," I told him. Jim not only worked for me, but he was also my friend. We had been through quite a few adventures together, and even though I knew he was up for this rescue, I couldn't justify putting us both in the kind of danger I was about to fly into.

"At least take my wetsuit and a lifejacket," he said, and I agreed.

Jim quickly stripped off his wetsuit, handed me a lifejacket, and wished me Godspeed and good luck. Wearing the wetsuit and lifejacket, I took off from Stephan Lake and flew straight to Devils Canyon.

Jay Hudson had somehow flown his Super Cub low enough into the canyon to make the successful airdrop of a radio; I knew that the only way he could have done this was by actually flying inside the narrow canyon walls, dropping to no more than fifty feet above the river. I was amazed; I thought that this part of the canyon was too narrow to possibly fly a plane through, but Jay had actually done it successfully. So, I reckoned it was possible to get my Helio Courier down into the canyon, close in on that river, and maybe—just maybe—by God's grace, I could land between rapids on the river, snatch Buckwheat out of there, and return home.

I ran through the plan in my head over and over. I pictured the whole thing happening at lightning speed, smooth as glass: Buckwheat would be ready as the plane swooped in and landed heading upstream into the current; he would run to the plane and jump in; we would turn around on a dime and takeoff downstream.

Piece of cake—perhaps.

I had been rescued by a helicopter pilot who had risked his life saving me in this very canyon earlier that summer. That's a debt that can only be repaid if I am willing to help someone else in peril. I can't explain this any better, but people who have been saved by someone who risked their life know the feeling of eternal indebtedness that comes with being rescued yourself.

I was terrified by the possibility of being back in the river, swimming in the rapids of Devils Canyon—but this time I also risked being trapped inside a wrecked airplane. No matter how I envisioned the rescue, this vision persisted in my mind; it was a very long fifteen-minute flight back to that canyon rim, with lots of time to reflect. I sure wished my gut would line up with my plan, but I wasn't exactly feeling it.

I flew over the canyon, circling above the rim, trying to radio Buckwheat. No response. The weather was deteriorating, and I had only minutes now to decide if I was going to fly down into this canyon or turn tail and go home. Logic told me to go home. The giant knot in my gut definitely told me to go home. But something better deep inside me said that I had to get Buckwheat out.

It was now or never. Buckwheat had already spent three cold, wet nights trapped in the gorge, with no fire or food. From above I could see him; he was not moving very fast, and he was still not responding to my radio calls. I figured he was hypothermic. I made another high pass in the bright yellow floatplane.

The spot where Buckwheat was trapped was deep in the canyon. The current looked to be moving at about twenty miles an hour, and the waves were three feet high. Devils Canyon is a notorious whitewater bounded on both sides by steep walls and cliffs; the only thing in my favor was that the canyon was fairly straight for about eight hundred yards, and the wind was calm; I would land headed upstream toward Buckwheat, who was stranded on a small gravel bar just below some rapids at the far end of my river runway. I was going to need every bit of those eight hundred yards to come to a stop, spin around, get enough speed built back up for the takeoff, and climb above the narrow spot in the canyon named Screaming Left Hand Turn.

Studying the river canyon as intently as possible from my aerial perspective, I thought that it might just be possible to pull off this rescue. I started descending at 1,400 feet per minute. If things went bad, I would crash in the middle of Devils Canyon. I figured I would survive the crash, but then I'd have to escape from a wrecked plane that would be upside-down in the river. I had my seatbelt tightened, but with the bulky lifejacket and wetsuit, I could not buckle my shoulder harness. I felt that if I were again forced to swim for my life, the lifejacket and wetsuit were more important than the shoulder harness. So, I re-tightened the seat belt and continued to descend.

There was no going home now. I had to put all doubt out of my mind and be one hundred percent focused on the landing.

One hundred percent in the moment now, thinking of nothing else but the job at hand, I set twenty-degree flaps, thirty percent power, and descend below the canyon rim and above the rapids known as Screaming Left Hand Turn. At three hundred feet above the rock walls, I set full flaps and chop the power. My rate of descent increases. Fifty feet above the river, the rolling waves seem to be growing in size; they now appear to be four or five feet tall.

Five feet above the waves, I add power back to sixty percent, then let her settle gently at first, just skipping from wavetop to wavetop. Slowly, I reduce power to fifty percent when I suddenly crash through a wave and come to a violent stop; on impact, I pitch forward and upward, slamming my head so hard that I see stars for an instant. Terrified, I fight to stay conscious; when my vision clears, I realize that the plane is being swept backwards, even at half power!

Quickly, I add power to seventy-five percent, but I'm still drifting backwards. I add full power and slowly start moving forward. Now every wave I crash through seems to explode as it covers the windshield; forward visibility is almost nonexistent, and I have to look out the side windows for reference.

Using full power, I maneuver upriver aiming for a small eddy one hundred feet from where Buckwheat stands transfixed. The water is calmer there. As I power upriver past Buckwheat, I yell out the open door, "You've got thirty seconds to be in this plane, because I'm leaving with or without you!"

I use a curse word or two. I am not sure of his condition, and I need to get him moving.

Reducing power, hoping to steady the plane enough for Buckwheat to climb in, I suddenly feel the floats hit solid and know I'm hung up on some submerged rocks. My Helio is really stuck now.

Buckwheat reaches the open door. He's not wearing his life jacket or kayak helmet; in his rush to get to me, he's left them on the bank.

"Go get your gear!" I yell. Since the plane is stuck anyway, we can afford those extra precious seconds I reason. If we don't make it out of here in the plane, we are going to be swimming for our lives; and I wanted Buckwheat to at least have a chance. While he runs for his gear, I have too much time to wonder if I've made the right decision. Yeah, the landing turned out okay, even though blood from the gash on my head is dripping down off my face. I also notice a couple of chipped teeth. I feel no pain, though; adrenaline has kicked in and is doing its job.

A lifetime of running whitewater rivers and 5000-plus hours of Alaska flying has prepared me for this. I will do this.

Finally, after what seems like terribly long, drawn-out minutes, but is probably only a couple, Buckwheat charges back to the plane wearing his lifejacket, helmet, and wetsuit. He gives me a shove as I add power and rock the elevator/stabilator forward and back producing loud grinding metal sounds. Slowly, we start to move. Buckwheat climbs in, and I begin taxiing as far upstream as possible. I still have to make the downstream eddy turn; if the upstream float catches in the current, it will dip the wing, and if the wing catches the current, we will roll over and instantly be upside-down in the middle of the river—in the heart of Devils Canyon—with absolutely no one to help rescue us.

"Get in the very back of the plane," I yell above the roar of the river. "Sit on the right side and be ready for a high side if the float starts to catch the upstream current!" I'm giving commands now; this is not a request.

"Okay!" Buckwheat's response is deadly serious, letting me know that he understands perfectly. He's a kayaker; he knows exactly what he needs to do. I give it full power, and slowly, we start to move upriver. The water rudders are down. I push full left rudder, then, for only an instant, I chop power. The current catches the right float and starts to swing the plane around. Then the float catches the edge and starts to sink. Instantly, Buckwheat high-sides, and I cram on full power—the torque of the engine helps on left turns. The legendary power of the Helio Courier and the huge ailerons all contribute; at this moment, the river, like some malevolent force tries to grab the right wing but can't quite get it.

Suddenly and mercifully, we're now heading downstream. The Helio seems to know the peril it's in and practically jumps onto the step. Soon we are skipping from wavetop to wavetop. I ease back on the yoke, and obediently, the Helio is airborne and free of the river. We are still in the canyon, though, and only need to climb above the rock walls before Screaming Left-Hand Turn. Everything has gone perfectly until this moment—thank you, God!

But wait! We aren't climbing fast enough! The rocks have put holes in the floats, and the water in the floats has made us too heavy to climb out of the canyon. Screaming Left-Hand Turn is too narrow—the wings won't fit. I need to be above those narrow rock walls.

Although my stomach feels like I swallowed a watermelon whole, I fight to stay calm. Suddenly I remember my extreme Helio training sessions with Ron Sutphin, the legendary pilot who helped perfect the use of the Helio for covert operations during the Vietnam War; it's time to use the skills Ron taught me. At the last moment, I force the plane onto its side using full left-aileron deflection; flying on the side with wings vertical, the rudder has effectively become the elevator and the elevator is now a rudder. True to its legendary status, my Helio staggers sideways through the narrow slot in the canyon.

As heavy as the floats are, and as slow as my airspeed is, in any other plane, we would have stalled and spun to our death. Ron's training—and the engineers who designed the giant ailerons, spoilers, and slotted leading-edge slates on the Helio Courier wing—have just saved two more lives.

The second we clear the narrows of Screaming Left Hand Turn, at my command, the Helio obediently turns back upright for me. Slowly we build airspeed, and very slowly she starts to climb; it seems to take forever to gain altitude, though. Finally, we're out of the canyon at last, and I breathe my first sigh of relief. I am totally drenched with sweat, and Buckwheat is still in the back of the plane. As he crawls forward to join me in the copilot seat, he sees that my face is covered in blood. Then we both notice vegetation hanging from the right wingtip. Really, no words are needed—we both know how close we were to death.

We were out of Devils Canyon, headed for Talkeetna, and we were both alive to tell our stories.

When we were finally within radio range, I notified Talkeetna radio that Buckwheat was safe and en route to Talkeetna. I also requested that my aircraft mechanics meet me at my floatplane base to check out the damage to the plane. I landed on the lake, but I knew that if I stopped, the plane would probably sink, so I kept her moving at about twenty-five miles an hour and headed straight for the beach. Just before we hit the beach, I chopped the power and let the plane beach herself.

Buckwheat was reunited, hugged, and kissed by waiting friends. As soon as I got my feet on the ground, I felt sick and had to sit down in the mud before I fell down; the adrenaline crash was intense. My mechanics looked like bees going over every inch of the plane and floats. They soon told me that I was grounded until repairs could be made. No argument from me, I thought. I can use a day or two off.

Buckwheat told the mechanics that he would cover the bill for the substantial repairs to the plane. I knew that he appreciated what I had risked on that mid-September day in 1995.

That night, I spent a quiet evening with my little boy, Jason. At bedtime, we said our prayers and thanked God for His protection and blessings.

I have had many close calls with death in my life, but now I had to think about being around for my son. As a single parent, it was very important for me to be there for him as he grew up. At the same time, being a man and doing what is right was also important.

I hope to never hesitate to help someone in need, as that is what I believe a man should do.

FlyHelio
simplemachines forum

New member
« on: November 26, 2012, 04:42:59 PM »
Hi everyone! New member to your site. I own N295JA H-395 s/n 514.I understand Paul LaPointe's dad owned this airplane at one time. Do you have some interesting stories or photos of your dad with this airplane? Happy to be a member.
Doug Johnson
Re: New member
« Reply #1 on: November 26, 2012, 06:17:17 PM »
Hi Terry,
Good to have another owner join. Below is what I have in my list on your Helio. Any corrections need to be made let me know. Do need 514's location. and if you can replace company names with owners' names it would be helpful.
If you want a mostly complete list of all 531 Helio's send me a personal message with your E-mail.
What is the deal on an H-395 having a registry of N295JA? I've heard the reason is that it has H-295 wings any truth to that.
Doug
construction number c/n 514, manufacture date 10/59, model H-395, originally N4162D (reused) used by factory until sold '61, Stolairco WA sold '63, export as OB-LKE-711 (Peru) American smelting & refining co '63, OB-M-711 American smelting & refining co '67, N4162D American smelting & refining co NY installed camera port '68 , XB-FEJ (Mexico) lease ASARCO Mexicana SadeCV '69, N4162D American smelting & refining co NY sold '69, Robert LaPointe MI sold '69, Jorl Sarnes CO sold '71, Mountain land construction CO sold '74, Joseph Steck CA deregistered sold by CA sheriff '79, Steve Murray CA installed glider tow hitch & Schweizer release sold '85, Edwin Dearborn LA sold '88, Juan Gomez Honduras '89, export as C-FEYZ Stan Stevens NT sold '94, registered N295JA Jerry Jacquez AK (Fugro Earth Map SD) placed on floats modified camera port put two camera mounts on fuselage sold '12, Terry Olson current owner location SD
« Last Edit: November 26, 2012, 08:05:07 PM by Doug Johnson »
Doug

Terry Olson
Re: New member
« Reply #2 on: November 26, 2012, 06:47:41 PM »
Hi Doug
No clue as to why N295JA was used. The logbooks show no change of the wings. Going to talk to Jerry Jacques to see if he might know. The plane is located in Rapid City, S .D.
Thanks!
Jerry Jacques
Re: New member
« Reply #3 on: May 16, 2013, 11:58:05 PM »
N295JA # 514 is a fantastic performing Helio! I have flown several Helio's and she was the best at short field work.
The N number 295JA was reserved for a H-295 that I also flew but we never got around to changing it over. When I bought #514 I tried to get N395JA but that was taken so I just used N295JA

I flew her mostly in Alaska on large tundra tires, skis and floats, and she always got me home safe.

Please take good care of her as she will forever have a soft spot in my heart.

#514 was used to rescue a stranded kayaker in devils canyon, landed on floats in whitewater in a deep canyon. In my opinion no other fixed wing aircraft other than a Helio could have made that flight.

#514 made many landings on MT McKinley

Doug Johnson
Re: New member
« Reply #4 on: May 17, 2013, 02:49:12 AM »
Thanks for the feedback Jerry, I've changed my list a little.
N4162D c/n 514 used by factory '61, Stolairco (Hunter Kindall dealer) WA '63, OB-LKE-711 Peru American Smelting & Refining co '63, OB-M-711 American Smelting & Refining co '67, N4162D American Smelting & Refining co NY installed camera port '68, XB-FEJ Mexico lease ASARCO Mexicana Sade CV '69, N4162D American Smelting & Refining co NY '69, Robert LaPointe MI '69, Jorl Sarnes CO '71, Mountain Land Construction CO '74, Joseph Steck CA de-registered sold by CA sheriff '79, Steve Murray CA installed glider tow hitch & Schweizer release '85, Edwin Dearborn LA '88, Juan Gomez Honduras '89, C-FEYZ (MacKenzie Mountain Outfitters) Stan Stevens NT '93, William Eglinski AB '94, N295JA Jerry Jacquez (Fugro Earth Map SD) AK (Jerry tried for 395JA but it was taken up it is a 295 in all but name because Jerry installed the 3800 lb up-gross using STC SA15899CE and a letter from Clarence Brent (Helio factory DER) re-configuring it to an early 1200 series Helio) installed a second camera port/mount on fuselage and reconfigured the first port & placed on floats sold '12, Terry Olsen SD
A picture of it in Alaska and one in a new color at Rapid City. Don't happen to have a picture of it in Devils Canyon do you?
« Last Edit: May 17, 2013, 07:02:13 PM by Doug Johnson »
Doug

Jerry Jacques
Re: New member
« Reply #5 on: May 17, 2013, 12:09:50 PM »
Sorry no photos were taken in devils canyon, too busy trying to just survive the flight.

I will look for the story that was written on what happened and send it along when I find it.

Jim Danish did a lot of work on the plane including the paint she now wears.

I had believed 514 was too low to get the 3800 GW but Larry Montgomery and Clarence Brent did the research and engineering and got #514 approved for the 3800 LBS GW.

Believe it or not I now own a DHC-2 Beaver serial # 514 so 514 must be my lucky number

TreeTopFlyer
Re: New member
« Reply #6 on: May 19, 2013, 11:39:00 AM »
Jerry Jacques can clarify this if I have it wrong...

Earthdata Aviation out of Hagerstown MD bought 514 from Jerry. They operated it for a number of years and sold it to Fugro (Horizon out of Rapid City SD, I think Fugro now owns Earthdata as well) Terry may have bought it from them.

It had a small camera hole and Earthdata had it enlarged to fit a Lieca RC30.

I flew for Earthdata at one point until 1999. Learned taildraggers in a C170 10 hours later jumped into the Helio/later decided perhaps I should get better training and went to JAARS for a week....(After ALMOST but not groundlooping 514).

I now own N295LA.

Fun Planes...would like to hear more about that Canyon flight. NO Jerry I'm not the pilot that coordinated the buy from you....LOL...but glad he did! (contributors 2013)

Bare in the Air

What Could Possibly Go Wrong?

One nice evening while driving back to my lodge in Talkeetna from Anchorage, I got a call from Kathy Sullivan, Ray Genet's widow, that her son, Taurus, who lives out on Pirate Lake near Denali, was out of food and needed a plane to bring out his supplies. It's an eighteen-minute flight for me, or a fifteen-hour walk from Taurus' place to the closest road.

I had a female pilot and mechanic by the name of Danielle Doherty working for me at the time. I had dispatched her in my Super Cub to one of my camps and did not expect her back until the next day. So, I was the only one left to deliver the groceries for Taurus.

Kathy met me as I arrived in Talkeetna where N70200, my Cessna A185E Skywagon on amphibious floats was parked. I had just enough time to comfortably make the flight and get home before dark, so we quickly loaded the supplies.

Normally, I would have changed out of my town clothes and put on a Nomex flight suit. But I was pressed for time, and it was a short flight. What could possibly go wrong?

I took off, retracted the wheels, relaxed, enjoyed the view, and landed a short time later, although the light was already slowly fading. Taurus and I quickly unloaded all the food and supplies so I could get home before dark.

Pirate Lake is a fairly small lake, amphibs are not good at getting off small ponds, so I needed to be on top of my game even though the airplane was now empty of the supplies.

I started the IO-520/300 horsepower engine, taxied to the south end of the lake, turned around, applied full power, and just got on step when I spotted two swans ahead and to my left that had just initiated their own takeoff. Unfortunately for both me and the swans, they weren't gaining much altitude—they were cutting directly across my flight path! I only had two choices, and neither one was great. I was either going to hit the swans with the left float or chop power and abort the takeoff. I chose to chop the power and came to a gliding stop, but I missed those two swans. I turned around and taxied back to start over. Now on my second takeoff attempt, I was on step getting ready to rotate, when the swans circled back to the lake, passing directly over me. That's when one of those huge, ungrateful birds decided to target me. He let loose a full bomb-bay load from his rear door and scored a direct hit on my windshield! An Ace could not have scored a more perfect hit.

Now a swan is a big bird and can weigh as much as thirty pounds. I do not know how much it can poop out at one time, but I can tell you that it's enough to totally cover the windshield on a Cessna 185.

Blinded by poop now, I had no choice but to abort the takeoff once again!

I was so close to the end of the lake that even after I chopped the power I slid to a stop in the shallow swamp at the end of the lake.

Now I was stuck at the north end of Pirate Lake. I was in the swamp with a major-poop-covered windshield. I started looking for paper towels in the plane to clear off the mess. They were not there… *oops!* We must have unloaded them with the supplies given to Taurus.

I pulled off my nylon-mesh jersey—no other options, I thought— and tried to clean the windshield. All my cleaning effort with that jersey did, however, was smear the poop around. While I was still poised for cleaning, standing on the float, I concluded that only cotton would do for this job. I was wearing nylon pants and knew they would not work either. That's when I realized that the only piece of clothing or anything else onboard made of cotton was my underwear. Taurus was out of sight on the other side of the lake, no worries. So, I just striped down and used the cotton briefs to clean the windshield. *Job well done!* I thought, admiring my own initiative.

I had to get unstuck from the swamp now. I was already naked and decided to just jump in the swamp to turn the plane around, but the second I hit, I was knee deep in mud and crotch deep in water. That's when I remembered that Alaskan swamps are full of leeches. I felt very exposed and really wished I had put on my pants to keep off the leeches.

Too late! So, I pushed and pulled on the floats, huffed, and puffed and finally managed to get the plane turned facing south down the Pirate.

As hard as I tried, though, I couldn't get it out of the shallow water to a point where it would float. Brilliantly, I decided to start the engine and use power to get unstuck. It might be a little tricky, but I knew I could do it.

Getting in from the copilot side, I pushed the control forward slightly and got the airplane moving. As I taxied back southward on the lake, I decided it was time to put my pants back on.

Oops! I had left them on the float, no worries. I opened the pilot side door and looked, Nope! They were no longer there. Propeller blast had blown my pants, as well as my underwear off somewhere back in the swamp.

Ugh! More decisions…It was getting really dark now, and I had to get airborne quickly, or I could spend the night on Pirate Lake with no clothes—or in soaking wet, muddy, leech-filled clothes, if I could even find them.

I was taking my first option. I did a high-speed taxi to the south end of Pirate, step turned around, and took off—bare in the air now and heading back to Talkeetna. During this short flight, all I could think about was, what if the engine quits? Surviving bare-ass naked would be no fun, or, if I did not survive an engine-out landing, what the heck would my family think of me flying around the Alaska bush wearing only a flight helmet and my shoes!

Then it occurred to me that I better check myself.

Gulp! Look down at my crotch, but I don't see any nasty leeches hanging around there. *Shudder and sigh of relief.* Soon enough, I was pumping the wheels down from the floats for a runway landing.

It was very late, so I was pretty confident that no one would be around. I knew that my hanger door was open, so my plan was to shut the plane down, run (streak) into the hanger, and jump into my Nomex flight suit. No worries—what could possibly go wrong now? I had made it okay so far, but, just as I was about to touch down, I hear a female voice on the radio.

"Talkeetna Traffic N4319Z turning base for landing 18 gravel Talkeetna," the voice advised.

Danielle is flying in my Super Cub and will land closer to my hanger than I will, or she will be only seconds behind me.

I am totally bare! I'm not wearing a stitch of clothing, and I've got a female pilot who's about to taxi in ahead of me or behind me—that's exactly what was going wrong right now.

Once more, the Lord was watching over me. I punch it in and land ahead of her with barely enough time to shut the engine off, run into the hanger, snatch my coveralls off the peg, and literally jump into them.

Danielle is actually taxiing up as I'm putting my arms into the flight suit. I'm still wearing my helmet.

I think I may have told her years later, but I didn't say a word about it at the time. I was pretty embarrassed about the whole incident. Part of my embarrassment was the fact that I've always been really cautious about how I dress for flight.

When I fly, I try not to wear anything flammable. I wear a Nomex flight suit, which is designed to help the wearer survive in case of fire.

I've always got survival gear in the airplane. I'm usually always very deliberate on my flights and a stickler about always being prepared. Unfortunately, and to my major embarrassment, this was one of those really rare flights I had rushed. I began this flight in Talkeetna woefully and dangerously unprepared in my highly flammable nylon garb, but it was only a short flight to help a friend, right…so what could possibly go wrong?

III.
Turn of the Last Century

Everything seemed to be changing rapidly at the turn of the last century. Except for the enduring majesty of landscapes like the outback of Australia, the wild African bush, and the towering snowcapped Brooks Range in the Arctic Circle, things were in flux, and Jerry's world was changing as well. Longtime friend, Dennis Samut and the already legendary Col. Thomas D. Smith III, offered Jerry the chance to help perfect a new long-range rifle scope while hunting feral donkeys in the Australian outback. Of course, Jerry said yes to this once-in-a-lifetime chance to shoot with such experts in their fields. He had seized yet another opportunity for adventure, slithering snakes and all.

Back from Australia for only a few short days, Jerry and Jason were scheduled to fly to Africa. But for the first time without his young son as his constant companion, Jerry ventured back to his seasonal guiding business in Africa. This safari trip would be his last, however, and he closed his business there.

Finally home hunting once more in Alaska, he found new love and a new family. His son, Caleb, was born in 2000. That same year, Jerry used his extraordinary bush-pilot skills to help save the life of his partner and friend, Rex, who lay gravely injured after a plane crash caused by the turbulent air over the Brooks Range.

*Fortunately for us,
all we need do to become immersed in these amazing adventures is turn the page.*

—CS Norwood

African Bush & Australian Outback

By 1992 I had spent enough time in Africa to earn my Professional Hunters license in South Africa.

In addition to my operations in Alaska, I had purchased a small hunting concession in South Africa and had several hunters booked for the month of March. One of my clients, Mike Abernathy, had a Cessna C-182 that he kept at Lanseria Airport RSA. Mike and I worked out a deal where I took him on free trips using my plane to Katmai National Park each year to see the grizzlies in exchange for the use of his Cessna anytime I wanted.

1996

Jerry & Jason on Africa safari with client Garry Hitch and his Kudu bull trophy

Being a single parent and a wilderness guide working on different continents was a challenge to say the least. It was a juggling act: running a business, traveling for work, and taking care of my young son Jason. Most times, Jason traveled with me, and this time as usual, he was excited about the prospect of another trip to Africa. The plans were set. Jolee, the African school teacher who was Jason's nanny on our last trip, was all set to help again. Jolee and her husband were to meet us at the airport in Johannesburg. From there, the drive would take four hours to my hunting concession.

Dennis Samut is a close friend with whom I had done several raft trips. Six weeks before my trip to Africa with Jason, Dennis called and invited me to join him in Australia for sixteen days.

The timing worked out as Jason was scheduled to be with his mom for two weeks during that time. After the Australia trip, I planned to fly back to Alaska, pick up Jason, and we would head back over to Africa together.

Dennis was one of those people who, when he got into something he liked, was driven to become an expert at it. I had introduced him to long-range rifle shooting in 1989. He took shooting as a personal challenge, spending vast amounts of time practicing. He attended several top shooting schools in the US and ordered ammo by the pallet. He personally shot $80K worth of ammo in just five years. He has far surpassed my long-range shooting skills and knowledge.

Dennis and Col. Thomas D. Smith III[1] were collaborating in the development of a new long-range rifle scope. Dennis wanted my input on the latest prototype rifle scope he and TD were working on, so he invited me to Australia, paying all my expenses. He did not need my help; he was just being generous, letting me be part of his project.

I flew from Alaska and met Dennis in San Francisco. From there, we traveled to the Northern Territories of the Australian outback where we were met by Bob Penfold, a professional hunter with an Australian government contract to cull a large number of feral donkeys in the Northern territories. The donkeys were an invasive species, causing environmental destruction in the territories. This was to be the proving ground for the new prototype scopes. Dennis had paid Schmidt & Bender of Germany to produce the first basic Christmas tree reticle scopes that he and TD Smith had designed.

We shot six thousand rounds of ammo using the prototype scopes mounted on custom rifles. The new-concept scope reticle worked fantastically out to six hundred yards.

TD was satisfied with the invention, but Dennis wanted more. A friendly argument took place with me stuck in the middle. I agreed with TD that the new reticle was perfect for hunting out to six hundred yards, but also agreed with Dennis that for longer ranges, something better was needed.

With Dennis' blessing, TD ended up getting a US patent on his invention, the TDS Trifactor Reticle.[2] This was a big improvement on anything yet invented. Swarovski and Schmidt & Bender both started to produce hunting scopes with the TDS reticle. For the average

[1] (TD Smith was an Olympic coach, world champion competitive shooter who set a world shooting record in the 1963 Pan American Games in Brazil) <u>TD Smith in the Oklahoman</u>

[2] <u>TDS Trifactor Reticle by Swarovski Optik</u>

hunter, the TDS Trifactor Reticle 5 is still a good option.

The last night that Dennis, TD Smith, and I were at the remote station in Australia's Northern Territories, we had discussed that we needed to leave by 5:30 a.m. the next morning as we had a fourteen-hour drive to get to Darwin. Dennis had assigned me to take the first shower, TD the second, and he would take the third shower the next morning.

The hot water at the station was heated by a wood-burning water heater. The electricity was provided by a generator which was shut off at 9:00 p.m. every night and restarted at 4:00 a.m. As scheduled, I was first up in the morning, and using a flashlight, made my way to the bathroom and took my shower. As I was getting out of the shower, someone had started the generator, and the lights went on. TD was next to use the shower, and, after he had taken his shower, he wound up in the kitchen where we were waiting for a quick breakfast to be served. Dennis was the last to enter the shower. TD and I were chatting over coffee when we heard a loud scream and then the pitter-patter of running feet on the cement floor coming towards us. Bursting into the kitchen stark naked with shampoo suds covering his hair came Dennis Samut. Wild eyed, he was stuttering *sn-sna-! Big f***ing-big f***ing snake!* TD and I looked at each other wondering for an instant if this was another one of Dennis' practical jokes. The fact that he was only in his birthday suit, and after looking into Dennis' eyes, we quickly realized he was serious.

TD and I got up and headed towards the bathroom and the shower stall. I was wearing my Colt 1911 lightweight commander in .45 ACP while TD had already packed his pistol away for the trip. Without thinking, the .45 made its way from the holster into my hand. Walking side by side with TD, it occurred to me that this man was the former world champion pistol shooter.

"TD! You're the best shot with a handgun I know. Here, take my pistol," I said as I handed it to him.

He took it, took one step, then said, "yes, but you know where your gun shoots," and handed the pistol back to me.

About this time, we were reaching the bathroom. We could hear the water running in the shower stall and see steam billowing out. With the .45 in my hand, I peeked my head around the cement wall and looked inside. Sure enough, there was a huge brown snake in the middle of the cement floor. Pushing the safety off, I started to take aim at the head and then paused. It occurred to me the shower stall had cement walls, cement floor, and the roof was heavy steel. If I had fired a round in there, the 230-grain ball projectile could easily have ricocheted around coming back at me.

I backed out of the shower stall and holstered my weapon. TD was peeking around me, seeing what was in the shower stall. Fifteen feet away was a door that led outside, and I had remembered there was a shovel and rake as well as other implements next to the door. I grabbed the shovel and headed back, but by the time I got to the shower stall, the snake had exited through a small hole in the wall. TD had watched it escape as I was trying to grab the shovel. This time I handed TD my pistol again, and I had the shovel. I retraced my steps out to the back door, went around to where we were opposite the shower on the outside and saw only the tail of the snake disappearing into a pile of bricks. TD handed my pistol back. I re-holstered, replaced the shovel, and went back to the kitchen. By that point, the cook had found a towel and Dennis had covered himself up.

"Did you kill that damn snake?" he asked. TD said, "No. It got away."

Dennis' only comment was, "Well, I'm sure as hell not gonna finish my shower then!"

Dennis told us that while he was showering and soaping up his hair, he felt something slide over his foot. Figuring it was one of the big green frogs that we saw frequently in the bathrooms and around the property he wasn't concerned for a moment. However, when he looked down and realized it was a huge snake coming out of a hole in the wall that had slid over his foot and was in the shower stall with him, he froze for a moment, watched the snake move away from the stream of water that was striking it, then slowly backed out of the shower stall. As soon as he was far enough away from the snake that he knew he couldn't get struck, he took off running towards the kitchen. When he saw TD and me there, he figured that we had our pistols on us, and that we would take care of the snake.

It was only after we had walked away heading towards the bathroom that he realized he was standing there, soaking wet and stark naked with a head full of shampoo bubbles in front of a room full of people. The female cook grabbed an apron and a towel, handed them to Dennis, and told him to cover up. After we left the next day, Bob Penfold killed the king brown snake[3] that had slithered back into the shower stall. He dispatched it with the flat-nosed shovel from outside the back door.

I arrived back in Alaska with only three days left before our scheduled flight for Africa. I had already purchased our tickets, but I was told that, while I was gone, Jason's mom had changed her mind about me taking him back to Africa. She had gotten a court order forbidding

[3] King Brown Snake

me from taking him out of the US.

With clients booked and on such short notice, I could not find a licensed African PH to replace me.

I had little choice but to leave my son behind with his mom while I continued to Africa. This was the longest time Jason and I had ever been separated.

I loved spending two months each year in Africa, but the separation was hard on both Jason and me, and since I could no longer take Jason with me to Africa, I decided to close my operation there.

With TD Smith off on other projects, Dennis wanted me to help him continue developing a reticle that would make possible hitting a target from 100 to 1000 yards without needing to adjust the turrets on the scope.

May

Dennis paid to have many prototype scopes made. He would test them and then send the ones he liked to me in Alaska to do my own tests. As the reticle got more complex, I suggested that the horizontal stadia lines have visible numbers next to them. Dennis incorporated that into all the subsequent prototype scopes.

Eventually, Dennis founded Horus Vision.[4] Many Horus reticles, ballistic calculators, and targets were patented by Dennis. Some of my ideas were adopted, but most of the development, and all the credit for the revolutionary Horus reticle goes to Dennis Samut. It was fun working on the project, and I consider myself privileged to have had a small part in the development of the Horus reticle.

Using the advanced Doppler radar system that rented for $20K a day, Dennis developed the first ultra-long-range ballistic program that worked for rifle calibers. The ATrag ballistic program[5] that he developed revolutionized the world of long-range shooting. This program was so good, it was copied by everyone in the shooting industry.

After returning from Africa, I loaded Jason and my kayak in the Helio Courier and flew us to Denali Park for a river trip on the Nenana River. A good friend, Jason Rucker and his three partners had a **rafting** and kayaking company. They had invited us to join them on a day trip. It was like an old-home week for me. Everyone liked four-year-old Jason, and Jason loved all the attention. We launched three rafts that day on the river; I was in my kayak. Jason Rucker rowed one of the rafts. My son, Jason was one of his passengers along with two female teachers and a nurse from Fairbanks with her two children.

June

---

4 https://www.horusvision.com/
5 http://www.snipersystems.co.uk/id30.html

There's a spot on the river that has a hole with a standing wave kayakers love to play around in. I knew the point well, so I sprinted ahead a couple of minutes and was surfing in the hole while they caught up to me. Normally, rafts just go around the play spot, but Guide Jason maneuvered his raft into the hole and intentionally ran into me. Before I knew it, he grabbed my kayak and pulled it into the raft with me still sitting upright.

"Rhonda, this is Jerry. Jerry, this is Rhonda; she's a nurse from Fairbanks," Jason said. I found out later that yanking me out of the water into the raft was a set-up by my friend Jason. He had decided to play matchmaker and thought this was as good a way as any to introduce me to Rhonda.

When we stopped for lunch, I noticed my son Jason and Rhonda's son, Matt, had become instant friends on the raft. Rhonda and I instantly hit it off as well and agreed to do another trip with the kids in two weeks. Over time, I saw Rhonda was a good mother; her kids Christin and Matt were nice kids, and everyone got along well; Jason loved being part of a family and having Matt to play with.

Rhonda and I were married in November 1997, and we traveled together as a family to trade shows.

Our son, Caleb was born in 2000. Now we all faced a brand new century, with all its new adventures, joys and sorrows, trials and tribulations.

Africa will always draw me & my family back.

Still, there's no place like home!

16.
Turbulence

Sheep and caribou hunting camp in the Arctic National Wildlife Refuge Eastern Brooks Range, was a huge, exclusive-use guide area that encompassed a million acres. I had a ten-man crew that consisted of myself two pilot/guides, a cook, four other guides, and two apprentice guides. The pilots were Zach Babat, Rex Maurer, and me. We would run two back-to-back, ten-day sheep and caribou hunts with six clients on each hunt.

Rex Maurer, who was both an experienced guide and bush pilot, had worked for me for a couple of years. After my divorce was settled, I was left in a dire financial situation. Rex had offered to become a partner in the hunting business. The investment he made enabled me to stay financially solvent, and I was now back on my feet. For Rex, guiding and flying were avocations; his real job was an executive with 3M, but he could take enough time off each year to fly and guide a month in the Brooks Range during sheep season and three weeks in Cold Bay for the brown bear season.

I have a policy that every client and pilot will wear a flight helmet whenever they are in any of my airplanes. What I didn't know was that whenever Rex was flying and away from camp, he never actually wore the helmet. It was uncomfortable, didn't look cool, and was just kind of a nuisance to him. Rex also had another habit that I didn't like. Whenever he would take off flying in my Cub, he would always forget to pack his lunch. Naturally, he would get hungry during the day but instead of having his own lunch, he would get into the survival food and eat his fill, and, of course, he always forgot to replace the food or tell me.

This accounted for the last two years of finding empty MRE bags in the survival area of the plane during my annual inspection. So this season, before Rex flew off in the Super Cub for the Brooks Range, I did not replace the MREs. Instead, I put two Ziplock bags of dried dog food in the compartment where the survival food is normally stowed. If anything happened with the Cub and we found ourselves in a survival situation, the dog food would certainly keep us alive.

The way we worked our hunts was to first establish a nice main camp, we flew a ton of gear, food, supplies, and fuel into a central location with an airstrip large enough to work the Cessna C-185. This is main camp where we set up a cook tent and large supply tent to store everything.

After main camp is set up and stocked with everything, we use the Super Cubs and set up satellite camps called spike camps. Each hunting client gets his own personal guide and has his own spike camp to hunt from.

The second day after we arrived at our main camp at Last Lake, Rex, Zach, and I spent the day flying gear to spike camps.

Late afternoon Rex landed back at main camp and stormed up to me and Zach. We could see that he was very unhappy.

"What the hell's the idea of having dog food instead of MREs in the plane?" he shouted.

Zach and I burst into laughter! We had been waiting for Rex to forget his lunch, try breaking into the MREs to eat, and finding only dog food in their place.

"I'm tired of finding empty bags of MREs and not having the survival food I packed for somebody who is actually in a survival situation and needs it," I explained.

He still wasn't happy, apparently.

Zach butted in even though he was the junior pilot. "Look Rex, if you'd only been replacing the MREs whenever you ate them, the problem never would have come up," he said.

Outnumbered, Rex just walked to the cook tent and got some food.

A few days later everything was set up in the spike camps and the guides were waiting there for the arrival of the hunting clients.

Rex and Zach flew their clients into their individual spike camps, and I flew the other four clients to spike camps where their guides were waiting to start the ten-day hunt.

Rex's spike camp was near the headwaters of the Sheenjek River on a tiny gravel-bar airstrip built by Joe Want decades before. Rex parked the Super Cub N82962[1] and proceeded to backpack with his client up into the mountains to hunt Dall sheep. Rex was scheduled to check in with me the morning of the fifth day. By early evening of the fifth day, I had not heard from Rex. I decided to go check on him and jumped in my Cessna 185. I flew from Last Lake camp on the Sheenjek River, upriver to the headwaters. As I flew up the valley, the headwind grew stronger, and I started to encounter extreme turbulence. You can feel the wind when you're on the ground, but whether or not there's turbulence in the air is hard to know.

Although Rex was an experienced pilot, this rugged mountain terrain was new to him. After flying the forty miles from main camp, I knew I was getting close to where Rex had the airplane parked. I could see the dust coming up from the gravel bar that indicated

---

[1] N82962 (Piper PA-18-150 owned by Jerry J. Jacques): Flightaware.com

Rex was taking off from that spot. It turns out he was moving the airplane four miles farther upriver to another small gravel-bar strip. I immediately jumped on the radio and started yelling.

"Do not go into that strip! The turbulence is too unpredictable there! It's not safe!" I yelled into the mic, but I got no answer.

Over and over, I yelled the same thing with no answer from Rex. After a moment of following him, I realized he was adhering to my policy for landing off airport: always have your master switch off. Should something go wrong, and you wreck the airplane, there is less chance of a fire with the master switch off. In horror, I watched helplessly as Rex tried to land the Super Cub and ran into windshear turbulence.

Rex tried to do a go around. He stayed airborne past the end of the strip. He was about a hundred feet off the ground, and, for a moment, it looked like he was going to be okay. Then he encountered what was probably a microburst, and it pushed him straight into the ground. He was in an empty Super Cub, light on fuel, at full power with a hundred and sixty-horse engine, and it still pushed him into the ground. I knew instantly that Rex and anyone in the airplane with him was either severely injured or dead. I did a sharp one-eighty-degree turn in the Cessna and headed back to main camp. Satellite phones did not work at that time in the Brooks Range, but I knew that the ELT in Rex's Cub should have been set off. The instant I landed at main camp, I told Christian Elwell, one of our guides who was also an EMT, to grab our major med kit, some extra sleeping bags, and a tent. I was going to fly the other Super Cub to where Rex had just crashed. The major med kit that I kept in camp was extensive and even included an IV kit.

"I'm going to fly into a spot that's going to be extremely dangerous. I fully expect that I'm going to wreck my Cub, but I want to get the major med kit and extra survival gear in to Rex," I said to Christian as I loaded the gear. "I recommend that you do not fly with me," I paused, "…but if you choose to, I would love to have your help."

If they're alive in the airplane, they're certainly severely injured. At this point, I don't know if it's Rex *and* the client or just Rex," I said, ready for takeoff now.

Christian instantly made the decision that he was coming with me and would accept the risk because he wanted to be there to help. The forty-mile flight wasn't fun. The wind had increased and so had the turbulence. I circled above the wreck a few times and made the decision that I thought it was possible to make the landing on the four-hundred-fifty-foot strip. I told Christian over the headset that I was going to come in hot to try to penetrate through the turbulence. I knew I would touch down much faster than normal.

"I expect to run off the end of the strip and into the willows

Christian came back over the headset. "I see movement at the Super Cub! Somebody's alive! Let's get on the ground."

I'll freely admit that I was scared to make this landing, but I felt I had no choice. Coming in from the head of the canyon, I kept a high rate of descent and touched down at around sixty miles an hour. That's twenty-miles-an-hour faster than normal touchdown in a Super Cub. The second my wheels were on the ground, I applied full breaks, and we started skidding the wheels. A sudden gust picked up the right wing, almost pushing the left wing into the ground. Wind tried to push the tail around, but I kept the airplane on the airstrip, regardless, and we skidded to the very end and into the willows. Those willows helped stop the Cub.

Christian and I were instantly out of the airplane. We grabbed the med kit and survival gear and ran at full speed the quarter mile to where the wrecked Super Cub had plunged to the ground. When we got to the wreck, Rex was lying outside of the mangled plane. One of our other guides was there, trying to assist. From the side of the mountain, the guide had also watched the wreck and had run down to help him. Rex was conscious but in bad shape. He was able to tell me that the client was not in the airplane with him.

Christian and I both triaged Rex and decided he probably had a broken back. There was no way for us to safely load him into a tiny Super Cub to evacuate him. I made the decision that Christian would stay with Rex, get an IV started if needed, and I would fly to Arctic Village, a hundred miles away. This was where the closest communications to the outside world was located.

I flew the Super Cub back to main camp, fueled up my Cessna 185, and flew to Arctic Village. That flight seemed to take forever, but as soon as I got to the health clinic, I used their phone to call for an emergency rescue. I gave the GPS coordinates to the Rescue Coordination Center (RCC) and let them know both the mechanism of injury and that Rex was in critical condition.

When the staff at the clinic found out I was flying back to camp, trying to get back to Rex, they asked if I needed anything. As my major med kit only had one bag of IV solution, I asked if they could provide a few more bags. They set me up with four bags of IV saline and the rest of the supplies I would need to administer the IVs. I flew back to main camp at Last Lake but, by this time, it was too dark to take the Super Cub back up to Rex. I needed to wait three hours for the sun to come back up.

Thankfully, within a couple of minutes, the Sikorsky Pave Hawk helicopter[2] the military sent for the rescue flew overhead and past us. The amazing rescue pilots using night vision gear went up into

---

[1] Pave Hawk in action

the canyon, landed, and rescued Rex. They flew him directly back to Fairbanks to the hospital. This amazing night rescue they performed without a doubt saved Rex's life. He was transferred later to Seattle Medical Center where he underwent major spinal surgery. Rex spent two weeks in the intensive care unit and undertook a long recovery.

The military flight surgeon got word that a civilian pilot was involved in a bad crash and had been wearing a flight helmet. He was surprised to hear that this pilot—a civilian—was wearing a helmet. Since I was the registered owner of the plane, the flight surgeon called me. He wanted to know details of what kind of helmet the pilot was wearing and why I required helmets.

After our conversation, he requested the helmet be sent to him for testing. It had been shattered and was junk anyway, so we shipped it to him. Later, after he had the results of his tests, he called me and told me that Rex never could have survived without that helmet.

When I was visiting Rex in the hospital he admitted that he never wore the flight helmet except for the day of the crash. Since he was late that day, he knew I might be coming to check on him, so he had put on the helmet.

He now wanted to buy one for himself and would never fly without a flight helmet again.

There are some good lessons here:

1. Flight helmets save pilots' lives. Statistics regarding VFR crashes show that, in a single engine, eighty-two percent of fatalities are preventable if you can avoid the head injury.
2. The crashed Super Cub had one of its gas tanks ruptured, and gas spilled all over Rex. Having the master switch turned off probably prevented a fire.
3. No pilot ever gets into a plane and thinks, "I am going to crash today." Do not get complacent. Have a flight plan filed with someone you trust, have good survival gear with you, wear your shoulder harness, and get a flight helmet and wear it!

Rex always wears a flight helmet when he flies his Cessna C-180 these days. After his accident, I bought his share of the company. We remain friends and stay in touch still today.

No matter where it happens, Alaska bush-plane wrecks are serious events. Injury and loss of life can happen, even though Alaska's bush pilots are long-known for their ability to "crack up easy" (Garfield 1982). Rex's plane wreck was a tragedy—one that took him a very long time to recover from.

I thank God that he survived and is still my friend today.

I have no photos of Rex's crash—these are NTSB photos of my leased-out Super Cub N4319Z. This wreck happened in Cold Bay on one devastating day in May 2004.

[For events surrounding this crash, read Chapter 20, "Tragedy in May."]

IV.
Cold Bay

*Arguably one of the most inhospitable places on the planet,
Cold Bay's siren song of pounding rain and howling winds,
coupled with its huge population of big grizzlies, roaming
wolves, and wandering caribou kept Jerry flying his clients into
the little village on the Alaska Peninsula every big-game season
for twenty-two years.*

*There are a few rare humans who choose to take
the rougher trail. They'll risk it all for a life
of hardship and adventure perhaps for the sole
purpose of discovering the depth of who they are
and their ability to survive, or,
perhaps it's just so they'll have an epic story to
tell their grandchildren...*

—CS Norwood

Cold Bay, Alaska

Home of the largest brown bear/coastal grizzlies on the planet and the world's worst weather.

In 1979, I made my first trip to Cold Bay to work for Master Guide Clark Engle. Later, I worked there for Larry Rivers and eventually bought the guiding concession from Larry.

Clark's guide area had lots of alder brush and all of his camp sites had sheltered places for the tents. Larry's guide area was more open country with not much alder, so most of his camps were in the open, exposed to the wind.

Cold Bay, Alaska, population sixty-seven, is the last village on the Alaska Peninsula and the starting point for the Aleutian Islands. Cold Bay in the late 70s and 80s was a wild place with high winds like no place on earth. Immense coastal grizzlies also known as brown bears, plenty of caribou, and wolves freely roamed, fished, grazed, and hunted this windswept wilderness and, sometimes, even sauntered through the town. In addition, plentiful marine life—whales, walruses, sea otters, seals, and sea lions, as well as red and silver salmon—ply the Bering Sea northwestward and the Gulf of Alaska waters on the south and east. My guide area started at Cold Bay and went to Unimak Island.

Navy Town, a few miles southeast of Cold Bay, was abandoned shortly after WWII. By 1978, it only consisted of about a hundred and fifty dilapidated steel Quonset huts that were half-buried in the ground. The old buildings were just barely standing as years of wind, blowing sand, and salt air had taken their toll.

Navy Town is now just a historical marker in Cold Bay, but back then, Larry Rivers used Navy Town as his base camp for his bear and caribou hunts.

When I first began work for Larry, he had all his guides scrounge through the huts until we had gathered enough material to make three of the huts livable. It was like being a kid and building a fort; nothing was level or square and everything was old and weathered, but the outcome was much better than living in a tent. This was only the base camp, however. Soon weather permitted Larry to use his Super Cub to fly one guide and one client into their own spike camp. Spike camp consisted of food for fifteen days, a two-burner Coleman stove and a small North Face mountaineering tent. These pup tents did not have room to stand and just barely enough room to sit up in. We lived in the pup tent until either we got our client a bear, the client quit, or the season was over twenty-one days later.

In the Aleutians, violent storms blow in off the Bering Sea or North Pacific quite often. Sustained rains with winds of over seventy miles per hour are common. There are no trees and many of the camps on beaches have no alder or willow thickets to block the wind.

I was a tough kid but even for me, the winds and weather were worse near Cold Bay than on Mt. McKinley. The North Face tents were the best mountaineering tents of the day, yet the Cold Bay winds often blow them to bits with alacrity.

During one season, a five-day storm blew in off the Bering Sea and destroyed the tents in five of the six of Larry's spike camps. My tent blew up on day three. My client and I were in the tent lying on our backs in our sleeping bags with our feet to windward. We were desperately holding the tent wall from collapsing in on us. The incessant roar of the wind even inside the tent, caused us to yell at each other just to be heard. We only had a few minutes respite before another rush came at us. We could feel it and hear it rumbling toward us like a freight train. As we felt the next big gust coming, we braced our feet on the tent wall into the wind, but when it hit the tent this time, the wind ripped half a foot of seam where the floor attached to the wall. My client and I looked at each other as we both yelled in unison, "That's not good!" We held fast, though, until after the gust subsided and the wind died down to a reasonable forty miles per hour. Then I tried patching the hole with duct tape. But before I finished the patch, we heard the next gust coming, and I knew we weren't going to save our tent this time. We could do nothing but brace ourselves as the tent completely tore away from the floor and departed up the valley. We must have looked pretty pathetic at that moment, sitting there, stunned and exposed on the tent floor looking at the sea grass yielding to the raging wind's onslaught. Grace was with us, however—it was not raining at that moment. Every piece of our gear that we had not secured was gone with the tent. Coming to our senses fast, we got out of our sleeping bags and started grabbing things. We wrapped everything in the tent floor and put big rocks over the bundle to hold it down. The food and some of our gear was already under a ten-by-fourteen-inch blue plastic tarp that was held down by twenty-five or so pumpkin-sized rocks. I remembered hearing stories from the natives that before the white man arrived, the native people in this area dug holes in the sandy soil and used driftwood to cover their subterranean shelters. I quickly found a spot on the side of a sandy grass-covered hill that looked like it would work and started digging. I screamed at the client to start dragging driftwood from the beach. The sand was fairly soft, so in an hour and a half of frantic digging I had a pit dug into the hill that measured four feet wide by eight feet long and four feet deep. I sloped the floor toward the opening so any water blown in could drain out. We covered the pit with boards and small logs we drug from the beach. Over the wood, we put a layer of tundra down then cut the tarp in half and laid it over the tundra roof. By the time we had finished our makeshift shelter, it was raining again. Of course, the wind was still blowing in ferocious gusts. Finally, we more carefully cut squares of sod and laid it down over the tarp. Now we had a waterproof sod roof. Essentially, we had constructed a small cave. I laid the second half of the tarp over the sand floor to keep us dry. After moving our things into the cave, I hung the tent floor over the front opening as a door. It was dark and damp inside, but it kept the wind and rain out. To our profound relief, our cave was also much quieter than the tent in the violent stormy winds.

We survived just fine in the cave for three days when Larry flew in with the news of how bad the storm had been. We were the last of his camps that he had checked. All but one of the camps lost their tents in the storm. Larry was used to this and left us with a new tent and the news that a new storm was brewing. Before I set up the new tent, however, I spent six hours digging a huge hole to erect the tent in. When I was done It looked like a bomb crater. The tent was now protected from the wind on all sides.

This storm hit us just as hard as the first one had. The tent in the hole was protected just fine, but the heavy rain flooded us out during the first night, so we moved back into our cave. The next morning, with the wind howling and rain blowing sideways, I took down the tent then dug a drainage ditch out of the hole. I had not thought it was necessary when I initially dug the hole, as it was sand, and I figured it would drain—not the case! After I had the tent set back up, we moved in again. That night, the storm hit full strength with winds roaring in again, only now at hurricane force of ninety miles per hour. The wind passed over the hole so fiercely that it created a vacuum effect. The tent actually lifted up as we lay in it! It was like lying on top of a giant, soft balloon. Each time the gust stopped, the vacuum-effect stopped with it, and we would drop back to the bottom of the hole.

Larry lived at main camp and flew by the spike camps in his Super Cub every few days, weather permitting. If we had a bear down, he would pick up the client and his bear hide, then return for the guide and bring him back to main camp.

One evening at Larry's camp at the old, abandoned WWII Navy base at Navy Town, I was reading a book in the fading daylight. Larry was also reading a book while another guide, Kirk, was cleaning his handgun. I walked outside to start the generator for the lamps so I could continue reading. The generator was a hundred feet away and at the top of a small hill. I bent over and pulled the starter cord once—nothing! On the second pull, the engine turned over but did not quite catch. As I was about to give it a third pull, I saw movement out of the corner of my eye. I stopped my pull and looked up at a sow grizzly moving purposefully toward me from only fifty short feet away. I stood up, making my presence known, but she kept coming straight at me at a very fast walk. I pulled my .45 ACP assuming a two-handed Weaver stance—she was still coming.[1]

"Get outta here!" I yelled calmly in a deep voice, but she kept coming. I took aim and shot a round in the ground in front of her paws. Still, she kept coming. I put a second round in the tundra in front of her advance. She was closing in on me fast now, with less than a dozen feet between us. I was prepared to put the rest of the magazine into her when suddenly, to my relief, she turned in an instant and ran off into the fading evening light.

A moment later as I was watching her, I heard footsteps coming in behind me. I hoped those footsteps were Larry and Kirk's. They were. There was no harm done, fortunately, just another close encounter of the furry kind, Alaska style.

Now Larry and Kirk have a slightly different version of this encounter.

They say that they saw me walk outside and head for the generator, then the lights came on for an instant. Then they heard a high-pitched squeaky voice scream, "get out of here you bitch," followed by two quick shots sounding almost like one shot as they were spaced so close together. Larry and Kirk jumped up, grabbed guns, and ran for the generator where I was standing with a smoking gun in my hand, watching a grizzly bear run off. Larry started the generator, and we walked back inside.

Inside, Larry told me he did not know my voice could sound so squeaky and still be loud. Kirk's head nodded in agreement as he asked if I had fired one or two shots.

So, I will leave it to the reader to decide whose version to believe. The biggest bears I have ever seen came from the Cold Bay area, and I loved hunting there. All total, I guided bear hunters out of Cold Bay one month each year for twenty-two years; nine seasons of that time I was working for Larry Rivers. The remainder of those seasons,

[1] https://en.wikipedia.org/wiki/Weaver_stance

I was on my own. In 1997, one of my clients, Marvin Winter, shot the new SCI world record bear. That grizzly scored 31 2/16" (skull measurement) and is still the largest bear ever shot. As of 2022, it still holds the all-time number one SCI record for the biggest brown bear ever recorded.[2]

Assistant Guide Jason (l) and I bring home the bearskin

I'm posing with Rex Maurer and my client, Marvin Winter's SCI record-setting brown bear.

[2] https://safariclub.org/the-biggest-bears/

18.
Cold Bay Journal

Date: 6/13/02 12:44:47 AM !llFirst Boot!!!
From: Talkeetnaairtaxi
To: Adventurous

In a message dated 6/13/02 12:05:58 AM !11First Boot!!!, Talkeetnaairtaxi writes:

I left home in Talkeetna on Sunday the fifth of May 2002 in my C-185 on amphibian floats. With two guides on board, we flew to Merrill Field, refueled, and picked up one more guide, sixty gallons of gas, one rifle, one handgun, and one large backpack. Two large pizzas later, the four of us re-boarded the plane. The C-185 was heavy on takeoff, and she wanted to stay on the ground.

We flew from MRI to Lake Clark Pass. The weather was nice, and the pass was very scenic with the waterfalls and glaciers contrasting against the sheer rock walls and volcanic peaks. On the west end of the pass, near Lake Clark it became turbulent. It made Lee sick, and the smell of secondhand pizza permeated the plane. Poor Lee had even been wearing the anti-sick wrist bands. Thank God for Ziplock bags.

Lake Iliamna, the largest lake in Alaska, was still frozen. Three hours after our departure, we landed in King Salmon. The landing was extremely difficult due to the very windy and gusty conditions. With two full Ziplock bags of blended pizza and Coke Cola, Lee, still green and shaky, headed for the terminal.

In the terminal, a guard saw Lee's .44 magnum and a security breach was started in place. Only in Alaska as it was no big deal, they escorted Lee out to the plane, and had Lee leave the gun in the plane. The guards warned me not to bring a gun into the terminal.

After fueling up, I decided that the wind was too strong and weather too marginal to continue, so we spent the night at the King Ko Inn. Dinner consisted of bar food and entertainment provided by the locals. They say an ugly woman gets better looking with each beer. Well, in Alaska, the farther into the bush one ventures, the better looking a homely woman becomes. Put that same homely woman into a bar in a bush community, and she becomes a gorgeous sex symbol. Drinking my orange juice and watching the goings on was certainly interesting. Then, as I was minding my own business and getting ready to leave, one of the local sex symbols danced over and told me that I was going to dance with her next. She outweighed me by at least twenty pounds, and her biceps were bigger than mine. I figured that I would just slip out while she finished her dance with the guy she was dancing with at the moment.

As I was starting to make my break, the old man that sold me gas for the plane stopped me. In a low voice he whispered into my ear, "You will not get out of here without her seeing you."

"So what!?" I challenged.

"She is a mean one, and she almost killed two guys in a bar fight in Montana a few years back. She put one person into the hospital since she arrived here. My advice to you is do not cross my little sister," he said.

The song ended about that time, and I saw her heading my way.

Gulp! Cold sweat and a sick feeling swept into my gut.

No wonder people drink in bars, I thought. Next thing I knew, she was in my face smiling with all thirteen of her teeth.

"Honey, go put some money in the jukebox, and we will dance," she ordered.

Feeling somewhat like a male black widow spider, I knew that I had better think fast. Telling her that I did not know how to dance did not seem like a good idea. Thinking she might take pity on me, I told her that I had a torn rotator cuff. Yeah, I knew it was a lame excuse, but I hoped it would work since she was at least partly drunk, and I do have a very bad shoulder that is very painful and not yet healed. She stared at me for a long time, and I thought I was in for a fight. Never in my life have I struck a woman, and I was not about to start now. So, I was at a loss what to do. Suddenly, she hit me in the shoulder (the one with the torn rotator cuff) with enough force to almost knock me over.

"Honey, too bad and no wonder you are single. Put some damn money in the music box for me anyway," she ordered again.

I did as I was told. Much to my relief, one of the local guys was talking to her when I got back. As they danced past me, I heard her tell him that poor guy had been injured, and he could not ever have sex again. I escaped into the night. As soon as I was out of the bar, I practically ran to my hotel room. Before I opened my door, I made sure I was not followed. I am afraid of no man nor any beast, but I must admit I am a little afraid of women. That woman certainly was no lady, and I had no clue how to deal with someone like that.

I unrolled my sleeping bag and was asleep on the floor in seconds. Two of my three guides came into the room a short time later. I asked where Todd was and got told that he was stuck with a big woman who was not letting him go. Three hours later, Todd stormed into the room.

He was mad as heck because we had abandoned him, and he had to face the thirteen-toothed Amazon female alone.

We departed the morning of the sixth and headed to Cold Bay. A headwind of thirty-five miles per hour made progress slow. Following the shoreline of the Bering Sea, we saw a big pod of gray whales, seals, sea otters, caribou, a few moose, and about a hundred walrus hauled out at Cape Seniavin.

Three hours and thirty minutes in the air later, we landed in Cold Bay. Over the last month, I had pre-mailed and shipped two thousand pounds of food and equipment to Cold Bay. We picked up all of our freight and mail, got plane gas, unloaded the plane, reloaded the gear, and I flew one of the guides, Jason, out to Boiler Point Lake and set up a camp. I saw one huge bear over ten-foot [tall]. Made a second trip with a second guide (Todd) to Hot Springs Bay. While landing in the salt water and taxiing up to the camp sight, I got hung up on a reef. Todd and I thought we could just carry the gear to shore from where we were stuck. Ten steps from the plane, Todd stepped into deep water and filled his hip waders. Not a fun way to start a nineteen-day trip on the Alaska Peninsula.

After getting Todd set up with his camp, I flew to the fishing village of False Pass and met with the Native Counsel. They are always happy to see me, mostly because I pay them $8K a year to hunt on their land. After our meeting, I flew back to Cold Bay. Brett and Riley had landed in my PA-18 Super Cub. It had taken them ten hours of flying time to get from Anchorage to Cold Bay. One of the town locals had taken them in for dinner and fed them. Alaska is still full of warm and friendly people. We all camped out next to Russell Creek for the night.

May 7— I flew five flights today. I put Gary Hudson at Deadman Bay; I put John Nicholas and Riley Pits at Little John Lagoon and stopped at False Pass to pay my yearly fee to hunt on their land.

May 8— I flew three flights. Two clients arrived: John Gullies and Garth Dal. I flew them out to camps on the ninth of May.

I flew nine flights: took off on my first flight at 7:00 a.m. and landed on my last flight at 11:45 p.m. Four flights in the float plane were very hard as the wind was twenty to thirty-five miles per hour and landing in the ocean is challenging with big waves. There is absolutely no room for error, and the smallest miscalculation can mean wrecking the plane. Flipping the plane into the Bering Sea or North Pacific is not a good idea.

The odds of surviving such a wreck are small. In high winds it is impossible to turn a float plane around, so I must land with precision and carefully pick my landing places. The flying I do here on the end of the Alaska Peninsula is high risk. I am the only one with a float plane operating from Cold Bay; no one else is crazy enough to want to work that hard or take the risk. I do it because I have a commitment to give my clients the best hunt that I can. Using my Super Cub on the tundra tires and having the float plane gives me a big advantage over any other outfitter. With the strong wind, I was taking off and landing the Cub across the runway instead of lengthways. The runway is a hundred and fifty feet wide and with a twenty-five mile-per-hour wind, that is plenty of length to land or take off. The Coast Guard crew that was stranded here, watched in amazement as the four of us guides landed and took off using fifty to one hundred feet of runway. My day finally ended at 1:15 a.m. when the planes were secured and tied down. I do not remember anything after I crawled into my tent.

May 10— I slept until 1:00 p.m. In the last ten days I have worked 176 hours, logged 51 hours flight time, and was totally fatigued. I had not had time to change clothes or take a shower since I left King Salmon on the morning of the sixth. I took two showers today and did my laundry. I was just given three huge king crab legs from Allen, the storekeeper, to take with me for dinner. They are fresh and will hit the spot tonight.

May 11— Was up early and was in the air at 6:00 a.m. Flew the beach in the Super Cub looking for anything new washed up. No walrus or whales have washed up on the beach lately. Saw a sow with two cubs, twenty to thirty caribou, and a few foxes. Checked on all six of my camps, and everyone was okay. Was back to Cold Bay by 9:00 a.m.

At 10:33 I flew the float plane with two clients from Cold Bay to Emmons Lake under Pavlof Volcano. Steam was coming out of the volcano covered in snow with a black ring around the vent hole. The majestic mountain looms over the entire area. The lake is at 2500 feet above sea level and was still frozen hard. There was no way to safely land the float plane on the lake, so I had to fly them to Sapsuk Lake instead. Sapsuk is also called Hoodoo Lake. I landed at the upper end of the lake and dropped off the two hunters.

Late this afternoon I received a message that one of my camp's propane cookstoves had stopped working. The storm outside was raging, and to be without a cookstove living in a tiny pup tent is not a

Sunday,
May 12, 2002

fun thing. I spent too many years on the ground as a guide, so I know what it is like to have the fifth most important piece of equipment fail. (Tent, sleeping bag, rain gear, and rifle are the first four on the list.)

I waited for a break in the storm, then took off from Cold Bay in my C-185 on amphibian floats. My mission was to deliver a new stove to Lee's camp at Hot Springs Bay. Just at the entrance to the bay, the weather turned very bad. A snow squall with strong winds made visibility drop to less than a half mile with a three-hundred-foot ceiling. I was forced to turn around and flee back to Cold Bay.

Before I got to Morzhovoi Bay, a squall was also in front of me. I turned around and tried to see if I could get back into Hot Springs Bay, but the entrance of the bay was still socked in. So I tried to get to the village of False Pass, but the turbulence was so severe that I was forced to turn around again. The visibility was very low, one-third of a mile at most, and the wind and turbulence were strong. To top it off, now I was starting to pick up ice. I had to find a place to land soon. The turbulence was now so strong, I was having a hard time keeping the plane in the air. The water below me was *way too rough* to land, so I had to find a sheltered place where the waves were not so big.

Hook Bay was close, and it may be as good a place to set down and wait out this fierce Aleutian storm. My windshield was iced up, and I could barely see the sand spit that creates Hook Bay. The spit lies between the Bering Sea and the channel that leads to False Pass. Picking a spot to land *now* was my only option! Things seemed to be working out as I touched down in the waves six hundred yards from shore. I will be on the beach and the plane on shore soon.

Thuuddd!

The very instant I thought I was out of trouble, I hit a sand bar, and I was stuck four hundred yards from shore. I got out and tried to get unstuck. *No way!* and the tide was going out. I was going to survive (at least until the tide came back in), but I might still lose the plane. If I lost the plane, I would be forced to swim for my life in the channel when the tide did come back in. I knew I would have to get to land before being swept out into the Bering Sea.

I was somewhat prepared to be in the frigid waters for short periods of time. I was wearing a three-millimeter set of neoprene chest waders. If I was in the water, this gave me at least thirty minutes of time that I can function. Without the neoprene, I had only seven to ten minutes of time that I could function. I put the anchor out and put tie-downs into the sand. The wind was at least forty knots, and the cold cut into my face and hands. My fingers, nose, and ears were growing numb very fast. The only choice I had now was to wait for the tide to come in and re-float the plane. I slept for a while in the plane.

Cub N4319Z near Cold Bay on Glen Island beach alongside the wooden remains of the two-masted schooner, Courtney Ford, wrecked in 1902.

The wind is now blowing from twenty to forty knots with gusts over fifty-two knots or sixty miles per hour. When a big gust hits, I wake up and hold my breath, hoping the tie-downs hold and keep the plane from flipping over onto its back. My laptop is with me, so I am writing down what has been happening. It is very dark now and the tide is coming in. Soon the water will be at the floats. The wind is steady at forty knots with gusting of at least fifty knots. Rain mixed with snow and blowing fog. The nose of the plane is, of course, facing into the wind. I hope as the water rises, the anchor and tie downs will hold. Only after the water is deep enough in front of me to get all the way to shore, can I cut the ropes and try to get to dry land. This is going to be a one-shot attempt. If I cut the ropes too soon and get stuck again before reaching the shore, I may have a gust strong enough to flip the plane since it will not have any tie-downs. Time to just wait and pray.

Money is tight for me after two different pilots each wrecked one of my airplanes, then with the $43K embezzled last year by my former secretary, I must save as much money as I can. I will not cut costs on the hunt as that would be unfair to both my clients and my guides. So, I only know of a few ways to cut costs: work harder and longer hours so I do not have to hire as many people. One of the ways that I am saving money is camping out on Russell Creek instead of staying at the Cold Bay Lodge or the Weathered Inn Hotel; that is saving me a hundred and twenty-five dollars a day.

Last night, some of the locals tried to rescue me; they drove out in the storm to Russell Creek and offered to take me back to their home and let me sleep on the couch. I did not accept the nice offer, though. I just want to be alone and enjoy the sound of the creek and watch the sun come up over the Bering Sea. I do not mind being alone when surrounded by spectacular beauty. Although, at times like this, I realize how lonely it is being single and wonder if I will ever meet someone. It is funny how clear things become when you do not know if you are going to live through the night. Many things are going through my mind. I have been blessed with a wonderful son, plus my mom, two brothers, and a sister who all love me. I have lived a life of extreme adventures and have seen and faced death plenty of times. It is time for me to try and spend the winters near my family. I want Jason to be able to spend more time with his cousins and aunts and uncles as well as his grandmother.

The plane is starting to rock. The water is rising fast now, and the floats will be floating soon. I can see the current is very strong. Soon it will be time to start the engine, cut the ropes, and then motor to shore. The wind is down to twenty-five knots, and this is going to work out.

Risking my life as a bush pilot may seem stupid to some folks. True, I have chosen a dangerous profession, but my job allows me the freedom to live my dreams. It's also true that, along with fighter pilots, crop dusters, firefighter pilots, and test pilots, on the spectrum of professional-pilot occupations, bush pilot resides on the extreme risk, far-wild-wilderness end. Couple bush pilot with wilderness guide, and the risk factor jumps exponentially.

Accepting the risk while being extremely knowledgeable and expertly proficient at what I do, I make a good living enjoying the lifestyle I love.

Life is more than work, though. It's made complete surrounded by those I love. From the beginning, all I ever wanted was to be in love with one good woman for the rest of my life and raise a family. I still believe it is possible to live a life filled with adventure and raise a family at the same time. I want to teach and show my family the wonders of the wilderness and the beauty of this planet that God created for us. Here, as a family-man and an Alaskan bush pilot, I believe I've succeeded. I have it all, including a wealth of friends. I'm rich beyond my wildest expectations.

I cannot get the engine to start. It tries, then dies as soon as I add power. The battery is almost dead. I am totally afloat. The three-eighths-inch rope that is attached to the anchor is stretched tight. That is the only thing keeping me from being swept out to sea. If the anchor pulls out or the rope breaks, I will be at the mercy of the Bering Sea.

The waves are huge only a half mile from where I am anchored, and they will pound my little plane to pieces. As it is, I am taking on water over the bow of the floats and have to keep them pumped out. Thankfully, all but two of the compartments are sealed. It is only the fish-hatch compartments that take on water.

It is time for me to swallow my pride, and set off the ELT and hope the Coast Guard picks up the signal. I left the sat phone in the Cub or I would also call for help.

At first light, I am trying to hand prop the plane because the battery is now dead. I saw that the air filter is covered with a sandy silt. It must have blown off the sand bar while I was waiting for the tide to come back in. The filter is completely clogged and will not let any air in, and that is why she will not start. Three quarters of an hour and I am still hand propping the stupid plane. I am about to invent new four-letter words for her and her stubborn Continental engine.

At last she fires and is running! We are inching forward into the wind. I cut the wing tie-down ropes with my knife as there is no way to remove them. The anchor rope is slack, so I start pulling in the rope being careful to stay clear of the prop. One big tug as we are past the anchor, and it is free. I jump into the pilot's seat, throw the anchor and rope in the back, then add half power. The shore is not far, and, to my surprise, she lifts off the water. Airborne, she seems to tell me *let's get the heck out of here and go to Cold Bay!* I am not prepared to be flying. The GPS is not on, my helmet is in the back, and my seat belt is hanging out the door, banging against the step. But we are in the air above the waves, so I turn her toward Cold Bay and hope the weather lets me make it there this time. In route, I open the door and get my seat belt on and set the GPS. It is 5:00 a.m. and no one is around when I land. I shut off the ELT, tie the plane down and crawl into the back and get back into my sleeping bag for some very-much-needed sleep. I wake up at 12:30 p.m. and what I just went through seems like a nightmare that did not really happen. But the dirty air filter on the copilot seat and my raw and bruised fingers from hand propping confirms it was all too real.

I have two clients arriving today at 2:30 p.m. I hope the wind dies down enough for me to get them out into the field.

The wind is too strong, and I remain grounded all day.

May 14— Today, Tuesday, the wind is still very strong and no flying for a while. Late in the afternoon, I try a flight with the Cub on wheels with a load of gear and no passengers. Wind is twenty-five knots with gusts to thirty-six knots. One of my hunters has a bear down, so I pick him up on my return and bring him back to Cold Bay. He gets sick in the rough air and fills a Ziplock with his lunch. The flight has gone okay, and I make a second flight with one of the waiting clients. The wind is picking up, and it is too rough to make any more trips, so I shut down and tie the plane down. The second client is understanding, and we eat dinner at the Cold Bay Lodge. At 8:00 a.m., the wind calms down, and we try again to get him out into the field. This time I get him out, and he is very happy to get into the field so he can hunt in the morning. I check on all the camps and everyone is okay.

May 15— First thing Wednesday, I flew Gary and his twelve-year-old son out to go beach combing for the day. Bill Martin and I took fresh food to three camps. The wind was blowing offshore at Deadman. I tried to land but the offshore wind made it too dangerous to land. Deadman has a whale washed up six hundred yards down the beach from the camp. With the offshore wind, I did not even try to go to the camp at Whale Bone as that is the most dangerous camp with an offshore wind. After the stops at the three camps, we flew to Unimak Island to look for steelhead and do some beach combing. We found a few Japanese glass fishing floats.[1] Saw lots of bears on the trip. Picked up Gary and his son at 9:00 p.m. They had a good time, and the weather was good for them. They found a hundred and seventy-seven Japanese glass balls and one of them was the larger, five-inch size.

May 16—I checked on all of my camps this Thursday, and everyone is fine. Jason and Garth were happy to get the fresh-food resupply. The camp at Hot Springs Bay with Lee and Rex as guides plus Riley as a packer and the two Cadwalter brothers are seeing a lot of bears. I dropped them off a full tub of food and talked to Rex for a while. The wind at Gary Hudson and John Gulious' camp was also blowing offshore. It was still not safe to land at John Harkey and Gerald Wernock's

---

[1] To learn more, see: https://en.wikipedia.org/wiki/Glass_float#History

camp at Whale Bone Cove, so I made a food drop to them as I flew over. The last camp I stopped at had a bear down, so I picked up the bear hide and brought it back to Cold Bay. Departing the last camp, I picked up a rock with the right-hand tire and threw it into the prop. The prop is ruined and no longer airworthy. I have grounded the Cub until I get a new prop. I left in the C-185 to go get the new prop for the Cub. Landed in Talkeetna at 12:30 a.m. Tired. I tied the plane down and got home at 1:00 a.m. Marie, the babysitter, went home as soon as I arrived. Jason woke up and was very glad to see me, and he sat next to me in my chair until 2:00 a.m. when he fell asleep. I carried him to his bed and tucked him in. It hurts me that I do not have a mother figure for him. I try to be a good dad, and I think I do an okay job, but I cannot provide him the things he needs from a mother. I believe that God intended kids to have a mother and dad who work together to raise the kids with love and guidance.

May 17— Jason and I slept until 10:00 a.m. this Friday. When I woke up, he was sleeping next to me on my bed wrapped in his blanket from his bed. We drove to Anchorage and did some food shopping for the camps. The new prop was not ready, so we saw two movies and spent the night in a hotel in Anchorage.

May 18— On Saturday, Jason and I went to the aviation trade show. We picked up the new prop at 12:00. I drove back to TKA. The C-185 has been serviced and the squawks fixed by my mechanic. I flew to King Salmon and landed at 11:30 p.m. Spent the night in the King Ko Inn.

May 19— Sunday, I flew to Cold Bay and checked on two camps. Very strong wind made it impossible to get to any other camps. I did airdrop some food to Jason and Garth's camp.

May 20— Monday. No planes had launched for a few days because of weather. Andy Greenblatt took off two minutes before me and headed to Little John. I was heading to a camp close to that, so we talked on the radio. It was too rough to get into that valley, so Andy turned around. I decided to continue and try a different camp to see if it was calmer there. I flew to Hot Springs Bay in the Cub and landed on the beach. Lee and Rex's clients both had bears. I loaded one of the clients named Bruce Cadwalter and his 10' 6" bear hide into the plane. Very turbulent, and it was a hard take off. The trip back to Cold Bay was very bumpy and rough. I waited an hour, then took a lady named Glenda and her fifteen-month-old grandson to her home in False Pass in the Cub. Bumpy ride. On the way back, I tried to land in Hot Springs Bay but, after two missed attempts to land, I headed home. I tried one more time and this time I got into Little John and picked up Jim Goff and brought him to the Cold Bay Lodge.

May 21— My first flight on Tuesday was in the PA-18 Super Cub. I flew fifty feet over the summit of Frosty Peak. This was an incredibly breathtaking view. Then I crossed Morzhovoi Bay near Egg Island. I then flew to Whale Bone Cove and Deadman Bay. I was not able to land because the tide and wind were not right. Then I flew to Hot Springs Bay. I was able to land and got the second client and took him to Cold Bay. The client was scared because of the turbulence, but it was the best flight I have had in a week. On my next flight, I flew the C-185 amphibian eighty miles to Sapsuk/Hoodoo Lake to get two clients and their two bears.

Cub flight to Little John/Morzhovoi Bay and picked up Todd, the guide. After returning from the two flights to Sapsuk, I made three flights in the C-185 to get Lee, Rex, Riley, and all the camp out of Hot Springs Bay. Then I made a flight to Whale Bone and Deadman in the PA-18 but was still not able to land as the tide was in all the way. I made airdrops of food to both camps. On the way back to Cold Bay, I made an airdrop of fresh food to Jason camp. This day started at 7:00 a.m. and finished at 12:45 a.m. the next morning. I flew 8.9 hours this day and made sixteen landings and three airdrops.

May 22— I worked on the PA-18. I changed the oil and changed a tail spring shimmy dampener. I replaced one spark plug and a few screws that had vibrated out. I was getting ready to take off when Andy Greenblatt flew in looking upset. He had one of his strips washed out and needed me and my float plane to fly out his client and guide. I agreed but told him to pick up my client and guide at Whale Bone for me while I got his two people. I had to do some maintenance on the float plane first. Andy returned without my client. The weather had rolled in and turned him back two miles from Whale Bone. The weather was so bad that we were grounded. One hour later, I got in the PA-18 and flew out to Whale Bone and picked up my client. The weather was okay for this flight.

I then got in the C-185 to try and get Andy's client. The lake that his people were on was fogged in, so I returned empty. Andy tried again to get my guide, but the weather was still bad.

May 23— Wind, rain, and a typical Aleutian storm is blowing forty-fifty knots with heavy rain. No flying today, and I got to catch up on my sleep. I slept an extra six hours this afternoon.

May 24— Grounded all day due to weather. Spent time in the Weathered Inn bar and had a good time playing shuffle board. I drank about three liters of water. The bartenders know me; as soon as I walk in, they get me an orange juice. The bar in Cold Bay is a gathering place for the locals and all who visit Cold Bay.

May 25— Last night at the bar, John from Flight Service told me about a pilot with one passenger who is missing and late on his return by three days. He is probably waiting out the storm, but they are getting worried. The Flight Service people tell me that the storm will last at least a day more. I talked to the guy on the radio as he was leaving, and he had never been to Unimak. I know him by reputation only, and he has a lot of Alaska experience. I may go out to see if he is stuck on the lake in the volcano on Unimak Island. He will be out of food by now. I will not be able to land but will do a food drop for him if I find him. I left Cold Bay with the storm blowing forty-plus knots with heavy rain. I had a wind of as much as seventy knots as I crossed over Apple Gate Cove at five hundred feet above the ground. Near Hot Springs Bay, the ceiling was down to two hundred feet and visibility was down to one mile. By the time I got to the end of Swanson Lagoon, it was getting better, and the wind was down to thirty knots.

Unimak Island is one of the most hostile places on earth, yet, at the same time, it is very beautiful. The plane was supposed to be somewhere on Unimak Island, perhaps near the Fisher Caldera. There are three lakes there; two are huge and one is a smaller one.

The smaller one is where I expected to find the missing plane as it is an incredible place and one of the wildest places on earth. It is the most beautiful spot on the whole island. That is where I would be camping if I were there in a float plane.

As I crossed over the ridge into the first lake, it became turbulent. I wanted to turn around and go home; I had a sick feeling in my gut, but I had this sick feeling since I knew I was to fly out here. One of the big bumps I hit sent the airdrop food flying around the cabin, and a can of chili hit me in the face. Well, it is lunch time, so a *Chili Smack* is appropriate I guess.

I was having trouble controlling the plane and started to turn around and run for home when it smoothed out. I checked out the shoreline of the first lake. No plane in sight. I checked out the shore of the second lake. Near the end of this lake, closest to the small lake, the plane was safely tied to a boulder on the shore. A tent was set up on the beach near the plane. I made a circle at six hundred feet above the camp and did not see anyone. The tent and plane looked to be in fine shape. I was not able to land and with no one in sight to drop the food to, I made a second circle with still no one in sight. The wind was at least forty knots on the ground. The spot that the pilot had picked out to anchor the plane and set up the tent was perfect with the wind blowing from the direction it was coming. I did not have anyone in sight, so I made the food drop from one hundred feet. It landed between the tent and the plane. I think they will find it. I suspect that they may be in one of the hot springs nearby. I returned the seventy-five miles to Cold Bay.

The weather really sucks, and I am glad to be on the ground. The Coast Guard helicopter that was looking for them had its navigation computer broken from flying in the storm looking for the missing plane. They are grounded in Cold Bay until they get it fixed. That is why I had to go out and continue the search myself. A C-130 from Kodiak just arrived bringing parts to fix the helicopter's navigation computer. They will be installing it now. After it is fixed this evening or in the morning, they will go to the coordinates I gave them and locate the pilot and his passenger to make sure they are okay. I believe they are only waiting out the storm. I do not know why they did not talk to me on the radio when I flew over. Perhaps they were out at one of the hot springs. The Coast Guard men and women are my heroes, they put their lives on the line constantly for the fishermen and pilots down here in the Aleutians. They fly day and night in the worst weather on this planet. They do rescues and body recoveries all the time.

Time for me to go to get some food and check with the FAA to see if anybody has any new info.

May 26— The missing pilot came to Cold Bay in his plane. I did not get to talk to him, but all was okay. Andy Greenblatt has a camp stuck on a lake. The storms have made his airstrip impossible to land on. I will fly his people out and in exchange he will do some of my wheel work with his Cub.

I made my first flight at 6:30 a.m. in the Cub, a flight to the camp at Morzhovoi Bay to pick up Jason and his client Garth Dal. The storm had pushed in kelp and made the beach unsafe and not landable for a plane on wheels, so I flew to Whale Bone Camp. Andy had picked up John Harkey, but there was still a load of gear to pick up.

My second flight was to Deadman to pick up Gary Hudson. It took three flights in the float plane to get Andy's camp and people out. Andy made a total of four flights in his Cub for me. I am thankful he more than made up for the flying I did for him in the C-185.

Now Rich Guthrie has camps stuck out because they are flooded. I made four flights in the float plane for him. The last flight, I landed in Cold Bay at 12:30 a.m. I still have one flight left for Rich. I have no daylight left so I will do it in the morning. I cannot leave people stuck out there. So the fact that I am doing this flying for him irritates me, especially when I came in on two of the four flights with a plane full of gear. I had to unload the plane by myself. Not a big deal, except it is not my gear!!! Rich and I have not always seen eye to eye but I must admit I am happier when I overhear Rich chewing out his guides for not making themselves available to help unload my plane.

May 27— At 6:30 a.m., I flew in and got the last person from Rich's camp in the float plane. The load is too heavy to get it all, and I left five full gas cans of outboard motor gas under his boat. Rich was upset that I left the gas. I told him to get them himself if they were that important to him. I only agreed to get the people out, and they were now out, and I did not care about his gas.

I made a trip to pick up some missed gear at Morzhovoi with the float plane. Now all my camps and gear and people were pulled from the field. My crew has been working hard getting the gear ready to ship while I have been flying.

May 28— Up early. I made a flight in the Cub with the Girl Scout coordinator. She has been trying to get to Nelson Lagoon for three days. I donated the flight because it is for a wonderful cause. Turns out that Heidi, the Girl Scout coordinator, and her husband are whitewater kayakers and have seen me in a few whitewater films. It's a small world sometimes. I did not get her to Nelson Lagoon. The fog stopped us halfway there, so I had to return. With everything shipped and mailed, we were ready to leave in the float plane at 3:30 p.m. I only had two guides to take home, Riley and Jason. I decided to offer Heidi another try at Nelson Lagoon. The catch was, if I could not land she had to go to Anchorage with us as I did not have time to return to Cold Bay.

She was out of time and was going to ANC anyway, so she jumped in for the flight as it saved the Girl Scouts six hundred and fifty dollars.

The wind at Nelson Lagoon was nineteen knots, a direct cross wind. Not good enough conditions for the heavily loaded amphib 185 to land on. We flew to Cape Seniavin near the Muddy River and saw over a hundred and fifty walrus. We saw beluga whales, gray whales, seals, sea otters, bear, moose, and caribou. Landed at King Salmon for gas and a bathroom stop. Flew directly to Talkeetna, and I landed at 11:50 p.m. on the lake next to my house. Jason was excited to see me, and I was excited to see him and be home. Marie, the baby-sitter took Heidi and the guide, Jason to Anchorage. Marie was happy to get home to her cats first and second to see her boyfriend.

Jason and I talked for a while, then I fell asleep in my chair. I woke up a few hours later, and he had covered me with a blanket and was sleeping on the couch next to me.

It is GOOD TO BE HOME.

A wild and rugged Cold Bay, Alaska, beach can be a lonely place to land a plane.

V.
Takin' It to the Next Level

The next chapters in Jerry's life exemplify his adventurous spirit to the max. From the devastating loss of family members and friends, to financial disasters compounded by ne'er-do-well business associates, these next chapters tell the story of love and laughter in times of disasters and hardships that few of us would recover from. Yet Jerry Jacques' perseverance in his plan to take life to the next level never included the words "give up."

Perhaps there's some inspiration in these next pages for all of us facing our own struggles to just laugh a little, love a lot, and—through it all— persevere as we take our own lives to that next level.

—CS Norwood

The Next Chapter

From its humble beginnings in 1978 when I was at my ripe-old age of twenty-one, the business had grown into a large guide and air service. With a lodge, cabins, tent camps, and aircraft operating in the Brooks Range, Alaska Range, Talkeetna Mountains, Iliamna, and on the Alaska Peninsula, my business was booming. It was large in scope, as well. Eleven hundred and eighty-three wild Alaska miles separated my farthest two camps. Since its beginning, countless incredible adventures had taken place all over Alaska, including dozens of first descents on whitewater rivers. The business was blessed and had become very successful. The downside was that I was always working, and my family suffered. This really hit me when my son Caleb was born January 2000.

The hunting business had changed over the years, I have no problem with hunting, it is a valuable tool for wildlife management, brings in a huge amount of money for saving and restoring wildlife habitat, and funds both research and management that is helping wildlife across the globe.

Making Plans to Get Out of the Hunting Business.

My issue is with a very small minority, a few wealthy hunters who have no respect for the wildlife. They are the hunters who only want to kill an animal for bragging rights and do not care about ethics; I detest this attitude.

As a professional hunter, I consistently led my clients to the largest bears and Dall sheep in Alaska, and, because of my reputation, I attracted many good hunters. Unfortunately, far too many of the disreputable hunters whose motivation for wanton killing of Alaska's big game (which I detested) also booked right along with those good hunters. There was just no way for me to separate the wheat from the chaff beforehand.

Over the years, it became apparent to me that I had grown to hate seeing bears die and often was rooting for the bears and not my clients' success. This was not fair to the ethical hunters. I knew I was no longer giving it my all, and it was time to get out of the hunting business.

As a starving young kid, Carl and Marge Jensen, highly respected *Dena'ina* elders, took me into their home in the village of Pedro Bay and became like parents to me. Carl had helped me get my start in the hunting business and taught me about the bears and how to survive in Alaska.

Twenty years later, I had this discussion with Carl and Marge—Mom and Pop to me now.

I told Pop that I wanted to get out of the hunting business.

At first Pop was upset!

"You are successfully carrying on a family tradition that I passed down to you and making a fantastic living," Pop said. "The hunting is the most profitable part of your business. Why would you want to turn your back on that?"

Pop wasn't happy. "You should just continue with the hunting."

Mom, however, interjected and said, "Carl! He is not happy and needs to follow his heart."

I'll never know what the conversation between them sounded like that night, but the next day at breakfast, Pop came with a smile and said, "Okay, I get it. Do what you need to do to be happy and take care of your family."

Exit From the Hunting Business

I had one very good cash offer from an outfitter who wanted to buy my hunting concessions. The problem was, he had no interest in keeping my crew working which didn't sit well with me. Ultimately, I decided to sell the hunting business to one of my guides. With no money down and a promissory note of payments over five years, we made the deal. I was only selling the hunting business but agreed to let him use my lodge in Talkeetna, so he had a base of operations. I also agreed to lease him my Super Cub during the hunting seasons. I structured the payments in such a way that the business could easily afford to make the payments. This was an interesting step for me as the hunting business was making me a very good living and was booked years in advance.

However, I just wanted to go back to my roots and passions of wildlife photography and river trips.

Rhonda and I also wanted to get sons Matt, Jason, and Caleb into a better school environment. A private Christian school near Grants Pass, Oregon, called Vineyard looked perfect.

I still needed to make a living, so I purchased Sundance Expeditions & Kayak School based on the Rogue River in Southern Oregon. My plan was to start running photo safaris in Alaska and river trips in Oregon and Alaska. Operating on the Rogue and other western rivers, Sundance was a respected whitewater rafting company and the oldest whitewater kayaking school in the west.

I felt this would be a perfect platform using Sundance's massive mailing list to advertise the non-consumptive wilderness trips in Alaska and continue its trips in Oregon. I did several three-day trips down the Rogue River and saw the Sundance crew was very solid and ran the trips just fine without me. This left me free to split my time between Oregon and Alaska.

Matt and Jason adapted well to school in Oregon and loved learning to kayak on the warm waters of the Rogue River. Caleb was still very young but enjoyed riding in the drift boat with me on the gentle sections of the Rogue.

I kept a personal Cessna 185 and a Piper Super Cub so I could run photography trips each summer in Alaska.

Back in Pedro Bay, Alaska, for a photo trip, I was sitting in the living room with Mom and Pop Jensen and said, "I need some help."

"How can we help?" Mom said.

I explained now that I was trying to attract photographers instead of hunters; the name "Hunt Alaska with Jerry Jacques" was not a good company name for what I had in mind now.

"Help me come up with a new company name."

Long before the white man came to Alaska, Pop's family called the bears *K'ahdil'ani*. Translated, it means large grizzly bear. Pop suggested Alaska K'ahdil'ani Safaris, but then said none of my prospective clients would know what K'ahdil'ani meant.

After a lot of thought, the three of us decided "Alaska Grizzly Safaris" was a good name. Pop and Mom Jensen were the epitome of who Alaskan's are.

"Thank you, Mom and Pop!" I miss them more than I can say.

"...it was time to get out of the hunting business."
—JJ

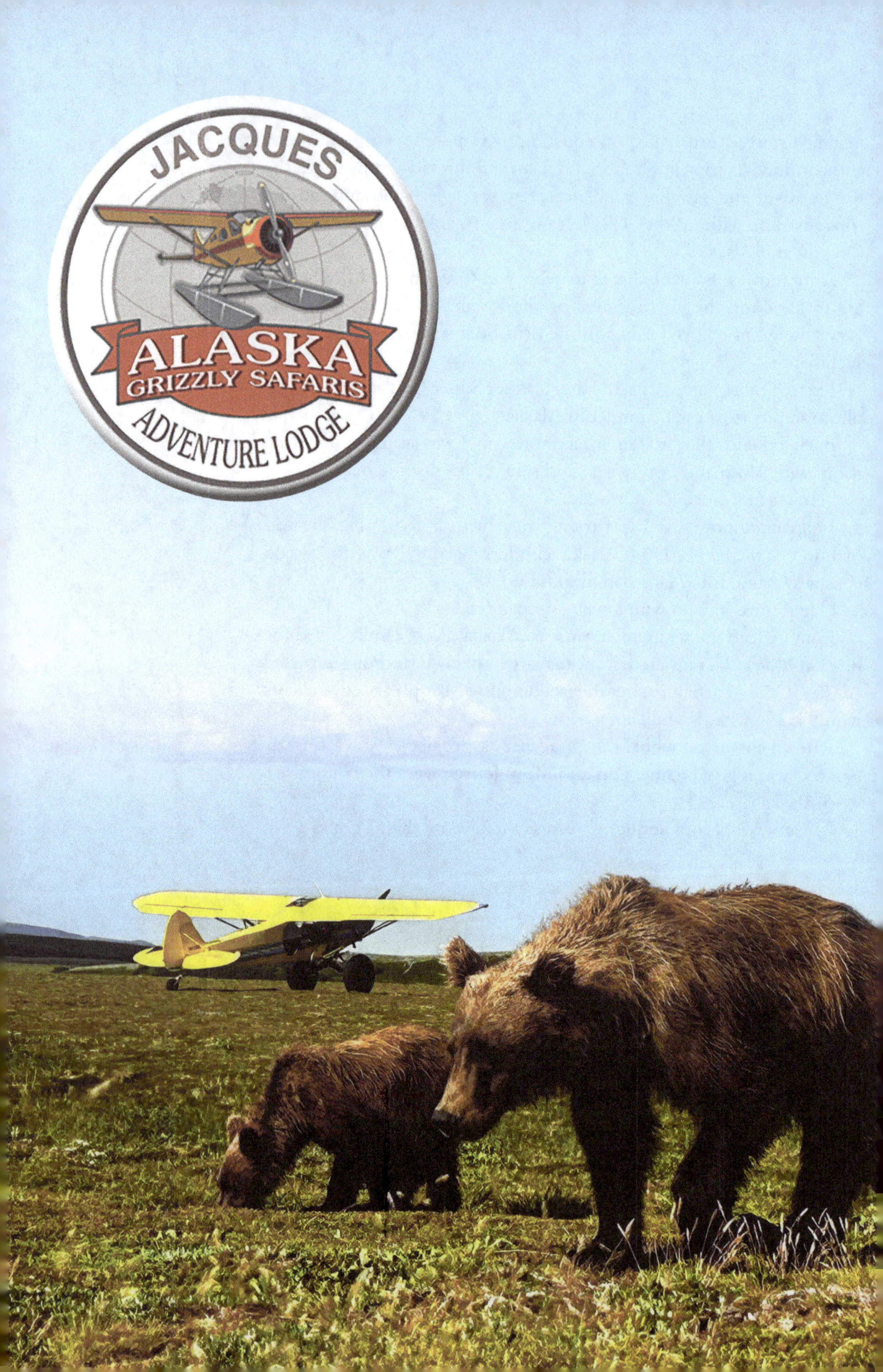
JACQUES
ALASKA
GRIZZLY SAFARIS
ADVENTURE LODGE

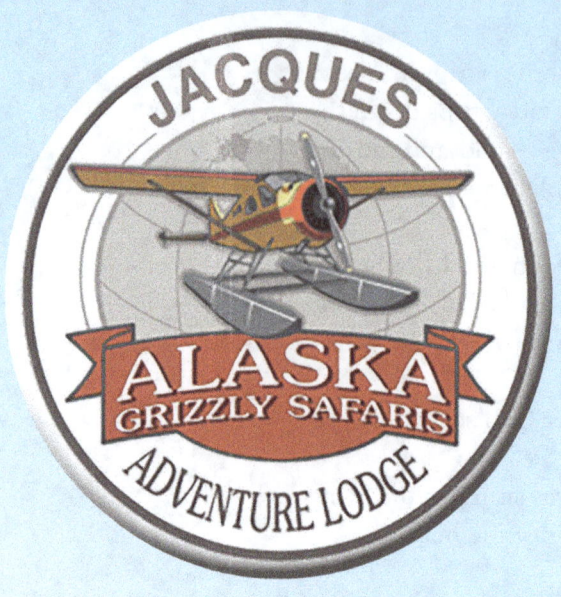

Tragedy in May

May 21, 2004—I got a call from the Alaska State Troopers that my Super Cub, N4319Z, had crashed. My friend and guide Gary Hudson had been killed, and the pilot was not expected to survive. I had sold the business but still owned the aircraft. The troopers were trying to locate and notify Gary's family. I volunteered to fly to Scappoose, Oregon, and personally deliver the horrendous news to Gary's family. Gary worked for me for eight years and became a good friend. It was one of the hardest tasks I had ever had. When I arrived at the Hudson's home, the whole family was waiting at the kitchen table: Gary's wife, two daughters, one son, and their respective spouses. They knew something bad had happened but were still hoping. Face-to-face, I broke the horrible news. Lots of tears and questions followed. I told them what I knew.

I had sold my company and had leased my plane to the new owner. He had hired a pilot who was flying Gary when the accident happened.

The state troopers contacted me as I was the owner of the plane.

I had gotten details from them and from people involved in the rescue. It was the last flight of the season; the pilot flying my Piper Super Cub had taken off from a small lake sixty-five miles from Cold Bay with Gary in the back seat. Ten miles from the destination float-plane pond, Blinn Lake, the pilot made a normal radio call to Flight Service. That was the last anyone heard from them. After a few hours, a search was started, and the wreckage was found. A volunteer rescue crew got to the plane and found the pilot, barely alive. Gary was killed on impact. They did not expect the pilot to survive.

I had talked to both the FAA and the NTSB and was shocked that they were not going to go to the crash site. ["The site of the accident was visited by the IIC and a FAA inspector on July 20. During an inspection of the wreckage by the IIC at a storage yard in Cold Bay on July 20, photographs of the wreckage taken at the accident site were provided by emergency responders who recovered the pilot and passenger." (NTSB page 4 of 8 ANC04FA056)].[1] Bill Martin, a legendary lodge owner and pilot who now lived in Cold Bay, told me that I should get there ASAP, the pilot said the engine quit and that's why he crashed.

Pete Huckins, who owned a King Air C-90, offered to fly me from

---

[1] For more information, search the Air Safety Network accident report for N4319Z

Oregon to Cold Bay so I could see the crash site for myself.

What Pete and I found was water in the left fuel tank; that must have caused the engine to quit.

At Blinn Lake, the floatplane lake, we found five-gallon gas cans that were used to fill the plane sitting outside in the rain, and two were not sealed. In Pete's and my opinion, sloppy fuel management let water get into the plane's gas tank.

From here things unraveled fast. The kid I had sold the hunting business to was due to make his first balloon payment to me, but he disappeared.

The valuable hunting concessions were taken away, two years of clients were booked, and their fifty-percent deposits had been spent by the kid who had disappeared. *Technically and legally, I was neither responsible nor obligated to honor those hunts*, but both my name and my reputation were used to book the hunters, and I felt responsible to fulfill the hunt contracts.

It would cost me every dime of my personal savings to honor those bookings at what was now half price—less than enough to cover expenses. My wife, Rhonda, was dead set against me spending the money or getting back into the hunting business. As a man, I felt that I was now a man without a choice, I had given my word that I would honor every commitment that was made using my name.

It was a Catch 22 situation for me.

With all the financial pressure, the threat of a lawsuit, and me working every waking moment, Rhonda decided that she had had enough. She took Matt and Caleb and fled the state. I can't say I blame her. It was a dark time.

She agreed to return when things settled down.

After a year, I was still head down and working nineteen hours a day trying to keep everything together. Rhonda was still out of state, lonely, and had found someone else. She wanted a divorce.

We had a simple, no fight divorce, and she remarried. Even though I was heartbroken, Rhonda and I remained good friends through it all, and she let Matt spend the summers with me as well as let me visit young Caleb as often as I could.

The next two years are still a bit of a blur for me. I was back to being a single parent, trying to run two businesses. Financially, things were tough; in the blink of an eye, I had gone from financially well off to being deep in debt. I was forced to take on contract-flying jobs in addition to running the two businesses.

After two years of hard, nose-to-the-grindstone work, I was steadily getting back on track and out of debt. The light at the end of this tunnel was such a welcoming sight.

I was at my lodge on Lake Iliamna in 2006, and we had a cook at the time named Saul. He would borrow my laptop pretty much every day for his own use. I was busy with my flying and everything else and didn't need it at the time. One evening when I didn't have to fly the next day, I came in and told Saul that I would like my laptop. He was all smiles, closed down what he was doing, and we got talking before I left and went back to my room with the laptop. I asked him what he was doing, and he said, "Ah, I've been on this on-line dating site." And I kind of took a step back and said, "I believe that stuff is really bad. Both my brothers are federal law enforcement, and they warned me to stay away from that stuff."

"Oh, no, it's not that bad. You just have to know how to do it… what sites to avoid. Yeah, there are some people on there that you have to watch out for, but there are some who you like."

"Well, you know, I have trouble meeting women. The fishing business is predominantly men. The hunting business is predominantly men. Besides that, I have a set rule for myself that I won't ever date someone I'm working with. I just feel like that's a bad scenario, especially in the seasonal business. I just think it's a bad idea," I said.

He said, "Yeah, I told her this."

I said, "No way!" I had been working with him for several months at this point, so he knew me a little bit. We talked for a while, then I took my laptop and didn't think much more of it.

About four or five days later, I went to grab the laptop back from him, and he said, "So, have you checked your dating app page?" I didn't know what he was talking about. Well, without my permission, he had put a bio up for me on a site called "Christian Singles," or something like that. At first, I was pretty mad that he'd done it. He assumed my identity without showing it to me. I was actually pissed to be honest. Finally, though, curiosity got the best of me. So I ended up looking at some of his responses of the ad that he put up for me, and there were about fifteen or sixteen responses. I found some of them looked interesting and went back on and talked to Saul and he said, "Ah, you can't do anything with this one. This one isn't real. It's a 'player' (as he called it), but these other two, I think they might be legitimate!"

So I responded to the two of them, and it didn't take long before Laura and I started chatting. Her brother had worked in Alaska as a guide for an outfitter that I knew. (I soon realized that I had met her brother.) We chatted for a while, and then I gave her my phone number, and we talked over the next month. I thought she sounded

And Then I Met Laura

interesting, so I used some of my contacts to get a background search to make sure she didn't have a husband. She was an attorney, and she was widowed. She had four kids. All of that checked out. After a while, I said, "Well, you know, if we're going to meet, you need to see what I do and what my lifestyle is like. It's very different than anything in the norm. So, I told her I'd buy her a ticket to Iliamna from Idaho, and she agreed to fly up to meet me.

When I told Saul that, he went nuts! He said, "That's not how you do this. You never do that! You either go see the lady, or she comes and sees you! You don't buy her tickets! That's bad!" He was all upset and got me second-guessing, but I wasn't going to go back on my word. I already bought the ticket.

Although Laura came up to the lodge towards the end of the season, it was still very busy.

I had arranged my schedule on the day her flight landed so I could meet her air taxi between my flights. When I got to the airport, I was informed that her flight was going to be two hours late. Well, that wasn't going to work. I had to go do my next flight; I had people out in the field to pick up. I was gone for about three hours, and by the time I got back to the airport, she'd already been waiting for an hour—probably not a great first-impression, unfortunately.

I gave her a private room at the lodge, and we spent the rest of the evening talking. I still had plenty of work the next day but finished it all

Laura,
the love of my life,
flying with me

early; then we had our first real date. My Super Cub with the big tires was parked in the backyard of the lodge. We jumped in and flew out to Katmai National Park, to one of my favorite wilderness locations to look at the bears.

There were lots of bears out on our first date. It was late in the evening, and we had one very large, aggressive boar who only came out late in the day. This behemoth did not like people, acted aggressively, and was very much a potential problem bear. As we were watching these other bears fishing and catching fish in the river, this big boar came out. He was heading straight towards the river with Laura and me in between him and his destination. I told her to stand up, but he didn't detour, and he wasn't deterred by our presence. He was coming straight at us.

"Get behind me," I told her, never taking my eyes off that big bear. Then I pulled out my handgun, something I rarely did with these bears. This guy just kept coming, though. I was pretty much in a face-off with this aggressive bad-boy, and it seemed like I was going to have to pull rank on him, until at about thirty feet, he finally decided I wasn't going to back down. He dropped his head and veered off. Going around us, he ambled down to the river and started fishing as if nothing had happened.

Laura and I went back to the lodge. I was impressed by how calm she was all during that potentially dangerous situation with this bear. She had never been close to grizzlies before, let alone an aggressive bear.

Laura loved the wilderness, and that impressed me, too.

On our second date, we went out and fished for silver salmon, flying out again in the Super Cub. This time I was landing on the beach on the outer part of Cook Inlet, also in Katmai National Park. We got a couple of silvers, and I filleted one and got a fire going. I had some spices with me and used a plank and cooked it right there on the beach. As the evening wore on, I realized that I was very much smitten by this lady and that she was everything that I had been looking for.

She stayed the week at the lodge. We did one more bear-viewing trip together and did some flying together in the Beaver. It was a fantastic week at the very end of the season.

It was time for me to get Jason back to school now, and I had worked it out so I could have a few days off. Jason, Laura, and I went back to Anchorage, caught a flight, and flew to Seattle together. Then she took a flight from Seattle to Boise, and my flight was back down to Oregon where I had Jason in a private school. He was staying in Oregon for the winter, and I had a small business, a kayaking school and rafting business called Sundance Kayak School in Oregon on the Rogue River, so I stopped there for a while to check on the business.

At the end of the season when it was all the way over and the lodge was locked up, I pulled my Cessna 185 off the floats, and it was now on wheels. I flew it down to Oregon and was there with Jason in school. We had one long weekend together in late September into early October, so we flew over to Twin Falls Airport where Laura met us. I had all the camping gear already packed in the Cessna, and we flew up to a hot spring in the Idaho backcountry. I actually had to make two flights with her and the four kids and Jason and all the camping gear. I took Laura and the younger kids in the first flight, and Jason, who was a freshman in high school then, and Laura's oldest daughter, Corine, stayed behind till I came back for the second load and got them. We had a great weekend camping at the hot springs.

By the end of our long weekend, we had gotten rid of enough fuel and food that the load on the Cessna was light enough that I could fly back all our gear along with everyone at once. I dropped Laura and her kids off in Twin Falls and Jason and I went back to Oregon so he could continue school.

On the sixteenth of December, three months after our first meeting, Laura and I were married.

Caleb's Mom   I was married to Laura now, but Caleb's mom, Rhonda, was dying. We had remained friends despite our divorce, but now she had become very ill.

Laura, my amazing new wife, graciously helped me see Rhonda through her final days, and I will be forever grateful for her kindness.

We may be able to stow away grief in order to continue our lives, but sadness like this never really remains hidden forever. Rhonda's passing is still hard for me to talk about.

One of the most difficult days of my life was the day I had to break the news to our young son, Caleb, that his mom had died suddenly of a pulmonary embolism.

Rhonda was loved, and she is missed.

21.
Hijack 'n the Bears

Email, June 24

Hello all,

Back flying in Alaska. Most days I love my job; it is a lot of hard work with long hours, but I thank God I can work and fly in this incredible land He created. Most days, I have the best job in the world. Yesterday was not one of Iliamna's wonderful days, however. The weather was horrible—strong winds, rain, and low ceiling. At 6:00 a.m., I gassed up my plane, and, by the time I had put the gas in, pumped out the floats, and pre-flighted the plane, I was soaking wet with the wind blowing the rain up my sleeves and down the back of my neck. My first flight was from the lodge to the mouth of the Iliamna River where it flows into Lake Iliamna on the east end of the lake. It was very cold and rainy, and, with the wind, it was hard to just launch the plane at the lodge. I had to unload the clients and have everyone help turn the plane around until I got the engine started. Take off in the big waves was very bumpy and scared one of the clients. He kept burping, gagging, and gasping into the mic on his headset—distracting and not very encouraging sounds.

The landing forty minutes later was also very rough, the wind was so strong the other plane could not get to the place where we had the boats parked. The boat had to go out into the lake and unload the clients on the lake while the waves pounded the plane and the boat. When I flew in to pick up that group of clients at 3:30 p.m., it was so rough the other plane could not land. I had to wait seven hours before I could take off again. I was soaking wet and cold the whole day. The seven-hour delay was not what I wanted. When I finally took off at 10:45 p.m., I was shivering and thankful to be able to have the heater warm up my hands. The landing back at the lodge was in big waves but was uneventful. Back at the dock, I found out one of the clients had thrown up in the plane on the trip—he had used my hat to throw up in. *Yuck!* I had to clean the plane and throw away my hat. One of the guides and one of my clients had to spend the night at the river, as it was too windy and turbulent for me to make another trip. They spent the night in a lodge located one mile upstream from the mouth of the river. The Guth Family owned the lodge and graciously took them in for the night.

It was past midnight before I got to the bunk house—wet, cold, and exhausted. I picked up my guide and client this morning and brought them back to the lodge.

On stressful days like yesterday, I thank God that no one got hurt. The weather was better today but still windy. I flew to the King Salmon Camp on the Nushagak River and took supplies to the guides there. I had to bring one of the guides back as he had cut himself with an ax; the other guide played doctor and put seven stitches in his hand—without anything for the pain. He needed to come in to get antibiotics and have the nurse look at his hand. I will fly him back in the morning. I am ready for an early bed tonight and hope to be asleep in twenty minutes or less.

July 23— This was the day my Jack Russel pup, Hijack, met his first grizzly. I had landed the Beaver on the Kamishak River along the outer Cook Inlet and dropped off three guides. They had taken one of the jet boats upriver to learn the river. I took the other boat and my pup downriver, just exploring the coastline for fun. After a few hours, I had to make a nature call. I was sitting on a log with my pants down around my ankles taking care of business, when an adult grizzly came

Me & my son, Caleb, with Hijack

walking up the beach. I first spotted the bear at ninety yards. This was a good teaching moment for the pup, so I started to growl. Hijack just looked at me for a few moments, until I swapped him around to face the approaching bear. The pup got the idea and started growling with me as the bear kept on its path in our direction.

This bear was not being aggressive, just walking the beach. As I was pulling up my pants, the bear was now forty yards away when little Hijack suddenly bolted ten yards forward barking as loud as he could. I stood up on top of the log and waved my arms. The bear was not concerned about us and just turned forty-five degrees and wandered off. The pup thought it had just run off the bear with its barking. He was the top dog—enormously proud of himself.

A few weeks later, we were in our room when the pup barked

once, then growled. I looked up from filling out my pilot logbook only for a moment, then went back to writing. Fifteen minutes later I heard a gunshot. I grabbed my .44 Mag, and the pup and I went out to investigate. Joe and two guides were standing on the trail between the lodge and the garbage pit yelling at something. When we got next to them, we could see the tail end of a grizzly with its head in the incinerator. Joe, who does not like my pup, Hijack, because he also gets into the garbage pit, said the bear would not leave and they could not burn the garbage, Joe had even fired his .357 into the air trying to scare the bear away but the shot had no effect. I picked up a rock and the pup and I took off running full speed at the bear. With my .44 in one hand and a rock in the other, we ran straight at the bear with the pup barking and me yelling like a wild man. The pup acted like he was going to bite that bear in the butt for stealing the food from his garbage pit. When we were twenty feet away, the bear turned and ran, but not before I hit it in the butt with the rock.

I think Hijack would have tried to take a bite out of the bear if it had not run away. He doesn't know he's a little dog; he seems to think he's the size of a bear. Jack Russell Terriers or JRTs are fast and fearless. Sometimes I think it's a good thing they're so small.

July 24— The pup and I chased the bear away from the lodge and into the alders near the lake. Forty-five minutes later, though, the grizzly was back. The pup barked and lunged toward the bear, but I grabbed him by the harness and handed him to the cook. Hijack looked at me as if to say, *"How humiliating!"*

With my .44 in hand, I went after the bear and hit it in the butt with a shot shell. It only stung the bear, and it ran into the lake to cool off its butt. The bear stayed clear for the rest of night.

July 25— The golden retriever and Hijack chased the bear away from the main lodge again today. The grizzly has been returning to the lodge at least once every day or during the night. She tears into the incinerator and drags garbage all over the place making a nasty mess. With clients going from the lodge to the cabins at all hours of the day and night, the bear has become a dangerous pest. I am afraid she's going to get shot one of these days, if not by someone from our lodge, then by someone at the lodge around the bay from us. This bear must learn very soon to stay clear of the lodge or she will have to be killed.

I'm trying to save her life by carrying a can of bear spray with me, hoping to catch her near the dump. If I can bear-spray her in the act of raiding the incinerator, I can teach her to stay away.

July 26— After two days of carrying the pepper spray around with me, I have not been able to get close enough to spray her. She has learned my scent and takes off running as soon as she sees or smells me. The rock and the bird shot in the butt taught her to avoid me.

I have killed over two-hundred bears during my career as a guide. I am not opposed to the use of deadly force, when necessary, but I do not want to see this bear die just because she has become used to getting into the dump.

This problem is man-made and not the fault of the bear. I have one last trick that I hope will work. I had one of the staff put bacon and Crisco on the can of bear spray. Then he hung the bear spray on the door of the incinerator. I did not want my scent on the can. Hopefully, when she comes in to dig in the incinerator, she will bite the can and get a mouth and face full of pepper spray. This may help to teach her to stay away. At least I hope it will.

Around eleven o'clock that night, the pup barked one time, then growled as I was reading. I hoped it was the bear as I wanted to see her reaction when she bit into the pepper spray, I grabbed my .44 and snuck out to the incinerator to watch. No bear, just a cold, wet butt from sitting on a wet log in the rain. I was cold, tired, and soaking wet when I got back to my room. My .44 was also wet, so I cleaned it and laid it next to my bed along with the .45 ACP lightweight Commander. I took a hot shower to warm up and was out before my head hit the pillow.

The grizzly returned to the lodge five hours later. I was sound asleep when the pup started growling. I grabbed my .44 and headed out the door wearing only my skivvies. It was just starting to get light as I stalked down the narrow trail through the alder thicket to the incinerator. Just as I was starting to see the outline of the incinerator in the poor light, I heard the sound of compressed air escaping from the ruptured can of bear spray. At once, the bear blasted all the air in her lungs out her nose; it sounded like a very loud half sneeze, half woof. The next thing I knew, she was crashing through the alder thicket—toward me!

What happened next is so embarrassing I have not yet admitted it to the staff, and I'm not sure I will until the season is over, if ever. After all, I am the Master Guide with thirty years' experience dealing with grizzly bears.

She broke out on the trail fifteen feet from me at a full charge. I had just enough time to raise and level my .44. I saw my front sight and was starting to pull the trigger while loudly yelling something I will not repeat. She heard the yell and saw me at the same time; she spun around, swapping ends so fast she was a blur, her feet spinning out as she did her best to get traction. She was so terrified, she squirted out a stream of the blackest, smelliest, foulest skat you can imagine. It plastered the trail in front of me and splattered my bare legs and feet. The whole thing was disgusting, but she had been scared off—gone back into the night.

It took me a minute to get my composure back before I turned and walked back toward the lodge. I used the hose in an attempt to rinse off my legs and feet. I suppose I wasn't entirely successful, though, because the minute I opened the door to my room, the pup growled just like he was growling at the bear. He wanted nothing to do with me. As I headed for the shower once again, I stood my .44 next to the bed. That's when I noticed the six rounds of ammo that I had unloaded earlier, before I had cleaned the gun hours ago—I had confronted that grizzly in my skivvies, with nothing between me and that surly bear except my own surly voice and an empty gun.

Email, July 31   Four clients and I flew the eight-seat de Havilland DHC-2 Beaver to the Kokolik River to fish. There is a short place to land a float plane on the river, and the lodge has a boat cached there. As we approached, we could see a grizzly bear in the middle of the landing spot; she was fishing for salmon. I added a little more flap, pulled back on the power a little more, and slowed the Beaver down, landing in true STOL fashion a hundred feet shorter than normal. She hadn't moved, so I taxied the plane right next to her. She did not like the plane, or the nine-cylinder, R-985 Pratt & Whitney engine (which sounds like a giant Harley engine) and swam to shore. When she got onto shore, two cubs came out of the willows and ran next to her as she half ran, half walked down the riverbank heading straight for the boat. We were also going downriver and stayed fifty yards from her. In forty-five seconds, she was next to the boat. This was the same sow with the trouble-making twins from last year that kept eating life jackets and pooping in the boat, leaving me a mixture of fish, white closed-cell foam, grass, orange nylon, and berries to clean up—what a stinking mess! But I was pleased to see how much the cubs had grown since last September.

As I taxied in to shore, the boat was between the plane and the three bears. Momma grizzly jumped right into the boat and started jumping up and down with all four feet, stomping like a kid throwing a temper tantrum. Still raging at our intrusion, she grabbed a five-gallon plastic gas can in her mouth and threw it out of the boat. The can, full of gas, sailed through the air, landing at least thirty feet back onto the tundra. Then she did the same thing to two more full five-gallon gas cans. Next, she jumped out of the boat, ran to the cans, and stomped each one into the tundra. Finished with her tantrum, she looked at us for a moment (I think she stuck her tongue out at us), turned her back, and wandered off with her cubs trailing behind. I had to stop laughing before I could beach the plane, After tying the plane up, we went to see the cans, they were half buried in the tundra with two leaking gas where she had bitten holes in them. Even at $6.98 a gallon with six gallons lost, I still could not stop laughing.

I am still laughing, so I thought I would share this with the rest of you.

August 26— Good News! The bear has not returned, and the pup is back to being my buddy again.

I have been privileged to fly over all of Alaska's amazing landscape and had the opportunity to kayak or raft more than twelve-thousand miles down Alaska's wild and wonderful rivers. Over the years and along the way, I've met up with many bears—a few sudden meetups were a little "touch-and-go," but these two funny encounters with cantankerous grizzlies remind me how truly blessed I've been in my life-long career as an Alaska master wilderness guide.

22

Escape from Chad

This news article appeared in the Shetland Times on 25 July 2008. I will neither confirm nor deny anything in the article, but I will admit that I've flown in Africa, and I did fly the Twin Otter into the Shetland Islands. Because of nondisclosure agreements, this is all I can legally say. Along with the fact that I just appeared in their airspace, my camouflaged TO was an unusual sight at Tingwall Airport, Shetland, UK, which prompted an interview and subsequent article from local reporter, Mark Burges.

Shetland Times
News Article

Shetland Times News Article

Pilot's desperate escape from Chad and chilling mid-air refueling stunt.

Shetland Times
July 25, 2008
By Mark Burges

The distinctive form and livery of the former Norwegian military de Havilland Twin Otter aircraft at Tingwall Airport over the weekend may have drawn an interested glance or raised eyebrow from passersby on the roads west or north, but few could have imagined the extraordinary story of the journey that took her to the calm and friendly Shetland airstrip.

Piloted by American Jerry Jacques to Shetland from Africa, the events that took him here are almost guaranteed to leave anyone in stunned admiration. Based in the USA, Jerry and his business partners were employed under contract to provide a transport aircraft to the relief operations in war-torn Chad by companies acting between relief agencies and the government. Chad is currently considered to be one of the poorest and most corrupt nations in Africa, with increased oil developments since 2003 doing little to stabilize a country under almost constant threat of revolution.

While flying there, it was necessary for Jerry to check the aircraft for bullet holes during daily operations transporting people, livestock, and food within the hostile country. After long months of no payment and constant danger, Jerry's open intentions to leave Chad with the plane were thwarted by a local agent's removal of his long-range fuel tank, charts, and survival gear in an attempt to guarantee that he and the aero plane remain in Chad.

In what is the stuff of aviation legend, Jerry spent two weeks planning an escape that would get him clear of both Chad and its equally hostile neighbors; and so it came to be that he took off from Chad one day with apparently innocuous barrels of fuel in the plane's cargo hold, some plastic tubing, a National Geographic map for navigation, some accumulated water bottles, rudimentary survival kit of an ax, knife, and whatever else he could conceal from what were effectively now his captors.

With the maximum range of the aircraft keeping him within the airspace of Chad his plan now took a turn for the heroic, or perhaps plain crazy. To guarantee his escape, he had to refuel the Twin Otter from outside the aircraft whilst in flight.

To facilitate this, he climbed above the range of the stinger missiles used in the region and, with no autopilot, trimmed the aircraft to fly straight and level. He then attached a rope from his webbing trouser belt to the cockpit harness and attached a length of hose to the barrel and exited the cockpit through the side door at 12,000 feet with the plane traveling at around 100mph.

With one hand holding him to the doorframe and standing on the tiny fuselage footstep, he used his other hand to feed the hose into the external fill point of the plane's underbelly tank.

As Jerry says, he was reasonably confident that had he slipped during this maneuver he could have hauled himself back into the cockpit, but the matter was far from certain, and he has understandably dreamt of these moments every night since.

All the more pertinent when you see the proximity of the Twin Otter's propeller to the position he was perched in. His success in this technique not only left him alive but also got him into friendly airspace, whereby he has hopped from country to country through Europe and Norway to Shetland.

This is roughly halfway home with a further 10 stops in prospect in Faroe, Iceland, Greenland, and Canada. Jerry remains remarkably un-fazed by this adventure, perhaps due in part to the nature of the routine flying he is engaged in back home.

He has spent all of his working life from 18 years old flying light aircraft commercially, splitting his year between Alaska and third world countries. In the rugged mountains and lakes of Alaska, he was chartered for hunting and fishing tours, flying to remote lakes in float-planes or flat ground or sandbars in wheeled planes to deliver hunters to their prey of moose or massive bears up to 700kg, anglers to monster fish, or to deliver whitewater rafters upstream to return via the river.

A typical governmental charter he relates is vermin control that requires pilots to fly between 25 and 50 ft off the ground while a gunner dispatches coyotes with a shotgun from the back seat at 60mph.

He has also flown for similar charters in southern Africa and swapped posts with adventure tour operators in central America. Even Jerry's aircraft, built in 1966, could tell many a tale and was equipped to carry the royal standard, for transporting royalty, during its time with the Norwegian Military. The twin-engine aircraft is ideal for skydiving charters which must seem surprisingly tame in comparison to its pilot's backwoods exploits. Jerry had actually retired four years ago before a change in his home life drew him back to aviation.

With great humility Jerry describes his home life as more exciting than flying and is eager to get home to the wife and 7 kids that await him in Alaska. He describes his time in Shetland as a lot of fun and enjoyable and "a really pretty place" that reminds him of the landscape and scenery of remote western Alaska, albeit much more developed. He expressed much gratitude to engineers John and Matt of Tingwall Airport and pilot Marshall Wishart for going out of their way to assist him on his journey. (Burgess 2008)

On the tarmac with the Twin Otter aircraft

23.
Notes from War Zones

After returning home from Africa I got a call from an old friend of Ron Sutphin's. He asked me if I wanted to fly for the US State Department as a special ops pilot in Afghanistan. I was all in. Flying US soldiers in and out of forward operating bases was fun and incredibly rewarding. Flying half the year in Afghanistan and spending the other half at home in Alaska, I had more time for family and time to play, yet I was flying meaningful missions again just for fun—although it *was* in a war zone. In 2008, there was a bounty offered by the Taliban of $25,000 for the head of any pilot citizens could turn in. By the time I left in 2010, the bounty had increased to $50,000 a head. That was a strong incentive to kill or capture special ops pilots as the average Afghani male outside of cities made, on average, $1200 a year. Looking back on my Afghan and later my Ukraine notes may provide a little insight into the life of a pilot in a war zone. I arrived in Afghanistan in 2009.

Afghanistan 2009

December 20— Did four flights today.

On the first flight, I saw another aircraft deploy its countermeasure flares in the distance. The flares are spectacular to see. We never heard anything of a plane being fired at, so the flares were most likely launched by mistake.

December 22— Afghanistan's Midnight Ice Follies—The show started at around 3:00 a.m. I got up, put my boots and jacket on, then headed out of my tent. As I walked outside, I noticed it was snowing and very dark. It was time for a long-postponed trip to the bathroom. From the squad tent I live in, the hundred yards [walk] to the bathroom is burned into memory so no flashlight is required. Besides, in the Afghan war zone, walking around outside at night with a flashlight is an open invitation for the Taliban to take a potshot at you.

I slowed my pace down forty feet before reaching the bathroom as the overflow of raw sewage is now a frozen sheet of slimy ice. In the total darkness, I was still aware of what is beneath my feet, and I did not want to slip and fall in that frozen yuck. But at the same time, the pressure on my bladder was telling me that if I did not hurry, I would pee my pants. So I was still at a fast, but kind of stiff legged walk when I ran headfirst into a GI who was walking from the opposite direction. Neither of us saw or heard the other until we collided. The ground was frozen and very slippery, and we had to hold onto each other to keep from falling onto that frozen slab of sewage. It was like hugging and dancing and groping each other trying not to fall. At first, running into someone that you did not know was there, was quite a shock, but after realizing what had happened, we both started laughing. That made things worse as we skated, slipped, and stumbled.

Somehow, though, we both stayed on our feet.

The other funny thing about the whole episode was that the laugh and voice of the GI were so familiar, but I still have no idea who it was that I was dancing with in our Afghan Midnight Ice Follies. The only reason I knew he was a GI was that he had his M-16 rifle slung over his shoulder and, at one point in our dance, I had his M-16 in my right hand holding on while we were both desperately hanging on to each other, trying not to fall.

December 23— Thirty days until I get to be home. Looking forward to being back with my family. Boy, do I miss them!

One of the neat things that happened while I was home last R&R was my oldest son, Matt, who is now twenty-two, moved nearby with his wife. It is sure nice to have them living within driving distance. Sounds like I may get to be a grandfather sometime in the future. That will be very cool.

11:47 p.m.—I was awakened by a loud blast that shook the roof of the tent. After the second round went off, we all knew it was outgoing Howitzer fire.

Don Lee yelled "Jacques! I told you not to eat the refried beans at dinner!"

Everyone in the tent was awakened by the first blast but had relaxed on hearing the second blast, and now we were all laughing except for the new guy in the bunk next to me.

"This is not funny! We should be getting into a bunker," he yelled.

We told him not to worry, it was outgoing fire.

"How the @!$#^! do you know that?" He replied frantically.

Someone told him, "You can tell it's outgoing when the tent tries to collapse from the shockwave from above. With incoming mortar or rocket fire, the ground shakes. You can feel the ground shake violently below you."

Then we heard one of the attack helicopters fire up and take off. Our base also fired a few flares into the sky, but I was too tired to get up and watch the fireworks and just went back to sleep. Now if small arms fire had also started, then I would have put on my body armor and armed myself.

December 24— We did seven flights today and moved over 11,000 pounds of mail by hand on and off the plane. I also flew fourteen GIs. Weather was good again. We get to sleep in forty-five extra minutes tomorrow morning; our planes will not launch until 6:45 a.m.

Well, it is the night before Christmas, and I am feeling very sad not being home with my family tonight—waiting for the kids to fall asleep, chasing them back into their bedrooms, and hearing them try to sneak out again. I will be home in twenty-nine days and can hardly wait. I have a schedule that lets me be home after three months. The GIs are gone for six to twelve months on their deployments. That must be very hard; being gone ninety days at a time is hard enough.

I hope everyone has a Merry Christmas. —Jerry

A Note From My Boss

Classification: UNCLASSIFIED
Caveats: FOUO
Team Afghan STOL,

I want to take this brief opportunity to wish you and your families a very Merry Christmas and best wishes for continued success, happiness, health, and prosperity in the coming New Year.

Your efforts, and the sacrifices both you and your families endure, have made possible immeasurable contributions to the war effort. But more importantly, we've made a positive, real, and measurable difference in the lives of the countless soldiers, sailors, airmen, and Marines who depend on us every single day for timely, efficient, and professional prosecution of airlift and airdrop operations. Even on our worst day, the level of mission accomplishment you have achieved, and continue to achieve, is nothing short of spectacular and you should all be very proud of yourselves and those who work at your side!

While we miss our homes and our families during this most blessed time of the year, I implore you to remain focused on your duties and responsibilities to ensure continued mission success whether it be fixing, flying, or supporting airplanes. In order to be an effective combat support capability, we simply have no choice but to remain at the top of our game and to avoid, at all costs, any and all human errors and aircraft accidents that might reduce or degrade our capability. Never forget we are at war and there are people out there who want to hurt us.

Therefore, we must always strive for perfection in everything we do, and we cannot accept a single lapse in judgment, attention to detail, or professionalism that might lead to an accident or injury, but I know you all already know this.

Thank you all for what you do, and know, beyond any doubt, that I have never been more proud to be part of any professional organization than I am now. As sick and demented as it might sound, I truly am living the dream. For those who are here, take care of yourselves and your teammates and the mission will take care of itself. For those of you at home, be safe in your travels and cherish the time spent with family and friends. Best wishes during this holiday season and God bless!

Sincerely and respectfully,
Brian
Site Manager
Blackwater Afghan STOL

February 27— Heading back to Afghanistan soon for my third tour. Looking forward to getting back with my team/friends. The comradery is something I do miss a lot when I am back home. Just not the same kind of connections with people who have not put their life on the line by living in a high-risk environment. I think that is why the Alaska bush pilots always tend to stick together.

Afghanistan 2010

March 2— Hello everyone.

[I] left home early in the a.m. headed back to Afghanistan. Had a good flight from Atlanta to Dubai. Weather had many flights canceled into Atlanta so the plane from Atlanta to the mid-east city of Dubai was only fifty-percent full. I had three seats to myself and was able to lay down and sleep; that made the long flight nice. Spent the second night in a nice hotel in Dubai, then next morning, got a flight to Afghanistan.

Security is a lot tighter at Bagram, it looks like they are expecting an attack and are ready for whatever may happen.

Started my yearly recurrent ground school and flight training as soon as I arrived in Bagram.

Took out the homemade moose jerky and smoked salmon for the guys to try. It was like magic, it disappeared in an instant and in its place was nine guys with smiles on their faces. Thanks sister Karla for the salmon!

March 6— Finished the flight training and did my yearly flight check ride. The check airman is an excellent instructor and is good to work with.

March 7— My first day back at work flying out of my assigned base FOB Sharana. Already missing my family and counting the days until I can go home. We had a rocket attack this morning with a few rockets hitting the FOB; thankfully, no one was hurt. The funny thing was after the second rocket hit, the siren went off and stayed on for a long time. Then it stopped and the voice on the speaker said, "Attack Over." Then within a few seconds, KABOOM!! as one last rocket hit. It was as if the Taliban was waiting for the siren to end before sending the last rocket at us. I guess they have a sense of humor.

Welcome back to Afghan greeting + fireworks provided, courtesy the Taliban.

March 8— Delivered mail to Gardez. Gardez is a forward operating base with an unsecured gravel airstrip three miles from the small base. The airstrip sits at 8500 feet above sea level. The poor GIs had not had a mail plane in close to a month and were very glad to see us. When they know we are coming, they bring three armored vehicles and secure both ends of the runway while we land. One vehicle with a trailer meets us on the runway and helps us unload while the other two armored vehicles stand guard on each end of the runway. Each box of mail or letters is looked at to see if it is for one of the crew helping us unload. They get very excited when a package is for one of them. After everything is unloaded the guys or gals that did not get a package look very disappointed.

On the ground at Gardez, we had small-arms fire hit within thirty yards of us as we had just finished loading the plane with outgoing mail. We did not stick around to find out what was going on or who was shooting at us. We took off with two GIs onboard and flew them to Bagram. They are going home for R&R and were happy to be getting out of the war zone for a while.

Every meal and at night I pray and give thanks to God for all the blessings that He has given our country. I am lucky and very thankful to have been born in the USA. Being in Afghanistan, I also pray to God that He takes care of my family and lets me get home safe. All of you that remember me in your prayers, Thank You! I am sure it helps keep me safe.

March 9— First flight of the day was to Bagram; we got within ten minutes and found out the runway had just been closed. Had to go back to home FOB Sharana and wait for three hours until they fixed the runway in Bagram.

Made five flights today, mostly carrying mail for the GIs. Flying was non-eventful for the day; that is the way it normally is. Even so, after every flight, we check the plane for bullet holes. Found out the shots fired in Gardez yesterday were actually from one of our own troops who had a negligent discharge with the .50-cal. BMG mounted on the MRAP.

March 10— I spent 6.2 hours in the air today and saw some new country that had nice rivers.

An uneventful day, and that was nice.

I got hurt during a military operation at forward operating base Sharana, Afghanistan. There was a rocket attack just before we landed. Two Chinook CH-47 helicopters came back for reinforcements and flew too low over my CASA C-212 Aviocar.

The chopper's hundred and fifty mile-per-hour rotor wash picked up a large rolling ladder with mechanic Stewart on it and flew it into me causing us all to tumble one hundred more feet across the tarmac. I sustained a severe neck injury. Stewart survived but was severely injured as well. After a year of physical therapy and, ultimately, neck surgery, I now have more good days than bad, but my days of flying in war zones or humping a heavy backpack are over.

2010: Final Note on Afghanistan

Anti-aircraft guns and airdrops in Afghanistan

Me at the Forward Operating Base of Farah.

FOB Sharana where I was based out of most of the time.

Notes from Ukraine and Poland

Although this is a contentious, hot-button issue in our country at the moment, I've chosen to record my experiences in Ukraine here for all who wish to read. Feel free to skip these notes if you choose. I make no apologies, and I stand with the people of Ukraine.

A few weeks after Russia invaded the Ukraine, I got a call from a friend who I had worked with in Afghanistan. He asked me if I would come over to help teach long-range marksmanship to a unit that he was working with. He remembered that I had told him my great-grandmother came from the Ukraine.

My answer was that, after getting hurt in Afghanistan, I promised my wife that I was done working in war zones.

He said it was not working but volunteering! I told him I would talk to my wife Laura but was sure she would say NO WAY ARE YOU GOING BACK INTO A WAR ZONE.

Now I have faced many dangers in my life but bringing up the idea of going to the Ukraine with Laura had me a little scared. This was a hot war zone with Russian troops quickly advancing and I thought she would be upset for me even asking her.

I procrastinated a few days but finally got the nerve to tell Laura about the call from the Ukraine. It was a Sunday on our way home from church. I told her that I felt led to go Volunteer. To my shock she asked if there was a way for her to also come help over there. Suddenly the shoe was on the other foot, and I couldn't handle the idea of my lovely wife going to a war zone. She made me promise to ask my friend if there was something she could do to volunteer. Still while driving home, we made the call and to my relief we were told this was no time to bring anyone into the country that could not effectively use a rifle. I was relieved and Laura disappointed.

Ukraine air space was closed and no flights to there were possible. The closest was Poland's Krakow or Warsaw airports and my friend agreed to have me picked up in Warsaw.

Within a few hours, Laura had made my airline reservations, and I was on my way two days later.

Things in a war zone seldom go as planned and this trip was no exception. My friend's unit had been called to the front lines as I was in the air over the Atlantic. I only found out when I changed flights in Amsterdam.

When traveling to a war zone it is wise to be hyper-aware of the people around you. I try to pick out the people who could be a threat

Called to Volunteer in Ukraine

or the people who make themselves a target. Someone wearing tactical clothing and carrying a military-style pack stands out, making themselves a potential target. Conversely, someone dressed in an expensive business suit carrying a nice briefcase is a potential kidnap target. It is good to not look like a US citizen as that may be enough to make you a target. It is best to blend in with how the average local person dresses, wearing nothing that makes you stand out. There are lots of articles on the gray-man approach and how to not stand out in a crowd.

Waiting to board my plane in Seattle, I picked out people I wanted to avoid, one was dressed in full tactical clothing, carrying a camo tactical pack and seemed to be the leader of a small group. He looked like a walking advertisement for a tactical, cool mail-order company.

As luck would have it, my assigned seat was next to Mr. Tactical and one of his friends. He was talkative and introduced himself as Brad. He was returning to the Ukraine for his second time with thirty-six sets of body armor to donate. He asked where I was going, and I told him Poland, purposely being vague. As Brad talked, I quickly determined this guy had a heart of gold and was doing what I wished more people would do and that is taking an active part in trying to help others in need. Thinking to myself, I decided I admired and liked this man but would avoid him at our destination.

Waiting for the next flight in Amsterdam, I distanced myself from Brad and his group; they attracted too much attention.

I also got a text that Yuri, my Ukraine friend, was being transferred from Western to Eastern Ukraine and would not be able to meet me. He would have a friend of his meet me instead. The next flight was to Poland. One of Brad's friends, Walter, sat in the seat next to me. I can't seem to get away from them, I thought. Walter said he was a Ukrainian who had been living in the USA for twenty years. He was helping Brad bring body armor and helping as an interpreter.

At Warsaw baggage, Brad had many duffel bags of body armor coming off the belt. I asked if they had steel or ceramic plates, he said ceramic, and my jaw dropped as the duffel bags were being dropped on the hard floor. When I informed him that the plates may be bullet proof but would be fragile if dropped onto the ground, he was surprised, but listened and had his friends handle the armor much more gently. Brad gave me his card and invited me to breakfast the next morning if I was still in town.

I was met by a former Polish soldier who had also worked in Afghanistan when I was there, but we had never met. It would be at least a week before he was heading to the Ukraine to help train drone operators. He could give me a ride then, but I did not want to wait a week. We went to the rental car companies, and they said no rental cars could cross into the Ukraine, and the Polish border guards were enforcing that rule.

Now what?

The breakfast that I had no intention of attending now sounded good. All of Brad's friends were not leaving Poland; they had helped bring the body armor this far but would go no farther.

Brad and Walter were to deliver body armor into Ukraine and said they could use help just moving the heavy bags.

I agreed to help and was now on my way to the Ukraine border. At the border, I met Salomon Smith, a former US Army Intel officer who was helping bring humanitarian supplies into the Ukraine. Salomon had worked in hostile and war zones before and knew his stuff. Now, Salomon thought like me on situational awareness and security. I joined his team. The trip was both educational and emotional.

Emails from Friends:

> God Bless the life of Jerry!
> I am sincerely praying for your safety, short and long-term my good friend Sir Jacques!! You're honoring your grandmother and everything good and righteous since! (Court Boice)
>
> Don't forget to bring Chuck Yeager's book & what you learned from it. CHECK SIX. Complacency will kill ya. Head on a swivel. How can I bust my butt, how can I prevent it and about 125 more :-) And keep writing yours, please. (Victoria Yeager)

Notes From My Second Trip to Ukraine & Poland

Once More— A friend said to me, "Volunteering and going to the Ukraine! You must have cancer or have a death wish!"

Well, as for that, I will say that I do not have any illness and I love life. I would love to see my one-hundredth birthday and want every minute of life that I can get.

I am incredibly blessed. My most desired dream and what I prayed for most in life was to have a loving wife and family.

I am blessed with a wife who is better than I deserve, seven fantastic kids, two daughters-in law, and three grandkids. I love every one of them, and when the good Lord calls me home, I hope to be very old and surrounded by my family. I also have many fantastic friends, as well as a business that I truly enjoy. I have everything to live for and plan to come back and enjoy everything.

Last week I was talking to Brent Cole, my attorney and friend for thirty years.

When I told him I was heading to Ukraine, he stated that I must be a saint. I laughed and told him I was many things but definitely not a saint, perhaps trying to make up for past sins.

At the end of my first trip to the Ukraine
After returning to my winter home KMVT/KSVT news interviewed me.

Kimberly man back home after giving humanitarian aid to Ukraine
"I truly believe that Russia, or nobody, will ever conquer the Ukrainian people. They may occupy the country, but they are resolute."
Idaho man returns home after humanitarian service in Ukraine
By Zach Bruhl
Published: Apr. 11, 2022, at 4:24 PM GMT-7

KIMBERLY, Idaho (KMVT/KSVT) — After spending decades in war zones as a pilot and host of sniper classes, Kimberly resident Jerry Jacques had a skill set that was needed in the war-torn country of Ukraine.

"I promised my wife and family I was done," he said. "I'd been asked by some friends of mine that have been over there for almost a month to come help teach a sniper class."

But on his way, an explosion at an ammo facility led to his sniper class being canceled, so Jacques had a change of plans.

He arrived at the Poland-Ukraine border and began offering help.

"I wound up finding someone that was delivering body armor and needed some help just lifting all the bags of body armor," he said.

That's how he met Brad Greer & Salomon Smith, men from Utah making a profound humanitarian impact.

"He's developing a network on the Poland side to find out what supplies are where. He fills his van with what is actually needed and goes back into Ukraine and is crisscrossing all over Ukraine delivering the supplies," said Jacques.

Jacques traveled alongside Smith for weeks, delivering food, medicine, body armor and other supplies into Ukraine, getting as close as 40 miles west of Kyiv.

"The people there were trying to go about daily lives, but you could see there was tremendous stress on them," said Jacques.

While traveling in the country, Jacques met hundreds of people, including one Russian man, who since moving to Ukraine has been displaced at the hands of Putin's army twice and is learning hard lessons about his home.

"He said, 'All my life I was told by Russia that America was my enemy, that England was horrible. Now, I'm seeing Americans and Canadians and British coming over with nothing but wanting to help. I now know who my true friends are'," Jacques explained.

Jacques tells me he learned many lessons during his time in Ukraine and, above all, he learned about the nature of the Ukrainian people.

"I truly believe that Russia, or nobody, will ever conquer the Ukrainian people. They may occupy the country, but they are resolute," he said.
(Bruhl 2022)

Yes, I feel led to travel to the Ukraine and will be in a dangerous active war zone. Why? I believe that the Ukrainian people are defending their homes and deserve all the help they can get. My great-grandmother came from Ukraine, and I have a skill set that is needed by the Ukrainian military.

I am not looking forward to rocket attacks and artillery fire aimed in my direction. Yes, those things scare me a lot. This is an adventure that I am not looking forward to and will be happy when I get home. I do feel strongly that volunteering for this cause is justified, so I am back in a war zone.

I plan to be back home working on my book, *No Sequel to Life: From the Heart of a Bush Pilot*, in four weeks.

Sincerely,

Jerry Jacques

I have seen the horrors of war in Africa, Afghanistan, and Guatemala, and now I am in the Ukraine and expect to see some very bad things. There is nothing good about war. Most Ukrainian people never expected their Russian neighbors to invade, attack, and inflict the horrors of war on them. But that is what is happening. The Ukrainian people are defending their homes and fighting for their freedom. They are not a threat to Russia.

The Horrors of War

To my fellow parents and grandparents out there: When your children wake up with a bad dream in the middle of the night or are afraid to go to bed because the boogie man is hiding in the closet or under the bed, we can calm them down and can honestly tell them that there is nothing bad in the house, and they are safe. Now imagine the parents in the Ukraine. Their children are afraid that a rocket, bomb, or artillery shell will come through the roof and kill them in their bed, or the Russian soldier/boogeyman will burst into the door at any moment to torture them and then murder them. A parent in the Ukraine knows this is a real possibility. What can they say to their beloved child? Think about that. Put yourself in that position. What would you say to your child?

To the young people out there who are most concerned with climate change and protecting our planet: War is an incredible waste of resources and causes more environmental damage than you can imagine. The young people of the Ukraine are just like you and had the same values as you. Now, though, instead of being in college or starting their careers, they are fighting for their very lives, living in a trench, and watching their friends being killed.

I have heard a few people in the USA say that the Ukraine has a corrupt government, and they are not like us, so why should we help them? I say to this: So, what! There are always a few bad apples in the barrel. You do not discard the whole barrel because of those rotten few. Yes, I am sure they have some corrupt politicians and government officials, and so does the USA. We are very much like the Ukraine.

I am sorry CS Norwood; I am supposed to be working on our book but am in a new adventure and cannot think about the past right now.

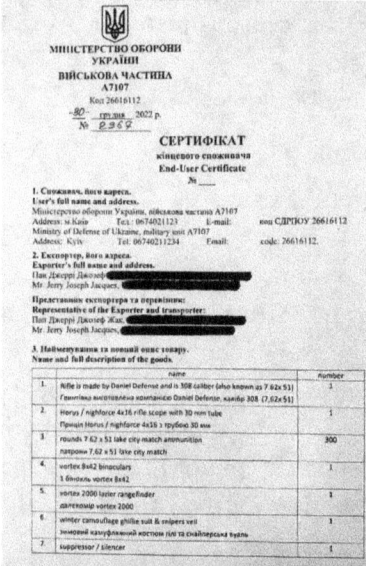

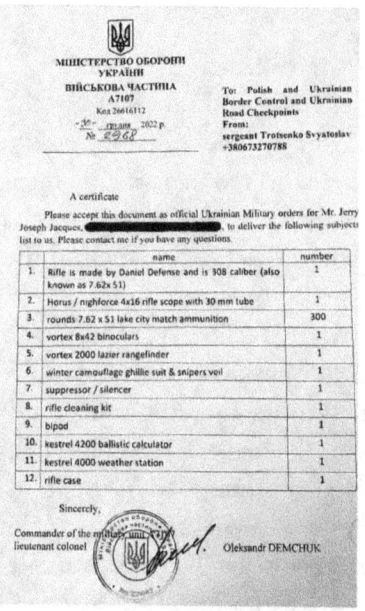

*My really
pesky papers*

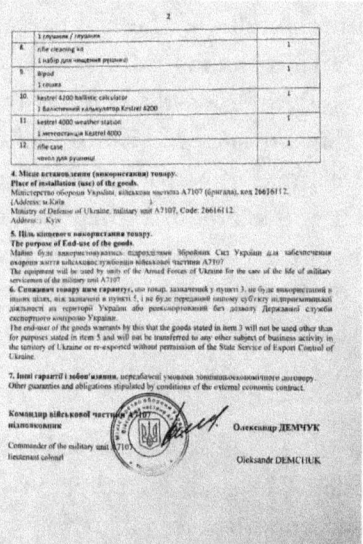

So I am adding to your already overworked pile of raw notes.

This is a trip of faith. For the last two months the paperwork for me to travel with rifles to Lviv, Ukraine, has been in the works. Far from the frontline, I am supposed to teach two back-to-back long range rifle classes.

Every few days, I heard that the firearm permits were supposed to be signed and sent to me, but they never came. Now the permits are promised to be waiting for me at Polish Customs.

I have decided to travel without the papers, even knowing I may get to Poland and be turned back home. I did the proper paperwork and checked the firearms correctly before leaving the USA.

I have arrived in Poland. There is no one to meet me with papers and no email with the needed documents.

My luggage arrived on time but no rifle case. After one hour, after all the other passengers left, passed through customs, my rifle case finally showed up. The customs guards just waved me through, only quickly checking my passport. I assume that the case was being held until they verified the papers that must have finally been sent.

I was now outside on the curb with a heavy rifle case, a backpack, a large camera case, and two large roller cases. Very few people are around.

Two nicely dressed men offered to help me and say they are "taxi with minivan." Something tells me not to trust them, they get aggressive, saying they "take me to border—less money than taxi." The gun case is a giveaway that I am heading to Ukraine. I hold my ground and insist that I am not going with them, and they quietly leave. They were probably just trying to hustle business, but I need to be careful and trust my gut.

About that time, a taxi drives by, and I wave him down.

Now at a nice hotel, I made a call to my contact and found out that no papers from the military in Lviv had yet been processed but were soon to be issued. How customs just let me through, I have no clue. My contact told me to stay in the hotel, and he would have me picked up soon.

Now it looks like papers may not come. So, I am stuck, I made a few calls to friends with Ukraine military experience and background, and they began trying to help. On a very long shot, I called Brad Greer, who I met on my last trip. He has no military or law enforcement background but has a friend on the frontline who is desperately searching for the equipment that I have, as well as someone to train his team with that equipment.

Four hours later, I have official orders to travel to the frontline to train a few of his men

A very nice young man in a taxi picked me up at 7:45 a.m. We left Kraków, heading to the border. He spoke a little English, and I enjoyed traveling with him. He is a new father and former Ukraine military sniper. He cannot cross the border as there are rocket attacks.

Things are at the highest level since the war started, and I am now headed to the frontline in the Donbas area. This was not the plan as I was only going to stay in the relatively safer western region to train people who would take the equipment to the frontline.

Across the river is Ukraine; this side is Poland.

Here, 20,000 Ukrainian refugee children are attending school in this part of Poland. It has been arranged that I wait until tomorrow in a Catholic Monastery run by nuns.

The last time I sat at a table with a mother superior I was seven years old and being expelled from Catholic school for fighting.

I am being given the royal treatment here, The Ukrainian people are so incredibly grateful to anyone who wants to help them retain their home.

A driver named Evon is to take me across the border tomorrow morning.

He is a wounded war vet who got shot during the war when Russia invaded Ukraine thirteen years ago. This part of Poland was part of Ukraine before the communist Russians took it over one hundred years ago and gave it to Poland. Most of these people here consider themselves to still be Ukrainian.

This tiny monastery helps refugee families and provides a temporary safe haven for them. The sisters are full of questions. It is very strange talking to Mother Superior and the sisters as they ask me questions about training snipers, but these nuns are supportive of my mission. Mother Superior actually wants to see my rifles, then tells me she was a competitive rifle shooter as a girl. She has two AK-47's just in case the Russians try to invade this part of Poland.

Polish Morning   The sisters fed us breakfast and invited me to join them to attend church with them. They also said that if I just wanted to stay and rest, that was fine. I gladly accepted the invitation to join them at church.

The church was a beautiful cathedral, and the mass reminded me of when I was a child attending a mass at St. Clair's Church in Santa Clara, California. Back then, the mass was in Latin, and I could not understand the words but could feel the presence of God.

I definitely felt God's presence here. When you are heading into danger, your faith often grows stronger.

After the service, several older men came up to me, shook my hand, and wished me safety and luck at the front in Ukraine. There are no men under sixty as the younger ones have crossed into the Ukraine to help stop the advancing Russians. Then Evon loaded his wife, two children, and me into his van and made the short drive to the border.

I presented my military orders to bring myself, rifles, and ammo to Ukraine, along with my passport.

After one hour of being searched and questioned, things got

uncomfortable. I did not have the correct papers for the gun and ammo in Poland; I was arrested, searched, strip searched, and put behind bars. They threatened that this offense was punishable by eight years in prison.

At the Polish Border

The Polish border guards were just doing their job. They acted very professionally and treated me with both kindness and respect. I still spent the night behind bars with everything impounded.

So, to sum up my day:
1. Breakfast with Catholic Nuns.
2. Mass in Catholic Cathedral spoken in a language I cannot understand.
3. Arrested and strip searched.
4. Spent the night behind bars.

Is this the "Luck of the Irish?" I don't drink, but I do have some Irish blood in me. It absolutely was an Advent-full Day.

The next morning I was taken in a prisoner transport vehicle to the prosecutor's office in town. He had been in touch with the colonel in charge of the Ukraine rifle battalion I was to be working with and understood I was volunteering for a good cause. I was interviewed again three more times by different Polish officials and, by late afternoon, released. Just before dark, I was allowed to walk out of Poland and go through no-man's land to the Ukraine. The Border Police were expecting me and just stamped my passport, smiled, and said, "Welcome Back."

Welcome Back to the Ukraine

I was picked up by Max and Opect and driven three hours to the town of Lviv. Opect is a pastor and one of my contacts here. Max is a young soldier with a wife and two young sons. He has been serving on the frontline since the start of the war. He is the soldier who Brad Greer and I delivered body armor to on my last trip.

Max has been assigned to take me to the sniper base; it will take us twelve-hours driving to get there. I will not disclose the location, but we drove through Kyiv, the capitol city, on our way. I saw first-hand more of the devastating effects of this war. Many buildings, apartments, shopping centers, and houses have been bombed, hit by rockets, artillery shells, or shot by tanks.

Ukraine was thriving as a modern nation before the invasion. Despite the carnage of war, its cities are still as modern as the cities in the USA. Kyiv has as much culture as Paris or New York City with much more architectural history than the Big Apple. Lviv is smaller than Kyiv but similar in culture. The country is a mixture of the old world and modern. In the larger cities, most people live in apartments, enjoying the advantages of urban life. Outside of the cities, more of Ukraine's old-world culture is preserved. Most houses have a garden, many raise chickens as well as other backyard farm animals. In hard times raising your own food can be the difference between starvation and staying healthy. When Lennon invaded the Ukraine in 1919, he sent all the food to Russia, and over a million Ukraine people starved to death. It was a planned genocide. The older people remember this, and it is reflected in the countryside.

Everywhere the Ukraine people give me the warmest welcome a person could ever receive. I am welcomed into homes, monasteries, businesses, and, more surprising, eventually welcomed into a tight-knit military team.

Going into an active war zone is never comfortable, and, because I do not speak the language, it added an additional layer of stress. I always know that this could be the last time I ever see my family, and that brings tears if I think about it for very long.

Me with the Priest and Nuns who showed me their hospitality.

An Interesting Week

I thought that I was heading to a Territorial Guard unit away from the front lines to help sniper training. Instead, we traveled across the country to a regular active army unit close to the border where the Russians are holding a position and spatially attacking. The base is not at all what I expected, I had in my mind a fenced military compound. Instead, the sniper base is just a private home that the residents had abandoned when they fled to a safer place and became refugees.

The unit I am assigned to has two mid-range AR platform 7.62 x 51 sniper rifles and one extreme-range 14.5 mm sniper rifle, some anti-tank weapons, a 105 mm recoilless rifle, several belt-fed machine guns, and lots of AK-47s and AK-74s. This twenty-two-man team splits its time between the front-line trenches and at the home base house. Half the team is always in position in the trenches, manning the guns. The second half of the team rests for twenty-four hours at the house but are on standby. A radio call from the trenches and we scramble to the trenches only a short distance away.

The battalion commander came to meet me and thank me for making the long journey and volunteering, he explained that it is a huge moral boost for his men to have an American care enough to personally show up. The welcome is warm and sincere. It is late at night when I open the cases of equipment that I have brought for them. The excitement is wonderful to see. The range finders, ballistic calculators, noise-enhancing earmuffs, binoculars, and spotting scopes are desperately needed.

The commander explained that tomorrow I will travel several hours with eight of his men to the main sniper training base where I will see their sniper program firsthand. After that, we will work on their long-range shooting skills.

Nothing is said to me, but I realize these soldiers do not know me or if I truly have any skills to teach.

It is a smart move on their part taking me away from the frontlines to a training base where they can assess me without putting anyone at risk

The Ukraine Sniper Program is very good, and in a three-week course, they accomplished the training that would usually take six weeks. Both the instructors and students are motivated by their will not only to survive, but to preserve their way of life. To say the least, their innate right to peaceful existence in their own country is their motivation to continue the fight.

Two Days at the Sniper Training Center

Most of the team has accepted me; at the range they saw that I can shoot and could help them improve their shooting.

But a few are skeptical as I have not been under fire with them, so I am unproven, will I stand and fight or panic is what is on their mind, again nothing like that is said to me but if I was in their shoes, I would feel the same way if some new guy suddenly just showed up.

Many of the team live in the area we are protecting, as we travel

Back on the Front Line and Living with Ukrainian Soldiers

back and forth to the trenches, I see firsthand with them the death and destruction of their families and their homes all caused by the Russians. This is the hardest, most emotional part of being here. Going to the cemetery with these guys who have friends and team members put into their graves recently and seeing the sad, often stoic faces of the people grieving was hard. I could see their pain.

When the Ukraine Army retook this village, the Russians were forced to retreat. Many Russians got separated from their units and fled into the woods. That was a fatal Russian mistake.

In the Ukraine old men over sixty-two and young boys under eighteen are excluded from serving in the military. But they know the woods in their backyards. Using shotguns with slugs they hunt deer and moose in these woods. Now they are successfully hunting Russian soldiers that are trying to hide there.

In the Field, What Is It Like Being a Sniper?

Most soldiers think the only requirement for being a sniper is to be a good shot. They think snipers have it easy, just lying around all day, safely waiting for an enemy to shoot at from the comfortably prone position and distance their very cool long-range weapon affords them.

The reality of being a sniper, however, is fraught with either mind-numbing stillness or deadly danger, with "mission accomplished" the goal, whether that takes sixteen minutes or sixteen hours to achieve.

Time for a reality check, and first and foremost on the reality check-list is that a Ukraine sniper has many enemies. The obvious one is the other guy trying to spot you and shoot you. Added to this, after you make your shot, Russians start lobbing artillery shells at your position, and now the latest tactical threat of a drone equipped for thermal detection spotting you is very real.

Think about getting into position before dawn, then lying motion-less in the same spot all day until it gets dark. You cannot move, you must hold your bodily functions from dawn to dark or pee your pants. Lying so still for that long, every joint in your body starts to hurt. Mentally you must suppress the desire to scratch the itch in your nose or whatever part of your body is crying for the relief of a simple scratch. This is agonizing.

You fight constantly with boredom and at times fight to stay awake. You fight the urge to turn your head and see if your partner is awake and still watching your back. (These guys desperately need a communi-cation device that has battery life for at least sixteen hours, an earpiece, and remote push-to-talk switch long enough to reach the trigger fin-ger). Your mouth and throat get desert dry, and you desperately want a sip of water. If you have a camel-back hose at your mouth, you must decide if the liquid intake is going to make you pee your pants later. The actual tears that run down your face when you are thinking about your family and how much you miss them have now left a crust on the upper part of your cheek, and it now itches so badly, but you dare not move to scratch. Here it is winter, so mosquitoes, ants, and snakes are not a problem, but the damn mice drive you nuts; they crawl down your back, chew on your ear, crawl up your pant leg or down your shirt. They are your worst enemy, trying to make you move and give your position away. You are cursing yourself for forgetting rubber bands to seal pantlegs at the cuffs and jacket at the wrists.

Then you see a flutter of movement at the edge of your vision and try to figure out if it was a bird or your enemy's movement that caught your eye. You also pray that no little birds are moving near you to attract a sniper's eye to your position. You wonder: Can I accurately make the shot in the split second when/if the opportunity presents itself. What will my firing solution be? Will I have time to move after the shot before they call in artillery fire on my position, or should I stay motionless and hold my position?

At the end of the day, when it is very dark, you crawl back into the treeline, and at last you can finally stand up. The urine flows easily, but the poop that you wanted to take for half a day will not come out because you are constipated from dehydration and lack of movement.

Being a sniper on the front line is a young man's work, I am too old for that kind of thing.

I did have a few tricks learned in Afghanistan and techniques from competitive shooting that I showed them. But the reality is, I learned more from them than they did from me. —JJJ

Me with a 14.5mm ultra long range sniper rifle

Warriors All   Tonight, I am with my team. They are all combat veterans who have been fighting on the frontlines since the war started. They are all types of guys: a few professional soldiers, but most are just normal men who joined up to protect their country and family. They are so diverse: skinny guys, fat guys, guys in fantastic shape, guys in poor health, and a father/son team.

They started out with thirty-six on their team and now have lost one third of the team members. I learn more about fighting from them than I will be able to teach them, but I can help them on the long-range shooting. They understand that I am here to give them support, and they have my back. I trust these men with my life. They are so appreciative of the fact that an American is here to volunteer and give them support. They also say if the USA is ever invaded, they will be volunteering to help us.

I expected to be eating bread, cheese, and some dried meat. They have a man on the team who is a cook with no prior military training, The locals bring him produce and live meat animals, he processes the animals himself to make sausage and dried meat. He also makes bread from scratch and stews that he cans. This food he prepares is for the men on duty in the trenches. When we are at the base house, he serves good hot home cooked style meals. A man like this is a vital part of a combat unit as it keeps men healthy and morale much higher. I still spend time in the trenches but most nights at home base. I know the commander is trying to take care of me and keep me as safe as he can. My grandfather's mother was from Ukraine, so I have Ukrainian blood in my veins and feel connected to these people. A few are Christians, there are Jewish men, Atheist, Russian Orthodox, Catholic and one Muslim man in our group. They all work together and get along well; they are totally united in the desire to not be conquered by Russia. These men are a team and watch each other's back. When we are in the trenches, they tell me they *will never retreat, behind us is our homes and families. We will stop the Russians here or die trying.*

When I was in Afghanistan, we always had the better equipment and superior forces. Here, the Russians have more men and equipment. Here, it is David v. Goliath. What I am personally doing is not going to make any difference in this war, but if enough people from the USA, Canada, and the rest of the world chip in to help together, we will make a difference, and Russia will not occupy Ukraine. This will also stop Russia from advancing into the rest of Europe and bringing the USA into a world war.

Goodnight from the Ukraine— To my seven children, two daughters-in-law, three grandchildren, and wonderful wife: Please know that I love each and every one of you. —JJJ

Today, January 6— At my request, Stan the company commander took me to visit a few villages that the Russians recently attacked. A lot of civilians were killed there.

First, the Russian paratroopers landed and secured a large airport used for cargo planes, then large aircraft landed with tanks, armored personnel carriers, and a large number of soldiers. They started shooting at anything they wanted, destroying houses and cars. There were simply not enough Ukraine military personnel to defend against all the Russians, so the government brought truckloads of AK-47s to the city center in Kyiv and gave them out to any civilian who wanted a gun to fight the invading Russians. Stan's nephew had just turned eighteen and was given an AK. He went back to his home village, which is the place we were visiting today, and they fought house-to-house trying to stop the Russians. At the cost of many lives the rag-tag Ukraine team succeeded.

Tomorrow I will be back on the frontline, in the trenches.

I now need to admit I was forced to abandon the sniper rifle I brought from home. I never thought that would happen to me, but it did. I feel like a failure; that rifle was going to be a gift to the team when I left and is something they truly need. I thought the commander would be angry, but he understood I had no choice and welcomed me back anyway. Since I do not have my rifle, the new job is to take photos and video on the frontline so I can show people at home the reality of what is happening here.; The Russian troops drive in tanks and armored personnel carriers, The Ukrainian troops drive in any civilian 4x4' or van they can get. They give it a quick coat of green paint and put their insignia on it. The artillery fire is not that far away, but since we are in the woods, we are safe from tanks, I will go back to the secondary line of defense at the house tonight.

My Choice— I have a choice to make: Without my rifle, I am carrying only my camera; I look like a journalist. The Russian soldiers have orders not to kill American journalists. I am told, if I do not carry a weapon, I am a lot safer.

Carrying a rifle takes the gloves off for the Russian soldiers and puts me in substantially more risk as I become a target.

I am living with this rifle team and, if necessary, will fight with them, so I now carry an AK-47 rifle that has been issued to me. I accept the risk.

Merry Christmas, January 7— The team rotates from the trenches to the house. Half the team remains on duty in the trenches. A radio call from them, and we will scramble to the trenches only a short distance away.

Christmas is celebrated on January seventh in the Ukraine, and this is the first time I have seen any alcohol since I arrived at the frontlines. The Ukrainian men do drink, but, like anywhere, a few will fall into alcohol abuse. I have seen only sober men in the trenches. This is a serious time, and every man stays ready.

At this Christmas dinner with my friends in the Ukraine, they propose a very nice dinner toast!

Four Toasts with the Same Drink— The first toast is to health. Men stand, and, if women are at the table, they remain seated because they are considered honored guests. The second toast is for whatever they choose. Tonight, it was for the women who are staying home, taking care of their families and homes so their men can fight.

The third toast is to all their friends who have been killed in this war; a few drops of the drink are spilled onto the ground to honor the fallen who lie buried in the precious ground of the Ukraine.

The fourth and final toast: "Hoping that no one will drink the third toast in our honor."

There are twelve men at the table with me, and each man has lost multiple friends in the war. The truth and absolute horror of war is that a few of these men I am with may not make it to see another Christmas as this war rages on. That makes me incredibly sad. I have been fully accepted by everyone on the team and consider them my brothers.

A sergeant who was skeptical of my motivation and capabilities at first, eventually accepted me as part of his team. He posted this about me, and I am very honored.

This is Jerry...Jerry Jacques.

This is Man with a capital letter "M".
A person with a big heart and a deep and beautiful soul.
Jerry is a veteran of two Ukraine military companies.
Volunteer Military sniper.
Jerry, a person who understands the essence and psychology of war and its consequences.
This is what drives Jerry to help those who may need his expert help and assistance as a person who knows whose side the truth is on.
A lot has already been done and he is doing even more as a volunteer, helping our combat unit.
Dear our brother Jerry!
We are sincerely grateful for your help and support!
And we are even more grateful for the fact that you continue to do this tirelessly and convey the importance of this information to others.

Your contribution to Victory is very important!
What you are doing is priceless!
A low bow and thank you for everything!
Honor, dear Jerry Jacques!

23 SRB (a separate rifle battalion)

—Sargent Andrew P.

Today I received the greatest honor of my life. Stan, the company commander presented me with their company flag. Everyone on the team chipped in to buy this for me. I have no words to describe the flood of emotions that I feel. Tomorrow is my last day at the front.

Monday, January 9— At the end of my stay, I visited St. Michaels Cathedral in Kyiv. The somber feel of the services being held for the soldiers killed in this unprovoked war with Russia was impossible to miss.

My wife, Laura, decided that she is joining me on this trip and will do volunteer work in Lviv while I return to the front lines with Rick McNurlin to deliver equipment. Rick is a Deputy Sheriff in Idaho and competitive shooter; he has volunteered to join us and help transport all the equipment that is being donated to the 23rd Rifle Battalion that I was with on my last trip.

Third Trip, Ukraine, March 31, 2023

Laura poses for me in front of a bombed tank which was brought into Lviv and positioned there as a reminder of the devastation throughout the country.

Since leaving the frontlines of Ukraine in January, I have been praying for the people of the Ukraine. Many of my friends in the USA have donated needed equipment and I feel led to personally deliver so it gets to the men who I know that desperately need it. Thirty-six hours before heading to the Ukraine, I took a misstep and fell down a flight of stairs injuring my knee. Having had many injuries in my life, I knew how badly I was hurt. The instant, excruciating pain told me that this injury would take months to heal and possibly require surgery.

I could barely walk, and, by the next morning, I could only hobble around with the use of a cane. Now the pain in both my neck and my knee made me even grumpier than normal. I'm not sure how Laura puts up with me when I'm in this kind of pain. She is better than I deserve!

I was sure that I would need to cancel my trip.

God's Timing and My Lack of Faith!!

The pain made me angry, even mad, not understanding how God would let this happen. The equipment I have is needed by my friends on the frontline, and I promised them I would return and get it to them!

Blessings come even in war-torn countries like Ukraine. I always feel blessed to meet a happy dog. This little JRT was wounded in a dog fight.

There was no way I could have made this rigorous journey if Rick and Laura were not with me to carry all the cases of equipment.

Every other time I have traveled to a war zone, I have been alone.

Could this be His timing?

When I invited Rick and Laura, I was walking normally; now I needed a wheelchair to get through the airport. I had to depend on others to do what had always been normal tasks for me. This was hard, and I was struggling to handle my emotions. I felt as though I no longer had control of anything! It was frustrating being dependent on others—so what is God trying to teach me?

Three days of travel and we finally arrived in the beautiful western Ukraine town of Lviv.

Another long train ride with Rick and Laura moving most of the equipment. Laura stayed in Kyiv to volunteer with a refugee program there, and last night my friend Max, a young officer, picked Rick and me up at our rendezvous point. That was the first time I could walk without a cane, although it was very painful to do so. Max was not happy to see my limp and did not think I should go to the front with him tomorrow.

Miraculously, this morning is the first time I have been pain free in my knee since my fall last week! Equally in the miraculous class, my neck injury, which has caused me constant pain since being injured in 2010 Afghanistan, does not hurt me at all this morning. Interesting timing?

I arrived in the Ukraine for the first time one year ago. This is my third trip and I'm looking forward to seeing my friends on the frontline and happy to have the specialized equipment they need.

It is 4:30 a.m. and time to leave.

We will not have any contact for at least seventy-two hours as cell and iPad are being turned off. —Jerry Jacques

Today,
April 1, 2023

I saw something today that exemplified the spirit of the Ukrainian people and the reason why Russia will never conquer these people.

In a once beautiful and historical city that has been devastated by Russian bombing, artillery, and small arms fire, the Ukraine Army has just managed to push the Russians back and free the city.

In the city square, Ukraine volunteers were cleaning up. All these volunteers were elderly people who were too old to fight. A few were using brooms to sweep the ancient cobblestone street. As they worked down the street, behind them was clean, ahead of them lay the dirt and debris.

One lady held my attention. She swept forward the dirt including pieces of broken glass and bits of trash, then stopped every few feet to sweep the debris into her partner's dustpan. The old man would empty the pan into the bucket he carried with him.

As I watched, a gust of wind blew a few cigarette butts out of the dustpan back onto the street behind her. Quickly the lady's broom rounded up the escaped butts, except for one which danced in the breeze down the clean cobblestone square until finding a resting place in a tiny crevasse. She could have just moved on with her work as it was only one tiny cigarette butt, yet this noble lady accompanied by her equally noble partner walked back twelve feet until she found the rogue butt and recaptured it with a flick of her broom into the dustpan. Satisfied, the pair walked quietly back to where they had left off their work, resuming the rhythm of their task. This simple action spoke

We Bear Our Cross to War

volumes to me about not only her pride and perseverance but that same resolve in all the Ukrainian people I have come to know and love. She reminded me of my grandmother who was displaced from her home so long ago, and an immigrant to Canada. The people of Ukraine love their nation. They see a future in their own homes, in their own country, swept clean and put back in order again.

Rick and I, along with Max, are heading into the lion's den—the meat grinder according to the Ukrainian fighters. I can't say I am looking forward to this, but I feel led to do so. The good news is I have kept my promise, returned, brought twenty-five sniper scopes and other requested equipment for the 23 SRB Rifle Battalion that I was with last trip.

I sent out an email asking friends to please pray for us as the next seventy-two hours would be intense. Rick and I made it to the front and met up with sergeant Andrew P and Commander Stan and were able to personally deliver the equipment we brought to donate. We were set to spend a few days with my old teammates, but the Russians started heavy shelling and advancing with a large force. The battalion was losing men and the commander ordered us to be evacuated. He did not want to further jeopardize our safety. To get away from the frontlines, we had to make detours avoiding advancing Russian troops but got out safely and headed back to Kyiv.

Now I am ashamed of my selfishness in thinking that I was the one bringing this equipment; the reality is that I only played a small part. God used many people for this mission.

My lack of faith in thinking simple knee injury was going to stop God's plan is hard to admit.

My three trips to Ukraine have shown me that the people of Ukraine are very much like the people of the US. To a large degree, they are a Judeo-Christian society that accepts all people and their different beliefs. They only want to remain a free and independent country

My Final Thoughts

The war in Ukraine is more complicated than we're led to believe by the US media. What is not complicated is the fact that Russia has invaded the sovereign country of Ukraine and is murdering thousands of innocent civilians there.

This is not a civil war. It is the country of Russia invading its neighbor and making excuses and false accusations to justify genocide. Russia is trying to recapture all the former Soviet Union countries and needs the resources in the Ukraine to succeed.

TVB7 Local News Article

Idaho man shares his experience on the front lines in Ukraine: 'To see the destruction and the carnage firsthand, it's heartbreaking'

This was Jerry Jacques' second trip to Ukraine to help.

Author: Shirah Matsuzawa

Published: 7:47 PM MST January 19, 2023

Updated: 7:47 PM MST January 19, 2023

Facebook Twitter

Idaho man shares his experience on the front lines in Ukraine: 'To see that the destruction and the carnage firsthand, it's heartbreaking' | ktvb.com

TWIN FALLS, Idaho — A Twin Falls man is back in Idaho, after he was on the front lines in Ukraine.

"This is really a David versus Goliath-type thing, and the sad thing is David is running out of rocks," said Jerry Jacques, who spent three weeks in Ukraine.

He told KTVB, while he was there, he witnessed rockets crashing into homes, air raids and destruction.

"They're fighting with minivans and Toyota pickups against tanks and armored personnel carrier," Jacques said.

He returned to Idaho on Saturday. This was his second time in Ukraine in the past year. Back in March, Jacques delivered humanitarian supplies to Ukraine and helped bring refugees back to a refugee camp in Poland.

Click here to watch video

Idahoan returns home after distributing supplies in Ukraine.

"This time, I went over there to help teach sniper class to the Ukrainian military," Jacques said. "Originally, I thought it was going to be to the territorial defense, which is their equivalent of our national guard, but by the time I got there, they actually decided they needed me to teach some team members that needed help right on the front lines."

What he saw was difficult, he said.

"Emotionally, it's incredibly tough," Jacques said. "The Russians are shooting a thousand rockets a month minimum into Ukraine and they're not targeting military installations, they're targeting power plants and homes and schools and businesses."

He said attacks can happen at any moment.

"The poor families, you can be sitting in your home with your kids at dinner and you don't know whether one of these huge rockets is going to come crashing through your house," Jacques said.

He adds, compared to his first visit to Ukraine in March, this trip he saw more carnage and a lot more homes destroyed.

"To see the destruction and the carnage firsthand, it's heartbreaking and then, at the same time, to see the Ukraine people, they are totally rallied around protecting their country, and fighting for freedom," Jacques said. "I think the thing that surprised me the most was every single Ukrainian I talked to, every one of them expressed gratitude, and how much they appreciated what the people of the United States were doing."

On the front lines with Ukrainian man and 105 mm recoil-less anti-tank rifle

Sunday, 8 January 2023, I'm presented with the Company flag

*Here, it is
David v. Goliath*

*Rick McNurlin &
me near the site
of yet another
destroyed tank*

War casts such a long shadow of desolation and destruction. Property is destroyed, lives are lost. These buildings can be rebuilt over time, but those lives are gone forever.

New Family Plan

Having spent time all over Alaska, my family's favorite place was always Lake Iliamna. Nestled strategically between Katmai and Lake Clark National Parks and the Bristol Bay coast, it has the world's best grizzly bear and walrus viewing destinations. Twenty million acres of incredibly diverse scenery in a true wilderness setting along with the largest salmon spawning grounds on earth made it a unanimous family vote to reopen the lodge on Lake Iliamna. We were concentrating only on what we still feel is the best of wild Alaska.

With the lodge having been closed for three years and ravaged by a winter storm, the place needed a ton of work. To our amazement, friends, past clients, and former guides started showing up at the lodge, working for weeks at a time on the renovation. Because of the incredible donation of hard work by family and friends, the lodge was again ready for guests the summer of 2011. My kids and the staff do all the work now while I get to enjoy the luxury of the lodge, eat gourmet food, and visit with our guests.

Float planes and boats dock in the front yard, aircraft on wheels park in the back yard. We are known for the best bear viewing on the planet as well as catching huge rainbow trout on a fly.

All was settled until an acquaintance told me that my old friend, Ron's manuscript had been published. Not long after, I received an email of

Alaska Grizzly Safaris Lodge on Lake Iliamna, AK

introduction from Ron's sister, CS Norwood. I read the story of her efforts in the front of Ron's book, spending a few years researching, editing, and compiling Ron's manuscript and finally publishing it in 2022.

I emailed back, linked her up with a recent podcast I had completed on Sam Carter's channel River Radius Podcast titled, "No Boat No Paddle on the Big Susitna River." She listened and suggested we get to work on my book. It's time, I think.

Laura and I watch the bears in Katmai National Park, AK

Call from a Friend

I got a call from our senior pilot at Bristol Bay Sportfishing Lodge. For forty years, Blake Larue has made his living as a bush pilot, flying all over Alaska. The last twenty-five years, he has flown Super Cubs and Beavers on the Alaska Peninsula.

I have never met a safer pilot than Blake and was excited when he started flying with us. The clients who have gone on the bush flying

Email Exchange

-----Original Message-----
Saturday, July 23, 2022 12:35 AM
Hello,
I wanted to touch base with you.
Just a quick note as we are in the busiest part of the season and flying 7 days a week until October.
I was lucky to have Ron as a friend. He was a huge influence in my flying career and helped me in so many ways that no words could ever express the gratitude I feel for him. On more than a few occasions the things he taught me saved my life .
I hope to be able to talk to you in October after I finish my flying season.
Sincerely
Jerry Jacques
Alaska Master Guide #110

Sent: Mon, Jul 25, 2022 6:05 am
Hello Jerry,
I'm hearing so much about you now. When I first heard your name in Jack Baker's post a few years ago in *FlyHelio*, I tried only briefly to get in touch with you. I'm sorry I never pursued harder.
I only knew Ron as someone in my childhood who I truly loved. I heard bits and pieces of stories and saw a few of the pictures I included in the book, but I was never able to put it all together until I had his manuscript. What an adventure! He's my hero, and I'm so glad to meet his friend. Thanks for contacting me, Jerry. I'm certainly looking forward to hearing more from you in October.
    Until then,
    CS

Sent: Tuesday, August 2, 2022 1:11 AM
Hello,
There is a 2-part podcast just released. It is about the 1995 Helio Courier rescue of a stranded kayaker in Devils Canyon Alaska.
THIS RESCUE COULD NEVER HAVE BEEN MADE IF RON HAD NOT TAUGHT ME TO FLY HELIO'S
    Ron knew the absolute limits of that aircraft; he pushed me as his student to fly the Helio to its limits. The lessons and advice Ron gave me saved both my life and the life of the kayaker that September day in 1995.
    The podcast is by Sam Carter. His channel is River Radius Podcast. It is a 2-part podcast titled No Boat No Paddle on the Big Susitna River.
    Jerry Jacques

Sent: Wed, Aug 3, 2022 3:20 pm
Subject: RE: Jerry Jacques old friend of Ron
Hi Jerry!
Thank you for sending this podcast. Kathy (one of my sisters) and I both listened to it. Amazing! That was a daring and bold rescue on your part. Even though Ron taught you to fly the Helio Courier, that tough little plane and, ultimately, your own skills as a pilot were what saved you and Buckwheat both, as well as the Helio itself! I felt completely involved in your drama while listening to it unfold. This story is so like Ron's, I think, a vignette in a larger-than-life adventure. If you ever want your stories recorded, let me know, and we'll get to work. I believe we're all a little richer when these stories are actually written down and preserved for the record. (The Library of Congress is a very good repository.)
    So, I'm going to write the River Radius Podcast a review. . . well done by everyone involved.
    Thanks again, Jerry. Please keep in touch.
    Very best,
    CS

safaris with him always come back to the lodge wide-eyed, talking about the incredible things they saw. Every pilot who is with him on a flight tells me they admire his skill and knowledge.

Sad News — When I answered the phone, Blake came right out and said what was on his mind.

"Jerry, I am hanging up my spurs, and you need to find another Beaver pilot for next season," he said. "No problems with my health or medical; it is just time after forty years to slow down and enjoy my family."

This news was hard to swallow, and a flood of emotions surged through me. I said, "I will respect your decision but will miss you." Then we both got choked up and had to end the call with the agreement that we would talk again soon. Realizing that I would not be working with Blake next summer made me extremely sad. Eventually it hit me that this was not a time for sadness.

Blake has had a successful forty-year career as an Alaskan bush pilot flying off airport in the harshest conditions that Alaska can dish out. He was the one making the decision for him to retire. That is the best thing that a pilot can hope for, a long successful career and that we are the one who decides when it is time to retire.

Time to Rejoice— A few days later Blake and I talked again. I will admit that call was still a little emotional for both of us. The end of a career for a fantastic pilot is sad. But then we agreed that Blake would stay current. In the spring, he would come to Iliamna and help train the new pilot. In addition, he would be a backup pilot should someone get sick or need a week off.

A Blessing for all. I am thankful for Blake's safety and the safety for those who flew with him for the last forty years. Good news I get to work part time with my friend, and the lodge has a fantastic backup pilot. Blake gets to spend most of the summer with his family and still gets to fly a Beaver in the wildest part of the Alaska Bush.

—Jerry Jacques

Family, friends, & crew at the lodge (© Michael V. Rainwater)

25.
Belize

Wednesday, December 7-9, 2022

All my adult life I have been dealing with bears and other dangerous land animals. I respect them but am not afraid of them. However, sharks have always scared me. Today in Belize, Erin, my daughter booked us a trip to swim with sharks in shark alley!

I was just going to humor her and get all my scuba gear together, and then I figured it wouldn't hurt to ride along with the family. Soon enough, though, the twenty-minute boat ride with a professional guide was at our destination in shark alley, and we were surrounded by these sleek denizens of the deep. From the safety of the boat, I could see multiple five- and seven-foot-long sharks circling beneath us. It was an intimidating sight—and I was fairly intimidated. Erin was first into the water off the back of the boat, but I was not sure that I wanted to do this. Reluctantly, I soon decided to give it a try, telling myself I needed to make my daughter happy.

I slid into the water from the front of the boat and swam to the back of the boat where the sharks and Erin were. As I got there, my wife Laura was entering the water. To avoid colliding with her, I moved closer to the nurse sharks and suddenly was surrounded by them; now the sharks were close enough to touch, but I was not actually tempted to do that.

Very slowly, I swam out of the center of the school, happy I was still in one piece. Soon four more people had entered the water.

Well, despite my trepidation, it turned out to be fun. The nurse sharks we were with are non-aggressive to people.

On Friday, we dove in a different spot and went down to seventy feet. That's the deepest I have ever been. Five of us were following trenches in the coral reef. The water was crystal clear, and we saw lots of incredible reef fish, including a few nurse sharks close by. I am now comfortable with them, but at a shallower depth in another trench, a six- or seven-foot-long reef shark swam very close and circled me twice. This, I was not comfortable with; I had to force myself to stay calm. After checking me out, the shark left me and swam over to check out another diver, circling him a few times before gliding off. Although this shark was truly magnificent and spellbinding to watch, I was not upset in the least to see it leave.

Lesson 19! Sometimes you need to get out of your comfort zone.

Remember, eventually, we are all going to die, what is important is to truly live before you cash in your chips. Although, I confess, I am still more comfortable around Alaskan grizzlies than I am swimming with sharks.

Thank you, Erin, for making these few days diving in the waters off Belize incredibly wonderful.

Nick & Erin with me & Laura in Belize

VI.
Hunting With My Sons

As everyone on this planet is unique, with their own experiences and life stories, so are my sons, Jason and Caleb. At young ages I introduced both boys to shooting and hunting. But they each had their own stories to tell of their Alaskan adventures, as well as unique stories of hunting big game with their father.

Although certainly not the only wilderness experiences I've had with my children, these are two fine stories written by two very individual boys.

—Jerry Jacques

Jason & The Bear

On my eighth birthday I got my first gun. It was a .22 rifle. I told my dad that I wanted to take my .22 and go on a grizzly bear hunt. Dad said I was not ready to hunt a bear, but we could start preparing for a bear hunt and some day we can hunt bear. I got my .45-70 Marlin for my Christmas present from Dad. We went cross-country skiing almost every day after school, and I carried my gun on my back. I shot lots of snowballs, icicles, and stumps. Dad and I pretended that these things were bears or moose or tigers. This was fun, but one day we got some big paper picture targets of bear. The pictures were as big as a real bear and fun to shoot at. We took my gun to the spring hunting bear camp, and Dad and I camped out and skied a lot. I wanted to find a bear, but Dad said I was not ready yet to hunt bear.

On my ninth birthday, I asked Dad if I could go to Cold Bay with him and hunt bear for my birthday present. I like shooting and only want to hunt a bear. I do not want to kill anything else.

Day 1, September 30— I am in Anchorage spending the weekend with my mom, and she is driving me to the airport at Merrill Field. I am finally going bear hunting in Cold Bay with my dad. We are waiting for Daniel, who is a pilot and mechanic working for my dad. He is going to pick me up in one of Dad's Cessna 185 airplanes, then we will fly to Dillingham for the night.

2001 Hunting Trip Diary

On the way, we flew past Susitna Flats, Beluga, Tyonek, Nikolai Creek, Big River Lakes, through Lake Clark Pass then over Lake Clark, then past Port Alsworth, Nondalton, then we stopped at Lake Iliamna for fuel, then to Talarik Creek, Levelock, then on to Dillingham. I have to follow our route on the map and keep these notes for Dad. It took us four hours to get to Dillingham. At the airport in Dillingham, we meet one of the guides named Christian; he is a friend of mine, too, and is a lot of fun, but he smells like a bear. We all stayed at the Beaver Creek Bed and Breakfast[1] for the night.

Day 2— In the morning, we went flying for five more hours. From Dillingham past Nakeen then to Naknek where we got gas, then in the air again to Egegik, Pilot Point, Ugashik Bay, Port Heiden, then to Cape Seniavin. At Cape Seniavin, we saw some walrus, then we

---

[1] https://dillinghamalaska.com/

went past Franks Lagoon, Bear Lake, Port Moller, Deer Island, past the Black Hills, Moffet Lagoon, and at last to Cold Bay to meet my dad. I learned that north is always at the top of the map. We had to dig ditches for tie downs to anchor the airplane. Daniel had to work on Dad's floatplane and Dad had to fly Christian to a hunting camp using the Super Cub.

Day 3— In the morning, I stayed at the hotel. I learned how to play shuffleboard in the restaurant / hotel / bar / general store / laundromat—all of these things are in the same building. After that, my dad and I went flying to a lake. When we landed on the lake in the amphib, which is a plane that can go on land and water, my dad had to get in a wetsuit, then go in the water and set the anchor, then screw in tie-downs to keep the plane from blowing away. I had to walk on the wings and help put the wing covers on the plane. We slept in the plane.

Day 4— Early in the morning, my dad got up and I was really tired. My dad thought he saw the sun starting to come up, and he started to get us ready to go out in the wilderness. I said I was really tired still so my dad looked at his watch, and it was 3:00 a.m. It was only the moon shining through the clouds that had fooled him, so we went back to sleep. Then we got up again at 7:00 a.m., ate, and I got on a wetsuit and chest waders so we could get to land. We will go hunting for grizzly bear. We will hunt for nothing else. I had my trusty .45-70 Marlin lever action gun and my binoculars. Dad has his big .416 gun and a big pack on his back. We were in a place that had no trees, but there were lots of alder bushes, some are as big as trees, and everywhere you step there were lots of ptarmigan. We saw a flock of swans and one red-tailed hawk. Then we saw lots of caribou. We looked at them for a while with the spotting telescope. One baby came right up to us to see what we were; when it got five yards away, it looked at us, then trotted off. We saw some cubs and a big momma bear, but we cannot shoot the mom because the cubs would die without her. So then we had a long hike back to the plane. We got to the plane just before it got dark. When we took off from the lake in the plane, we saw a big bear! DARN! So we flew back to Cold Bay and spent the night at the hotel.

Day 5— In the morning, my dad got up, but I was too tired from all the hiking the day before, so my dad let me sleep more while he went to fly and check on all his guides and hunters. Then I got up at 1:30 in the afternoon. We ate lunch at Mary's Lodge.[2] Then we flew to the same lake as before. We had to get the plane tied down and the wing covers on, and then Dad fixed us dinner, and we got to sleep in the plane.

Day 6— In the morning, I got up, but Dad was too tired and would

2 http://www.coldbaylodge.com/

not get up, and I had to wait. DARN! So now we got up finally and ate dried fruit for breakfast. At 8:00 a.m., we started walking and hunting. I had my trusty gun so I could kill the bear we spotted yesterday. We got to a top of a hill and, with binoculars, we searched for the bear. First we saw the mommy bear and her cubs, then we saw the bear at the other end of the lake. We had to walk fast for a long while to get to the bear. We had to crawl on our bellies and sneak up to get close enough. Dad was always checking the wind direction. Finally, we were sixty yards away; the bear was slowly walking, and he was sideways to us. Then the big moment came to kill the bear with my gun. Dad told me to wait until the bear stopped walking. I took careful aim; the bear turned away from us, stopped, and BLAM! I hit the bear in the butt because he had turned as I was pulling the trigger. He ran into the alder thicket. Dad made me wait in a big alder tree while he went in to look for the bear for a few minutes. Then he came back, and we went back to the plane and drove it across the lake. Dad made me wait in the plane while he looked for the rest of the day in the alder thicket for the bear. Dad heard the bear roar at him while he was tracking the bear in the thick alder. Dad could not get the bear to come out of the alder, and it kept moving, so he could not get a shot to finish it. I felt horrible and cried because I had wounded the bear. After a long time, Dad came back, and we flew to Cold Bay. On the way, we saw at least a hundred seals on a beach and at least a hundred and seventy-five sea otters.

Day 7— We ate breakfast at the Cold Bay Lodge, then Dad, Christian, and I flew back to the lake to look for the bear. Dad and Christian tracked the bear in the alder while I watched from the top of a hill. The bear had left the alder and was headed for the beach on the Bering Sea a few miles away. We flew back to Cold Bay and spent the night there.

Day 8— Dad went looking again for the bear; this time he was alone. He came back at 2:00 p.m., and he told me that he knew where the bear had gone, and we were going to go after it again. This time, we were going to have to backpack a long way to get to where the bear was. We got into Dad's yellow plane with the big tires; I think it is a Super Cub, and we flew to a beach on the Bering Sea. Daniel flew the plane back to Cold Bay.

Dad and I started walking. I had to carry my rifle and binoculars and rain jacket. Dad had a huge backpack on his back and his big .416 Rigby rifle. We walked along the beach, and a seal was following us in the water for a long time. Dad called him our pet seal and said he would bring us good luck. Just before it got dark, we started looking to find a place to camp.

We were trying to find an old Native Village site with ruins. Dad had spent a night there before I was born. We were lucky one of the ruins was still standing. It looked like a grassy hill with a few caves in it. The walls and roof were covered with sod and grass, so it was kind of buried. We did a lot of work to fix it up enough to stay in it for the night. My dad had to find a bunch of wood and rope on the beach to fix the place up. While inside, I cleaned the old wooden bunks out. A lot of dirt, sand, and rabbit poop was covering the old wood bunks, and it was hard to get it all out. Dad used two garbage bags to put down on my bunk, then my sleeping bag on top. He used his poncho on his bunk. It was spooky sleeping in the old ruin that night, but it was dry and out of the wind and rain. We ate Mountain House dried food for dinner and a candy bar for dessert.

Day 9— In the morning, we had a little breakfast. Then we started walking and hunting for my bear. We saw a sow with two cubs. After a long walk, we saw a very big bear that Dad said was about nine and a half feet. This bear was leaving the whale carcass on the beach and stopped one mile away. The big bear was sleeping in the tundra and Dad said it was not my bear as it was a lot bigger than the one I had wounded. After one hour, that bear left and went farther away from us. Then a different bear was near the creek out on the tundra; we stalked this bear. We did a lot of crawling and had to keep moving to stay downwind of the bear. Finally, the bear was in range, and we looked at it with a spotting telescope. Dad said it was not my bear, so we just watched it. The bear kept getting closer to us, and when it was twenty yards away it saw us and ran away. I could have easily shot this bear but was only looking for the wounded bear.

After that, we went down to the beach and saw the whale carcass. The dead whale was about twenty-five feet long and it was very, very stinky. I found a piece of baleen that was from the mouth of the stinky whale. We think it was a humpback whale. There was an old skull and two ribs from a giant whale on the same beach about a hundred yards away. This must have been a monster of a whale. The ribs were over eleven feet long. This was a gray or blue whale.

Dad thinks it was getting late and we did not see my bear, so we started to hike back to the ruin. A big storm was coming in from the north. Then we saw the big bear heading back toward the whale. Then Dad saw a different bear that we had not seen yet. This bear was very scared and kept looking all around. It did not act like the other bears we had seen. It cautiously made its way to the beach. Dad studied the bear with the spotting telescope. It was limping and had dried blood on its butt, and dad was sure it was my bear. We walked, and we ran, and we crawled, and finally we were forty yards away, looking down on the bear that was eating the stinky whale.

Laying down with my gun on Dad's backpack, I took careful aim, then shot it. I killed it with my first shot. The 540-grain Garrett custom bullet went all the way through, breaking both shoulders and killing him almost instantly. He was an eight-and-a-half-foot bear.

We knelt beside the beautiful animal and said a prayer for the bear. I was excited and felt sad at the same time. Dad says that it is okay to feel sad at the death of any living creature. He says they are all God's creatures, and we should respect them. We thanked the bear for giving up its life for us and asked God to bless its spirit. After the prayer we admired the bear, then took pictures.

Then the bad news. We had to skin the bear, and it was total darkness before we were even one quarter of the way through. I had to hold the flashlight for Dad while he finished skinning, and I had to keep looking to make sure a different bear did not sneak up on us.

When it was done, we carried the hide for a half mile and hid it, so another bear did not eat it. I found a glass ball on the beach where we hid the hide. Then we walked out onto the tundra.

The wind was blowing so hard it kept knocking us over. The hail stung my face and hurt a lot. We had to set up a tiny tent that was in my dad's pack. This was very hard and, because the wind was blowing so hard, it kept blowing us down. We found a little low spot in the tundra, but the wind still blew the tent everywhere, and we had a bad night in the storm. Dad said that the wind was seventy knots, and it was the worst storm of the season. It was so loud I had to yell in Dad's ear for him to hear me.

Day 10— In the morning we had no breakfast. The wind was still blowing, and it was raining with ice pellets in it. Oh well, we started walking back to the ruins. We got there and got our gear off. Then the pilot that was going to pick us up flew over and we had to get our gear back on. We never should have taken it off, I thought. Then our plane could not land because of the wind and high tide. This happened several times and we had to keep walking trying to find a beach that the plane could land on. Finally, late in the evening, a different pilot came back and landed to pick us up. We had to leave the bear hide because there was not room for all of us in the plane. We flew to Cold Bay and got there after dark. Dad said that we had walked at least fifty miles during our hunt.

Day 11— Dad flew out and got the bear hide and from the stinky whale he got two of the ribs and two of the backbones. I was tired and wanted to stay in the room and read my book.

Day 12— I flew to Anchorage with Larry, who was one of the hunting clients that hunts with Dad a lot. He flew on a big two engine plane and my mom met me in Anchorage, and I spent the weekend with her. Then on Monday she took me to Dad's house in Talkeetna so I could go back to school.

Jason's trophy photo signed by Gen. Chuck Yeager, Joe Engle, and Pres. George H. W. Bush

Caleb's Caribou Hunt

My father is a guide and bush pilot. That means he's rugged, and a little rough around the edges. He's brave, fair, and good. He's always been a great man, and the people around me have always admired and idolized my father. I, however, know many of his secrets and embarrassing stories, and I still respect him.

I moved back in with my dad when I was eight. It was just days before my mother died. I don't remember the surrounding days very well, just lying on the couch until he put a boot in my rear and told me it was time to get moving again. My dad has never been one who enjoyed sitting around.

Three months after I moved in with him, he got called to serve in Afghanistan, and I was left alone with a family I barely knew. I was an outsider to their group. That was hard. When he came back, things were different. I was in trouble all the time, and life was uncomfortable. I despised my older siblings, who were awful to me, and I wanted more than anything to return to my home in Alaska, which no longer existed.

While I couldn't return to my life before my mother died, my dad promised to take me back to Alaska for the summer when he came home. He also promised my youngest sister, who was a year older than me, that she could come too. She was the only sibling I liked at the time.

I loved waking up, packing up the tent, and exploring and being a boy out in the woods with my dad. We spent the summer exploring the western regions of Alaska, fishing in remote creeks like Amakdedori. It was fun, and I got to know my father for the first time in my life. However, not every day was all sunshine and treasure hunting. Often the weather was awful, which made the flying bumpy, and a little scary for a nine-year-old who grew up hearing how dangerous aviation was.

I learned a lot: how to fuel an airplane, how to shoot, fish, hunt, take down a tent, and put one up. It was a good time, though difficult. Eventually, the summer ended, and we dropped my sister off at Ted Stevens airport, and she went back home to be with her mom, my stepmom.

I wasn't ready to go home yet, and my dad gave me a choice. I could either stay with him and get to hunt a caribou, or I could fly back to Idaho. I chose to stay. At this point, we were staying at the large log cabin my dad built in his early days in Alaska. Of all the houses I have lived in, it was my favorite, and I still miss it. The cabin smelled of pine and wood smoke, and the scent constantly reminded me of my dad. I'd visited the cabin once before and stayed with my dad there. I must have been six the first time. I was enjoying my time in Alaska, and I chose to go on the hunt with my dad. The thing about that was we wouldn't be staying at the comfortable cabin. It meant flying up to the Brooks Range and camping from the airplane as we had done much of that summer.

When the weather was good, camping was comfortable, and when the weather was bad, camping was very uncomfortable. Camping out of the airplane meant stale everything: bagels, yogurt that made me sick, and oatmeal I had to choke down. It also meant pitching the tent and taking it down in the morning.

When you are young and have gone through trauma, travel can be difficult to recall as you tend to zone out to make time move faster. I don't remember the trip up to the Brooks Range or where we stopped first. I wasn't much for reading maps or remembering names when I was that young. I spent much of my young life trying to make time move faster.

I do remember the hunts themselves, though, and the dressing, fleshing, and packing of the meat. That, to me was the exciting part.

On the first day we landed somewhere, I am still not sure where, but I'll ask my dad who will know. We talked with a lady there who pointed out an injured caribou in the rocky, windswept valley we had landed in. We camped there, and the next day we hunted that lone caribou for many hours. So many that my legs ached, my belly hurt, and my nose ran like a leaky faucet. It was cold, and we never got closer than five hundred yards to the caribou.

My father was tired, and dark would be closing in within a few hours, so he made the tough decision to shoot the caribou himself. I remember the shot. We positioned downwind of the animal, and my dad lay down while I crouched behind him with binoculars. I heard him breathe out slowly after figuring out the range and getting in position with his sniper rifle. The rifle was a tan camo, heavier than most hunting rifles, but also more accurate, and my father was accustomed to it. I heard the breath leave his lungs, and I jumped when the loud bang came. I watched the caribou take a few steps and then tumble to the ground. It stopped there and never stood again.

I don't recall why, but when we approached the animal, I teared up. That was the first animal I had ever seen die, and I will never forget it. I don't love killing animals, death is not pleasant, and it is always sad. I didn't cry immediately; I was too excited. I remember asking my dad to pray for the animal. We said a small prayer. And then he taught me to skin and break down an animal.

I remember that lesson, but not the packing of the meat afterward. If you pack enough in your life, it all turns into a blur of walking and sweating. Packing meat is very boring.

That was one of three caribous we killed that summer. Dad 1, Caleb 0.

The next thing I remember is flying into a new strip a day or two later and meeting Larry Rivers, and his two daughters Fern, and Robin. I liked them. Larry was as hard a man, maybe harder than my father. I wanted to be like Larry when I grew up because Larry had taught my dad, and my dad seemed to respect and love Larry.

Larry's two girls were like no other girls I'd ever met. They were all enthusiasm and smiles. That was the first time I had ever met girls I liked to be around.

That morning we ate oatmeal, which I hated, and then set off to hunt the herd we'd seen while flying over the day before. Fern, Larry's oldest daughter, ended up leading me the next time we went out to hunt caribou, and I got so nervous I missed a three-hundred-yard shot. My dad wasn't upset, even though I expected him to be.

Larry, my dad, the two girls, and I made our way to a hill looking out over a half dozen caribou. My father coordinated with Larry and the two girls, and I got into position to shoot. After a few seconds of coordination, the countdown started, and two of us shot as it reached one.

My caribou dropped almost immediately. I still remember the numbers on the range finder that day, three hundred thirty-six yards. I also remember the range of my father's next caribou, which was seven hundred and ninety-eight yards. I remember that because my dad was showing off to Larry what his sniper rifle was capable of doing. I remember skinning my caribou and starting to break down the meat into quarters, taking out the backstrap, breaking down the ribs, and getting the tenderloin. It was a long process and would have been longer had Larry not gone back for his Cub and landed closer to the animals. We flew meat out for the rest of that day. One of the girls, I don't remember which, kept a lens from the eye of her caribou. I also ate a bite of the raw heart of my caribou, as that is what Larry and my dad said was tradition after killing your first animal.

I will always treasure these memories, even as I get older and remember fewer and fewer specifics. What matters is that I spent an entire summer with my dad learning how to be a boy. Larry and my dad taught me more about how to be a man on that trip than I ever learned from school or books. From Larry telling me to drink my hot cocoa despite the mosquitoes that wound up in the cup, to Fern telling me to close my eyes and breathe and relax before taking my next shot. I will always remember those lessons. I hope to pass on the same lessons to my boys one day. My only wish is that I could go back and experience that again now that I am older and better able to appreciate all the uncomfortable things I wasn't able to then.

That is the thing about growing up with a dad like mine. You miss the good old days without ever knowing you were living in them in the first place.

That is the most important lesson of my life. If you are born with noble parents who are equally wise and hardened by life, enjoy their company, enjoy their scolding, because one day you won't have them anymore, and you'll wish you could have had just one more scolding, one more lesson, one more anything. Losing a parent so young is hard, and it teaches hard lessons. The best lesson it taught me was to appreciate every second you have with the people you love while you have them. The second lesson it taught me is to appreciate what you have. I have the best dad ever.

Scan the QR to link to Caleb Jacques' YouTube Channel

*Caleb's first caribou,
Brooks Range*

VII.
From the Heart of a Bush Pilot

The following chapters are true and fascinating stories from a bush pilot who's experienced it all. Jerry Jacques is an Alaska master hunting guide who proudly holds #110 in rank order, a whitewater explorer and guide, and a bush pilot who's experienced just about everything the unpredictable Alaskan weather can dish out, as well as unforeseen mechanical failures. Here are stories of the beautiful ups and the terrifying downs of being a bush pilot in that vast and wonderful land, Alaska.

From fun and harrowing hunts, to stories of lifelong friends and a few foes, these chapters are written to touch your heart—and they will. After all, they come straight from the heart of a bush pilot.

—CS Norwood

General Chuck Yeager

When I met General Chuck Yeager, I was in my early twenties; I was a young guide and pilot taking way too many risks.

He took me aside, away from everyone and chewed me out. He said if I did not listen that I was probably going to get myself killed in a plane crash. Then he gave me advice about risk management for flying. Funny, Ron Sutphin would give me a similar talk. .

He told me this years later while visiting me at my lodge in Iliamna. From a note he wrote to me:

> *"Jerry, I remember you as a cocky young pilot unlikely to survive. I sat you down and gave you some stern advice. You listened and, since then, we have had many wonderful Alaskan flying adventures together. Over the decades, I watched you become one of Alaska's most experienced wilderness guides and pilots."*

> *"Good job Jerry.*
> *Fly safe."*
> —*General Chuck Yeager*

Our first meeting was in 1980 or '81 at the SCI (Safari Club International) National Convention; I had heard a rumor that General Chuck Yeager was going to be there. I hoped to maybe get a glimpse of him. During a lunch function, I was invited to sit at a table with several senior Alaska Guides. Also sitting at the table was General Yeager, I was introduced to him and shook his hand. I listened to him interact with the other guides. I never said a word as I was overwhelmed even being invited to sit at the same table with some of the people who I admired most in the world.

The next time I met General Yeager was on a fishing trip. I did not fly him on that trip, but I did fly myself to camp in my Piper Cub. I tried to show off my skill by buzzing camp low-level, making a steep one-eighty-degree turn with my wing tip twenty feet above the ground, then landing as short as I could at the camp. I was pleased that I nailed the landing and got stopped short. I was very disappointed when my boss and General Yeager never said anything about my low-level one-eighty degrees or the short landing that I was so proud of.

That next day the real fishing guides were still not in camp, so I was assigned to be General Yeager's guide for the day.

I had never been much of a fishing guide and quickly learned that

General Yeager was an expert fly fisherman. All I did was get him to the best fishing holes, net his fish, and release them. I was shocked when he requested me to be his guide the next day. He caught both Dolly Varden trout and grayling, and he was fun to be with. The third day I was not only to guide him, but I was also tapped to fly him—I was actually going to fly General Chuck Yeager; I was very nervous and could hardly sleep that night.

I did my best to make my little Cub perform and show off my flying skills that day; I really wanted to impress General Yeager. He said nothing about the flight when we landed, though, but the fishing was fantastic for dry-fly grayling, and he said he had a good time.

The next morning, I asked General Yeager if he had any flying advice for me.

"Let's take a walk," he said.

When we got away from the camp, in private, he chewed me out and read me the riot act for taking unnecessary risks, for being too abrupt with the controls, hard on the airplane, and just pushing the limits when it was not necessary. He told me I was going to get myself killed if I didn't change my ways and calm down.

I had impressed him all right—but not in a good way. I listened to his every word. After all, this was Gen. Chuck Yeager offering me some much-needed advice. Of course, I was crushed when he said he would not fly with me again unless I promised to calm down and stop taking stupid risks.

"Son I see excellent potential in you as a pilot."
—General Chuck Yeager

I was privileged to be General Yeager's pilot and guide in Alaska on many occasions, and, when I had a booth at the SCI or FNAWS convention, he would always come to visit with me. Over the years we became friends, and I saw the man behind the legend. Oftentimes in life when you see the person behind the curtain it is disappointing. With General Yeager, the more I was around him, the more respect I gained for him. He was totally honest; if you asked him a question you always got a straight answer, even if it was not what you wanted to hear. He was one of the most amazing men on every level that I have ever met.

He was kind, loyal, funny, curious, talented, and unbelievably observant. He loved the USA and loved life. He truly lived life to the fullest.

After decades of knowing Gen. Chuck Yeager, I realized that if he had never been a famous pilot and unknown to the world, he would still have been a hero to me. He was everything a man should be.

The first time I met Victoria Yeager was at the lodge in Iliamna with a group of visiting VIPs. I guided the General and his wife for three days and was impressed with Victoria, she was tough, a fantastic fly fisherman, and loved being in the wilderness. I also saw that the General was a lot happier with Victoria in his life.

Gen. Chuck Yeager with his "favorite wing- man," wife Victoria Yeager

Over the years my wife and I got to hang out with both Victoria and General Yeager for weeks at a time. We both saw that they were a good team who truly loved each other. By the time the General hit ninety, he was starting to slow down a little physically. Victoria now reminded me of Nancy Reagan. She became very protective of the general, and the strong woman she is showed through.

I noticed a few people who did not like the fact, that unlike before when she was always in General Yeager's background, she now stepped up to take the lead for her husband. I was, however, extremely impressed, as her motives were only to do what was best for the man she loved so dearly. Seeing how she now ran point for the general put a smile on my face, if only every man could be so lucky as to have a smart, strong woman like Victoria Yeager at his side! Gen. Chuck Yeager gave so much to our country—he deserved the best, and he got the best with Victoria.

I was incredibly happy for my old friend to have a fantastic wife like Victoria Yeager at his side.

I had to fire our chef and send him home. In three days I have six guests arriving at the lodge, all expecting to be eating fantastic food. I am now scrambling to find a new cook.

I called my close friend Ace Dube and asked if he could fill in as the lodge chef until I could find a permanent replacement.

Ace has bailed me out many times over the decades and agreed to

It All Began on August 12, 2000

help. He said, "I can stay for the rest of the season if you want!"

My problem was solved.

August 14— Ace, along with Donna, his wife, just arrived. He immediately took over the kitchen.

Ace Dube has been a friend for decades. He's worked with me both as a whitewater rafting guide and a hunting guide. He is the rifle coach at West High School, a certified explosives expert, and a cook who knows his way around a commercial kitchen.

He and Donna had helped me a tremendous amount in the raising of my son Jason. In short, Ace and Donna are the kind of friends who, if you are lucky enough to have, you're blessed to have them as friends for life.

Ace is an iconic Alaskan, he was born and raised on a gold mine in a remote corner of Alaska where bears were a constant problem. His mom cooked for the twelve-man mining crew and dad ran the crew Being home schooled at the remote mine, there were limited resources available.

The two books that were used to teach Ace to read were the *Dupont Blasters Handbook* and *The Better Homes New Cookbook*.

By the time Ace was thirteen years old, he was the powder monkey at the mine, which meant he was the one setting the dynamite charges for the miners. And, when his mom was sick, Ace cooked full meals for the twelve hungry miners.

He's a big powerful man with a full beard, soft spoken, well read, and always wears a S&W .44 magnum model 29 on his hip. If you can picture what a Klondike gold rush Sourdough from 1898 looked like, Ace fit that image.

August 15— Today General Chuck Yeager, Victoria Yeager, Dr. John Gurden, Karen Gurden, Roy Zettel, and Shirley Zettel arrived.

We picked up all of our guests at the Iliamna airport and brought them out to the lodge. The crew was out front to meet the arriving guests. Everybody was excited to meet General Chuck Yeager. After introductions, the crew helped get the guests' bags into their cabins and then we headed into the main lodge.

When General and Victoria Yeager entered the lodge, Ace had fresh chocolate chip cookies coming out of the oven. The aroma was wonderful and immediately had the general's attention, Ace was looking forward to meeting General Yeager and was pleased when the general asked if that was cookies he smelled.

Ace invited General Yeager into the outer part of his kitchen and served him a steaming hot chocolate chip cookie.

Ace does not allow anyone in his kitchen and that includes me.

When he's in his kitchen mode he moves quickly and efficiently, often with hot pans, boiling water, or knives in his hand. He can maneuver around the kitchen with his eyes closed and still get his work done. But seeing that he invited General Yeager into his kitchen I decided that this might be my chance to snag a cookie and still keep all my fingers, so I followed the General and Victoria into the forbidden zone.

Ace looked up from his discussion with the general, knew what I was after and growled, "OKAY JACQUES just this one time and only one cookie."

He went back to chatting with the general, and I quickly snagged a cookie before Ace changed his mind and ran me out of his kitchen.

After a few minutes, Ace excused himself saying that he had dinner to prepare and went back into the inner part of his kitchen and was at the cutting board chopping. The general could see more cookies on the cookie sheet and decided that he was going to help himself to another cookie and stepped into the inner part of the kitchen. About that same time, Ace turned around and almost bumped into the general.

Ace flinched, took a step back, and said, "Excuse me General. Sir! I do not allow anyone in the inner part of my kitchen as this is my workspace, and I'm constantly moving with knives, hot pans, and boiling water. Sir! I respectfully must ask you to stay out of this part of my kitchen!"

Victoria and I met eyes, both astonished as no one talks to Gen. Chuck Yeager that way. I held my breath, but all General Yeager did was take a few steps back, after which we all retreated out of the kitchen. Neither General Yeager nor Victoria said anything about the incident to me. I hoped that when Ace served the delicious dinner, all would be forgiven.

August 16— Today in the Beaver, we flew out to Brooks Falls to do some fishing and watch the bears. Victoria Yeager sat in the copilot seat, and Gen. Yeager sat behind me; my father-in-law Roy Zettel sat next to General Yeager, and Dr. John Gurden sat next to Roy. In the rear sling seat was Shirley Zettel and Karen Gurden. The rainbow-trout fishing was fair, but watching the bears was fantastic.

Back at the lodge afterwards, General Yeager sat across the table from me and nonchalantly asked, "What's your cook's name?"

Uh oh! Here it comes, I thought, cringing a little inwardly.

"Ace," I replied, and now I was waiting to hear a complaint from the General. His reply was classic Gen. Chuck Yeager, however.

"Yes, Ace…he's a grumpy old fart. I like him."

Today we're going to the Kamishak River to fish for silver salmon.

At breakfast Ace informed me that we were having prime rib for dinner, and he needed to know what time I would be back with the guests.

"I'll shoot for 6:00 p.m., but no later than 7 o'clock," I replied.

Today's plan is to take three guests and fly the Cessna 185 on floats. The passengers will be Karen Gurden, Victoria Yeager, and Gen. Chuck Yeager.

We flew the thirty minutes to the Kamishak River. The river is on the Katmai coast, in the outer part of Cook Inlet, which has some of the most extreme tidal differences in the world. The place we land the floatplane is near the mouth of the river, which is an estuary. The estimated tidal difference today is nineteen feet but, at extreme tides, it can be as much as twenty-six feet difference. We keep a boat anchored to a buoy there.

Docking a floatplane after landing in a flowing river is tricky. When you're docking the plane, there's no reverse and no brakes, so you have to time the engine shut-off. You need enough forward momentum to get to your docking point which, in this case, is a boat tied to a buoy. If you don't have enough forward momentum, the current just sweeps you away, and you have to get back in the airplane, restart it, and try again.

If you have too much momentum when you shut off the engine, you can't stop the plane and you overshoot the docking spot. So, in other words, in a float plane with river current and wind, trying to time it correctly to pull up next to the dock, or, in this case, the boat, the person tying off—me, the pilot—has to have time to get out of the airplane and tie the floats to the anchor buoy. Having General Yeager in the airplane with me, I wanted to make sure that I didn't miss and have the embarrassment of floating back downstream, getting back into the airplane, restarting, and trying again. Thankfully, the docking went fine on the first try.

The four of us got into the eighteen-foot Jon boat powered with a forty-horsepower Yamaha jet and motored several miles upriver. We stopped at a deep pool and fished for a few hours. General Yeager caught seven or eight chum salmon on his fly rod. Chums are also known as dog salmon. Victoria and Karen each caught a couple. Dog salmon are fun to catch but not the best eating of the salmon. We then boated farther upriver and got into a spot where we could catch some silver salmon. Catching silvers on a fly is a whole lot of fun. Pound for pound, they're the hardest fighting of the salmon, and they can be aerobatic when hooked. Even though silver salmon are outstanding to eat, we released all the fish that day. We motored the boat back downriver, expecting to tie up to the buoy and fly back to the lodge.

When we got to the airplane, unfortunately, the tide was still out, and the airplane was sitting high and dry on the sand. Because of the extreme tides, judging the tides is always a guess, and I had miscalculated when the tide should have been high enough to depart. So, now we had time to kill.

General Yeager had fished here with me a few times before. He asked, "How is the Dolly and grayling fishing on the Little Kamishak?"

I smiled. Instead of pointing out my tidal miscalculation, he was just suggesting another spot to fish until the tide came back in.

So we motored on downriver past the airplane about a mile to the confluence with the Little Kamishak River.

The plan was now to travel up the Little Kamishak six or seven miles where the entire river flows over a thirty-foot cliff, forming a beautiful waterfall that dumps into a big pool. There is good grayling fishing in the pool below the waterfall.

As we pulled onto a gravel bar at our destination, the General asked, "How accurate are the gas gauges on your boat tank?"

"They're not accurate at all," I said.

General Yeager said, "I noticed that you haven't checked that gas tank during our entire trip."

I explained to him that I had personally filled the gas tank to brim two days before and the boat hadn't been used since then, and we had plenty of fuel to get back to the airplane. But of course now I was curious, so I jumped back in the boat to visually check the tank. It was empty! There couldn't have been more than two cups of fuel left—not enough to get down the Little Kamishak and certainly not enough to get back up the Kamishak River to our airplane. The general then handed me a sticky note that he had just found in the bottom of the boat. It read:

> *"Jerry, We were short on gas and borrowed some of your boat gas, I will replace it in a few days."*
> —*Kacy Long*

The little piece of paper was floating in the bottom of the boat, the general had picked it up as he got out of the boat.

Victoria helped me paddle seven miles downriver to the confluence of the main Kamishak. Of course this took two and a half hours longer than if we'd use the motor. When we got to the main Kamishak, I started the motor and used the last of the fuel to get us upriver to the airplane that was now floating in six feet of water. As we were loading the airplane, it occurred to me we were going to be three hours late for dinner.

Ace would not be happy with me. We flew back, landed on Lake Iliamna in front of the lodge and taxied to the dock. The crew was there to help. Standing on the top of the dock, however, was Ace with his hands on his hips, glaring at me. Before I could even tie the airplane up, Ace had turned on his heels and headed back to the kitchen.

One of the crew asked, "Is Ace unhappy?"

They all pointed to what was on the landing. A doghouse had been moved there. Ace had used yellow paint to write my name, Jerry, on the front of the doghouse. Conspicuously in front of it was an old fashioned windup alarm clock with the time set for 6:00 p.m., the exact time I was supposed to have returned. I knew Ace probably wouldn't talk to me for a day or two, and getting any dessert was now out of the question. So I decided, *"Well, maybe I can make fun of the situation."*

I crawled inside the doghouse, handed one of our guides my cell phone, and had him take a picture of me with just my head sticking out of the doghouse door. I sent the guide with my cell phone to show the picture to Ace. By the time I got to the dinner table, Ace had calmed down.

He came out of the kitchen and asked, "You didn't just stay late because the fishing was good?"

"No! I ran out of gas in the boat and had to paddle back to the plane."

"All right I can live with that, but no dessert for you tonight," he said. At the end of a nice meal that we all enjoyed Ace still served me dessert.

Lesson learned!

Besides preflighting your plane, a preflight of your boat is worth your time. It could also keep you out of the doghouse.

"ACE! I'm in the doghouse now..."

Over the years I was Gen. Chuck Yeager's pilot and guide in Alaska on many occasions.

Dinner at the lodge with the General, Victoria, & friends

I am proud to say General Chuck Yeager was my friend. —JJ
To learn more about this great American hero, visit his website at https://www.chuckyeager.com/ and scan the QR Code to shop The Right Stuff Store for General Chuck and Victoria Yeager books and more.

29.
First Airplane Crash

Preamble Having survived twenty-thousand-plus off-airport landings,[1] nine engine failures and thirteen airplane wrecks, I wish I could claim my survival was due to being an outstanding pilot. The truth is, I survived my early years not because I was good but because I was lucky and by the grace of God. Unfortunately, over the decades, several of my friends who were better pilots than I was, died in plane wrecks or were injured so badly that they never fully recovered. (One old friend survived many crashes in his long flying career. He was always able to "walk or hobble away" from them all—except for that last one.)

Most of my wrecks were one hundred percent my fault. I can attribute them all to poor judgment, poor risk management, or just my lack of experience. Most bush-flying accidents are preventable. Early on, I flew a lot of worn-out aircraft that had shoddy maintenance histories. Those planes were barely airworthy, so a few of my wrecks were the result of mechanical failures. Being young and invincible—desperately wanting to fly—it was my choice to fly those planes. I was putting myself in risky aircraft and risky situations that could and should have been avoided.

Older and wiser now, I just want to pass on some insights and a few lessons that I've learned the hard way.

My Very First Wreck I had logged little flight time as a pilot when I bought my first plane. It was what I could afford, a used plane to build my flight hours in. It was a 1971 Cessna 150L, fixed wing, single engine aircraft with registration number N1773Q.[2] It was the cheapest plane for sale in Alaska. Not my dream plane, but it was something I could own and fly.

One of Don Sheldon's pilots, Mike Fisher, was a flight instructor who checked me out in my newly purchased plane the same day I bought it. I had flown it three or four times before a week of steady rain and low visibility kept me grounded.

As soon as the weather cleared, I was ready to get back in the air, so I drove over to my new plane, parked in Talkeetna at the Village Airstrip. Cliff Hudson had a sideways sloping tiedown that he let me

---

1 I had about 14,000 hours of flight time at the time I wrote this (over 16,000 hours now). Ron Sutphin had over 40,000 hours by the end of his legendary career, but he told me that I had many more takeoffs and landings than he did.

1 https://onespotter.com/aircraft/fid/814219/N1773Q

use for free, and my Cessna had been secured with it through the rainy weather. Fred Blackie, a high-flight-time pilot was to join me and give me some pointers. I did a good preflight, and Fred did his own pre-flight, looking the plane over carefully for mechanical issues. When he was satisfied, he helped me push the plane out. Shortly after takeoff, however, the engine began to sputter and run ruff. I knew the Parks Highway was in glide distance and turned in that direction. But just as I lined up on the highway, the engine completely quit. Fred asked to take the controls—I agreed.

"I am sorry, but I am going to wreck your plane," he said.

With that said, he turned away from the road and headed toward a large swamp we could see ahead and to the right. His touchdown was smooth; we rolled one hundred feet before the plane's wheels dug in. We lurched forward then violently tipped over. We were suddenly upside down, hanging from our seat belts in the middle of this Alaskan swamp.

We both exited the plane fast, grateful we weren't hurt.

"Why didn't you go for the road? We had lots of altitude to make it!" I asked, sort of perturbed. I was looking at my plane, lying there right in front of me, belly-up in the swamp.

"Yes, we had the altitude," he said, "but with the trees blocking sight of the road, I couldn't see if there was traffic or power lines on the road. Taking the large open swamp was the safest bet. Planes can be replaced, people can't." That was a fantastic lesson.

Lesson Learned

When in doubt, go for the safest place, and do not worry about damage to the plane.

What Caused this Crash?

Cause of the engine to quit: Water in the gas.

How could that happen? I had sumped the tanks and so had Fred, so the tanks had actually been sumped twice before we took off.

As with most crashes, there was a series of events that caused this aircraft accident.

First, the mechanic who rebuilt the plane after the wreck found the entire fuel system and gascolator full of water. That happened when the engine was running. He also found that the gasket around one fuel cap was missing. Instead of replacing the gasket, someone had just bent the ears down on the gas cap, so, although it appeared to fit tight, it wasn't sealed water-tight with a gasket. The plane had been a rental before I bought it, so that guilty party is still unknown.

Second, a week of heavy rain let water flow past the gas cap that had no gasket and into the gas tank.

Third and finally, the angle that the wings sat in the sloping tiedown let one wing sit way low. So even though we sumped that tank twice, it did no good. The low wing let the water settle outboard of the sump.

Always, always have a good mechanic thoroughly inspect the engine on your new-used aircraft, and make sure that your wings are level when you sump your tanks on preflight. Water always settles to the lowest point, and, if the wings are not level and the low point is outboard of the sump, even if water is in your tank, none will show up in your preflight.

The next day after the crash, I was feeling sorry for myself—like I did not have what it took to be a pilot; I began telling myself that flying may not be for me. After all, my very first plane on one of its first flights, was now lying upside down in the local swamp, and it was a wreck—my first wreck.

That same day, Larry Rivers, a Talkeetna hunting guide and bush pilot, tracked me down. He had dual controls, and he put me in the right seat of his Cessna 206 as we flew supplies to his cabin twenty miles away. After he took off again, he had me take the controls. For the next two hours he showed me how to do tight maneuvers and practice emergency landings. At first, I was very nervous, but after about an hour, I started to relax, and the second hour was actually fun. Larry told me his whole purpose was to get me to climb back up on the horse that had thrown me. By doing this, Larry quickly helped me get over my fear from the crash before it festered. Thank you, Larry! If he had not done that, I may never have started flying again.

The next day, I started the crash-recovery process of getting my plane out of the swamp. Damage assessment included one wing that was badly damaged, the prop was bent, and the windshield broken.

To my surprise, Fred bought me a good used wing and helped me rebuild the plane. Only four months later, I was back in my plane, flying again.

30.
First Super Cub

My little rafting and guiding business was growing, and I needed another plane to keep up with the operation. I already had a Cessna 180, so on the advice of one of my flying mentors, Master Guide Larry Rivers, I decided to buy a hundred and fifty-horsepower Piper Super Cub with big tundra tires. Searching via Trade-A-Plane, I looked at many Super Cubs in the lower forty-eight. I eventually found one for sale in Alaska on Kodiak Island. I flew to Kodiak in my C-180, N7813A[1] to take a look at the plane. A couple of Coast Guard aircraft mechanics had rebuilt a Cub. It was beautiful, came with a belly tank that held thirty-two extra gallons of fuel and had two sets of tires. Foolishly, I bought this very pretty Cub without getting a buyer's inspection. A week later, I took the ferry to Kodiak and picked up the Cub. Flying it back to Talkeetna meant crossing open ocean, so I had brought along a wet suit and tiny raft.

N7813A my Cessna 180

On the flight between Kodiak and the mainland, my new Cub started running rough and was burning an excessive amount of fuel. I was glad that I had the extra thirty-two gallons, or I would not have made the crossing without running out of gas. I landed in Homer and looked things over but could not find the problem. A mechanic also

---

[1] N7813A is a 1956 Cessna 180A fixed wing single-engine with a four-seat capacity currently owned by Kvichak Lodge, LLC in Anchorage, AK.

looked and could not see anything wrong with the engine other than two fowled spark plugs, so we changed those. He did point out a few things that were not correct with the rebuild, but they were not safety issues.

Taking off from Homer in route to Talkeetna, again the fuel consumption was twice normal. Because it started running rough midway; I diverted to Merrill Field in Anchorage where Ward Samonos, a mechanic that I knew, worked on the plane. Ward had me pull the carburetor off, and he rebuilt it. Then Ward had me reinstall the carburetor and test fly it. Same problem. He again had me take off the carb and this time sent it to a specialty shop. They said it had corrosion issues internally that could only be seen with a special tool. After Ward put on a new carb, the engine purred like a kitten, and the fuel consumption was back to normal.

A week later Ward helped me put on the tundra tires that came with the plane, They were actually drag-car racing slicks with modified wheels and brake adapters. Ward was not a fan of the slicks and tried to talk me into buying a set of Gar Aero Tundra twenty-nine-inch wheels or a set of thirty-inch Airstreak tires, but my budget was too tight, and I decided to run what I had.

Ward told me to do five or six landings to test the newly installed tires and brakes; I did only one test landing and thought they were fine.

It was a nice day, so on the spur of the moment, my old friend Robert and I jumped into the Cub and took off for Chakachamna Lake near Merrill Pass. A wheel strip had access to a spot for king salmon. The landing spot was a very narrow dirt peninsula just wide enough for the wheels. It was my secret spot for king salmon that very few pilots seemed to know about. I had landed there a few times in my C-180, so I was confident that it would be fine in the Cub. I was wrong. There was a five- to ten-mile-per-hour crosswind over my landing site. So, brakes were important. As I landed, the left brake failed. Without the brake and in that crosswind, I was not able to stay on the narrow peninsula. I went into the swamp. The plane nosed over and over and finally flipped, landing upside down in the swamp. A more experienced Cub pilot would probably have been able to pull off the landing, and a smarter pilot would have spent more time testing the new wheel and brakes.

In a life-and-death situation, fifteen seconds can seem like an hour. Crashing my Piper Super Cub into a swamp was one of these time warps.

Hanging upside down, suspended by our seat belts, the first thing that went through my mind was that I had forgotten to file a flight plan. Next I remembered we had no ELT, and to top it off, our radio antenna was now in the water, so we had no method of communication.

We released our seat belts, landed on our heads, and collapsed into a pile inside the tiny cabin of the two-person plane, with water starting to seep into the cabin, of course, the only door was jammed shut.

Robert started laughing and said, "If we can't get out of the plane on our own, a bear will eventually drag us out."

Now we were both laughing. We kicked out the side window and crawled out.

There is no equipment to lift a plane in the bush; to get a plane that is resting upside down on its back flipped back over onto its wheels is a big issue. One method is to take the wings and the tail feathers off and roll the fuselage. The other option is to dig a big hole around the engine, lift the tail up so the engine goes into the hole and the entire plane rotates on the leading edge of its wings a hundred and eighty degrees and comes back to rest on its wheels.

Robert, who had helped me rescue my first wrecked plane, knew the procedure; we took out the battery, dug a hole in front of the engine, and took off the prop spinner. But in spite of our efforts, we could not get the plane turned back over. We needed help.

Old Alaska Bush Pilot Saying:
"Fly an Hour or Walk a Week"

We had just flown an hour into the Alaskan wilderness, crashed the plane, and no one knew where we were.

Robert stayed with the plane and fished for the three days it took me to get back to him. Hiking out, I had to make my way across a glacier, so it was slow going that first day. I made it across before nightfall, but that first night away from the crash site was extremely cold and lonesome. The next day, I made better progress, spending a comfortable night under a spruce tree with a small fire to keep warm. On day three, I finally got to the dirt strip at Nikolai Creek in a tiny community called Shirleyville. I was able to use their radio and get a message to Don Lee. He came and picked me up in my C-180, and I flew home from there.

Early the next morning, Ward the mechanic, his helper with his aircraft rescue tools, got in his C-180, while I flew my C-180 to my wrecked plane. It was stressful flying toward the same spot that I had wrecked my Cub only four days before, but my landing was fine. The four of us got the plane turned over and back onto its wheels. Using four pieces of three-quarter inch plywood cut into two-foot by eight-foot strips under the wheels, we pushed the plane back to dry ground. Amazingly, the plane had no real damage. A dented spinner, cracked

Plexiglass, and small dents on the leading edge of the wing was all we identified. The soft swamp had cushioned the plane so well that, when it flipped, no damage had happened.

Ward pulled the wet carb and mags off, dried, and reinstalled them; Robert and I drained the oil reservoir and gas tanks, then poured in fresh oil and gas. To my amazement, the plane started up with no issues. It was back at Ward's shop that night.

The Cub continued to give me problems as there were corrosion issues that kept cropping up. Eventually, the rudder hinge failed on takeoff which caused me to wreck the plane again. It was on a remote dirt strip in the Alaska range. Larry Rivers rescued me. I was okay, but that time, the Cub was a total loss.

Lessons Learned!

First Lesson— This was just another case of my overconfidence causing big problems. If I had followed Ward's advice and done the five or six landings on a big airstrip, the brake failure would have occurred in a place where it would have been easy to control the plane. The problem could have been fixed with little effort and not cost me a month's worth of wages.

Second Lesson— Have a good mechanic do a buyer's inspection and listen to your mechanics advice. Do not let a pretty paint job and nice interior fool you into thinking that the actual structure of the plane is sound. Never let your emotions influence your decisions in aviation.

First Helio Courier

I was trying to buy my first Helio Courier. I found six for sale in the US, two in South Carolina at Larry Montgomery's, and four for sale in Alaska.

In my search, I learned that there were two others for sale in Alaska. One was owned by Johnny Walker, a hunting guide from Nome or Kotzebue. He was selling a Helio H-250 asking $54K, which was in my price range.

Ron Sutphin also had two nice Helios for sale, but they were out of my budget. When I talked to him, he told me about an H-295 that was not advertised. It was owned by Jim McGowan in Anchorage. Ron told me that Jim would take $62,000. It was a stretch to come up with that much money, but I could make it work if I stayed on a tight budget and ate moose meat and potatoes all winter.

The last Helio was also an H-295 in Anchorage listed for $67,000 by an aircraft broker at Merrill Field, Anchorage; that price was more than I could afford.

I did not know what to look for in Helios and asked Ron if I could pay him to do a buyer's inspection on the Helios. I was surprised that he said he would be happy to inspect the planes but would not charge me anything. He said I could buy him dinner instead. That was a fantastic offer, and I quickly agreed. I had met Ron several years ago when he taught Charley Connell and I how to fly a PC-6 Porter. I knew Ron was a legend in the Helio world and a fantastic instructor. He was the person to teach me how to fly a Helio Courier aircraft.

Ron talked me out of buying the H-250 because he said it would not carry the heavy loads that I needed.

The other H-295 that I looked at, looked good to me, but Ron wanted to fly it to see how it performed. Jim, the owner, agreed but wanted to be in the copilot seat and get his biannual flight review from Ron.

Jim's wife and I rode in the back.

Ron took off and put the plane through its paces, Jim was shocked at what the Helio could do with Ron flying and so was I.

Over the next hour, Ron gave instruction to Jim; there was a giant improvement in what Jim could do with the plane, his landing distance was cut in half, and his takeoff distance also got shorter.

When we landed, Jim told Ron he had owned the plane for years and had three different high-time pilots teaching him to fly the Helio. Jim never knew it could perform like it did and, after Ron's teaching him the tricks on how to make it perform, he didn't want to sell the plane.

Jim apologized to me as he was no longer willing to sell his Helio, although, he did let Ron give me one hour of dual instruction while he rode in the back seat.

After the hour-long lesson from Ron, I now wanted a Helio more than ever.

In our conversation over dinner, Ron told me that a Helio would not go everywhere that I could take my Super Cub. "But it will far outperform a Cessna C-185 for short field work and load-carrying ability," he said. Ron was a big fan of the Helio but also knew its limits and was realistic about what the little plane could do.

"When you do buy a Helio, you should get more dual instruction before putting it to work with heavy loads," Ron said. "The Helio is not like the Pilatus PC-6. It takes a long transition to really learn how to fly the Helio."

The last Helio I found advertised for sale in Anchorage had an asking price of $67,000, and that was $5K more than I could possibly come up with.

Ron knew the plane and told me it was a good-flying Helio and in good mechanical condition. He told me that I should pay no more than $60,000 for the plane, though. Ron also told me he did not trust the aircraft broker that had the listing.

"Be very careful dealing with him," Ron said.

I made an offer of $60,000, and the broker rejected the offer.

A month later as I was getting ready to head over to Africa to work as a safari guide, out of the blue, the broker called me and asked me if I was still interested in the Helio. He said the owner had dropped his price and would now accept $62,000.

I said I would buy it for that price and bring him the money in four hours, so I flew my Cessna 180 from Talkeetna to Merrill Field and parked at Jayhawk Air where the broker had an office. I then went to the bank and withdrew $62K in cash, which left me two hundred and fifty in my savings and a hundred dollars in my checking account.

When I got back, George was looking at my C-180 and asked me if I wanted to sell it.

"Sure!" I said.

I gave him my bottom-line price of $32,000. He said he had a buyer who wanted it and could make a quick deal.

I gave George $30,000 cash for the deposit on the Helio and flew back to Talkeetna. The next morning I dropped off the Cessna 180 with the log books and left for Africa for the safari-guide job. The deal was done. At last I had a Helio! My only problem was that now I had to wait until I got back from Africa to fly my new plane.

Seven weeks later, returning from Africa and landing back in Anchorage, I called George to arrange for me to pick up the Helio; I planned to fly it back home to Talkeetna.

He then informed me that the sale of my Cessna had fallen through. I said, "I deposited the cash that I had in the bank, and it will take me a few days to get home to Talkeetna and back to Anchorage with the money."

George said, "Just come by my office Monday or Tuesday."

Tuesday morning, I went to his office with a cashier's check for the $32,000 balance.

When I walked into the broker's office, he just handed me a check for $30,000, along with my Cessna keys and log books. I was stunned!

"Here's the $32,000 for the balance! We had a deal in writing!"

He just shrugged his shoulders. "I sold the Helio to someone else yesterday."

Two days later I found out that a doctor from Palmer had bought the Helio from the broker for $67,000.

Talking to Doc, we figured out that it was only a few days after I had left for Africa. Doc later told me that George told the previous owner of the plane that it had been sold for $62,000 (not $67K), and George had taken his ten-percent commission out of that amount, and not the $67K. George only paid the seller $55,800 and not the $60.3K he was entitled to.

Boy was Ron correct; I should never have trusted that broker!

I ended up operating my C-180 and two Piper Super Cubs until the end of 1991.

After the '91 guiding season was over, I called Ron to see what Helios were available. He told me that he had three Helios for sale and that I might be interested in one.

When I landed in Oregon, Ron picked me up in the Helio, flew me around in the plane, and gave me some additional instruction.

I asked him to give me the straight story on the plane, and he told me everything that was wrong with it, as well as the things that were good.

Ron suggested I have an independent mechanic do a buyer's inspection, but I trusted Ron and that his knowledge of Helio Couriers was second to none. I paid him for the plane. And, for the next seven days, Ron trained me. We flew into all kinds of bush airstrips with him teaching me how to really fly the Helio.

After leaving Ron, I flew the Helio all over the US, doing trade shows to sell my Alaska hunting and rafting guided trips.

Returning to Alaska in early spring, the Helio was a big improvement over the Cessna 180. It hauled fifty percent more gear and would land on short bush air strips that I would never attempt with any Cessna. It could land as short as a Super Cub but needed an additional hundred feet of airstrip to take off but, with that extra one hundred feet, it could haul twice as much as the Cub. If it had eight hundred feet of runway, it could haul what it would take a Super Cub three trips to carry. I was set.

My First Helio Wreck

Yesterday I wrecked my Helio near the head waters of the Talkeetna River. It was a hot day; I had a heavy load of rafting gear and was getting ready for the flight when a New Zealand pilot showed up at my hanger wanting a ride around Mt. McKinley. I told the pilot I was heading in the opposite direction to a seven-hundred twenty-six- foot-long rough and narrow gravel-bar strip. He asked if he could ride along. I agreed.

What Caused the Wreck

Pretty simple! Pilot error on my part.

My first mistake was agreeing to let him ride along with me. The plane was already heavily loaded. His extra two hundred pounds was more than I had ever flown with for a short strip landing. I should have removed two hundred pounds of gear when I added the passenger.

My second mistake was trying to show off my skill and what the Helio could do. I tried to land extremely short to impress the Kiwi pilot.

My third mistake at the approach end of the strip was a four-foot cut bank. On short final approach, I got too far behind the power curve with the heavily loaded plane. Checking the descent rate with power is a normal procedure with a Helio Courier but, when you get too heavy, the amount of power needed increases exponentially and must be added earlier than normal. The result was that I got too low and did not add power soon enough. The main wheel on the right side hit the edge of the cut bank. Hitting the bank that hard, it sheared the landing gear bolt and the gear collapsed. Soon after, the right wingtip started dragging in the brush and we came to a very fast stop.

Having been in a few plane crashes already, I was not concerned about a fire or being rescued. I wanted to shut off the gas, master switch, and mags.

The Kiwi however was panicked and wanted out before I could even shut off the fuel and master power switch. A Helio does not have a door on the copilot seat, so he crawled over me to get out of the plane through the pilot door.

After assessing the damage and seeing there was no fuel spill or leakage, I was not worried. We had tent, sleeping bags, and lots of food. The radio still worked, and I knew a plane would eventually fly over or someone would come looking for us. All I needed to do was turn on the radio and talk to a plane that was in line of sight. The Kiwi was, however, still quite shaken up and wanted to set off the ELT for an emergency rescue.

"No way!" I said, "We're not hurt, and this is not an emergency."

"What do you mean? We just crashed and we're stuck in the middle of nowhere!" He yelled angrily.

I told him we were just delayed. "If I need to, I can row one of my rafts back to Talkeetna in a couple of days."

"But I will miss my train ride back to Anchorage tomorrow," he whined.

I had just done $20K damage to my plane, so I didn't have much sympathy for a hitchhiker on a schedule.

After a little while, I decided to see if there were any king salmon in the nearby creek. I took the handheld radio and went for a short hike. I was only gone fifteen minutes—no fish yet—so I went back to the plane. I noticed the gear had been moved in the back of the plane. Looking closer, I saw that the ELT had been set off. I shut it off and questioned my New Zealand passenger/pilot. He told me that he had set it off so we would be rescued. I was not happy, telling him again that this was not an emergency—only a delay.

A few minutes later, he turned it back on. Now I was furious! This time I took out the ELT and kept it with me.

After another hour, a commercial jet flew over at 30,000 feet on its way from Anchorage to Fairbanks. I was surprised that I was able to get the pilot on the radio. He gladly relayed a message to Talkeetna for me asking for my pilot, Paul Rodrick, to come and pick us up. I cleared a new place to land on an open gravel bar a quarter of a mile away. Paul got the message and flew my Super Cub in to pick us up later that afternoon.

The Helio could have been flown out with a few days of field repair, but my mechanic decided that it was safer to hire a helicopter and lift the plane out and back to Talkeetna. Since I was now in the spotlight with the FAA, I needed to be smart.

It was a week later before the helicopter could give my Helio a lift. After the last shackle was secured and it was twenty-five feet in the air, it started to spin. The helicopter was now in danger, so the chopper pilot hit the emergency long-line release, and, in what seemed like slow motion video, I watched my plane drop straight down and hit the ground with a sickening thud. Now my already crippled Helio was really wrecked—it was now a total rebuild project that would take at least a year to complete.

Immediately after I finished the season using my Cessna 180 and my two Piper Cubs, I started looking for another Helio Courier to buy.

A wrecked Helio is a very sad sight

Boris and the Big Bear

I wrote this story years ago and have it somewhere in my notes. I'm recording this from memories of this event some thirty-five years ago. This is the best memory I have of the worst hunter I ever guided. I'll change the name to protect the guilty.

We were on a brown bear hunt in Cold Bay. I was working for Larry Rivers at the time. I had flown my Cessna 180 to Cold Bay with Larry paying for the gas. I picked up two guides along the way and all our gear before landing in the little town of Cold Bay, Alaska.

At this stage in my flying career, I did not have enough experience to be flying around and landing on the beaches in the severe conditions that Cold Bay presents, so after arriving at the airport, I parked my plane, and Larry flew everybody in his Super Cub or Cessna 206 out to the individual spike camps.

The morning of October sixth, I was getting my personal gear together and waiting for him to fly me out when Larry told me to go to the Weathered Inn and meet my client.

"His name is Boris," Larry said. "Make sure that Boris has the correct equipment for the hunt.

"I'll fly you out in about an hour and a half, and then I'll come back and pick up Boris and fly him to the spike camp."

When I walked into the little restaurant at the Weathered Inn, it was easy to pick Boris out. He was the only person sitting there. I walked up to him and asked if he was, in fact, Boris. He confirmed. We talked for a minute until the cook walked out.

"Whadda'ya want? Make it quick; I'm a cook, not a waiter."

Boris ordered two extra-large deluxe breakfasts. I was pleased; I figured Boris had ordered a breakfast for himself and one for me while we were waiting for Larry to return. I would get a nice hot meal—I was wrong.

When the food came out, Boris pulled both orders right in front of him and proceeded to eat every scrap off both of those huge, piled-up plates of food. While I sat directly across from him, watching the spectacle in front of me, I studied the man a little closer. Even while he was seated at the table, I could see Boris was, in fact, a huge man. The bigger shock came when he stood up, though. Boris was only five feet tall but weighed at least three-hundred-and-fifty pounds! He was at first glance the most out-of-shape hunter I'd ever seen in my life! While he ate his two breakfasts, Boris told me that he had hunted in Africa many times.

"Don't let my size fool you," he said. "I'm a very tough, hard hunter, and I can hunt hard."

I had my doubts. To say I was unimpressed with this guy at the first meeting is probably an understatement, but I kept that to myself. I was relieved when I heard Larry's Cub fly overhead. It meant that I had to get over to the runway and get my gear along with the camp gear into the back of Larry's Cub so he could fly me out to the camp.

On the way, Larry mentioned that he was going to have a tough time getting Boris in and out of the Cub—another understatement. I didn't think Larry could do it.

This guy was so wide and so fat that his belly hung over where he couldn't even pick up his legs more than a couple of inches off the ground. He kind of had to shuffle or waddle to walk.

Larry instructed me to gather some driftwood and find some pallets on the beach and build a ramp so we could unload Boris when he got there. I had about an hour and a half before Larry returned with Boris, and that gave me time to set the tent up, stow my gear into the sand dunes about a hundred-and-fifty yards from the beach, and scrounge up some pallets and driftwood to make a ramp. Larry buzzed me, landed, and taxied right up to the pile of wood. He actually had to take the pilot seat out of the Super Cub, which he had done just an hour and a half before, so he could get Boris into the airplane.

Even with our makeshift ramp, it probably took thirty full minutes to get Boris out of the Super Cub. He was so wide and cumbersome that it was almost comical.

After we managed to get him out, Larry grabbed part of his gear, and I grabbed the rest of Boris' gear. We carried it up to the tent while Boris waddled behind us and immediately crawled into the tent.

In those days, the best mountaineering tent on the market was made by North Face. It was called an Oval Intention. Technically, it was a four-man tent which meant there was just enough room for four people to sleep. There was no room for any gear, so that meant the Oval Intention was a cramped, small, two-person tent for a hunting camp. You couldn't stand up in it, but there was enough room to put your gear, as well as the client's gear out of the weather inside the tent and survive the notorious Cold Bay storms.

Especially crucial when you're looking for the big, old brown-bear boars who are very smart—they don't get big and old by being dumb—is to manage your scent. Larry and Clark Engle had taught me one of their tricks which is that you never poop or pee where the bears can smell it. The way to accomplish this is to go to the surf line with a shovel. Dig a little hole, do your business, bury it, and let the surf wash everything away. That way, you disguise the scent. It was a trick that I'd learned that not many guides used. It definitely helped and was probably a pretty ecologically sound practice.

So, bright and early October seventh, my client and I were up and ready for opening day of brown bear season—at least I was. Before daylight, I was out of the tent, and had my gear ready by flashlight. First things first, though. Shovel in one hand, rifle slung over my shoulder, and binoculars around my neck, I went down to the beach to do my nature call. I squatted at the line of the surf, did my business, and buried it there. There was just the tiniest hint of daylight breaking as I completed my task. I stood a moment to survey my surroundings, and as I looked along the beach, I saw movement. I put my Swarovski 10X40 binoculars to my eyes as they gathered more light than my eyes could see without them. Sure enough, there was a bear about one hundred yards down the beach. I was still too far away in the dim light to judge the bear's size, but it definitely was a bear.

The wind was blowing offshore, so the bear was not getting my scent, and it was still dark enough that I didn't think the bear would see me. I made my way as quickly as I could to the tent, opened the tent door and told Boris that we had a bear on the beach. "We need to get out there right now cause the bear's working its way down the beach. When it gets even with us, the wind's gonna carry our scent to it. It'll bolt when it gets a whiff of us, and it'll be gone! You gotta hurry. All you need is your rifle," I said.

"Well, I got to change," Boris said.

Unbelievable!

"No you don't! You don't even need shoes!" I told him in exasperation. "Just run down through these sand dunes eighty yards, and we'll lay down and when the bear comes by, we'll shoot it. We'll be right there!"

Boris would have nothing of it. He very painstakingly took off his pajama top. He took off his pajama bottoms, took off his socks, and then proceeded to change. What should have been thirty seconds at most to grab a rifle and get out there took him ten minutes. I was going nuts! I knew as soon as the bear got our scent, it would be gone. Well, as luck would have it when I'd seen the bear at first, it was actually busy digging in a big pile of kelp and driftwood that had washed up and was looking for scraps of food. He was after old fish, maybe eating some of the kelp, I couldn't tell. But the bear was in the same place that I'd first seen it. Over ten minutes later, when I got to the edge of the sand dunes with Boris was about when the bear looked like it had finished. He started walking down the beach in our direction. When it got parallel to us at about forty-five yards, I could tell this was not a Big Bear; it was a young bear about eight feet at absolute most but probably closer to seven-and-a-half feet.

"This bear's too young. It's not big enough to shoot," I told Boris. "I can't let you shoot it."

This launched Boris into a pretty intense tirade.

"Well, any bear in West Virginia would be a Big Bear, and I wanna shoot it," he argued in what I came to know as his West Virginia accent.

"We're not in Virginia now," I said.

"It's West—by God—Virginia!" Boris was almost shouting now.

"I told you no!" I argued back. "If I let you shoot that bear, I'll be fired, and I'll be the laughingstock in the guide business. This is the land of the biggest bears on the planet and I'm not gonna let you shoot a %#@ little bear! Larry will fire me. You cannot shoot this bear."

Well, the argument didn't last very long because the bear had ambled even with us, got our scent, put its head up, and trotted down the beach another couple of hundred yards away from us.

Boris was pretty mad at me now.

"I should have shot that bear! Any bear in West Virginia would be a Big Bear!" he growled. But it was too late, he couldn't do anything about it, and I was relieved. Boris went back to the tent.

I would have been on bear watch immediately that first couple hours of light, as then and the last few hours of daylight are the prime hunting hours. Boris, however, insisted that I cook him breakfast. He is the client, so he's the boss when it comes to such matters. So, against my better judgment, I left off the bear watch to cook him breakfast. As soon as he finished, I was ready.

"Let's go out and hunt awhile," I said.

"Nah," he said. "You go up to the top of the dunes and watch for bears and you come get me when you see something."

Boris just wasn't like any other client I'd ever guided. Especially on opening morning, every hunter I'd ever guided was excited and ready for the hunt! This guy just wanted to hang out in the tent! *Well, so be it*, I thought in pure consternation. About a hundred-and-fifty yards away was the tallest of the sand dunes. From the top, I could see the whole valley beyond the tent, as well as up and down the beach. I had a pretty good three-sixty-degree view. Shortly after getting on the dune and glassing up the valley, I spotted a few bears, then one in particular came into view. This was probably the biggest bear I'd ever seen! This was a huge, massive bear who really lived up to the Big-Bear moniker. When I spotted him, he was about a mile up the valley and had just come off the stream where he'd apparently been fishing. I kept watching as he walked uphill to the side of the valley and laid down. He was resting in some very light willows and was still very easy to spot. There was no doubt; even as far away as I was; I didn't have to size this bear. There was no guesswork to it. This was a monster bear! I ran down to the tent, got Boris, got his rifle, and started trekking up the valley, Boris trailing in my wake. On my own, it would have taken me about twenty minutes at most to get within shooting range, but I was in my twenties and in great shape. With one of our average client's, it would have taken about thirty-five or forty minutes to get there. So that's what I figured with Boris—within forty-five minutes we would be within range of this bear. Two and a half hours later, Boris was still pathetically slow-waddling. He couldn't step over the hummocks. He couldn't step over rivulets or creeks. It was a miserable two and a half hours, and we were still only halfway to the bear!

I was going crazy!

"You need to pick up the pace!"

The offshore wind had died. The only time the wind dies in Cold Bay is when it's going to shift. If it shifted to onshore, that bear would get our scent and immediately be gone. I had carried Boris' rifle and his little day pack ahead with me and had gotten about a hundred yards away from where the bear lay sleeping. I laid the pack down with Boris' rifle on the pack with the crosshairs centered on the bear lying broadside to us. Then I went back to Boris in order to encourage him along. I was so frustrated, I grabbed him by the hand and tried to pull him with me. For the fourth time, I told him that he needed to pick up the pace. I felt doomed to the wind. I just knew it was going to shift, and I told him so.

"I ain't willing to get all sweaty for a bear," was his only comment. "We'll just have to go at my pace."

This made absolutely no sense whatsoever to a twenty-year-old hunting guide.

By the time we were two-thirds of the way to our bear, Boris and I had covered the mile distance in a whopping three hours and thirty minutes! This marked the total time from when we'd left the camp. This should have only been an easy thirty-minute hike, not tough at all.

Suddenly the wind shifted. I threw my binoculars up at the first light gust of wind shift. The bear got that gust of wind, sat up, and sniffed. I could tell that he thought he smelled something but wasn't sure what it was. The wind gusts had not yet carried our full scent to him. He laid back down and went back to sleep.

Meanwhile, I was just going nuts trying to get Boris to hurry. He wouldn't and, moreover, he couldn't. He just was not physically capable of picking up the pace, period.

Unfortunately, the next gust of wind coming off the ocean took our scent straight to our quarry. Big Bear stood up, sniffed, dropped down to all fours and immediately started walking off at a fast pace. I watched him go all the way to the head of the valley up through the snow fields and out of the valley through avalanche zones where no human could follow before he disappeared. He was gone. We would never see him again, at least not during that hunt.

I was pretty frustrated, but I wanted to see just how big that bear really was. This was a landmark point in my hunting-guide career—I'd never seen a bear that big. I left Boris and walked to where I could find a good set of tracks. Sure enough, the width of the front pad was over ten-and-a-half-inches wide. This was a huge, huge bear. I had taken some big bears on Kodiak before while hunting with Jim Bailey, but I'd never seen a bear so massive.

Still frustrated, I went back to Boris. I was carrying his rifle and his pack along with my pack and rifle. The whole event was painful, and now I had to painstakingly walk next to him as he waddled his way back to camp and crawled into the tent. He insisted that I cook him dinner, which was fine with me. Boris never left the tent after that. He would pee in a can and poop in a can and would not get out of the tent. I was repulsed; I was not gonna sleep and live in a tent with that man! It was disgusting. I wound up digging myself a cave in the sand dunes and made a shelter to keep me out of the weather. At least I would not have to be sleeping next to someone peeing in a can two or three times a night next to my sleeping bag. This had turned into *the hunting trip from hell* for me.

Every morning I would get up before daylight, go to the tent and cook our breakfast; I'd leave his breakfast plate there for him. By the very first light, I would be on top of the sand dune, glassing up the valley.

We were in some nasty weather. It was a big storm with the wind blowing onshore. That didn't matter; I still had to do my job. I spent all day on top of the sand dune on bear watch, glassing, hoping that a bear would come close enough for me to encourage Boris to waddle within range.

I was starting to second guess myself at this point, though. Maybe I should have let Boris shoot that bear, the one that had walked down the beach opening morning. Boris sure wasn't letting me forget it, either.

"I should have shot that bear! You should have let me shoot that bear!" He was really letting me have it at every opportunity. "Any bear in West Virginia would be a Big Bear!"

"We're not in Virginia."

"West—by God—Virginia!"

I spent all day, day-after-day, up on the bear watch. About two-and-a-half hours before dark, I would come back in and fix myself a bowl of Top Ramen soup to warm up and then go back up for the last two hours of daylight.

An early-warning alarm to the bears must have gone out on the wind because no bear came within any kind of reasonable distance that Boris could manage. The wind was wrong. It was blowing up-valley anyway. The few bears I was seeing were at the head of the valley, far away and beyond the distance that Boris could hike or waddle. The bears were contentedly fishing, usually in the first hour in the morning and the last hour in the evening.

With the winds blowing about thirty miles an hour onshore and up the valley, I used my shovel to carve several chairs into the top of the very steep sand dune. I had a reclining chair that I could sit back and be comfortable with my legs up carved into the sand dune; I had an upright chair for kind of stretching and trying to stay awake and a third chair that was just kind of a chair that kept me down out of the wind. I had my 375 H&H with me at all times, no round in the chamber, what the Germans call underloaded, full magazine empty chamber, and that rifle was always either in my hand, next to me, or slung over my shoulder.

I was idly scanning the view when I started feeling kind of weird, like somebody was watching me. I turned around and looked up and down the beach behind me. I saw nothing, so I turned my attention back towards the valley. But that creepy, being-watched feeling wouldn't go away. This time I sat up straighter, pulled my hood off my rain jacket, and turned all the way around. I looked up and down the beach and then right at the very base of my sand dune—the bear was looking straight up at me. We made eye contact with only my head poked up above the crest of the dune. About the time we made eye contact, the bear charged me, coming like lightning straight up my forty-foot dune. It was full speed and closing amazingly fast.

I grabbed my rifle and worked the bolt—things happened so fast, but everything seemed in horribly slow motion in those seconds. Just as the bear hit the top of the dune, literally three feet from me, I managed to get the rifle round in the chamber and pulled the trigger.

It was point-blank range. The 350-grain Barnes projectile hit center mass. The bear made a grunting sound, hit the barrel of my rifle, and over the dune it went. Suddenly the top of the sand dune collapsed underneath me and that bear. The way I'd cut out my chairs and the life and death struggle that bear and I were engaged in caused the dune to lose any stability it had. As soon as the bear hit my rifle, it started sliding down the other side of the sand dune, while I was desperately trying to regain my balance while atop this avalanche of sand. I got my balance and grabbed my rifle back. I was starting to work the bolt action for the second shot when the dune collapsed again.

I was on my back now, sliding down the front side of the sand dune, feet in the air, rifle in hand, looking back up at the dune as I'm sliding down. At the same time, the bear crested the sand dune, coming back at me again.

I'm sure %#@ now! I don't remember if I even had time to think those words; I sure felt them, though.

As upside down and confused as I was, with everything happening so fast, I only had time to react instinctively. I managed to fire a second round from about fifteen feet as the bear was above me, just cresting the dune and coming down fast. It would be on me in a second. That second round hit solid through its chest and into its spine and took all the fight out of it. I was still sliding backwards down the dune now with that bear sliding down right behind. I was trying with all my might to roll out of the way and work the bolt for a third round. After what seemed like an eternity, but was only a fraction of a second, I finally got the bolt worked and fired a third round into the bear. At that point, it was probably already dead, but I wasn't about to take any chances. The bear slid all the way to the bottom of the sand dune and was finally lying dead at my feet.

Great, I thought, *I just killed the only possible bear that this client could shoot.*

It wasn't huge either. It was probably an eight-and-a-half-foot bear at most, and probably closer to eight feet. I was sure it was bigger than the bear I wouldn't let Boris shoot, though.

I was just standing there, pondering my dilemma when the adrenaline rush hit. I've got a dead bear and a client who I know is gonna show up any minute and be furious that I shot his bear. Thankfully, I was wrong, though. Because of the steady howl of the high wind and the fact that he never stuck his head out of the tent unless it was to empty the slop bottle just outside the tent, coupled with his practice of playing music on his state-of-the-art Sony Walkman, Boris never heard my shots.

I still knew that I was in trouble here. I had a dead bear, a client who couldn't walk, and, to top it all off, I was gonna have a boss who would be mad as a hornet at me.

Slowly, with the adrenaline rush fading now, my devious mind started working.

I had a dead bear. The client didn't hear a thing, and he never showed up.

Maybe, just maybe I can save this.

I painstakingly erased all the tracks going up the hill and the sand dune with a couple of chunks of alder that I cut. Then I rolled the bear over to a log and got it into a position where it looked lifelike, or as lifelike as I could make a dead bear look. Finally, I erased all the tracks on my trail to the dune as I went back to the tent. It actually was my normal time to come in. I got my cup of Top Ramen soup warmed up and then walked back out as it started to get low light. I played it as if nothing had happened. My plan was to stay out for a while, run back, get Boris, and have him come out into the twilight where he could barely see the bear's silhouette, shoot the bear (even though it was already dead), and claim his trophy. I hoped he wouldn't figure it out.

That's exactly what happened. It was a perfect plan that worked perfectly.

I hurried back for Boris just at low light and managed to get him going. He waddled out to the beach and saw the sleeping (dead) bear silhouette I pointed out.

"This is late-evening light," I whispered to Boris, so as not to disturb the bear that I was pretty sure was dead asleep anyway. "You're just gonna have to start shooting. As soon as you shoot. I'm gonna start shooting, too. We can't risk it."

Boris was fine with that, so he started shooting. He shot twice into the barely visible outline of the bear. I fired three shots, purposely missing, because there were already three bullet holes in this bear.

It was all over pretty quickly. Boris had fired his two shots, and I'd fired my three shots.

"Huh, it's dead," I said squinting across the dim light at Boris' bear. "It's dead. I guarantee you one hundred percent that that bear is dead!"

My practice was to never make that guarantee, but I was able to make an exception this time.

I was expecting Boris to be right behind me as I walked up to the bear lying barely forty yards away. When I turned around to see his reaction, I was surprised to see Boris still standing where he'd shot from. He was holding his rifle by the barrel, butt stock in the sand.

"Is it dead?" Boris yelled across the distance.

"Yeah," I yelled back, "it's dead! Come on over and take a look."

"Nah," he said as he turned away. "It's cold out here. This is windy miserable. I'm going back to the tent."

He never even walked up to the bear, which was probably a good thing cause rigor mortis had set in. The bear was stiff and cold by this point.

I watched in quiet amazement as Boris waddled off into the fading light. Then I took some pictures of the bear and started my process of skinning it out that night under the glow of my flashlight while Boris nestled himself snugly inside the tent. I didn't really mind Boris' absence all that much at this point, though. I was just doing my job.

Twenty-five years passed before I mustered the guts to tell Larry Rivers what actually happened with me and Boris in Cold Bay. I was too chicken early on, I suppose, but I no longer worked for Larry; I was a Master Guide in Alaska now with my own thriving business. Larry and I are still friends; we were never competitors. He is someone whose friendship I will always cherish. So, when the opportune moment finally arrived that I did tell him, I understood when he gave me this stern look as he listened quietly and patiently to my whole confession. When I gave him that final look that said I was sorry and I was so glad to get that whole affair off my conscience, Larry just burst into laughter!

Boris was not only the worst and most out-of-shape hunter in my career, but he was also the worst and most out-of-shape hunter in Larry River's career—ever, period, exclamation point!

The sport of big-game hunting in the Alaskan wilderness is not for the faint-of-heart or the out-of-shape. No matter what size you are, it's seriously challenging. Please keep this in mind before you book your next trip. Guides always want the best for their clients; please go on any wilderness adventure as fit as you can be, well equipped, and with as positive an outlook as you can muster. Alaska Master Guides: Your success is their business.

The Glen Hunter

This hunting season has been my best season ever. I started in the Brooks Range guiding two hunters for Larry Rivers. Isolated and undisturbed, and basically at the northern extent of the treeline, the Brooks Range is home to Dall sheep, grizzly bear, black bear, gray wolves, moose, and caribou. My two clients took two sheep and four caribou on this hunt. Then I began working for an outfitter in the Talkeetna Mountains. Farther south in Alaska, the Talkeetna Mountains rise just east of the town of Talkeetna and the Susitna North River. I guided four clients, three from Germany, and one from New Jersey in the lower states for this outfitter. One of the clients took a grizzly and a moose, two clients took only grizzlies, and one client took only a single moose. It had been my most successful season yet. It was one of those seasons that game was plentiful, and I seemed to always be in the right place at the right time with good clients who could all walk and shoot straight. After the third moose was down, killed by the client from New Jersey, I led the packers to the kill site then headed back out to the point that the outfitter picked me up in his floatplane.

I was done here and had a week before I went to Cold Bay down on the Alaska Peninsula to work for Larry Rivers during the brown bear season. The outfitter flew me back to the lodge with only one day remaining in the moose season. We arrived at the lodge just before dinner. As I was heading for my first hot shower in a month, old timer John Ireland, a hermit/hunting guide and mountain man, came paddling up to the lodge in his canoe. I do not remember if I saw him coming or smelled him first. John was a legend in the Talkeetna Mountains; he only went to town once a year. His one-week trip was to buy his supplies for the year and take his once-annual hot bath. I ran to the shore and met him as he pulled in. This gruff old sourdough had been the one who had taken me under his wing and taught me about Dall sheep hunting. John was also a Bible scholar and devout Christian.

Right off, John wanted to know how the outfitter's client, Glen Hunter, had done on his hunt. I told him I didn't know and did not know any client named Glen. It was my first time back in the lodge in a month. He growled, "Where is he?!" When I indicated the direction, he stormed off in pursuit of the outfitter.

Still from a distance, I could see John and the outfitter engaged in a heated conversation about something. It didn't take long to learn that John had taken Glen Hunter up the mountain to a remote cabin at the outfitter's request. John had agreed to guide Glen for only two days. He was to get another guide for Glen and relieve John. John did spend the two days guiding Glen including one extra day; but finally had to get back to his own cabin. He left Glen alone at a high-mountain trapper's cabin. John then walked down at night to the lodge and informed the outfitter where he had left Glen. He assured John that Glen would have a guide by the next morning. Confident that the outfitter would take care of the situation, John paddled his canoe back through the night. It was six miles to his cabin, and waiting for him there was his client who had already been dropped off. John had been with his client a week before he killed a moose. As soon as the client left, John paddled the six miles to the lodge, intending to meet up with Glen and see how his hunt had turned out.

When the outfitter admitted that Glen was still alone at the cabin and had never been provided a guide, John came unglued. John made threats to him about it being illegal to leave Glen without a guide on a guided hunt. The outfitter was in a panic. With only one day remaining in the moose season, he asked me if I would agree to guide Glen for a few days; I was willing, skipped the shower and dinner and got my gear together. The outfitter flew me to the cabin in his Piper Cub. On the way flying up the valley, I saw the largest group of moose that I had ever seen—at least forty cows and eight bulls, and four of those bulls were huge. "I know where Glen and I will be at first light," I said.

"Glen's too feeble to get that far down that valley to those moose," he said.

"I'll carry Glen's pack and rifle, and we'll go as slow a pace as Glen needs to," I said.

"It's too far to pack a moose, and I don't have any packers available anyway. They're all still packing the last two moose my clients shot," the outfitter persisted.

"It's the end of the season, and I'll pack out the moose by myself if I have to," I said. "I still have a week before I have to leave for Cold Bay."

"It's impossible to pack the meat that far uphill!" He was starting to be a little too persistent now by my reckoning.

"I'm willing to try," I told the outfitter. I'm sure I sounded a little defiant at that point.

Now he got mad.

"Glen got a deal on the price of his hunt and under no circumstances do I want him to kill a moose!" He issued this command over the sound of the Cub's engine. "Just stay at the cabin and hope a grizzly walks by," he instructed.

"That's pretty unlikely, and you know it," I said, a little hot-under-the-collar myself. This was my reputation at stake. I had been hired to guide my client, no matter what deal he had made with the outfitter.

"Glen is just a working stiff and a nobody. I have important clients coming next year, and I'm going to save those moose for them!"

I was shocked by this statement. The outfitter landed the plane at the cabin. While he was still taxiing, he turned and said, "Do not let him go down the valley for any reason, and do not, under any circumstances, let him kill one of those moose. If you do, I will fire you, then blackball you from ever guiding in Alaska again."

Our conversation had to end there as Glen was walking toward us, almost to the plane. As soon as the door of the plane was open Glen stuck his hand in my face and introduced himself with a big "Howdy! I'm Glen!" He grabbed the sack of food out of the plane, and I grabbed my pack. While I was getting my rifle out of the scabbard on the strut, Glen carried the food to the cabin for me. The outfitter scowled at me and growled, "NO MOOSE! or you are done as a guide." Then he took off.

This put me in an extremely awkward position. I was the assistant guide, and my name was now on the hunt contract that listed 'Moose, Grizzly, and Black Bear.' I was obligated to do my best for both the client and the outfitter I was working for, yet the Outfitter had ordered me to not let my client kill a moose, even though Glen had tags for moose, grizzly, and black bear.

Before leaving the lodge, I had repacked my gear and had to run to the plane. I had missed dinner as well as my long-awaited shower. I suspected I smelled like John Ireland, but Glen just ignored my rank body odor.

This was the first cabin I had ever hunted out of. I was used to hunting out of a pup tent. A cabin was nice!

Glen found out I had not eaten and insisted on cooking me dinner. I was the guide, so it was my job to cook and clean up afterwards, but he would not let me near the stove and insisted I let him cook. I thought to myself, this is a nice guy, and I am under orders not to let him take a moose! If I do, I will get black-balled out of the guiding business.

We ate and talked until late. He was a very nice man. It did not take me long to decide that at first light we were going to be down the slope trying to find the biggest bull moose in the valley for him. The hell with orders; I was going to suffer the consequences and do everything in my power to help Glen get his moose.

The way I saw it, the outfitter had signed a contract with Glen to provide him with a guide for sixteen days, and the contract and Glen's tags said he could hunt grizzly and black bear, as well as moose. My name was now on the contract as the guide. I felt that I was obligated to do everything in my power to get Glen any animals on the hunt contract. At that moment, I did not know where any grizzlies were, but I did know the location of a whole herd of moose.

One hour before first light, we were walking down the valley. We hunted hard. Glen was very slow, but he did not know the word quit. He just kept up a slow, steady pace. We searched all day and only saw a cow moose with a calf and a few small caribou. Around 5:00 p.m., I made the call that we had to head back up the valley. I had failed to find Glen his bull moose, and it would be after dark by the time we reached the cabin. I felt bad for Glen, but he had a good attitude and said, "We tried, but that's hunting."

Shortly after we started our hike back up the valley, though, we heard horns crashing against horns. Two bulls fighting? We made our way over a small hill, searching the landscape below, but there was no sign of a moose. The willow and alder were very thick here, blocking a clear view, but we glassed and walked from hill to hill. Nothing!

Glen and I kept our voices low, still stalking. We whispered to each other that we were both sure we had heard two bulls fighting, even though the sound of clacking antlers lasted for only a few seconds.

Most people who have never been around moose or studied them in the wild, don't realize that they are not very bright. But God did give them a good nose and unbelievable hearing. They are huge, powerful creatures with legs like stilts, yet, despite their size, they can move silently through the brush when they want to. Moose, both bulls and cows, are solitary creatures, except when the cows raise their calves.

In the Talkeetna Mountains, the moose start moving to the high country sometime in September. They seem to like the transition zone at the edge of the timberline. The valleys with alder and willow below the alpine and above the trees is the place they seem to like the best. This is where the rut takes place. The bulls and the cows without calves meander this way sometime in September. Before the bulls start collecting their harem, the smaller bulls do a lot of sparing with each other. As rut gets going, the bulls start collecting their harem and protecting them from other bulls. Now the fun is over, and the biggest, most powerful bulls fight for keeps. The big bull will drive out any smaller, weaker bull that gets close to his harem. This is how the herd stays strong. Many people believe the older a bull gets the bigger his antlers become. Not true. The bull will grow his antlers the largest during his prime years. After he gets older and past his prime, his antlers get smaller and often become slightly deformed. Soon he can no longer defend a harem; it becomes the younger, stronger bull's turn to keep his own harem.

Glen and I waited and listened. Again, the primal sound echoed through the valley—yet again, for only a few seconds. We waited a moment, then whispered together; what we had both heard echoing across the quiet wilderness was the sound of two bulls clacking antlers in battle.

Just then, my eye caught movement. About four hundred yards downhill and to my left, I saw a huge bull chasing a smaller bull at full speed. They had broken into the clearing with the smaller bull running in the lead. But just as suddenly as they had appeared in the short clearing, they both disappeared into the willows—that small bull crashed into the thicket full speed, running for his life with the big bull closing in.

I grabbed Glen, turned him, and pointed a hundred and fifty yards away to a clearing directly below us and said, "They'll come out there! That big bull chasing the small one is heading for the clearing! Don't shoot the small one. He'll come into view first. Aim for the big bull." Glen jerked a round into the chamber of his 8-mm Wildcat mag at the same instant the small bull appeared in the clearing.

"Don't shoot that one!" I whispered.

The big one followed a second behind. He was magnificent. Glen took aim, led the bull, and pulled the trigger.

I watched the impact of the bullet as it hit its mark. Water flew off the hide from the bullet impact.

A perfect hit, I thought. Then the bull, still at a full charge, disappeared into the alder, still chasing after that smaller bull.

It was raining, so a blood trail would be soon washed away, and it was late in the afternoon. The normal process is to wait at least thirty minutes after an animal is hit, then follow it up. That way, the animal will bleed out and lie down not far from where it was shot. If you charge right in after the shot, the animal may spook, and with the adrenaline pumping, he is off and running. Mortally wounded big game can cover a mile or more before dropping dead, and they can be hard to find that way.

This was not a normal circumstance, however. I told Glen to get up the hill and watch the area; if the bull went up valley, he would see it. Leaving my pack, I took off at a full charge carrying my 1898 Mauser chambered in .375 H&H. I ran straight to where the bull had disappeared and followed at full speed. After two hundred yards into a heavy willow and alder mix, I broke out into a grassy opening about the size of a football field. I halted my chase in shock. Before me in the clearing, huddled in a tight group only fifty yards to my left and slightly uphill from me, stood at least twenty-five cow moose staring at me. Standing fifty feet from them was a huge bull moose, looking at the cows. There were also two other big bulls off to my right about a hundred yards. Their horns were positioned and in a fighting stance. Also, fifty yards directly in front of me was a huge bull lying down next to a small, stunted spruce tree.

This scene: the rain, the cows with the lone bull watching over them, the fighting bulls, and Glen's downed moose is still etched vividly in my mind. It felt prehistoric. I quickly worked the bolt and chambered a 300-grain Barnes bullet. This broke the silence and at that moment the cows bolted, and, unexpectedly, the bull by the tree lunged up like lightning and charged me. I had no idea if this was the bull Glen had shot, but he was actually charging me! I felt confident. I was a good shot and had a .375 H&H in my hand.

I raised the rifle and calmly shot him at thirty yards. He went down instantly like everything I had ever shot before with the .375—but to my complete shock, he jumped back up fast, almost as fast as he went down. I worked the bolt quickly and shot him again at fifteen yards and he went down again. This time I was not so calmly working the bolt. He was up and coming again from eight feet! I fired my remaining round and dove out of the way as he fell where I was standing seconds ago. I was fumbling in my pocket for more ammo as the bull was struggling to get up and finish me. His eyes were red with rage! He was going to squash me like a bug. He did not get up, but he did hook me behind the leg with one antler and send me flying backward. I held onto my rifle and nerve as my hand finally pushed a .375 round into the chamber. I closed the bolt and fired again, this time only three feet from the bull, and it was over. Backing up thirty feet, I grabbed another round and put it into the chamber—I stood ready—my mind racing to catch up with what had just happened.

As my adrenaline rush abated, I heard Glen yelling off in the distance. He had heard the snorts of the charging bull and the shots. He was screaming, "Are you okay? What the hell has happened?"

I finally got my breath back enough to shout back to him. "I'm okay! It's over."

Glen found me ten minutes later; I was still standing where I had stopped thirty feet from the dead bull; Glen was very much out of breath, and I was having the shakes from my adrenaline crash. Together, we were a mess just at that moment.

I was not at all sure if this was the bull he had shot, but I kept that thought to myself. I climbed the same small tree that the bull had been next to and put a ribbon of survey tape near the top to mark the kill so I could find it again easily, then I looked around; there was no sign of any of the other bulls. When I got back to the moose, Glen was sitting next to the kill, sobbing. I did not know what to do so I just kept quiet.

He looked up finally and said, "Nothing is wrong. It's just that this is the fulfillment of a promise." He asked me to sit for a minute.

"My son would be the same age as you, Jerry. When he graduated from high school, he asked me for a moose hunt in Alaska for his graduation present." He paused a moment and then said, "He went to summer school in San Diego first, then, in the fall, we were coming to Alaska to hunt a moose for my son and a grizzly for me. On the way to San Diego, the plane he was in had a midair collision with a military plane and everyone on board was killed, including my son."

This hunt was Glen's way of fulfilling his commitment to his son—his only child. I was also crying after hearing the story.

But I still had to deal with the moose. It was getting late, and I was beginning to worry about getting Glen back to the cabin.

I had been taught not to gut moose as it was a waste of time; I was taught to butcher and quarter without gutting. But there was not time for that, so Glen helped me, and we quickly gutted the moose. I would return and quarter the moose the next morning. We left the kill site and started back to the cabin; I could tell Glen was exhausted. He was very slow, but he kept going. As we hiked, he told me that he had heart bypass surgery a few years before. He did not tell the outfitter or me before because he did not want it to keep him from hunting. I was worried this was too much for him, but we eventually got to the cabin in the dark. It was sometime after midnight.

Sunrise came too soon for me, but I heard Glen at the stove. He was up with the sun and cooking breakfast. As I got ready to go to the kill site, Glen told me he did not think he could make it back down the valley to the moose. I was relieved, as I was sure he could not make another round trip.

I went down the valley and, for two hours, searched unsuccessfully for any sign of a second bull, I found no indication that a second bull had been shot. At last, I went to work on the bull, caped out the head, quartered, and butchered the moose. During my processing, I recovered an 8-mm projectile; that was the moment that I knew, one hundred percent for sure, that the bull that charged me was also the same bull that Glen had shot. I was much relieved. It was going to take a long, hard week to pack out just this one moose, but to have to pack two moose up the valley by myself was something I was really hoping to avoid. The last job I had at the kill site was to tie the moose cape and one tenderloin onto my pack frame before making the long pack to the cabin. It was dark by 9:00 p.m., so the last two hours of my trek were in the dark. I got back to the cabin at 11:00 p.m. Glen had a nice dinner waiting for me, and I was so grateful; I was totally exhausted after packing that moose cape six miles up the valley.

I had seven more loads to do to get everything packed up to the cabin. I was starting to feel that the outfitter was right—it was impossible to pack a moose up the valley to the cabin.

I am against boning out the quarters as the meat will not hang or age properly. I told Glen this when we discussed my next load for the morning. Reluctantly, he agreed that I should not bone out the meat.

The next day, after bringing the moose cape to the cabin, I was awakened by Glen as he handed me a cup of hot chocolate. Breakfast was on the table. It was hard to get up, but I had no choice. Glen packed me a lunch; as I was eating my breakfast, he went outside the cabin with a role of survey tape.

He had used ashes from the stove outlined with orange survey tape to make seven-foot-high, twelve-inch-wide letters on the green tundra that spelled out:

BRING MEAT PACKERS

I asked if he was trying to get the message to the jets that occasionally fly over or was it to the outfitter?

By 8:00 a.m., Glen was fleshing the moose cape, and I was walking down the valley to get a hindquarter. At noon, the outfitter flew over the cabin and circled three or four times. Then he flew down the valley and found me. He circled low with the door open as he flew by, and I could see him shaking his fist at me. As a parting gesture, he flipped me off, then left. I knew I was not going to get any help packing out this moose.

It took me until 8:00 p.m. to get back to the cabin with the hindquarter on my back.

The next day around noon, with the last hindquarter on my back, I was so physically exhausted I knew I could not make it up the valley with the load. I was at a loss of what to do. I did not have the physical strength to make it the rest of the way up the valley with the hundred-and-twenty-pound load on my back. I stumbled and was on my hands and knees and could not get up. With all the strength I had, I tried, but I could not get to my feet with the load. At last, I gave up and started praying. I knew without a doubt that I could not do this on my own.

I believed the only way the meat was going to be salvaged was if God gave me the strength to do it. After a long time praying on my hands and knees, I was able to struggle up to my feet. I was given enough strength to make it to the cabin just before dark. When Glen lifted the pack off my back, he was positive it weighed a hundred and forty pounds. For the rest of the week, I went down to the kill each day and made a trip back with a heavy load. Each day I got to the point where my strength failed. I tried to do it without His help and failed each time. Only when I prayed for strength from God was I able to make it to the cabin with a load. Each evening when I got to the cabin, Glen met me with a cold glass of Tang and helped me take off the pack and hang the meat. He also had dinner waiting for me.

The outfitter had flown over a few times during the week but never landed.

The last load I made was the lightest load I had made, so it did not take me as long to get back up the valley. I was at the base of the hill that the cabin sat on, taking one last short rest when I spotted what looked like a grizzly on the side of the mountain above the valley. It appeared to be a mile away. I left my pack at the base of the hill and ran up the hill to the cabin. I was used to Glen meeting me as I crested the hill, but he was not there. I thought he must have seen the bear from the cabin and was on his way after it. I figured I had better find Glen and fast. I decided to exchange my handgun for my rifle still in the cabin. I burst through the door of the cabin and ran smack into Glen who was heading out the door with a cup of Tang in his hand. Now covered in Tang, I told Glen that there was a bear on the side of the mountain. We grabbed field glasses. It was a grizzly all right and one of good size. The bear was feeding on blueberries across the mountainside as we started up. We knew we only had a few hours of daylight left. Glen was very slow going uphill.

After an hour, he was struggling, sweating, and breathing hard, and the bear was still uphill and still five hundred yards away. Glen told me he could make a four-hundred-yard shot from a prone position. I was young and inexperienced back then. Now I do not believe in letting a client shoot at a bear any farther than a hundred to a hundred and fifty yards at the absolute max.

When we got to three hundred yards, we stopped. Glen got his breathing slowed and heart rate down to normal, got into prone position and slung up. He was steady as a rock. He fired the bullet, hit the bear, and it went down and rolled into some low willow bushes. After a few minutes, I told Glen to watch the hillside. I had to cross a deep creek with steep rock walls then climb up to where the bear was. When

I got there, I found a blood spot where the bear had been, but there was no bear. It had been hit hard and solid. I was sure it could not have gone very far and must be within a few yards. I started following the spoor and went about forty yards before I lost the trail for a minute. Then I saw a patch of blood on the tundra thirty feet in front of me. That meant the bear was in the thick alder patch ahead. I knew I must go in after it. I slowly walked to the edge of the alder patch, rifle ready. I knelt trying to see under the foliage. A freshly broken twig and a slight depression in the ground told me I was on the right track. From this low stance I could see thirty or forty feet ahead, but still no bear in sight. With the rifle in front of me ready for a charge, I stepped into the alder. At that instant, I heard a rush of air behind me. As I started turning around, my rifle sling hung up in the alder. The grizzly was behind me at full charge and had me dead to rights, and my rifle snagged and tangled hopelessly in the alder. In that split second, I knew I was in serious trouble, but in the next second as the grizzly lunged, he collapsed onto the ground beside me. Instantaneously, I heard the report of the shot Glen had just made, saving my life.

Glen, from three hundred yards away across the creek, had watched me following the grizzly's trail, then watched the bear come out from the low willows, stalking me from behind. Just as the bear started the charge for me, Glen's bullet hit the bear, stopping him in mid-charge. The momentum of the charge had carried the bear to within five feet of me. I finally broke my rifle free and fired, but another shot was not needed, the bear was dead from Glen's last shot. The reason I heard the shot after the bear went down is that the bullet was traveling at around 3,200 feet per second, three times the speed of sound. So, the bullet had hit the bear before the sound had reached me.

It was very late again, and I knew I had to get Glen back to the cabin. I gutted the bear, then left him there, planning to come back the next morning.

On the way back down the mountain, it started snowing. We got to the cabin around midnight. Glen did not look good, and I was worried his heart would fail him. He was concerned and said so when we got inside the cabin. He told me he had completed his mission and was ready to be with his son. I was terrified he might die during the night. The next morning, though, we both awoke with four inches of fresh snow on the ground and the color back in Glen's face. I went back to the bear and skinned it out. It was an eight-footer with a beautiful hide. As I was packing the hide down off the mountain, The outfitter landed in his Cub. I watched from a distance as he and Glen got into the plane and flew off. I was getting close to the cabin when he landed for the second time.

He was tying on the moose rack and loading the moose cape into the Cub when I arrived. The outfitter was furious with me for letting Glen shoot a moose and even madder because he also killed the bear that I had spotted. I had to walk out in the snow to the lodge as he refused to fly me; he also refused to pay me for the eight days I spent in the cabin with our client.

Glen was not at the lodge when I got there the next evening. He had a flight to catch. The cook gave me a note from him. Glen said he was very embarrassed that, after tipping the cook and John Ireland, he had no money left to give me a tip, but he would make it up to me after he got home. I sent him a letter from Cold Bay telling him I had felt honored to have been his guide and his friendship was the best tip I could ever ask for. Five weeks later when I got home, there was a box waiting for me from Glen. In the box was a progressive Ponsness/Warren rifle reloading press. It was something I had always wanted but never could afford. Glen had also enclosed a note.

The moose is 69" and will qualify for Boone & Crockett Club Record Book. My taxidermist scored it 229 and another taxidermist scored it 232 B&C.
I refused to let it be officially scored because I don't want that SOB outfitter, to get the credit or get good press out of it.

—Glen Hunter

The outfitter did try to blackball me. He succeeded and delayed me for a year from getting my registered guide license.

Larry Rivers told me there are two things in this world no one can ever take away from you—your faith in God and your integrity. Only you control those things.

Larry Rivers and Clark Engle went to bat for me with the guide board, and I did get my registered license the next year.

Glen and I remained very close friends for the rest of his life. He helped me get my start as an outfitter and personally recruited my first six hunting clients.

Glen passed away in 1999. I felt privileged to have been his friend.

It is hunters like Glen who make being a big game guide worth all the hard work.

Packin' Out   People have no idea how huge an Alaska moose is. For a big bull moose, these are the following loads to be packed out:

One cape weighs, 75-90 lb,
Two front quarters weigh, 75-90 lb each,
Two rear quarters weigh, 90-110 lb each,
Neck meat and tenderloins weigh, 70-80 lb combined,
Back straps and ribs weigh, 70-90 lb combined, and
Freshly killed, antlers with skull weighs, 50-80 lb.

The last load is the antlers still attached to the skull. The problem is carrying a fifty- to seventy-inch-wide load through the brush. It's extremely awkward and always hanging up on something.

The One-Legged German

The first bear hunt I ever guided was for a German doctor while I was employed by Sunny Headland and Carl Jensen. We were hunting near Lake Iliamna.

Doc Schmidt, the client, had a fused knee which had no movement in it. He had taken a round from a US machine gun in World War II when he was a young boy. Doc had no animosity toward the US, only anger toward the Nazis.

Doc was a joy to be with in the wilderness; he never complained. Walking through swamps or over logs was hard for him. Understandably, it took a lot of effort and energy for him to navigate through the rugged Alaskan wilderness, yet he was always cheerful. The gun he was using had been his dad's. This was his dad's dream hunt, and he was making it to honor him. His dad's last wish was for his son to do the hunt in his place using his old 7x57/1898-model Mauser rifle, fulfilling a dream I suppose they both shared. Initially, we used a skiff then walked hours with full packs.

We watched a small bull moose play in a swamp and attack a birch tree with vigor, like it was a rival trying to steal his sweetheart. Doc loved having a campfire at night and enjoyed his tea. I told him that the light from fire reduced his chances of seeing an approaching grizzly.

"Some things in life are worth the risk. In German woods, we are not allowed to have an open fire," he said.

Four days into our hunt, we spotted a big bull moose. Doc lined up on the moose from a hundred yards and squeezed off a round. It was a perfect shot. The moose never knew what hit him. He was very respectful of the dead moose and made a nice ceremony honoring the life of the moose, asking God to let the consumption of this magnificent animal give us strength, which it did. I lived off that moose meat for the rest of the winter.

After I field dressed and butchered the moose, we hung the meat in a tree. Doc stayed with the meat while I hiked back to the lake, took a boat to Pedro Bay, and recruited my friend Kevin and one of the Jacko boys to help me pack the moose meat out.

It took three days to pack all the meat out to a lake where it could be boated to camp. Doc rested and fished while we packed the meat.

On the last trek back to the kill site, I saw movement at the head of the valley just above treeline, three or four miles off in the distance, so I checked with my field glasses—yes, a grizzly feeding on blueberries.

The doc was really excited when I got back to the lake and told him. Carl Jensen was waiting at the skiff, and the three of us made quick arrangements. Carl took the meat by boat back to main camp. Doc and I checked our packs, taking our tent and food enough for only three days.

We hiked up through the trees, coming out above the bigger trees into the low brush and berry bushes where I had spotted the bear. We looked for two days with no sign of the bear. We also watched the gut pile from our high ground to see if the bear was attracted to the scent of our kill, but he never showed there either. On the other side of a pass was another valley the bear had been feeding toward when I had first glassed him. Another guide and client had taken a bull moose in that valley a few days before Doc shot his moose, so there would also be a gut pile there. Doc talked me into hiking to that next valley over so we could take a look. We had a day's food left, and, despite the foraging bears, there were still lots of blueberries above treeline. We still might be able to bag this bear, but I was very reluctant because of his leg as well as his age. Doc was game, but not really in great physical shape. His idea was sound, but I did not think he could make the trek.

We talked; I lost. I had never before tried to argue a stubborn German out for bear!! Doc was determined to fulfill his dad's dream on this hunt, and it was my job to help him realize that dream, so onward toward the valley we hiked.

Cresting the pass, we saw some Dall sheep, all ewes and lambs. It was the closest I had ever been to Dall sheep. I was starting to get a little tired after a long day's hike, so I knew Doc was probably feeling pretty weary. At last, we climbed to an ideal spot—a hill overlooking the moose-kill site in the next valley. It looked like a bear or wolf had been working the gut pile. Resting a moment, checking our options, we decided to set up camp on another hill across from the gut pile. There was a deep canyon bottomed out by a fast running, rocky, shallow creek about fifty feet wide between us and the moose kill spot.

To my surprise, Doc had packed in some extra food he shared with me, and I killed a few ptarmigan with my slingshot. We gathered some blueberries along the way, so we ate well that evening. On the morning of the last day of our hunt, the bear showed up on the gut pile. Doc and I made a slow, careful stalk, finally advancing to within range at about a hundred yards. I put my pack down, and Doc laid his rifle on it, ready for prone position. We watched our bear for over an hour, both of us admiring the magnificent beauty of this alpha predator, but the light was fading quickly now.

"Doc, you have to make the shot soon or I won't have enough light to track that bear if you miss the kill shot and only wound him," I said. Doc looked at me with a funny smile, then opened the bolt on his rifle. He emptied the ammo from the magazine and laid it on my pack. Dock then got into prone shooting position and took aim. I thought this was strange, but I got ready to back him up if the bear charged. He pulled the trigger and CLICK! No bang—only click. I thought the round in his chamber had misfired.

Doc looked at me with a calm smile written across his face. "My aim was steady, and the shot would have killed the bear," he said. "My gun is empty. I was not going to shoot that bear."

So we sat there then, watching the bear rummage and feed until it was too dark to see anymore. Doc had decided not to kill the bear.

"I have already shot a big old bull moose," he said. "You and I have hunted hard, and I was close enough to make a clean kill on the bear. This has been the hunt of my dreams, and my dad would have been proud of the big moose his son shot with his old gun."

He told me he planned on a special place in his home to mount the moose antlers with his father's rifle hanging just beneath them.

"My daddy's gun has fired its last shot," he said finally. Next morning, at first light, we walked to the lake, boated back to main camp, and then the float plane took Doc away to Anchorage. He was headed home.

That winter, in a letter from Doc, he told me he missed his flight from Anchorage to Germany and had to wait in Anchorage a full week for another flight. We exchanged a few letters over the years, never really losing touch, but it had been a long time now since I had heard anything from him.

Then, in 1996, I got another letter from Doc. He wanted to take his grandson hunting and wanted to know if we could hunt by boat as he could not do much walking. I was guiding part of the winter in Africa then and suggested a safari. Two months later, Doc, his grandson, and I were on safari in Africa, and it was fun! Doc's grandson took some nice plains' game, and Doc shot a big warthog. We ate well.

One night, as we all sat next to our fire under a brilliant African sky, Doc told me that this was his last hunt. He told me that the moose/grizzly hunt we shared was his most prized hunting memory, and he thanked me with tears in his eyes.

I'm so grateful Doc decided to save his grizzly that day...

35

Larry Keeler

For quite a few years, I was privileged to work with one of the most experienced hunting guides in the state of Alaska. His name is Larry Keeler. He got his registered guide's license in 1953 working for Alaska's first Master Guide Hal Waugh.

I first met Larry at an Alaska Professional Hunters Association meeting during a coffee break. He introduced himself but had such a bad stutter that he was having trouble even saying his first and last name. He used a finger on his hand to spell his name out for me. That's Larry Keeler. Of course, I just stood patiently and listened to his introduction, and then I introduced myself to him. He glued himself to me during the lunch break we took with several other guys. It was a nice lunch, and we all talked a little bit.

Then the same thing happened after the meeting; he kind of glued himself to me as we went to dinner. As the multi-day meetings progressed, I found out that he had been working as a guide for Ray McNutt (Master Guide #38) in the Wrangell Mountains.

Ray was president of the guide board, and an old-school horse outfitter. He was a tough boss and an outstanding outfitter.

Larry said that after twenty years working for McNutt, they had a falling out and he was looking for work as a guide.

At the time, I didn't need any guides, but as it often happens in the guide business, just weeks before the season started, one of my guides called me and said he couldn't go to Cold Bay. So. I thought about this guy Larry, I called Ray McNutt, and his wife answered. Ray was not home so I asked her about Larry Keeler. Her response was just what I wanted to hear.

"OH MY! He and Ray had a falling out, but he is the best guide we ever had and a peach of a man. If you have the opportunity to hire him, do it," she said.

I asked what the issue was between Ray and Larry. She paused as if, I thought, to look around and see if Ray had returned, then told me that the last season Larry worked for them, Ray was drinking too much.

"One morning Ray was so hungover he was stumbling. Ray wanted to fly Larry out to a camp in the Super Cub, and Larry refused to get in the plane. Larry told Ray that he was still drunk, and his drinking was out of control. Ray did not take this well because no one had ever stood up to him before.

"What Larry said sunk in, though, and probably saved my husband's life," she said.

It's noteworthy that, after losing Larry as a guide, Ray quickly got control over his drinking and never again got into his plane unless he was totally sober.

I called Larry and offered him the guiding job.

Very Special Forces

Two weeks later, Larry and I were in my Super Cub, flying to Cold Bay to hunt brown bear.

I put him with a client, who was a well-known international hunter. The client was very impressed with Larry! He said Larry was the best guide he had ever had, even though he didn't get a bear. He was just really impressed with how great a guide Larry was and wanted Larry as his guide on his next hunt.

That said a lot to me about Larry Keeler. Most times, when a client fails to get an animal, he blames it on the guide. So for Larry to be good enough, this client didn't rail at him for not getting his trophy… this was, to me, a feather in Larry's cap. I hired him to work for the entire fall season in the Talkeetna Mountains.

When we first met, I thought Larry was in his fifties, but soon learned that he was actually sixty-three years old. That's no spring chicken for doing the work of a hunting guide.

I had six clients coming in September when hunting season opens for Dall sheep, black bear, moose, and grizzly. Each client gets his own personal guide and camp to hunt from.

All my camps and guides were set to go before the clients arrived, but one client arrived a day later than the rest. When I looked at his contract, I thought that it said he was fifty-six years of age. I figured he was the oldest of my clients, so I was going to put him with Larry. By the time the client arrived at my lodge, all the other clients were out with their guides at their respective camps.

As it turned out, this client wasn't fifty-six—he was twenty-six years old! Yeah, I had misread his age on the contract. To top that off, he had just gotten out of the Army as a Ranger. His family tradition was that all their kids always went into the military and served at least one tour of duty. When they got out of the military, the family would buy them an African hunting safari, sort of as a reward and respite before their college grind began.

This kid didn't want to go to Africa to hunt, though; he wanted to come to Alaska. And that's how we ended up with this young man

I flew him to the hunting spike camp where Larry was waiting and left them to their hunt, thinking with a little trepidation that I had probably not made the best match-up of guide and client. Two days later as I was airborne, Larry got me on the radio. In his stuttering voice, he said, "We've got an animal down."

My sixty-three-year-old registered guide led that twenty-six-year-old Army Ranger on a nonstop hike up a steep, barren rock mountainside. Two days, and they already got the ranger his Dall sheep. That's the most strenuous hunt Alaska has to offer!

Larry was fleshing the hide when I walked into the camp to get their animal. The hunter was there, and he looked up with this kind of special-forces stern look on his face.

"I've got a bone to pick with you," he said.

Uh-oh, I thought.

"I'm twenty-six years of age. You've put me with a sixty-three-year-old man, and I just got out of the Army Special Forces! I am in as good or better shape than any professional athlete. And I wanna tell you, I can't keep up with that ***. He's out-walking me!"

I kind of gave Larry a second look.

Oh! That's impressive, I thought. And there he is, not saying anything, just fleshing out this sheep hide.

Those two, my kid-client and my over-the-hill guide, had the most incredible fun. Every other day, I'd fly over, and they'd hit me on the radio.

"We've got another animal."

They killed two black bears, one Dall sheep, a grizzly, and a moose in sixteen days. It was incredible! Every time I walked into the camp, Larry would be busy finishing up fleshing the hide as the client helped me load the meat into the plane.

About the third time I walked in. The client said, "I'm finally happy! Now I can keep up with Larry. That's been my biggest accomplishment of this whole hunt—being able to keep up with Larry."

Larry just smiled and said, "Yep, he's got his tundra legs now."

The last time I walked into their camp, the client came strutting up to me and said, "I will have you know. I have out-walked Larry today."

Larry stopped fleshing the hide he was working on. Looked up and cross-ways at me, got a funny smile on his face and said, "Yep, he's finally able to out-walk me. It's as it should be."

The young man said the best accomplishment of the whole hunt was to out-walk his guide who had out-walked him every day, except the last two.

The Souvenir &
the Sweetheart

There's another part of the story with Larry that's both a little gross yet very heartwarming.

After Larry's wife passed away, he started corresponding with a lady by the name of Ruthie.

Ruthie lived in Naknek at the time, but as a child, she lived with Larry's family. The two of them went to school together. Larry graduated from eighth grade, which used to comprise a relatively standard level of education.

Larry spoke to Ruthie on the phone and corresponded with her through letters, but they had not seen each other since they were school-age kids.

At the end of one Cold Bay hunt, Larry and I were flying home in the Super Cub when we spotted a dead walrus on the beach. A walrus skull with the tusks attached is considered one of the ultimate finds for a bush pilot or guide. However, a decaying walrus is the worst, most disgusting smell I have ever experienced—bar none! It is horrendous!

Without a second thought, I immediately circled and found a safe spot to land as close to the walrus as possible. In order to harvest the skull from a rotting carcass, you do have to detach the head…we had an ax.

Hmm...

Swinging an ax while chopping on a putrid, rotting carcass…the larger and sharper the ax, the better.

So Larry got the ax and got there ahead of me. I watched him take the first five or six swings and hits. Then he walked over to me, handed me the ax and threw up. So far, I was still holding it together. I walked up to the walrus, took maybe three or four swings and hits with the ax, then it was my turn to hand over the ax and go throw up. Oh yeah, we did this disgusting routine till we had the head off. Alaskan bush men aren't easily deterred when it comes to collecting rare souvenirs.

Normally I would have tied our stinky, severed souvenir onto one of the Cub's struts, but I already had a backpack on each strut so there was just no place to tie it outside the plane.

Larry's suggestion:"Let's just put it inside in between you and me." *I'm okay with that,* I thought; I didn't have anything left in my gut to throw up anyway.

Larry got inside the aircraft with my raincoat covering his lap, and I handed him the walrus head. He put the tusks down on the floor right next to his feet and rested that gross, stinky head on his chest which was, after all, protected by the raincoat. All good.

Our next stop was Naknek, were Larry wanted to visit Ruthie, his lady friend. He hadn't seen her for decades. We stopped, and Ruthie showed up at the airport with a brand new pickup truck that had just come in on the barge that week.

We'd forgotten about the stench of the walrus. By this time, our nostrils had burned out, and we couldn't smell anything. Ruthie never said a word. She loaded us into her new pickup truck, took us to her home, and fed us lunch. When I walked into the bathroom, I noticed my face covered with little chunks of rancid meat and blubber from the walrus. I spent a little time cleaning up. Larry did the same thing.

When Ruthie dropped us back off at the airplane, she gave Larry a big hug and kiss.

Amazing!

That kiss was the start of a relationship that lasted for of the rest of their lives.

Well, the next season we went back down to Cold Bay, Larry said, "Ruthie says we're welcome to stop at her place, and she'll feed us lunch—provided we're not covered in walrus blubber and stench."

Hoarfrost

It was the twenty-first of September. Up high in the mountains, Larry had been hunting sheep with a different client and had back-packed to a spot which actually used to be a good airstrip. Not used much, it was overgrown and in bad shape now.

I hit Larry on the radio to ask if the strip was okay to land on and he said, "No. I don't think you should."

After a few passes, I landed anyway, but it was really marginal. Larry was right it was too marginal.

I said, "Look, I'll take the client now.

"I don't have enough daylight to come back and get you, and I'm not gonna pick you up here. You have to walk down the valley. There's a better strip down there."

"Yeah, okay," he agreed.

We loaded the client up and flew back to Talkeetna.

It was now the twenty-second of September, and it was cold in the high country. It's the time of hoarfrost, which means it's so cold the water freezes, pushing up in tiny little sharp spires oozing out of the ground. They look like miniature stalagmites It was all over, covering the entire tundra.

The word hoarfrost, comes from the word "hoary," which means "getting on in age." Yeah, hoarfrost was on the ground—an amazing sight to see.

At first light, I flew back to where Larry should have camped on the airstrip, but there was no tent up on that cold, early morning with the tundra covered in hoarfrost.

I circled again and spotted Larry on that second pass. I landed on the wide spot in the Tundra.

The first thing Larry said when he walked up to meet me was, "Here's your tent," and he handed me the bundled tent! "I dried it yesterday because the weather was nice, I didn't want to get it wet so you could put it away dry for the season."

"Good man!" I said, "but where did you sleep?"

"Oh, I just slept in the tundra," he replied.

"So now *your* sleeping bag's gotta be all wet," I said.

"No. I didn't wanna get my sleeping bag wet either. So I just put on my rain gear and just crawled into a depression in the tundra."

It was twenty degrees and colder still for his night on the tundra. He suffered cold and damp to give me a dry tent at the end of the hunt. I probably looked a little bit stunned when he told me this, but I was thinking, *Wow! Just an amazing, tough man!*

Larry felt that every client should have the experience of what he called a *siwash* or what climbers call a bivouac of being out away from camp and just spending the night out with nothing—no gear, no provisions. He steadfastly believed that every client should experience that once during their hunt, and he would always make that happen. He would just stay out so late in the evening they couldn't get back to the camp before nightfall. It's one of those little things I loved about this man.

At the end of that hunting season, I had a couple of young guides working for me who did not like Larry. They confronted me together and said, "We're not coming back to work for you if you hire Larry back.. He smells, and he's old, and we just don't like him being a guide."

I looked at these two young guys for a long moment and said, "Well, don't let the door hit you in the butt on the way out, because Larry's a great guy and he's got so much experience and knowledge to offer; we can all learn from him. Larry stays."

One of those two guys actually did quit. The other guide stayed on.

Larry worked for me for years. When his eyesight was starting to go in his mid-seventies, I put young assistant guides who had good eyesight with him so they could look out for him while they learned from the master.

Eventually, one day when Larry was in his late seventies, he came to me and said "Jerry, I'll do one more, one more season for you, but I'm gonna have to hang it up after that. My old bones…it's too hard for me sleeping out on the ground."

We stayed in touch for a long, long time after he quit guiding.

36

Uncle Satch

My dad was a good carpenter and woodworker, but he was not mechanically inclined. When I was growing up, there were neither mechanic's tools in our home nor the opportunity for me to learn anything about being a mechanic. My crazy uncle Satch, however, raced motorcycles, cars, had a 1943 Willys Jeep and did all his own maintenance. He also had guns that he let me shoot. Satch was one of my heroes, and I was heartbroken when he moved away from Reno to Alaska.

My first time working with tools came when Robert Reid had me help him work on his motorcycles in his dad's garage. He told me to get him a metric Crescent wrench out of the toolbox. I was so naive, it took me at least five minutes of searching before I figured out that an adjustable Crescent wrench fits both metric and SAE bolts! Mr. Reid was very patient.

Fast-forward a decade or so: Now I was in my early twenties, and I, too, was living in Alaska, struggling to build a rafting business. Uncle Satch was always magnanimous and let me stay at his house whenever I was in Anchorage; this was a huge help for me. I had a place to sleep, a shop I could use to keep my truck running, and a dry place to patch my rafts or weld broken rowing frames.

Satch was smart enough to never get in an airplane with me, as I'm sure he remembered me as the wild kid who was always getting into trouble. He also knew that I had limited mechanical ability. After hanging out with him in his garage, watching him work on his race cars, and with him helping me maintain my old four-wheel-drive pickup, I continued to learn the basics of being a mechanic.

On one occasion, my mom Lois, and Uncle Satch decided to join me on one of my five-day whitewater rafting trips down the Talkeetna River. Satch still wouldn't get in an airplane with me as the pilot and made the decision to fly with Cliff Hudson to the put in for the raft trip. (I guess Satch was not as crazy as my parents always said he was—but he was watching.) A year after the whitewater trip, he decided that he might live through an airplane ride with his wild nephew. (After all, I had singlehandedly hauled him out of the Talkeetna River back into the raft—not once but twice!)

One day Satch asked if I wanted to fly him out and go fly fishing. I was absolutely thrilled that finally my favorite uncle was willing to get into an airplane with me! The next Friday we got into my 1947 PA-11 Piper Cub N4740M and made the three-hour flight to lower Talarik Creek where it flows into Lake Iliamna. Our weekend target—the huge rainbow trout for which that creek is famous. Fishing sucked that weekend, but spending time in the wilderness with my uncle was fantastic.

It was a cold Sunday afternoon when time to leave. My old Piper Cub had no electrical system—and no starter; the only way to start this aircraft was hand-propping. The method is simple, but a little scary. Satch got into the back seat to hold the brakes, turn on the magneto switch, and work the throttle. I stood in front of the airplane, cautiously pulling the propeller through the compression stroke hard enough to spin it, then quickly stepping out of the way.

I tried and tried and tried, but I just couldn't get the aircraft to start.

"Satch, change positions with me," I shouted.

We switched jobs, and he tried pulling the prop several more times until he exhausted his arms without even a sputter from that engine.

We opened the engine cowl and checked to see if it was getting spark and fuel. Everything looked good, so we tried hand-propping again—again with no success.

Then Satch just walked away from the airplane, started a fire, and instructed me to take the spark plugs out of the engine. He carefully heated the spark plugs over the fire, then quickly reinstalled them into the plane's engine. He explained that sometimes just warming the spark plugs could be enough to help get the engine started.

Now, Satch wasn't an airplane mechanic or pilot, and this wasn't a race car or a motorcycle, so I was a little skeptical. He had me get in the airplane, give it a little fuel, turn the magneto switch on, and, of course, the first time he spun the prop, the engine started! Another lesson learned!

This is a trick I've used a few times over the decades since, to start both a plane and a stubborn outboard. Every boy and young man should be lucky enough to have an Uncle Satch in his life.

Zach Babat

I got a call from a young man by the name of Zach Babat who was looking for work as a guide and wanted to meet in person. A few hours later, Zach showed up at my place in Talkeetna and introduced himself.

He was a young Jewish boy who had been guiding fly-fishing trips and running boats, and he was now working on his pilot's license. I really was impressed with him. He was a smart, straightforward, clean-cut kid.

Zach had been working as a fishing guide for Ron Hayes, Alaska's most notorious poacher. He didn't know that Ron was this big-time poacher when he went to work at Ron's lodge.

Ron was caught by Fish and Game and convicted for poaching bears and moose then sentenced to prison, so Zach no longer had a job. He was embarrassed about his past history of working for Hayes and hoped I would not hold it against him.

I agreed to give Zach a chance and hired him for the spring bear hunting season.

Well, that was probably one of the best business decisions I ever made. Zach turned out to be not just smart, but brilliantly smart and just a great, great young man.

Even though I thought well of Zach, until he had actually guided a couple of hunts, I couldn't really decide how good a guide he was. He went out on a spring hunt and did great. The clients as well as the other guides liked him. He was young and inexperienced, but definitely top-notch.

Before coming to Alaska, he worked for an outfitter in Montana, so he had a couple years of hunting experience which definitely helped, plus he had a lot of natural and instinctual ability.

The very next fall season, another young man came to work for me by the name of Christian Elwell. Christian had also been working in Montana as a guide and had gone through a Montana guide school. Christian was also a really hard working, smart, nice young man. Well, Christian and Zach immediately crossed swords and were rivals. They were both the new kid on the block, both trying to prove to me that they were gonna be the best guide I'd ever had. Initially, they did not get along. They were trying to out-compete each other.

Fortunately for all of us, that didn't last very long. Pretty quickly they realized they were both outstanding guides, and they became great life-long friends. Zach and Christian really liked my old-time guide Larry Keeler. They respected Larry's history and experience and were willing to learn from Larry.

Zach and Christian, along with Larry Keeler, Greg Smith, Jason Rucker, and Rex Maurer were my go-to guides and all dear friends.

During this time, Zach had finished his private pilot's license and obtained his floatplane rating. He was flying with me a lot—flying right seat in the Helio Courier or back seat in the Super Cub.

Zach came to me for advice one day. He wanted to be more than just a guide; he wanted to be a pilot guide. He needed to build flight time. He had been saving his money and wanted to buy an airplane to accomplish this goal. Together we looked at a bunch of different airplanes. Ultimately he bought a very nice Luscombe 8E *Silvaire* Deluxe 85 HP tailwheel airplane.

With his newly acquired 1949 aircraft, Zach started building time and becoming proficient in a tailwheel aircraft. Any chance or excuse he had, he was in the air with a huge smile on his face.

As his skill increased, I would pay his gas, and he would fly himself and his personal gear out to my remote camps. This took him to places like the Brooks Range, Iliamna, Dillingham, and Cold Bay.

He didn't have enough experience to fly clients yet, but it was helping him build time and real Alaska flying experience.

He also wound up buying a piece of property close to my lodge and started building his own cabin. I was really happy and proud of him, because this showed long term planning and commitment; this kid was going places.

One funny thing that happened was that one day he came over from his cabin. It was mid-winter, and he asked me if I would get his rifle out of my gun safe for him.

"Sure!" I said.

As I was working on opening the safe, I asked, "What do you need the rifle for?"

"Well, I have to shoot my dog, Cody," he replied, sounding kind of forlorn.

I stopped opening the safe. Cody was a beautiful husky-malamute type dog, and I knew how much Zach loved him.

"Why do you have to shoot Cody?" I asked, really puzzled now.

"Well, he's killed a couple of your geese and your favorite turkey, and now he's killed somebody else's chickens, and my neighbors are all telling me that because he gets himself in trouble, I have to shoot him."

"So when you let him out to go potty in the middle of the night or early in the morning, just put him on a chain and let him do his business on a chain," I said.

"I don't know. My neighbors are pretty adamant I need to shoot this dog."

"Zach, I'm not gonna get you your rifle. You think about it overnight. If you come back in the morning and still want your rifle, I'll give it to you then, but I'm not giving it to you now."

He wasn't very happy with me at this, but he didn't come back the next morning for the rifle. Ultimately, Cody lived for fourteen more years and died of natural causes. Cody was just a little bit of a mischievous dog, but he had a sweet nature and didn't have a mean bone in his body when it came to other people.

Zach continued with his flying and continued guiding and eventually started flying my Super Cubs. He was becoming a very essential part of my business, being able to fly and guide. I could now send him into town with a list of supplies, and he was smart enough that, if there

Zach & me by the Super Cub.

wasn't something exactly that they had, he could find substitutes that could make it work. He helped me in more ways than I can say.

Zach was also great with my young son, Jason. As a single parent, I had to rely on Zach and Christian occasionally as well as Larry to help me take care of Jason when I'd go out for a flight. They all got along. It was kind of like a big, extended family with Zach and Christian and Larry being like uncles to Jason.

Over time, though, I noticed that in spite of being a nice looking, well spoken young man that girls just flocked to, he never wanted anything to do with them. He sort of pushed them away as if he didn't want anything to do with them. Some of these girls were quite beautiful, but he wanted nothing to do with any of them.

Zach and I were flying up to Anchorage one day and had some time together to talk. I said, "Zach, you know, you've got all these beautiful girls fawning all over you, and you don't want anything to do with them. I don't care, but I'm curious. Are you gay?"

"No," he said with a slight smile.

"When I was working in Montana, I met a girl there, the boss's daughter. She's very, very smart, really a neat girl, and we fell in love. Her name is Kerry Pride. Before she graduated high school, though, her parents broke us up because they wanted her to go to vet school. That was her goal, and they didn't want her hanging out with some bum hunting guide. It broke my heart.

"She followed her parents' advice and went away to college. I moved to Alaska. We haven't talked since, and every time I look at another girl, all I can see is Kerry. My heart's still broken..."

I felt really bad for him, but there was not much I could say. I had gone through a divorce that had broken my heart and could relate.

Eventually Zach became a very skilled bush pilot. He flew both my Cessna C-185 and Super Cubs and managed one of my camps.

Forward a Few Years

Zach came to me with a stack of letters in his hand.

"What are these," I asked.

"Remember that girl I told you about, Kerry? I told you her parents broke us up."

"Yeah."

"Well, she's been sending me letters. I haven't opened them. I just can't force myself to open them."

There were about five letters in the stack.

"Why don't you just open them?"

"I can't bring myself to do it. I'm just afraid of what she's said. I don't wanna go through this hurt again. I still haven't gotten over her, but I've stopped wanting to move on. I just can't..."

"Zach," I said, "you've gotta read the letters."

"I can't do it! I think I'm just gonna burn 'em."

"You can't burn 'em before read 'em, Zach! You'd wonder the rest of your life what she wrote you!"

"Well," he said, "Would you read them for me, or at least read the first one or two and see if I should read the rest of 'em? If they're bad, I don't wanna know."

So I opened one of the letters he gave me and read through.

"Zach, you need to read them all! This is not anything bad." I handed him the rest of the letters back, and he went back to his cabin.

Apparently, they talked on the phone shortly thereafter. A week or two later, Kerry sent him a plane ticket to Louisiana. She was in her last semester of veterinary school there, and although he was still uncertain and scared, Zach was hopeful now, as well.

When he returned it was so neat to see a sparkle in Zach's eyes.

"How did it go?" I asked him.

"Oh, better than I could have ever hoped! I'm still in love with her, and I see a future!"

Zach and Kerry were married a year later, and they had just this great relationship. Kerry is such a wonderful young lady. They were very much in love.

Soon after they were married, Zach bought his first Super Cub and then came to me.

"Jerry, I want to go off on my own in the guiding business, but I don't wanna hurt you or our friendship."

"Zach," I said, "I'll be disappointed not having you around, but I'm totally excited for you to continue with your life and continue building your own business. You're a great, smart kid. You're married now, and you should go off on your own, and I'll help you in any way I can."

I was able to continue being a mentor to Zach, and we stayed in close contact. He worked for several air taxis. He gave me as a reference, and they all called me for a recommendation. I always gave him two thumbs up.

He and Kerry eventually sold the cabin in Talkeetna and moved into a place in Palmer. Then, after a while, Zach was back in Cold Bay, helping to guide there. One fall day, we were all gathered at the bar in the Weathered Inn, Cold Bay's small hotel, restaurant, laundromat, general store, and bar all rolled into one. I was having my double orange juice, and the guys were drinking beer when Zach made an announcement to everybody.

"You know, I think I'm gonna quit guiding for a while and concentrate on my art work."

Well, none of us had ever even seen Zach do a scribble, a doodle, or a drawing of any kind, and we all laughed so hard, some of us fell off the barstools.

Undeterred by our disbelief, Zach did exactly what he said. We had no clue. Within three or four years, he was becoming a well-known artist doing his unique Alaska-style wildlife watercolor canvases. His work was fantastic.

Zach decided to make the change complete and sold his Super Cub. He and Kerry bought a small ranch in Montana, but still kept his hand in the guiding and flying a little bit. It was really cool to see him happily married and with his own ranch and art studio.

A neat thing happened one year while I was doing an outdoor recreation show in Boise. Zach decided he was going to do that same show with his artwork. Up until that time, I'd only seen a couple of photos of his paintings. He had the booth right next to me, and as I was setting up my booth and he was setting up his booth, I watched his paintings go up, and my jaw just dropped. His work was incredible!

I kept scratching my head wondering how I knew Zach for all those years and had no clue he had any artistic ability at all, and now he was a world-renown western wildlife artist. It was so cool.

Zach was still flying and guiding summers in Alaska. My business with fishing and photography had grown again enough that I wanted Zach to come back to work for me. I had the perfect position that would work for him and me both. He'd be flying a Beaver on floats and be the backup fly-fishing guide and could work as short a season as he wanted and still do his artwork. I even told him that I'd give him a small room that he could use as a studio to do his artwork whenever he had time off through the guiding season. Kerry could come up anytime she wanted and stay as long as they wanted. It was just this perfect scenario—and he turned me down!

"No," he said, "I've been working for Wade Renfro, who's really a good guy, and it's too close to the start of the season. I'm not going to leave Wade hanging like that.

"I'll tell Wade that it'll be my last season and then I'll come back to work with you, and I'll probably finish my flying career working summers with you in Iliamna and doing my art work in Montana during the winter."

So I was excited. Zach was excited. I knew Wade wouldn't be very happy, but he would understand. Wade has a great reputation, treating people who work with him really well too.

That same year, Zach was flying for Wade in Super Cub N82452.

He had dropped off a passenger at the village of Holy Cross in the Yukon area and was bringing a guide out to one of the camps. He was going to drop that guide off and pick up Christian Elwell and bring him back to Renfro's Alaskan Adventures home base. Christian was also working for Wade because I was long out of the hunting business by that point.

August 31, 2016

I'll never forget the day I got a message from my chef that Christian Elwell had called on a satellite phone.

"Christian says it's important, and you need to call him back as soon as possible," Chef told me.

I was loading my Beaver at the dock with passengers about to depart. I tried to return the call but could not get a connection on Christian's sat phone. Larry Rivers was next to me when I made the call and said he would get hold of Christian while I flew my clients out.

That was at the start of my flying day, but I was plagued throughout the day by this horrible gut-feeling that it was about Zach. I went out, did my flying, and came back to Larry Rivers waiting for me at the dock.

"I've got horrible news," Larry said.

I just looked at him and said, "Is it about Zach and flying?"

"Yeah. How did you know?"

"I couldn't get it out of my mind all day long…I had this horrible feeling. What is it?"

Larry told me that Zach had been in a midair. "There were no survivors," he said.

Christian accompanied Zach's body from the time he was taken away from the crash site all the way back to his home in Montana. It really deeply affected Christian, as well as Larry and me.

I was very blessed to have had Zach in my life for as long as I did.

Very heartbroken, I went to the memorial service in Montana and was one of the speakers at Zach's funeral.

I miss him so much. It's still hard for me to talk about. To this day I can't stop crying when I think about Zach.

According to the NTSB Form 6120.1: "The aircraft departed Bethel Alaska at 0907 destined for a location approximately 85 miles Northwest on a 350 heading. The sky was bright and clear with the sun to the east of the aircraft. The two aircraft collided approximately 7 miles west of Russian Mission." Both aircraft were total losses. Five people, including Zach and his passenger lost their lives in the midair collision.

Scan this QR Code to view some of Zach Babat's amazing artwork.

Epilogue   I have a lot of joy and much to be thankful for at this time in my life, but what's sunshine without shadows? I keep my own measure of sorrow trailing along like a shadow. Sometimes it's behind me, and I don't pay it much attention. It's when I look away from the sunshine in my life that it presents it's full measure, and sometimes it's pretty deep and dark. Choosing to live and work five decades in the wilderness of Alaska—an extremely high-risk environment by any measure—has come at a cost. I've lost six friends in kayaking accidents and in war zones abroad. Incredibly, I've also lost twenty-two friends in aircraft accidents—most of them in Alaska plane crashes.

Alaska Department of Labor statistics show that being a bush pilot is by far Alaska's most dangerous profession. Bush pilots, sadly, have an accident death rate two-and-a-half times greater than that of workers in the commercial crabbing industry, and I can personally and very sadly attest to how tremendous the loss of my bush-pilot friends has been to me. They're not always in front of me, but they're always with me, and I will always carry their memory around like a shadow of myself.

Don Lee & Larry Rivers

Friends to the Rescue

It was the middle of hunting season, the busiest hunting season I've ever had up to that point. I'd gone to Anchorage where I bought supplies and spent the night.

Just before dawn the next morning, I got a call from my brother-in-law that my dad had suddenly passed away of a heart attack.

My dad was sixty-two years old, and his death came as an unexpected shock. When I last saw him, he was in what appeared to be good health, although he did smoke three packs of cigarettes and drank two-to-three liters of soft drinks a day, not to mention his horrible diet.

I was dazed and distraught by the realization that my dad was gone. There had been no opportunity to say goodbye and seek his forgiveness one last time. I thought of all the issues we'd had over the years. I had been a young punk kid and not a very good son to my dad. It seemed the only bright spot would be that we had patched things up and our relationship had continually gotten better in recent years.

Suddenly, I came back to the present and the reality that I had camps with guides and clients spread out all throughout the Talkeetna Mountains and Alaska Range. I knew I had to deal with that, and I didn't see any way I could even get to Dad's funeral.

I needed to just put my emotions and grief on hold and get back into a frame of mind that I had a job to do. I could think of nothing else now; so I drove to Merrill Field, loaded the supplies, jumped in my Helio Courier, and flew back to Talkeetna.

As soon as I got to my hanger, one of my assistants helped me fuel and load one of my Super Cubs.

Off I flew, concentrating only on the job at hand, landing at each camp, delivering supplies, checking on their statuses.

I flew the Cub back to Talkeetna in the fading light and landed in the dark where Don Lee and Larry Rivers were waiting for me at my hanger.

Don and Larry told me to get my topo map and show them where all my camps were located.

"You're not flying anymore right now. We're gonna do your flying for you," they said.

"You're both flying full time with your own businesses. You're too busy to take on my work!" I protested.

"We're doing this for you! You have some things to take care of right now," they told me, and that was that.

They had already taken the keys out of all three of my airplanes.

Flat out, they said, "There's no choice; we're gonna cover this for you. Go down to the lower forty-eight, be with your family, and be there for your dad's funeral.

"We'll cover everything. It's not gonna cost you anything. We're just going to keep you safe, and you need to be with your family."

So I caught the next flight to California, and, for five days, they covered all my flying; it was pretty amazing. They were both busy with their own businesses. It was the busiest time of year for them both, yet they chipped in and took care of all my camps so I could go to my dad's funeral and be with my family for a few days.

They're both amazing men, and I'm blessed to have friends like Don Lee and Larry Rivers!

39.
Coca-Cola Only

The following is the reason my staff, clients, and visitors will only find Coca-Cola products in my lodge; I never purchase any other brands, only Coca-Cola products.

I had a client by the name of J. Frank Harrison III. His grandfather, J. B. Harrison, is the person who came up with the idea of putting Coca-Cola in bottles; prior to his idea, Coca-Cola was only available from soda-fountain dispensers. Mr. Harrison's company, Coca-Cola Consolidated, Inc., is the largest bottler of Coca-Cola products in the eastern USA. In the mid-1990s, Mr. Harrison brought a group of business associates to Alaska to hunt moose. They had flown in via his private Gulfstream jet to Anchorage where we picked them up and brought them to my lodge.

Greg Smith, who was working for me as a guide and pilot at the time was assigned to guide Mr. Harrison and his associates. They flew out to a hunting cabin that I owned located deep in the wilderness.

Mr. Harrison wound up shooting a monster bull moose on this trip. Back at my lodge at the end of the hunt, Mr. Harrison approached me for a private conversation. He told me how impressed he was with Greg and that he would like to offer him a flying job in his business, he would put Greg through a considerable amount of school and get him up to speed so he could fly both their company helicopter and become a copilot on the company jet. He wanted to know if I was okay with that because he didn't want to steal a great employee from me.

I was overjoyed! This was a fantastic opportunity for Greg.

Greg and his wife soon moved to Charlotte, North Carolina. I had certainly lost a good guide and pilot, but Greg was also a friend, and I wanted the best for him. We stayed in touch.

Many years later, Frank Harrison wanted to bring another group to my camp in the Brooks Range to hunt caribou and Dall sheep. Greg made all the arrangements. He was still flying for Mr. Harrison's company but now as a captain on the Gulfstream.

I had just returned from California before Mr. Harrison's hunt started. My mom was battling cancer and I was able to stay with her for an entire month. My son, Jason, was with me as well, so I considered this precious time with my family. Jason and I took her to her first few chemo treatments, but by mid-July, I had to get back to work. We returned home to Alaska. Before leaving, I had talked to Mom's doctor who told me that she was terminal; she should make it to Thanksgiving, and, if we were lucky, perhaps even through Christmas.

One of my brothers moved into her house. My plan was to return to California after my hunting season, then my brothers and sister and I would all take turns staying with her.

Three weeks later, I was in the Brooks Range at my hunting camp on the east fork of the Chandalar River when Mr. Harrison and three of his business associates arrived. My guides were already waiting in the spike camps. Mr. Harrison asked me to get his friends out into their individual spike camps first, and then I would fly Mr. Harrison out to where his guide was waiting.

While we were making those arrangements, an airplane flew in and landed on my little gravel strip. A pilot from Ft. Yukon got out and handed me a note. The note from my brother said that Mom had passed away suddenly due to complications from her chemo.

"Her funeral is on August the twenty-first, at 1:00 p.m." the note concluded.

Being in the remote Arctic, it had taken a full week for this sad message to get to me. The funeral was the next day, and it was already 6:00 p.m. in the evening on August twentieth.

I got on a satellite phone to see if there were any flights that I could get, but it was too late; there was no possible way I could get to the funeral.

Obviously, the walls of a tent are not soundproof. Mr. Harrison overheard what was going on as I was trying to get a flight from Fairbanks to California. He had his own satellite phone that I did not know about.

Fifteen minutes after I knew for certain that there was no flight available that could get me to the funeral in time, Mr. Harrison came into my tent.

"Fly yourself to Fairbanks," he said. "My jet and my crew are standing by, and they'll fly you through the night directly to Stockton. There'll be a rental car waiting for you when you land, and that should give you plenty of time to get to the funeral."

I was absolutely shocked. "I don't know what to say!" I stammered.

"Fly your plane to Fairbanks and attend your mom's funeral." He said again this time with finality in his voice. "I'll cover all the costs."

There was now only enough time to drop Mr. Harrison off at his spike camp then fly Jason and I directly to Fairbanks International Airport. With Mr. Harrison dropped off, Jason and I flew into Fairbanks and parked the Helio Courier there about midnight. One of

Mr. Harrison's flight crew ushered us into the waiting Gulfstream jet and flew us nonstop to Stockton, California.

There were two Chevy Suburban's waiting right next to where the Gulfstream stopped. The flight attendant told me one of the Suburban's was for me and to meet them back at the airplane at midnight. Because of Mr. Harrison's generosity I was able to drive the thirty-five miles to my mom's funeral service and get there two hours early.

Jason and I attended the funeral and spent the remainder of the day with my brothers and sister and the rest of family. Finally, we drove the Suburban back to the Stockton airport, got in the jet and flew directly back to Fairbanks.

Being so far north, by the time we landed it was already starting to get light. We fueled the Helio, and, two hours later, Jason and I were back in my hunting camp. I have no clue how much fuel that jet aircraft burned and how much that flight cost Mr. Harrison, but I know that it was probably way more than what he paid for the hunt for himself and his friends.

That act of kindness from Frank Harrison is something I will never forget and that's the reason why, at my lodge, the only products I buy are Coca-Cola products, and as long as I'm running the lodge, that will always be the case. So, if you come visit me in my home or at the lodge don't ask for anything but a Coke…or, I suppose you could have a glass of water.

Larry Rivers

Larry Rivers was an amazing mentor to me and is still my dear friend. He taught me how to survive the challenges of flying as a bush pilot in the Alaska wilderness. He taught me how to properly run and manage a small business, and how to be competitive in the business world and still maintain my integrity as a Christian man.

Larry had one of his hunting camps located on the east fork of the Chandelier River inside Arctic National Wildlife Refuge in the Brooks Range. Flying in his fully loaded Cessna 206 on his last flight of the season, he was halfway between his remote camp and Fort Yukon when his airplane experienced catastrophic engine failure. One of the cylinders had completely separated, immediately spitting out all of the engine's oil with some of it covering the windshield. Larry's incredible skill as a pilot and his ability to remain calm was now essential for saving both his life and the life of his passengers. He knew he only had a minute or two before the engine completely seized up from lack of oil. He also knew the country extremely well and knew that there was no way he could make the big open sandbars on the Sheenjek River, twenty miles away, so he made an immediate right hand turn heading for about a mile toward a small lake. Larry knew the country here was heavily treed and he knew that this lake had a wide section of tundra between the lake and the tree line.

He lined up on this semi-flat straight section of tundra and put the plane down. He had about a three-hundred and fifty-foot ground roll with everything going fine until the nose wheel dug in and hit hummock. At this point, the nose wheel folded under, and the airplane flipped up and over onto its back. Larry and his passengers experienced only minor injuries that probably would have been fatal for a lesser pilot. Everyone was rescued safely, but the plane remained upside down where it had landed.

Two months later and the Arctic tundra was hard-frozen, and the little lake with Larry's little plane resting beside it was frozen solid. Alaska bush pilots are a separate breed, and Larry exemplifies the spirit of that breed. Never one to leave a perfectly good aircraft lying upside down in the frozen wilderness, Larry recruited mechanic and pilot Ed Gunner to fly Ed's Cessna 182 with tools and equipment to the crash site to attempt a rescue of the downed Cessna, and I got word the airplane's rescue was underway.

Larry had done so much for me throughout the years, including rescue me from one of my wrecks, that I considered this an opportunity to help out a friend who was always there to help me. I immediately volunteered to join the team which provided two planes headed out to the Cessna.

Between the two airplanes, we loaded a new engine, a new prop, chain hoist, chainsaw, tent, food, and tools. Both planes were loaded to full gross weight when we took off from Talkeetna. We fueled up in Fairbanks and then flew out to the remote lake on the south side of the Brooks Range. Since I had skis on my plane I landed first, but there was only half an inch of snow on the lake so there was no problem for Ed to land his tricycle-gear Cessna on wheels. While Ed assessed the damage and came up with a game plan, I was sent with the chainsaw to cut three large straight trees for poles. After we dragged the limbed trees over to the airplane, we chipped and scooped out three triangularly-spaced holes in the ice to set the poles in for our tripod. This certainly wasn't Ed Gunner's first upside-down-aircraft-in-the-wilderness exercise. With his expertise on retrieving airplanes, and a lot of sweat, blood, and tears, as well as some swearing from all of us, we got the airplane turned over and upright. Over the next five days, with Ed giving directions and all three of us doing different tasks, the plane had a new engine and a new prop installed. The tail section was banged out and made straight, then aluminum pop-riveted over to reinforce it. All the dented leading edge of the wing and the wing's aluminum was pushed over then drilled and pop riveted.

The temperature ranged anywhere from fifteen-degrees-above- to thirty-five-degrees-below zero by the lake where we worked and camped. In the span of those five days, I made one trip back to Fairbanks for some needed supplies while Ed and Larry continued working.

After a week's worth of steady work, Ed's last job was to bolt on the vertical stabilizer which had come from a salvage yard in Anchorage. It was supposed to fit that make, model, and year of 206. The only problem was that it didn't fit. The angle was wrong. The bolt holes in the rear attachment point fit, but there was a four inch gap where the front attachment point needed to be.

To add insult to our "damned-part-doesn't-fit" injury, the weather was starting to change. The forecast was bad, and the storm was coming in fast. To my way of thinking, the only option was for us to leave the airplane, go back to Fairbanks, get a new vertical stabilizer, and return once the storm cleared. Ed didn't think that was the only option, however. Being both creative and a phenomenal mechanic, he had a better idea. He grabbed the chainsaw, marched out to one of the fresh stumps that the poles had come from, and cut out a block of wood. The stump was old-growth, tight-grained spruce, which means the block Ed cut out was relatively strong wood even though trees in the taiga don't get very tall. He made a spacer with the block and attached the stabilizer using the spacer with the original bolts, and it worked perfectly. We fueled and checked the oil in Larry's new engine, and we were finished!

I took off first in my plane while Ed stayed on the ground. I circled and watched Larry take off. The plan was as soon as he was safely in the air and things looked okay, that we would all head back to Fairbanks. Ed was to follow Larry right on his tail. I was going to fly to Fairbanks, top off my fuel, and then fly home as I had a trade show to attend in the lower forty-eight. Larry and Ed made it safely to Fairbanks, fueled up, and spent the night, then flew their planes home to Talkeetna the next day. When I asked Larry how the flight went, he told me he kept it slow, only cruising at about eighty miles an hour. He said that it needed all the rudder that his leg could stand for the long flight because it did not fly straight. In fact, he told me it flew horribly. More repairs were needed before Larry's Cessna 206 was safe to fly in full service again.

The entire experience, however, was very rewarding and educational for me. I learned how to take a wrecked, upside-down airplane with a bad engine, bent prop, and banged-up fuselage and tail and make it right-side up and flyable again. The things I learned and the lessons I learned from Ed Gunner's salvage of that airplane have helped me many times over the years to retrieve other wrecked airplanes.

The week we spent camping out in the Arctic where the temperature never rose even close to the freezing mark was pretty tough. I was always miserably cold, and my fingers felt frozen. But, even in my misery, all my thoughts were centered on all the things that Larry Rivers had done for me and how happy I was to have this chance to help my mentor and my friend for a change.

Along with my old friend, Ron Sutphin, Larry Rivers taught me to fly safely in some of the most dangerous weather conditions on earth and takeoff and land on some of the harshest terrain on the planet. Larry never missed an opportunity to teach me something new from his wealth of wilderness and bush-pilot knowledge—his lessons saved my life on more than one occasion. For this and many more reasons, I will be forever grateful for Larry Rivers, my friend and my mentor.

Larry Rivers
My Mentor & Friend.
(Photo © Larry Rivers. All rights reserved. Used with permission.)

Number One-Ten

Becoming a Master Guide in Alaska? So, well, it's a process. You have to have put in the time. Assistant Guide comes first, of course. In order to get an Assistant Guide license you have to work for two years as well as have the recommendation of a Registered Guide or a Master Guide who will sign off for you. And then that allows you to get your assistant guide license. You have to guide for three years minimum as well as guide three clients minimum for each of those three years with an eighty-percent favorable letter of recommendation from every client who you guided as an assistant guide.

Becoming Alaska Master Guide #110

Then you're allowed to take the Registered Guide test after all of that. The test is an extremely difficult written test that goes along with an oral exam. As a rule, it usually takes a person five to seven years of working in the business in Alaska to become a licensed Alaska Registered Guide.

The two test and exam judges are either registered guides or master guides who have been in the industry for a significant length of time and then, in the past, it was usually somebody from Alaska Fish and Game. That was the third person on the board, and they could ask you any questions under the sun. There was only about a ten- to fifteen-percent pass rate on that portion on their first try. I think it was like twenty-five or thirty percent passed on their second try and most people that took it a third time seemed to always get through.

After acquiring your registered guide license you had to have guided and outfitted for a significant number of clients, fifty or a hundred clients with, again, an eighty-percent favorable letter of recommendation from all the clients that you had guided and outfitted for.

Prior to me getting my Master Guide license, another requirement was you had to be considered a leader in the industry as well as a positive influence on the guiding industry overall. Just before I got my registered guide license, that requirement was taken away because they felt it was too ambiguous.

An applicant for Master Guide also has to have twelve years with no kind of Fish and Game violation of any sort. So as a rule, from the beginning, it takes an average of about twenty years to go from a novice through the registered guide license to get an Alaska Master Guide license.

I am Alaska Master Guide #110 and I think there are now about two hundred and fifty master guide licenses that have been issued. I think there are only about twenty-five or thirty master guides with numbers lower than mine still alive today. Larry Rivers, Alaska Master Guide #68, and Alaska Master Guide Clark Engle helped me more than I can say.

...now, being a Master Guide as well as a high-time bush pilot in Alaska—well, that has to come from the heart.

After Words

Lessons Learned

Wilderness & Life Lessons I've Learned

First lesson— Don't count on food to be there when you need it, you'd better make sure you have the proper kind of food that's stored in a very secure way, or you will go hungry.

Second lesson— Make your egress plans before you head off into the wilds and have at least two good contingency plans.

Third Lesson— Birch bark, snow, or small pinecones do work to wipe your posterior but make a very poor long-term substitute for real toilet paper. At -20°F, your butt will freeze to a wooden toilet seat in the outhouse. Styrofoam will make using the outhouse much less of a pain in the butt over an Alaskan winter.

Fourth Lesson— Packing boots with two sets of liners or bunny boots are necessary items working outdoors in cold and snow environments.

Fifth Lesson— A .22 rifle or pistol is a must-have firearm in the wilderness.

Sixth Lesson— Clothing made for loggers, surveyors, and commercial fisherman may be heavy, but it passes the test of hard wear over a long haul a lot better than sporting gear. Filson is the best.

Seventh Lesson— Make sure you have a source of vitamin C.

Eighth Lesson— If you do bring a weapon in from the cold, strip it down, dry it, and clean it. I quickly learned to leave my rifle outside next to the door for most of the winter and only brought it in to clean.

Ninth Lesson— Being able to at least hear what is going on in the outside world helps your mental attitude a lot. A radio to listen to the news is vital.

Tenth Lesson— Tape the muzzle of your rifle to keep snow out of the barrel when you take the inevitable header into the snow. I use electrical tape or put a condom over the muzzle of all my rifles in the field to keep everything out of the barrel. It will not affect accuracy unless you are shooting over 300 yards.

Lesson 11— Cross country skis are no substitute for snowshoes.

Lesson 12— In a frigid winter climate, use no oil in the bolt or trigger assembly of your rifle—it could freeze.

Lesson 13— Any outlet or inlet of a frozen lake may have thin ice.

A warm spring or any number of other anomalies can cause thin ice.

Lesson 14— Always have the kindling and all the fixings of a fire ready, especially any time you leave your cabin. You never know when someone may be at the end of their strength and need to get a life-saving fire going.

Lesson 15— Moose are dangerous, especially in late winter. Give them the right-of-way.

Lesson 16— Grizzly bears do not truly hibernate and may be out of the den during any month of the year. Over the years, I learned that if a bear is away from its den in the winter, it will be hungry and grumpy—and nothing to underestimate.

Lesson 17— Quick draw holster v. northern woods obstacles of snow and mud. In the Alaska bush, you want your handgun in a full flap holster or in a normal holster worn under the last layer of clothing. Getting your handgun into your hand fast is of no use if it will not fire when you need it.

Lesson 18— Select holsters that will allow you to always carry your handgun with you comfortably and will protect the weapon from the elements.

Lesson 19— Sometimes you need to get out of your comfort zone. Remember, eventually, we are all going to die, what is important is to truly live before you cash in your chips.

Lesson 20— I've learned many lessons over this long and storied life I've been blessed with. Some have been hard lessons, not easily learned, but I have tried to live my life honorably. I have a few regrets, but a lot of happy memories, as well. If I can leave you with my best lesson, though, it's to look for a little adventure now and then, live life to the fullest and to the best of your ability—honestly and faithfully—and, in the end, you won't regret the fact that there really is no sequel to life.

Acronyms

ACP .... Automatic Colt Pistol
AK .... Alaska
ALCAN .... Alaska Canada Highway
ANC .... Ted Stevens Anchorage International Airport, AK
ANWR .... Arctic National Wildlife Refuge
ATrag .... Horus Vision accurate targeting calculator software
BLM .... Bureau of Land Management
BMG .... Browning Machine Gun
BO .... Body Odor
CDP .... Census-Designated Place
CFS .... Cubic Feet per Second
ELT .... Emergency Locater Transmitter
FAA .... Federal Aviation Administration
FNAWS .... Foundation for North American Wild Sheep
FOB .... Forward Operating Base
FOUO .... For Official Use Only
GED .... General Educational Development
GI .... Government Issue
GMUs .... Game Management Units
GPS .... Global Positioning System
H&H .... Holland & Holland
H&R .... Harrington & Richardson
ID .... Identity Documents
IIC .... Investigator-in-Charge (senior investigator for NTSB)
IV .... Intravenous
JRTs .... Jack Russel Terriers
LDS .... Latter Day Saints
MRAP .... Mine-Resistant Ambush Protected
MREs .... Meals Ready to Eat
MRI .... Merrill Field, AK
NTSB .... National Transportation Safety Board
OSCE .... Organization of Security & Cooperation in Europe
PE .... Physical Education
PH .... Professional Hunter
R&R .... Rest & Relaxation
RCC .... Rescue Coordination Center
REI .... Recreational Equipment, Inc.
RSA .... Republic of South Africa
SCI .... Safari Club International
SAE .... Society of Automotive Engineers
STOL .... Short Takeoff and Landing
T&Ls .... Takeoffs & Landings
TDS .... Col. Thomas D. Smith III
TKA .... Talkeetna Airport, AK
VFR .... Visual Flight Rules
VIPs .... Very Important Persons
VK .... Vladimir Kovalik

Bibliography

Alfonsobouchot - Trabajo propio, Dominio público, https://commons.wikimedia.org/w/index.php?curid=8687075

Art Wolfe, Inc. "Nature & Cultural Photography 1-888-973-0011." Art Wolfe. Art Wolfe, Inc., March 12, 2015. https://artwolfe.com/. Accessed November 8, 2022.

ArcticHokie - Own work, CC BY-SA 3.0, https://commons.wikimedia.org/w/index.php?curid=17513526

Bing. "Confluence of Yellow Jacket Creek with Talkeetna River AK." Microsoft Bing, 20 Jul. 2023, https://www.alaska.org/detail/talkeetna-river.

Bruhl, Zach. "Kimberly Man Back Home after Giving Humanitarian Aid to Ukraine." https://www.kmvt.com, April 11, 2022. https://www.kmvt.com/2022/04/11/kimberly-man-back-home-after-giving-humanitarian-aid-ukraine/. Accessed September 9, 2022.

Burgess, Mark. 2008. "News>Pilot's desperate escape from Chad and chilling mid-air refueling stunt." *The Shetland Times.* July 25. Accessed September 6, 2022. https://www.shetlandtimes.co.uk/2008/07/25/pilots-desperate-escape-from-chad-and-chilling-mid-air-refuelling-stunt.

Collier, Zach. 2022. "Remembering Vladimir Kovalik." *Whitewater Guidebook.* February 24. Accessed September 10, 2022. https://www.whitewaterguidebook.com/remembering-vladimir-kovalik/.

"Don Sheldon." Don Sheldon Alaska Piloting Legend. Sheldon Air Service, 2022. https://www.sheldonairservice.com/About-Sheldon-Air-Service/Don-Sheldon-Alaska-pilot. Text from: Don Sheldon: Bush Pilot Extraordinaire, by Todd McClamroch

Garfield, Brian. *The Thousand-Mile War: World War II in Alaska and the Aleutians.* Toronto: Bantam Books, 1982, p. 50.

KCAM Radio. 2022. "Caribou Clatters/Bulletin Board." KCAM Radio>The Voice of the Copper River Valley. Accessed September 10, 2022. https://www.kcam.org/caribou-clatters-bulletin-board/#.

Kovalik, Kyle, & Steiger, Lew. Vladimir Kovalik. Boatman's Quarterly Review, 18(4) (Winter 2005-2006): 1, 26-36, 38, 40, 42. [Transcript of portions of an oral interview with Kovalik in January 2005, with editorial interjections; and with separate sidebars of interviews with others, "Kyle Kovalik", pp. 37, 39 (ITEM NO. 2.10503); and "Karen Kovalik", pp. 41, 43 (ITEM NO. 2.10504).] https://static1.squarespace.com/static/61d3bc4beef7c3126df06d78/t/61f720a4adb6ec0f97380290/1643585705209/18-4.pdf.

Legacy.com, and Legacy. "Carl Jensen Obituary (1928 - 2016) - Anchorage, AK - Anchorage Daily News." Legacy.com, November 8, 2016. https://www.legacy.com/us/obituaries/adn/name/carl-jensen-obituary?id=17746762.

Medina, Marilyn. 2022. "Why Do Salmon Swim To The Ocean?" *Sweetish Hill.* August 7. Accessed October 16, 2022. https://sweetishhill.com/why-do-salmon-swim-to-the-ocean/.

OBrien, Sam. 2021. "Different Classes of Rapids Explained - The International Scale of River Difficulty." *Water Sports Whiz.* December 22. Accessed September 7, 2022. https://www.watersportswhiz.com/classes-of-rapids/#:~:text=Class%20III%20rapids%2C%20known%20as%20%E2%80%9CIntermediate%2C%E2%80%9D%20are%20characterized,irregularly%20%E2%80%93%20and%20can%20easily%20swamp%20a%20kayak.

Outward Bound. 2022. "Northwest Outward Bound School>Wilderness Courses." *Classic Out-*

ward *Bound Wilderness Courses*. Accessed September 2, 2022. https://www.nwoutward-bound.org/programs/wilderness-courses/.

Pacific Coast Air Museum. 1996. "Pacific." *Home>Aircraft>Stinson 108 Voyager*. Accessed October 21, 2022. https://pacificcoastairmuseum.org/aircraft/stinson-108-voyager/.

Ricraider - Own work, CC BY-SA 3.0, https://commons.wikimedia.org/w/index.php?curid=20425074

Sheldon Air Service. "Kahiltna Glacier Basecamp." Sheldon Air Service, 2022. https://www.sheldonairservice.com/Denali-Air-Taxi/Kahiltna-Glacier-Denali-Base-Camp.

Sutphin, Ronald J. *Covert Skies: Ron Sutphin's Road to Civil Air Transport (CAT) and Covert Operations in Laos*. Edited by CS Norwood (Bay Minette, Twin Falls: AWI adventure writers ink) on Amazon.com.

Wheat, Brent. 2016. "The Weaver Stance: Combating the Misinformation." S.W.A.T. Survival Weapons and Tactics. January . Accessed October 17, 2022. https://www.swatmag.com/article/weaver-stance-combating-misinformation/#:~:text=The%20Weaver%20stance%20is%20a%20two-handed%20shooting%20position,arm%20is%20bent%20and%20the%20elbow%20pointed%20downward.

Wikimedia Commons contributors, n.d. "File:StanislausNF-Rafting.jpg," Wikimedia Commons, https://commons.wikimedia.org/w/index.php?title=File:StanislausNF-Rafting.jpg&oldid=474767085 (accessed July 19, 2023).

Wikipedia, contributors, n.d. "CASA C-212 Aviocar," Wikipedia, The Free Encyclopedia, https://en.wikipedia.org/w/index.php?title=CASA_C-212_Aviocar&oldid=1128539938 (accessed December 21, 2022).

—. n.d. "Barter Island." *Wikipedia, The Free Encyclopedia* . Accessed October 17, 2022. https://en.wikipedia.org/w/index.php?title=Barter_Island&oldid=1084018391.

—. n.d. "Brooks Range." Wikipedia, The Free Encyclopedia. Accessed September 16 , 2022. https://en.wikipedia.org/w/index.php?title=Brooks_Range&oldid=1096598741.

—. n.d. "Cold Bay, Alaska." *Wikipedia, The Free Encyclopedia* . Accessed October 16, 2022. https://en.wikipedia.org/w/index.php?title=Cold_Bay,_Alaska&oldid=1105871111.

—. n.d. "Dennis the Menace (1959 TV series)." *Wikipedia, The Free Encyclopedia*. Accessed September 2, 2022. https://en.wikipedia.org/w/index.php?title=Dennis_the_Menace_(1959_TV_series)&oldid=1107615915.

—. n.d. "Ray Genet." Wikipedia. Wikimedia Foundation, December 4, 2021. https://en.wikipedia.org/wiki/Ray Genet. Accessed September 2, 2022.

—. n.d. "The Beverly Hillbillies," Wikipedia, The Free Encyclopedia, https://en.wikipedia.org/w/index.php?title=The_Beverly_Hillbillies&oldid=1174982401 (accessed September 19, 2023).

Yeager, General Chuck and Leo Janos. *Yeager: An Autobiography*. New York: Bantam Books, 1986.

Yeager, General Charles E. "Chuck" and Victoria Yeager. *101 Chuck Yeager-isms: Wit & Wisdom from America's Hero*. The Right Stuff Publishing, 2022.

Yeager, Victoria. *Chuck Yeager: What a Ride! My Amazing Life with The Original Right Stuff, Chuck Yeager*. The Right Stuff Publishing, 2024.

About the Authors

Jerry J. Jacques

Alaska! There was no other place on earth he wanted to be. From hearing his grandfather's stories of wild days in Alaska and the Yukon Territory to hitchhiking his way into his own true story, Jerry Jacques grew up living the life most people can only dream about. He had to make a living, though, so Jerry discovered the perfect pathway to his success. He shared his adventures by becoming a bush pilot and wilderness guide, leading rafting and kayaking tours, hunting trips, and ultimately flying photography safaris deep into the Alaskan wilderness, the breathtakingly beautiful place he calls home.

Now, still flying, traveling to war-torn Ukraine, and leading grizzly safaris, all the while writing his first book, Jerry spends every possible moment at his Alaska Grizzly Safari Lodge on Lake Iliamna in Alaska. Among his many, many accomplishments and *firsts*, Jerry is proudest of his family and his life of adventure as Alaska Master Guide License #110. *(Photo: Jerry & faithful flying companion, Katmai)*

CS Norwood

CS Norwood recently completed editing her brother's memoir, *Covert Skies: Ron Sutphin's Road to Civil Air Transport (CAT) and Covert Operations in Laos*. She currently lives in Alabama, spending her retirement writing, researching, and helping others complete and publish their adventure books under the imprint of *AWI adventure writers ink* and *ALP adventure large-print* editions. *(Photo: CS & faithful writing companion, Jack)*

Contact

Summer (May - November)
Jacques Adventures
P.O. Box 164
Iliamna AK 99606
(907) 571-6524

Winter (December - April)
(907) 570-1459

While you're creating your own adventure story,
scan the QR code on the right to visit our website
https://awi-adventurewriters.com/.

Index

7:07

.ıll 5G

← **Replies** 🔍

 41 years ago I was mauled by a small bear, I had a 45 acp and that probably saved my life although my arm and shoulder were never the same. After that incident my dad bought me the 4" model 29

on Mon   **Like**   **Reply** 👍😮🤗 15

Jedidiah Wick
Jerry Jacques I remember the teeth marks in your arm and the bald skull of the sow where your shot her in the head while she tried to pull you out of the window

on Mon   **Like**   **Reply** 👍😮 4

 Jedidiah Wick
Jerry, I was 4 1/2 years old when you and my dad came back from that trip- I think it was 37-38 years ago 😄 1986ish Y'all had the bear strapped to the front of the blue jeep, I remember when you got out at the cabin we lived in (Sheldon's)and you had your arm bandaged up and blood was seeping through where her teeth clamped down on your arm. unforgettable for a young boy

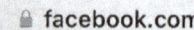 Write a reply…   GIF @ ☺

🔒 facebook.com

We hope you enjoyed the adventure!

www.ingramcontent.com/pod-product-compliance
Lightning Source LLC
Chambersburg PA
CBHW080836120626
46553CB00009B/2450

* 9 7 9 8 9 8 8 4 4 7 0 8 5 *